ENDING VIOLENCE AGAINST WOMEN

Oxfam GB was founded in 1942. It is a development, relief, and campaigning agency dedicated to finding lasting solutions to poverty and suffering around the world. It believes that every human being is entitled to a life of dignity and opportunity, and it works with others worldwide to make this become a reality.

From its base in Oxford, England, Oxfam GB publishes and distributes a wide range of books and other resource materials for development and relief workers, researchers and campaigners, educational establishments, and the general public, as part of its programme of advocacy, education, and communications.

Oxfam GB is a member of Oxfam International, a group of 12 agencies of diverse cultures and languages, which share a commitment to working for an end to injustice and poverty – both in long-term development work and at times of crisis.

www.oxfam.org.uk

ENDING VIOLENCE AGAINST WOMEN:

A Challenge for Development and Humanitarian Work

Francine Pickup

with Suzanne Williams
and Caroline Sweetman

Oxfam

First published by Oxfam GB in 2001

© Oxfam GB 2001

ISBN 0 85598 438 4 (paperback)
ISBN 0 85598 458 9 (hardback)

A catalogue record for this publication is available from the British Library.

Available from Bournemouth English Book Centre, PO Box 1496, Parkstone, Dorset, BH12 3YD, UK
tel: +44 (0)1202 712933; fax: +44 (0)1202 712930; e-mail: oxfam@bebc.co.uk
and from the following agents:

USA: Stylus Publishing LLC, PO Box 605, Herndon, VA 20172-0605, USA
tel: +1 (0)703 661 1581; fax: +1 (0)703 661 1547; e-mail: styluspub@aol.com

Southern Africa: David Philip Publishers, PO Box 23408, Claremont 7735, South Africa
tel: +27 (0)21 674 4136; fax: +27 (0)21 674 3358; email: orders@dpp.co.za

For details of local agents and representatives in other countries, consult our website: http://www.oxfam.org.uk/publications.html, or contact
Oxfam Publishing, 274 Banbury Road, Oxford OX2 7DZ, UK
tel: +44 (0)1865 311 311; fax: +44 (0)1865 312 600; e-mail publish@oxfam.org.uk

Printed by Information Press, Eynsham

Oxfam GB is a registered charity, no. 202 918, and is a member of Oxfam International.

Francine Pickup would like to dedicate this book to

Livio Zilli and Suzanne Williams

Contents

PART 2 Strategies for challenging violence against women

Preface
Suzanne Williams

Emerging from the Silence

Ending violence against women is one of Oxfam's priorities. It is a central strategy within Oxfam's overall goal of promoting gender equity throughout its international programme, and it is central to Oxfam's mandate to relieve poverty and suffering. This prioritisation is the fruit of a long, although often obscure, history of Oxfam's support of work to address violence against women around the world. It has often been obscure because it is in the nature of the issue of violence against women to be hidden, to be silenced, and to be encircled by fear, shame, and violence. It is a difficult and dangerous area in which to work. Located as it is, in the majority of cases, within the family or household, it has been regarded as a private and domestic issue, inhabiting terrain where development agencies have feared to tread. If anything, it fell within the realm of the charitable and welfare projects that characterised much of Oxfam's programme in the 1950s and 1960s.

Oxfam's early support to community organisation and development, legal education and legal aid, and women's groups and organisations, is likely to have had an impact on the extent of violence in the lives and relationships of women and men that has never been documented. It has not been documented because it has only relatively recently appeared in the language of development aid, and been regarded as a legitimate development concern. As has been recorded by Oxfam staff, a focus on women's particular rights was felt to be divisive and potentially alienating to partners who did not themselves raise the issue, particularly in the context of community-based or political organisations striving for social justice. So while it may well be that Oxfam has indirectly and unknowingly contributed to attempts to stop or lessen the incidence of violence against women, it is likely that interventions were supported which may have brought about – or worsened – the violence meted out to women. A key issue that is addressed in this book is that unless development and relief agencies are aware of the ways in which women are subordinated within their beneficiary group, and take measures to address it, their interventions will probably exacerbate it.

One of the earliest projects in the organisation's archives dealing directly with one of the many aspects of violence against women was supported by Oxfam in Brazil from 1971 to 1983. The Centro Educacional Bem Me Quer was a social and educational centre for prostitutes and their children, founded by three social science graduates in the town of Aracaju, in northeast Brazil, in 1969. Oxfam funded a day care centre for the children. At the time of writing up the first grant, the Oxfam Representative referred to it as 'pioneering' work, and wrote, 'This, I believe, might appear an unusual project for Oxfam to support. But perhaps we should think not only about water supplies, selected seeds, nutrition, etc.. Prostitution, as a problem, is as endemic a symptom of underdevelopment in Northeast Brazil as subsistence agriculture or lack of water.' By 1978 Oxfam was supporting several programmes working with women in prostitution, and funded a seminar for prostitutes within the national context of the organising of sex workers. In 1982 Oxfam sponsored a mission by the Anti-Slavery Society to West Africa to find ways of supporting local efforts to combat what was then known as female circumcision. In 1984 Oxfam funded a study on 'the hidden crimes against women' in India, and in1989 Oxfam supported a national conference on the anti-dowry movement in Bangladesh. These are only a few examples of many programmes addressing different aspects of violence against women that developed during the 1970s and 1980s.

Over the last two decades, given considerable impetus by the two United Nations World Conferences on Women – in Nairobi in 1985 and in Beijing in1995 – and the UN World Conference on Human Rights in Vienna in 1993, Oxfam's work with women became increasingly informed by a gender and human rights-based analysis. A strong publishing programme on gender equity gained force over this period, with a range of books, working papers, and a journal. The publication of this book, following on from the International Oxfam Workshop on Violence against Women held in Sarajevo in 1998, is part of the systematic documentation of Oxfam GB's work on gender. This book is a celebration of the difficult and dangerous work undertaken by our partners in countries around the world, and a contribution to the work now being undertaken by many international agencies to address violence against women within the context of development and humanitarian aid.

A crime against humanity

As this book will show, it is only in the last decade that violence against women has emerged from the shadows to be seen in the full light of day as the fundamental human rights abuse it constitutes. The statistics are shocking: across the world, it is estimated that between one-third and one-fifth of the world's population of women and girls are the victims and survivors of rape, sexual assault, murder, slavery, mutilation, and physical and emotional torture of the most diverse forms. It is a global crime, affecting millions of women and girls. Insofar as such violence is meted out to women because of their gender, it is systematic. Where these violations of women's human rights are promoted or enshrined by formal or customary law, or where the legal system routinely fails to protect women, it is systematic. Where army troops or militia commit rape or sexual torture as part of war strategy, violence against women is not only systematic, but planned, and sometimes part of a policy.

Crimes that fulfil these criteria – being widespread, or systematic – meet the legal definition of crimes against humanity as codified in the Statutes of the two ad-hoc war tribunals – the International Criminal Tribunal for the former Yugoslavia (ICTY) and the International Criminal Tribunal for Rwanda (ICTR). These tribunals broke new ground in trying cases of rape as genocide, and as crimes against humanity. The ICTY established that each individual who commits rape as part of a widespread attack can be prosecuted as guilty of crimes against humanity. The Statute of the proposed International Criminal Court (ICC) follows these models, and has gone further, breaking the legal association between crimes against humanity and war crimes. Thus, while in the context of armed conflict, rape and sexual violence have been prosecuted as crimes against humanity, the definition of sexual and gender crimes as crimes against humanity in the context of peace will have extremely far-reaching implications.

However, violence against women is not only in the legal, but also in the moral sense of the term, a crime against humanity. Humanity itself is diminished by the fact that difference between the sexes is the site of oppression and violence, in which one half of the human race systematically attacks and subordinates the other. The humanity of each one of us cannot be whole while women are subjected to violence because they are born women, while men perpetrate violence as part of their expression of manhood, and while both women and men turn away and by their inaction, condone it. Inaction can also form a pattern, become habitual, and become systematic.

A systematic violation – a systematic response

In the face of a problem of such monumental dimensions, it is difficult to see what a relatively small international development organisation such as Oxfam can do. Certainly, there is almost nothing it can do on its own. The effectiveness of Oxfam's interventions depends entirely upon the quality of the partnerships it forms with community-based, national, or international organisations in the countries in which it works, or with individuals and groups mobilised to help carry out operational work in emergencies. Nothing that Oxfam does can be solely attributed to its own efforts. Oxfam defines, and achieves, all its goals in partnership with others. This book describes those goals and the partner organisations that work at different levels and in different ways in many countries across the world. There is further work to be done to strengthen alliances with organisations and agencies working to eradicate violence against women. New alliances also need to be built, because to tackle violence against women means addressing it systematically, at every level, with a range of strategies appropriate to particular contexts, and with interventions that can be sustained over a long period of time.

The first step is to recognise the systematic ways in which violence against women forms part of the fabric of human society, and human institutions. Violence against women is necessary in order to maintain the institutions of patriarchy: that is, the structures, beliefs, and practices that maintain male dominance over women. There is abundant evidence – some of which is presented in this book – that when women begin to challenge this dominance, be it through taking up educational opportunities, or joining organisations, or increasing their status in any way, they often meet with male violence. In a study that attempts to understand the motives of male sexual murderers, Deborah Cameron and Elisabeth Fraser state:

> ...*violence against women, exemplified in practices like rape and incest, is not just a collection of randomly vindictive acts, but a social institution which is crucial in reproducing male power by keeping women in a state of fear and unfreedom. This view gains credence when we look at the ways in which violence against women is covertly condoned: rape victims find their own morals on trial, battered women cannot trust police to protect them, social workers respond to incest with concern for the 'family' which may entail a girl risking further abuse within it, men who bludgeon their wives to death are praised for their 'devotion'... is the violence really aberrant, or is it somehow in tune with the workings of our society?*

(Cameron and Fraser 1987)

This book describes the ways in which violence against women is promoted, defended, silenced, and tolerated by the practices and policies of social institutions – from the household and family to the community, the State, and within international organisations. It is at these two levels, the level of thought and the level of action, that violence against women needs to be challenged. This is a far-reaching project, requiring fundamental changes in the relations between women and men. A number of initiatives in the field of international human rights have created a favourable international climate within which to take this work forward. This means not resting upon one's laurels, but redoubling efforts to make sure that gains are not lost, and that the momentum for change is maintained. It is at this point that Oxfam GB finds itself, on the occasion of publishing this book.

In recent years, Oxfam GB and its nine sister organisations around the world, forming a consortium of agencies known as Oxfam International, have begun to work together more systematically to improve the quality and increase the impact of their work. A rights-based approach to development is intrinsic to the way the aims of the programmes of Oxfam International have been defined, and brings to the programme the consistency of a set of international standards. These strategic programme aims are framed in terms of rights – such as the right to the basic services of health and education, and the right to a sustainable livelihood. The strategic aim related to gender equity states, 'women and men shall have equal rights.' Within this aim, violence against women is recognised as not only the starkest expression of gender inequity, but as its cornerstone, and has been taken up as a programme priority in most of the regions in which Oxfam works. Programmes are being mapped out to address it in different ways in several countries – some of the work that is part of these programmes is described in this book. Oxfam will address violence against women within three main areas – violence in the context of conflict and crisis, trafficking of women and girls, and domestic violence. Domestic violence is something of a misnomer in this context, because the category includes community-based violence that involves perpetrators outside the immediate family or household, including, for example, so-called 'honour killings' in parts of the Middle East, dowry murders in India, and female genital mutilation.

A further dimension of the increasingly systematic way in which Oxfam is structuring its international programme is what is known as the 'one programme approach', which means that all programmes are required to work in an integrated way in the three spheres of humanitarian response, development work, and advocacy and campaigning. This creates new opportunities to make links across programming areas that are usually quite separate, and apply a consistent analysis and planning framework to violence against women in different contexts. There have also been recent developments with regard to campaigning and humanitarian work. Within Oxfam GB there is an increasing emphasis on campaigning, with a plan underway to launch a campaign on gender equity in the South Asia region. Within the humanitarian programme, which has traditionally focused on assistance, Oxfam will be developing its expertise on humanitarian protection. Particular emphasis will be placed on the protection of refugee and displaced women and girls, and on specific protection from sexual and gender violence.

Finally, a new framework for the identification and measurement of the changes Oxfam GB wants to achieve through its programme interventions is being implemented. This framework seeks to clarify the changes in the policies and practices of institutions – from the household to international organisations such as the agencies of the United Nations or the World Bank – that will be required in order to achieve the desired results of the programme. Recognising that changes at the practical level are not likely to be sustainable unless more profound social and cultural change underpin them, programmes will also identify key changes in ideas and beliefs that will have to be promoted and achieved. These are ambitious goals, and have very different implications for different parts of the world. Oxfam GB's overall vision is of a number of 'global programmes' that will draw together the best and most relevant work from its regional bases, working at local, national, and international levels, to effect real changes in the lives of the people with whom it works.

A famous dictum of criminology cited by Cameron and Frazer (1987) is that 'society gets the crimes it deserves'. Violence against women, as a universal crime, has its origin in a global society that preserves the domination of women by men through fear and physical aggression. It is this society which must change.

Acknowledgements

This book would not have been possible without contributions and support from the Oxfam country offices and women's organisations that participated in the Oxfam international workshop on violence against women in Sarajevo in November 1998. Both were instrumental in Oxfam's decision to commission this book, and were also a great source of inspiration to me.

The book owes much to a number of people in Oxfam – especially field staff who provided much of the material used. In particular, I would like to mention Lina Abou-Habib and Omar Traboulsi, then from Oxfam's Middle East Programme in Beirut; Nelly Claux, then from Oxfam's Americas Programme in Lima; the Eastern Europe office in Sarajevo; and the Publications Team. I would also like to thank staff at Amnesty International – in particular, Liz Hodgkin, Leanne MacMillan, Tania Baldwin-Pask, and Angelika Pathak for their advice. I am indebted to Judy El-Bushra, Deborah Clifton, Deborah Eade, Judith Large, Adam Leach, and Sarah Totterdell for the time they gave to carefully read through earlier drafts. I would like to thank Livio Zilli for his intellectual rigour, which has made this a much better book, and for his patience and encouragement throughout. Last but not least, my gratitude goes to Suzanne Williams – whose brainchild this book is – for the wonderful learning experience and great fun this project has been.

Francine Pickup, June 2001

List of abbreviations

FGM	Female genital mutilation
GAD	Gender and development programmes and projects
NGO	Non-governmental organisation
PASF	Project Application Summary Form
STDs	Sexually transmitted diseases
WID	Women in development programmes and projects

Regional intergovernmental organisations

CoE	Council of Europe
OAS	Organisation of American States
OAU	Organisation for African Unity

United Nations bodies and instruments

CEDAW Committee	The Committee on the Elimination of Discrimination against Women, established under the terms of the Convention on the Elimination of All Forms of Discrimination against Women adopted by the United Nations General Assembly in its resolution 34/180 in December 1979
EXCOM	The Executive Committee of the United Nations High Commissioner for Refugees' Programme. It acts as the governing body of the United Nations High Commissioner for Refugees. Composed of 57 member states, the EXCOM holds an annual plenary session, in Geneva, Switzerland in October.
ICC	International Criminal Court
ICCPR	The International Covenant on Civil and Political Rights. Adopted and opened for signature, ratification, and accession by the United Nations General Assembly in its resolution 2200A (XXI) of 16 December 1966, entered into force on 23 March 1976.
ICTR	International Criminal Tribunal for Rwanda
ICTY	International Criminal Tribunal for the former Yugoslavia
ILO	International Labour Organisation

Torture Convention	The Convention against Torture and Other Cruel, Inhuman or Degrading Treatment or Punishment, adopted and opened for signature, ratification, and accession by the United Nations General Assembly in its resolution 39/46 of 10 December 1984, entered into force 26 June 1987.
UDHR	The Universal Declaration of Human Rights, adopted and proclaimed by the United Nations General Assembly in its resolution 217 A (III) of 10 December 1948.
UNDP	United Nations Development Programme
UNHCHR	United Nations High Commissioner for Human Rights
UNHCR	United Nations High Commissioner for Refugees
UNICEF	United Nations Children's Fund
UNIFEM	United Nations Development Fund for Women
UNRISD	United Nations Research Institute for Social Development
WHO	World Heath Organisation
Women's Convention	Convention on the Elimination of All Forms of Discrimination against Women adopted by the United Nations General Assembly in its resolution 34/180 in December 1979.

Women's organisations and projects fighting violence against women

CEDMUJER	Centro de Desarollo para la Defensa de los Derechos de la Mujer (Development Centre for the Defence of Women's Rights)
CISAS	Centro de Información y Servicios de Asesoría en Salud in Nicaragua
CLADEM	Comité de América Latina y el Caribe para la Defensa de los Derechos de la Mujer (Latin American and Caribbean Committee for the Defence of Women's Rights)
CMV	Colectivo Mujer Vida (Women and Life Collective)
CSVR	Centre for the Study of Violence and Reconciliation
DMV	Domestic Violence Matters project
FIDA	International Federation of Women Lawyers
GAP	Corporación Grupo Apoyo Pedagogico
KZN PSV	KwaZulu Natal Programme for the Survivors of Violence
NCTPE	National Committee for Traditional Practices of Ethiopia
NOVIB	Oxfam Netherlands
PADV	Project Against Domestic Violence
POWA	People Opposing Women Abuse
WCLAC	Women's Centre for Legal Aid and Counselling
WVV	Women Victims of Violence Project
YWCA	Young Women's Christian Association

Introduction

'I can kill you whenever I want. I could kill you and no one would ever do anything about it.... I have eaten human livers... raw.' That is what he said to me after he punched me in the face with such force that he knocked out my four front teeth and split my gum. While the blood poured from my lips, he returned, laughing, to his friends and his card game. My children and neighbours watched.... Each day he beats me several times. He punches me, he whips me with bamboo rods. Many times he has held a gun to my head and threatened to shoot me. Fear of my husband haunts my thoughts every day. If you ask me whether I feel like a servant or a slave, I will tell you that I am more like a dog.
(A survivor of violence, Project Against Domestic Violence, Cambodia)

More and more development agencies are acknowledging that unless they confront the massive and deeply entrenched problem of gender[1]-based violence, the 'empowerment of women' will be a hollow slogan. Sustainable human development must rest on the shared conviction that unless women and men resolve together not to tolerate violence against women in their homes and their communities, development will not be human, and it will not be sustainable.
(Bunch, Carrillo, and Shore 1998)

Why is violence against women a central concern for development? The publication of this book reflects a growing, broad-based consensus on the need to address violence against women among policy-makers and practitioners in both human rights and development organisations. The 1994 United Nations Development Programme (UNDP) Human Development Report notes:

In no society are women secure or treated equally to men. Personal insecurity shadows them from cradle to grave. In the household, they are the last to eat. At school, they are the last to be educated. At work, they are the last to be hired and the first to be fired... and from childhood through adulthood, they are abused because of their gender.
(UNDP 1994, 31)

1

Violence, and the fear of it, limits women's choices in virtually all areas of their lives, in every community worldwide. Violence against women is pervasive and widespread; it is usually planned, and often systematic. It threatens women in the workplace, at home, in school, in community spaces, and in state institutions. When women survive the violence to which they are subjected, they may suffer long- and short-term consequences, physically, emotionally, and socially. Violence against women detrimentally affects women's ability to gain an education, earn a livelihood, develop personal relationships, and enjoy fully the human rights to which they are entitled. Wherever development and relief agencies work, violence against women is present, hidden or evident, in the populations that they hope to assist.

Over the last decade, major developments in the field of human rights have resulted in the recognition of violence against women as a long-ignored and fundamental abuse of women's human rights. In June 1993, the United Nations (UN) World Conference on Human Rights, held in Vienna, placed violence against women unequivocally on the human rights agenda. The final document of the Conference, the Vienna Declaration and Programme of Action, states, 'The human rights of women and the girl-child are an inalienable, integral and indivisible part of human rights.' (Section I, paragraph 18) Success in placing women's human rights on the agenda at Vienna can be attributed to the collective action of women in the years and months leading up to the conference.

In December 1993, the UN General Assembly's adoption of the Declaration on the Elimination of Violence against Women added to the gains made at Vienna. The Declaration condemns physical and emotional violence against women in the home, the community, and when condoned by the State, as an abuse of women's fundamental human rights.

The momentum created by the Vienna Conference led to calls for women's rights to be mainstreamed within human rights discourse. In March 1994, the UN Commission on Human Rights created a thematic mandate on the elimination of violence against women, entrusted to a Special Rapporteur on violence against women, its causes and consquences.[2]

Finally, the Fourth UN World Conference on Women, held in Beijing in 1995, reinforced what was said at Vienna. The Beijing Platform for Action – the final document to come out of the Conference – reinforces the commitments to eliminate violence against women at Vienna and notes:

> *Acts or threats of violence, whether occurring within the home or in*
> *the community, or perpetrated or condoned by the State, instil fear*
> *and insecurity in women's lives and are obstacles to the achievement*
> *of equality and peace.... High social, health and economic costs to the*

individual and society are associated with violence against women.

(United Nations 1995b, paragraph 117)

The international attention generated by the atrocities committed in Rwanda and the former Yugoslavia during the last decade of the twentieth century has resulted in further attention to violence against women, both in the context of internal or international armed conflict. The Statutes of the International Criminal Tribunals for the former Yugoslavia and Rwanda (established by UN Security Council resolutions, to try those responsible for genocide, other crimes against humanity, and serious violations of international humanitarian law), were both potentially equipped to deal with gender-based crimes more effectively and ensure justice for women. Both tribunals have resulted in progress in international criminal law, so that it tackles violence against women. As a result, rape and sexual abuse, under certain circumstances, have been found to constitute a war crime, genocidal act, or crimes against humanity.

In an unprecedented judgement in September 1998, the International Criminal Tribunal for Rwanda (ICTR) convicted Jean-Paul Akayesu on charges of genocide. The Tribunal stressed that rape and sexual violence were an integral part of the process of destruction of the Tutsi ethnic groups. The Tribunal found that numerous Tutsi women seeking refuge from the massacres were systematically raped by armed local militia. In December that year, the International Criminal Tribunal for the former Yugoslavia (ICTY) convicted Anto Furundzija, a former local commander of the Croatian military police unit, of war crimes. The Tribunal judged that aiding and abetting in outrages upon personal dignity, including rape, constitutes a war crime.

Following the achievements of feminist human rights activists at Vienna and Beijing, and the establishment of the two ad-hoc Tribunals, States' representatives agreed the Statute of the International Criminal Court (ICC) at the Rome Conference in 1998.[3] The effective inclusion of crimes of sexual violence in the ICC Statute was the result of years of negotiation and active lobbying by the Women's Caucus for Gender Justice and other NGOs. The Statute codifies rape and other forms of sexual violence as war crimes in international and internal armed conflict, and as crimes against humanity when committed on a widespread or systematic basis, and significantly, when committed in the context of peace as well as war. The ICC Statute also provides measures to protect the safety and physical and psychological well-being of victims and witnesses, particularly in relation to crimes of violence against women. The Statute is not yet in force, requiring further ratifications.

In a landmark judgement on 22 February 2001, the ICTY handed down the first ever convictions for rape and for enslavement – including in particular enslavement for sexual purposes – as crimes against humanity.

These developments establish that under certain circumstances violence against women constitutes a crime under international law, and help in the fight towards its eradication.

Currently, a growing number of policy-makers in development are acknowledging that violence against women is also a development issue. This recognition reflects a wider awareness of the links between poverty, human insecurity, and violence, and the need to develop strategies to address these holistically. It coincides, too, with growing realisation of the common roots of poverty and marginalisation in industrialised and 'developing' countries. Many argue that the process of economic 'globalisation'[4] at the start of the 21st century is generating more human insecurity throughout the world (UNDP 1999), including increasing violence and conflict at household, community, and national levels. The UNDP now defines the two essential elements to human security as freedom from fear and freedom from want (UNDP 1994, 24). This is a significant shift from the vision of development common in mainstream development agencies until recently, of the efficient promotion of economic growth and 'modernisation' in developing countries.

This shift began a decade ago, when the 1990 Human Development Report (UNDP 1990, 10) broke new ground in connecting human rights perspectives to development concerns. It defined human development as widening the range of choices available to people, according to principles of equality of opportunity, sustainability, and empowerment. It stated that, 'Human development is a process of enlarging people's choices. The most critical are to lead a long and healthy life, to be educated, and to enjoy a decent standard of living. Additional choices include political freedom, guaranteed human rights, and self-respect.' The report also stated that people must be able to make these choices safely and freely. The role of development organisations – including state institutions at both national and international levels, as well as non-governmental organisations (NGOs) of different kinds – is to provide the conditions in which people can claim these rights and make these choices. In line with this, the 1994 UNDP Human Development Report called for a new development paradigm that 'puts people at the centre of development, regards economic growth as a means and not an end, protects the life opportunities of future generations as well as present generations... [and that] empowers people – enabling them to design and participate in the processes and events that shape their lives.' (UNDP 1994, 4) International governmental and non-governmental organisations are increasingly adopting a 'rights-based approach' to development that aims not only to relieve poverty and suffering, but to address its causes.

Most recently, the Human Development Report has stated that, 'The mark of all civilisations is the respect of human dignity and freedom.' (UNDP 2000, 1) Freedom from fear of physical violence is recognised as a fundamental and common principle shared by human rights and development concerns. The Report goes on to argue that amongst the worst personal threats are those to women (op. cit., 36). Rape as a weapon of war, trafficking in women for the purposes of prostitution, female genital mutilation, domestic violence, honour killings, and the sexual abuse of girls are all highlighted in the Report as forms of physical violence that threaten women's security.

The violence to which women are subjected, predominantly by men, jeopardises their freedom to participate in the social, economic, and political life of their communities, and marginalises them from the processes and events that shape their lives. Such violence not only terrorises individual women and destroys their lives, but damages the social fabric that is essential for trust and co-operation between human beings. By eroding the vital social relationships between individual women and men, and between groups of men and women, violence against women perpetuates – and worsens – poverty and vulnerability. While only some women actually experience violence, the fear and threat of it is common to all women, influencing their thoughts and actions at all levels: from the most intimate aspects of life at home, to participation in public political and economic activities.

Oxfam's work on violence against women

Staff in Oxfam GB have been working in different ways on the issue of violence against women since the 1970s. As stated in the Preface, the centrality of violence against women to development was recognised in Oxfam's organisational Gender Policy, ratified in 1993 by Oxfam's Trustees. The Gender Policy states, 'Violence against women constitutes an infringement of basic rights, undermines their self-determination, and their ability to participate fully in and to benefit from development.' (Oxfam Gender Policy 1993, 2) However, while innovative and useful work has been done in some contexts, progress in translating this principle into action has been patchy. In 1997, Suzanne Williams, then Oxfam's Policy Adviser on Gender and Rights, instigated a year-long research process to map Oxfam's experience on violence against women across its international programme, with a view to developing a coherent strategy on the issue. Francine Pickup, the principal author of this book, was the researcher on this project. The research began with the collection of information about the projects and partner organisations supported by Oxfam that work on issues of violence against women. The research also involved attending workshops and conferences, and collecting information on women's movement initiatives to end violence.

The research process culminated in a five-day international workshop on violence against women, held in Sarajevo, Bosnia, during the internationally recognised 'Sixteen days of no violence towards women' in 1998. The event brought together 60 participants from 26 countries, spanning Eastern Europe, Latin America, the Middle East, Asia, and Africa, all of whom were practitioners or policy-makers in the field of violence against women. Some participants were Oxfam's own staff; some came from organisations supported financially by Oxfam; others were from organisations working with Oxfam in a non-funding relationship. The research and the workshop have had a substantial impact on the work on violence against women within Oxfam GB and partner organisations, and form the basis for this book.[5] A report of the Sarajevo workshop has been published by Oxfam (Oxfam GB 1998b). As a result of meetings of the Latin American participants at the workshop, CLADEM has published, with support from Oxfam GB and NOVIB, an analysis of violence against women in 17 countries in the Latin American region based on detailed case studies of State and NGO responses and strategies.[6]

The Sarajevo workshop represented a landmark in the development of Oxfam's understanding of the nature and impact of violence against women both in peacetime and during armed conflict. Strategies to tackle violence within development, relief, and human rights interventions were discussed at the workshop, which explored the experiences both of women survivors of violence, and of those working with them in development and human rights organisations. It enabled insights to be shared across differing cultural, economic, and political contexts. Until the workshop, much of this vital information had remained fragmented and invisible to many. The workshop generated tremendous energy, challenging Oxfam to participate in the ongoing global struggle to end violence against women, and resulted in Oxfam's development of a global programme on violence against women.

What you will find in this book

This book argues that all organisations involved in development should challenge violence against women, and work to end it. It does not, however, set out to offer a blueprint for this work. Rather, it considers different views of why violence against women exists, and the various types of response to such violence that are open to development organisations. The first half of the book attempts to synthesise some of the contradictory explanations for violence against women, to give development policy-makers and practitioners a better sense of the beliefs and values that underlie different policy options. In the second half of the book, policy-makers will find a discussion of different practical responses to violence against women, drawing on a wealth of case studies from many organisations working in different parts of the world. Many of these have been supported at some point by Oxfam GB.

Chapter 1 begins by exploring definitions of violence against women and related concepts. It considers ideas about power and their implications for discussions of violence, and discusses the terminology of victimhood and survival. It presents a gender relations framework for understanding violence against women and shows how this framework allows us to ask questions about men who are not violent as well as women who are. The chapter draws out some links between violence against women and poverty. It then turns to a framework for understanding responses to violence against women. Different kinds of policy responses are discussed. The chapter shows how individuals, groups, and institutions can violently resist attempts to transform gender relations, and considers the ways in which development organisations can help to prevent such violent male backlash.

Chapter 2 reviews the human rights and development responses to violence against women. These responses differ considerably, with the human rights response focusing on physical violation, while the development response focuses on the costs to the community and State. We consider the advantages of, and limitations to, these different responses. The discussion stresses the importance of rejecting artificial distinctions between political and civil responses on the one hand, and social and economic ones on the other, in order that the many aspects of violence against women may be understood, and that women's interests may be addressed holistically.

Chapter 3 reviews evidence of the extent of different forms of violence. It considers the physical, mental, emotional, and social impacts of violence on women victims, on witnesses of violence, on perpetrators of violence, and on communities and societies. It concludes by drawing out the implications for development workers.

Chapter 4 addresses four institutions – the family, the household, the community, and the State – where values promoting women's subordination may be advanced and where violence against women takes place. It considers the ways in which these institutions perpetuate violence against women, and asks what development workers can do to change this. The chapter then discusses economic hardship and armed conflict, contexts within which violence against women is often reported to increase. It asks why violence increases in these contexts, and elucidates the implications for development workers.

Chapter 5 concerns strategies that provide direct support to survivors of violence. It begins by looking at the options open to women, and the barriers to them seeking assistance. The chapter analyses the different kinds of services that are provided by women's and development organisations to meet women's needs, and considers the tension between western, feminist-dominated models and indigenous, locally-specific forms of support.

Chapter 6 considers ways of challenging violent men. It first asks why we should work with men at all. It shows how women's empowerment in their close relationships may be one way to challenge men's violence. The chapter addresses strategies advanced by development organisations and NGOs that aim to challenge men's behaviour directly, rather than waiting for this behaviour to be challenged by changes in gender relations brought about through other means. It considers the advantages and limitations of four different types of response: traditional healing and reconciliation mechanisms; psycho-social therapy; psychological treatment programmes; and education.

Chapter 7 explores how attitudes and beliefs in public culture can condone violence against women. It asks how these attitudes may be challenged so that community level institutions support rather than stigmatise women victims of violence, and challenge men's violent behaviour. It addresses various strategies used by development and women's organisations to raise public awareness of violence against women. These include: research and collection of information; the use of national and local level interventions that aim to harness media influence; and training influential community members to act as agents for change.

Chapter 8 discusses the responses to violence against women available to the State, and considers the role of women's and development organisations in ensuring that the State fulfils its commitments to protect women.

The final chapter draws out some planning implications, and considers the links between violence against women and social change. It summarises the feminist analysis used in the book and its planning implications, both for directly supporting women, and for challenging the institutions that perpetuate violence against women.

PART 1

Exploring violence against women

1 Explaining violence against women as a development concern

[Male partners hit women] when they are sober, when they have work, when there is no reason for jealousy, for questioning authority, when there are no disagreements on childrearing, when they have finished all the household chores... so for no reason at all. In these cases, women are left baffled by the inequality in their relationships. What they do know for certain is that their partners can hit them when they feel like it, and that they accept it as normal: that is what happened with their parents, and that is what goes on in other families.

(Paulina Gonzalez Sanchez, Corporación Grupo de Apoyo Pedagogico (GAP), paper presented at Oxfam international workshop on violence against women, Sarajevo, 1998)

1.1 Defining violence against women

Violence against women is not unusual. Nor is it committed only by abnormal, psychologically disturbed individuals. On the contrary, it is perhaps the most pervasive form of abuse: a universal phenomenon that cuts across all divisions of class, race, religion, age, ethnicity, and geographical region. However, there is no universally accepted definition of violence against women. Rather, definitions vary according to different perspectives, and are reflected in different policy responses from human rights and development organisations.

The first definition reproduced here focuses on physical harm – an example of a narrow definition. International definitions are broader, encompassing physical, emotional, and psychological harm as well as the threat of such harm. Oxfam GB uses the UN definition set out in the Declaration on the Elimination of Violence against Women, and in the Beijing Platform for Action, adopted by 189 countries at the Fourth World Conference on Women in Beijing in 1995, as an appropriate policy and advocacy tool and framework for direct interventions.

> *[Violence against women includes] any physical or sexual act against
> a woman (or girl) which meets or surpasses a minimum level of force,
> including pushing, hair-pulling, hitting, smacking, slapping and being
> held down by a man's weight so that the woman cannot move, and
> which denies the woman ability to control contact.*

(P. Sen 1997a)

Narrow definitions, such as the above, focus on the infliction of physical
hurt. By defining violence according to objective and measurable criteria,
this definition makes physical contact an essential element of violence,
therefore distinguishing it from psychological abuse. Non-contact forms of
violence such as flashing, depriving women of resources, sexual
exploitation of women through prostitution, and the impact on women's
lives of the fear of violence, are not included. This allows researchers and
policy-makers to demarcate physical violence from other acts clearly, and
address these as a priority. However, such definitions exclude psychological
and verbal abuse, which may be as injurious as physical violence in some
cases.[1]

> *Violence against women means any act of gender-based violence that
> results in, or is likely to result in, physical, sexual or psychological
> harm or suffering to women, including threats of such acts, coercion
> or arbitrary deprivation of liberty, whether occurring in public or
> private life. Violence against women shall be understood to
> encompass, but not be limited to, the following:*
>
> a. *Physical, sexual and psychological violence occurring in the
>   family, including battering, sexual abuse of female children in the
>   household, dowry-related violence, marital rape, female genital
>   mutilation and other traditional harmful practices to women,
>   non-spousal violence and violence related to exploitation.*
>
> b. *Physical, sexual and psychological violence occurring within the
>   community, including rape, sexual abuse, sexual harassment and
>   intimidation at work, in education institutions and elsewhere,
>   trafficking in women and forced prostitution.*
>
> c. *Physical, sexual and psychological violence perpetrated or
>   condoned by the State, wherever it occurs.*

(United Nations Declaration on the Elimination of Violence Against
Women, adopted by the General Assembly on 13 December 1993)

This broader definition of violence against women recognises not only
physical, sexual, and psychological violence, but also threats of such harm.
There is a danger in employing very broad definitions. If the term 'violence'

is used to describe practices or norms for which other words already exist, this may result in the power of the term 'violence against women' being diluted. A narrower definition, that distinguishes between different forms of violence, can provide greater clarity about the nature and specific contexts of the violence at issue.

The Inter-American Convention on the Prevention, Punishment and Eradication of Violence Against Women, adopted in June 1994, states that:

> *For the purposes of this Convention, violence against women shall be understood as any act or conduct, based on gender, which causes death or physical, sexual or psychological harm or suffering to women, whether in the public or the private sphere.*
>
> *Violence against women shall be understood to include physical, sexual and psychological violence:*
>
> a. *that occurs within the family or domestic unit or within any other interpersonal relationship, whether or not the perpetrator shares or has shared the same residence with the woman, including, among others, rape, battery and sexual abuse;*
>
> b. *that occurs in the community and is perpetrated by any person, including, among others, rape, sexual abuse, torture, trafficking in persons, forced prostitution, kidnapping and sexual harassment in the workplace, as well as in educational institutions, health facilities or any other place; and*
>
> c. *that is perpetrated or condoned by the state or its agents regardless of where it occurs (Article 1 and 2).*

One can speculate that use of the word 'conduct' in the Inter-American Convention definition could include behaviour that constitutes the threat of violence (threat being mentioned explicitly in the UN Declaration on the Elimination of Violence Against Women). The word 'conduct' could also be construed to encompass an act of omission. For example, the failure to intervene against the perpetuation of practices harmful to women such as lack of safe access to contraception and abortion, laws and policies that perpetuate women's socio-economic subordination, discriminatory food allocation, and lack of critical healthcare provision could be within the scope of the Convention. The logic underlying these radical definitions is that violent acts are not only those inflicted directly on individual women or girls, but include those that lead to omission or deprivation, including polices and customs that result in gender discrimination and that harm women physically or mentally. The advantage of such definitions is that they link violence against women to the broader economic, social, and political contexts in which it occurs. The disadvantage is that they use the vocabulary of violence for acts other than those that directly injure human bodies and minds, and may therefore diminish our appreciation of the nature and importance of such direct injuries.

> [Violence against women includes] *any act involving use of force or coercion with an intent of perpetuating/promoting hierarchical gender relations.*
>
> (Asia Pacific Forum on Women, Law, and Development 1990)

Definitions of violence against women also vary as to whether they consider that violence is being applied in order consciously to perpetuate male control over women. The definition provided by the Asia Pacific Forum on Women, Law and Development stresses the intent of the perpetrator. Other definitions focus on the harm caused by violence, in the belief that such harm reinforces women's subordination whether or not this was the conscious intention of the perpetrator.

However, a focus on the harm caused may lead to disagreements about what constitutes harm. There is considerable disagreement about definitions of sexual violence against women. Some sex worker activists have vehemently criticised the way in which 'sexual exploitation' as a term has been understood by some to include commercial sex work and pornography. They consider that this places sex work in the same category as incest and domestic violence, so that non-consensual sex is extended, by implication, to all commercial transactions involving sex. One example of an organisation that defines sexual exploitation in this way is the Coalition Against Trafficking in Women, a North American NGO (NGO Coalition Against Exploitation of Women 1995). Helen Vicqua, a sex worker activist from the Scarlet Alliance, an Australian organisation that promotes sex workers' rights, states, 'To equate professional prostitution with domestic violence is to diminish the horror of the helplessness; to equate choiceful sex work with the violence of criminal greed is to deny the value and dignity of the work some women choose to do.' (Cited in Murray 1998, 61)

Whichever definition they adopt, researchers and policy-makers should state which they are using. Lack of clarity on definitions leads to confused dialogue about the issue, and results in prevalence statistics that cannot be compared and contrasted. When wrongly cited, they may underplay the issue, or lead to charges of sensationalism.

1.1.1 Recognising violence in contexts of intimacy: who defines violence?

> *We are so fed up. The man comes home in the early hours and you just have to submit. What can we do? Culture just demands that we open up for him at whatever time. And with the AIDS epidemic, how safe are we?*

(YWCA 1994, 25)

Is what this woman describes sex or is it violence? It may be difficult for readers to decide what they think about this – but it can be even more difficult for women themselves to recognise and name violence against them.

Coercive sexual activity is perhaps the most difficult-to-recognise manifestation of violence against women, both for women themselves, and for development workers. In the case above, the sexual activity involves two people who are sharing a bed and a home. The woman displays no physical resistance. In this sense the act is not physically violent; yet the woman shows disapproval of her partner's behaviour, recognises that it is physically dangerous to her, and states that cultural norms constrain her ability to challenge it.

Defining violence within marriage and other intimate relationships is particularly difficult, since women do not universally recognise such violence as abuse. Such violence may even be understood as a vital part of the relationship in some cases. Cultural norms have developed over time to justify, sustain, and perpetuate men's sexual coercion of women, as well as other forms of violence towards them. Jealousy and violence may be considered by many women to be a vital sign of a husband's commitment to the marital relationship. Sex and violence may not be mutually exclusive ways of relating, and experiencing violence during sex may not be definable in terms of consensus or non-consensus. It may be more accurate to say that many women experience their personal relations with men in terms of a continuum from choice, through psychological pressure, to force (Kelly 1988). Women may experience coercive sexual relations without physically confronting their aggressor, as a result of the normative constraints surrounding – and economic consequences of – dissent. But such women do not necessarily tolerate or consent to violent behaviour. In such cases, to make a simple distinction between whether the act involved physical coercion or not is inadequate.

For example, some popular beliefs dictate that women who sell sex cannot be raped, because they have already agreed to have sex, albeit for money. Legal definitions, which play a central role in defining what counts as rape, tend to deal in clear dichotomies – freedom or force, non-violence or violence. Evidence of rape is limited to visible marks of force in or on the body of a victim after the event. In a study in London, UK, sex workers contradicted the idea that rape always involves force. The sex workers distinguished between two main types of sexual and violent relations. On the one hand there was sex as work. This sex was alienated from the person, was priced, circumscribed in space and time, involved restricted activities, used condoms for protection, and was disassociated from pleasure and reproduction. On the other hand, there was sex for pleasure, integral to the self. At work, intentional removal of the condom or non-payment were perceived as violence. Such broken agreements constituted 'rape at a distance'. Rape outside work was 'close-up', because women invested personal and moral integrity in the relationship (Day 1994).

Some perspectives emphasise that women's own perceptions of violence should be the starting point of work to end violence (Hanmer and Maynard 1987). However, the fact that women in different cultural contexts may not recognise forms of violence discussed in the definitions as violence makes it essential to bear in mind some kind of objective definition. The language of the debate may be alien to women in different contexts. Equally, it is not wise to assume that people can or will express their views candidly on such a sensitive issue.

It is very important to recognise violence as such in advocacy or public campaigning work, in order to gain the attention of decision makers at all levels. Some feminist approaches to violence hold that it is also important for individual survivors, and those around them, to name violent behaviour inflicted against them as such. Such approaches consider that this helps women's psychological healing processes, and may also oblige others to offer support, and condemn the behaviour of the perpetrator. However, women may suffer from such approaches where their societies do not consider what they have experienced to be violence. A woman who no longer faces violence, but must live with its memory, may not welcome the additional pain caused by feelings of confusion or alienation from society, and rejection or stigmatisation. One British Oxfam staff member attended an international conference on female genital mutilation (FGM), with an Ethiopian friend who had undergone this.[2] The use of the emotive term 'mutilation' in the presence of women survivors, and the revulsion expressed by international activists who considered women who had undergone FGM to be 'incomplete' or 'disabled', appeared to be another form of abuse.

A World Bank study on all forms of violence in Jamaica (Holland and Moser 1997) aimed to identify the extent to which communities saw violence as a problem, the priority they gave to violence relative to other problems, and the perceived gravity of different types of violence. The study looked at all forms of crime and violence instigated by men and women in all contexts. Using participatory urban appraisal (PUA) methodologies, communities identified 25 different types of violence. While there were significant distinctions between communities and different groups within communities, the report contended that overall the groups ranked gang violence using guns as the most serious form of violence, followed by rape and drug related violence. Other interpersonal forms of violence were considered the least serious, although this was the most prevalent type of violence in the communities.

These definitions raise several points about priorities and who establishes them. There are dangers in solely relying on local people's standpoints. Violence against women may not be accorded high priority because of women's secondary status; a community may lack appropriate conceptual or linguistic frameworks within which to express ideas about violence against women; and the assumption that participatory appraisal techniques will enable people to express their priorities may be a false one. What women and men say is context-dependent and to varying degrees constrained by gender identities (Jackson 1996). Gender identities shape our perceptions of what constitutes violence, and which forms of violence are prioritised. In contexts or relationships where women are expected to give sex, or where the abuse of women is seen as normal behaviour, certain forms of violent behaviour may not be named as violence. Development policy-makers and practitioners are well aware of the need to distinguish between the perceived priorities that participatory methods bring out, always assuming that women are able to express any priorities at all, and those that an outsider may see more 'objectively', although these are of course also perceived.

Women may often develop their own strategies to deal with violence, and these may not involve the direct 'naming' and condemnation of it. In a recent study conducted in Calcutta, the majority of women expressed their belief that violence was bad. Most women demonstrated either regret, pain, anger, sorrow, or disapproval. The study noted, 'This disapproval does not always involve unequivocal condemnation of violence or approval of all attempts to resist male violence, but most women found ways of making known their dissatisfaction to their husbands or to others.' (P. Sen 1998b, 151) Finally, women may not see violence as the most pressing issue facing them, but as one issue among other issues facing the community.

1.2 The causes and the perpetrators

There are many myths about violence against women that attempt to explain or justify it. Common myths include the following:

- Women are subjected to violence by a minority group of psychotic men;
- The ravages of poverty or war lead to attacks on and abuse of women;
- Violence against women is caused by abuse of drugs, including alcohol;
- Violence against women is an inevitable part of male-female relations;
- Violence against women is an inherent part of maleness, or a natural expression of male sexual urges.

Such views can lead to a perception that violence against women is rare or exceptional, and/or that it is caused by factors outside men's control. They place onus on women to ensure that they minimise the chances of their behaviour instigating violence. Men as the perpetrators of violence and the violators of human rights know, by and large, that they will get away with it.

Explanations stressing psychological factors

Some explanations of violence against women focus on psychological aspects of men who abuse. Some researchers have argued that men who abuse women have an 'impaired masculinity', which is often said to have been learnt as a result of growing up in a violent household.[3] In this view, it is likely that people exposed to violence in childhood may in turn consider it as an option for resolving conflicts.

However, psychological explanations for violence often fail to appreciate the role of wider inequalities in the relations between women and men, and the need to transform these. It is not simply the case that if one sees or experiences violence as a child, one will in turn abuse others. Girls are three to six times more likely to experience sexual abuse than boys, yet the vast majority of sexual abuse is perpetrated by male, not female, adults (Kelly *et al.* 1995). The processes by which witnessing violence as a child affects one's adult relationships are themselves gendered.

Explanations stressing external factors

At the other extreme, violence against women is seen by some as the result of men's experience of external factors including poverty, conflict, or rapid economic or political change. While evidence from women themselves in many different contexts indicates that poverty and crisis exacerbate violence against women, in particular marital violence, poverty is not in itself the cause of violence against women. Rather, it is one of many factors that may aggravate or increase the violence that already exists. Overwhelmingly, evidence suggests that violence against women cuts across socio-economic boundaries. The fact that not all men in poor households are violent indicates that poverty is an insufficient explanation of violence. To over-exaggerate the role of poverty also negates people's agency in making choices about the way that they react to factors outside their control. Later in this chapter, we will examine the relationship between poverty and violence against women in more detail, since it is of key concern to development policy-makers and practitioners.

Conflict and rapid change affect the extent of violence against women in a society, but they do not cause it. It is true that existing rates of violence against women often increase during times of social instability, and that new patterns of abuse can be triggered. Men's unemployment and women's entry into the workforce during times of economic restructuring, or the lack of opportunities for demobilised soldiers after a war, are two situations that may pose a challenge to men's sense of themselves as powerful. In contexts where individual men feel that their sense of masculinity and power is threatened, and violence against women is condoned in law or in custom, such violence may increase in intensity and frequency, as men struggle to maintain a sense of power and control.

Many women understand the connections between the humiliation and low self-esteem experienced by unemployed men, and violence against women. One woman in a study in the Eastern Cape of South Africa reported, 'Many men are being retrenched. Many men are unemployed. They have nothing to do. They are looking for excitement. So they cause trouble. A man gets depressed over his wife's success. It causes jealousy. At home, if the man is unemployed and his wife is employed he will be resentful. Alcohol is leading to more abuse of children.' (Hirschmann 1998, 235)

Explanations from gender and development approaches

Gender analysis of human development shows us that the root cause of violence against women is not psychological damage to individuals, or external economic or political factors. Rather, it lies in the unequal power relations between women and men, which ensure male dominance over women, and are a feature of human societies throughout the world.

Feminists have termed this inequality 'patriarchy' (literally, the 'rule of the fathers'). Violence against women has been termed one of six 'structures of patriarchy', which control women and consolidate men's political, economic, and social dominance (the others being the household, employment, the State, sexuality, and culture) (Walby 1990, 21). Violence against women is the ultimate weapon available to men wishing to assert their masculinity or to ensure continuing control over resources and decision making at all levels of society, including within the household, the market, the State, and development organisations. Violence itself, and the threat of violence, are fundamental to creating fear of – and compliance with – male domination in women. 'Victims are chosen because of their gender. The message is domination: stay in your place or be afraid. Contrary to the argument that such violence is only personal or cultural, it is profoundly political.' (Bunch and Carrillo 1991, 8)

Eliminating violence against women is a profoundly political challenge, because it necessitates challenging the unequal social, political, and economic power held by women and men, and the ways in which this inequality is perpetuated through human institutions at all levels of each society.

1.2.1 Men who reject violence: resisting 'hegemonic masculinity'

Not all men are violent to women. Despite the fact that no society is free from it, male violence against women varies in degree and intensity according to specific circumstances; it is not monolithic. There are many ways of being a man, and individuals are able to exercise free will over their actions.

The concept of 'hegemonic masculinity', or a dominant ideal of masculinity (Hearn 1996), explains how many different masculinities may co-exist within a society. In any given society, however, particular forms will be seen as most desirable, and as offering men the most power. These are 'hegemonic' masculinities. Opportunities for individual men to conform to or differ from the models of hegemonic masculinity in their particular society vary according to structural factors: class, race, sexuality, and other aspects of identity.

Many men do choose to reject dominant stereotypes of violent, controlling masculinity. There is an important role for men who reject violent aspects of masculinity to work in solidarity with women against violence. However, the fact that individual men may decide not to conform does not mean that they do not indirectly benefit from women's fear of male violence, because violence is one of the ways that men's dominance is maintained in the institutions that structure society.

1.2.2 Women who are violent: 'bargaining with patriarchy'

Numerous studies have shown that cases of male violence towards female partners constitute the majority of cases of violent conflict in the household. In the small number of cases where women are violent to men, this is usually in self-defence (Dobash, Dobash, Wilson, and Daly 1992; Brush 1990). However, some types of violence against women are perpetrated by women. If we accept the idea that violence against women is the ultimate method of male control over women, how do we explain why some women are violent to other women? While men have something to gain from conforming to dominant notions of what it is to be a man, the reasons for women's participation in violent acts are less immediately apparent.

'Bargaining' with patriarchy refers to the various strategies in which women engage to ensure their own survival and security, within a social, economic, and political context that is shaped and dominated by men (Kandiyoti 1988). Although women who undertake such strategies may sacrifice the long-term interests of women as a category by supporting the status quo, as individuals they may be guaranteed economic, social, or political rewards. Sometimes, the bargain they strike requires them to collude with men in episodes of violence against other women. These episodes are the logical outcome of women's conformity to the rules of a game that has been designed by men.

The range of bargains with patriarchy made by women shows the complexity of structural relationships between women. Gender inequalities are cross-cut by inequalities created by age, position within the family, class, race, and sexuality, to produce conflicts of interest between women as well as between men and women.

In some societies, older women may display violent behaviour towards their daughters-in-law. These women may consider their daughters-in-law as posing a threat to their position of influence with their sons, on whom elderly widows depend for resources. In addition to exhibiting violent behaviour themselves, older women may also encourage their sons to behave violently towards their wives (Gallin 1992). The effect is to strengthen the ties between mother and son, in a context in which women are the property of the husband and his family. The ability of older women to initiate violence in these ways partly reflects young wives' own lack of recourse, either within the marital family, or to her natal kin – who may be distant or may regard it as no longer their concern.

In a gender training workshop, traditional Indian midwives (*dais*) reported that that no mother would willingly kill her daughter, but that mothers who do not yet have sons may consent to female infanticide. They do this because they realise that, within the household and more widely, the status of women with daughters but no sons is lower than that of women who have sons or both sons and daughters. The *dais* themselves argued that they were forced to kill baby girls even though they did not wish to, because their poverty and dependency on upper-caste households forced them to do so (Murthy 1996).

Race and class may also interact to cause violence against women, when these are factors increasing the vulnerability of women. Upper-class women who are socially and materially dependent on their husbands may use violence against their domestic workers to protect and assert their position as wives.

In some situations, the bargain that a woman makes with patriarchy may be on behalf of a daughter or other female dependant, and in the dependant's own perceived best interests. For example, it may be a rational – and even loving – decision for a mother to decide to genitally mutilate her daughter in a culture where she will stand little chance of finding a husband otherwise, and where there are few economic alternatives to marriage.

The notion of the patriarchal bargain also helps to explain why struggles to end violence sometimes meet resistance from women, as well as men. The type of bargain a woman makes with patriarchy varies according to the institution to which she is loyal. If a woman sees her best interests being served by upholding the status of the family, she will protect that status even if doing so perpetuates violence against other women. Shakti Shalini, a grassroots NGO in Delhi, India, opposes dowry-related violence. In the late 1980s, NGO workers told a member of Oxfam staff that older women dislike the organisation's approach to dowry because they fear that women who are in contact with the organisation will start speaking for themselves, become activists, and even leave their households. In particular, the older women criticised Shakti Shalini for taking extreme cases of violence to court, because in a court case the honour of the family is questioned, and its reputation jeopardised (Piza-Lopez, no date given, Oxfam internal document).

While the concept of the 'patriarchal bargain' can enable understanding of why women inflict violence on other women in a social, political, and economic structure which furthers the interests of men, this is not the same as absolving women from all responsibility for their violence. Women, too, have agency – albeit to a limited extent in some situations – and many resist the social pressures on them to be violent. As agents of the State, in particular, women have been guilty of appalling violations of women's human rights, inflicting torture or ill-treatment on women for whom they are responsible. As officers of the South African State and wardens of prisons, women inflicted torture on imprisoned women (Goldblatt and Meintjes 1998), and female prison officers in Northern Ireland have also been directly responsible for administering torture and humiliating treatment of a sexual nature on women political activists (Cullen 1994, cited in McWilliams 1998).

This section has conceptualised violence against women as a strategy that men, and sometimes women, use to assert power and retain control over women in male-dominated social, political, and economic contexts. Individual men – and women – may choose to employ violence in their different relationships with women, according to their particular context. While poverty, conflict, or crisis may trigger a rise in the incidence of violence against women, these factors do not cause it: violence against women exists in all societies, and individual women experience it in every social and economic group. Similarly, psychological explanations that emphasise that individuals who have been exposed to trauma and violence are more likely to be violent cannot explain the endemic nature of violence against women.

Despite the fact that many of the organisations that respond to violence against women have focused on psychological support to women and girl survivors, the explanation for violence against women outlined here suggests that a more holistic response is needed, one that addresses both the perpetrators of violence, and the institutions that promote and sustain gender inequalities between men and women. Above all, this explanation points to the need for a radical shift in power relations between women and men. For this reason, many development organisations are working not just to provide support to individual women victims of violence, but are asking how to transform the unequal gender relations that pervade societies' values and institutions.

1.3 Poverty and violence against women: exploring the links

Since International Women's Year in 1975, international and national development organisations of all kinds have focused on women in many different ways. An early interest in 'integrating' women into development led to 'women in development' (WID) and later, 'gender and development' (GAD) programmes and projects. In order to analyse the ways in which development organisations had worked with women, Caroline Moser (1989b) created a typology distinguishing between five different policy approaches: welfare, equity, anti-poverty, efficiency, and empowerment (for more on this, see pp. 31–32). Development organisations have tended to under-emphasise the feminist goal of promoting equality between women and men in favour of the goal of poverty alleviation (Jackson 1996). Most development interventions focusing on women or on gender issues do not aim to challenge gender power relations or shift unequal workloads from women to men; rather, they aim to encourage women in production. Few development organisations have been willing to consider working on interventions that aim to get men to undertake reproductive work, or to challenge violence within the family or household.

Reluctance on the part of development organisations to address violence against women is likely to be due to a range of concerns, many of which are dealt with at more length in Chapter 2. These include fear of intervening in the 'private sphere' of the family and household, and concern about being charged with breaking up the family, or interfering with the institution of marriage. More pragmatic concerns include the concern that misplaced interventions may leave women more vulnerable to violence through empowerment strategies that encourage women to step out of culturally ascribed gender roles. There is indeed evidence of a link between economic and social change, shocks to gender power relations, and increased violence against women, which should not be ignored. This will be examined in more detail later in this chapter.

Our analysis of violence against women shows that we cannot sustain a vision of poverty as separate from equality. Poverty affects individuals differently according to their gender, and other aspects of their identity. Women who struggle to live free from violence speak of economic deprivation, but also of social and political dimensions, including their exclusion from participation in society, their lack of self-esteem, and their sense that they lack autonomy. Living in poverty makes women particularly vulnerable to male violence against them. Economic need may compel women to accept income-generating strategies that make then vulnerable to violence. In societies where women are seen as contravening gender norms by leaving their homes, women who work outside the home for pay are particularly likely to encounter such violence.

In Bangladesh, women who have to leave home because they cannot afford to obey demands that they remain in *purdah* (seclusion) in the home are vulnerable to harassment, abuse, and violence from men, because they are perceived as transgressing the norms of female decency (Kabeer 1994). In contexts of extreme economic crisis, women may place themselves at appalling risk by undertaking work that is a form of violence in itself. For example, women of the former Soviet Union who are trafficked for sex work, may do this out of desperation to reach countries where work is rumoured to be available but legal immigration is not an option. Research by the UN Special Rapporteur on violence against women, its causes and consequences, reiterates a finding already known by many human rights activists in the United States, namely that the vast majority of women in prison are there for drugs smuggling. These women are paid to use their bodies to smuggle drugs; many are coerced by their families, who are offered considerable financial rewards by drug traffickers (Coomaraswamy 1999c).

Some grassroots organisations are responding to poor women who face violence in the 'public sphere'. The Israeli Coalition against Trafficking of Women, in conjunction with other NGOs, including the Israeli Women's Network and Amnesty International, successfully lobbied the Israeli Parliament to amend the Penal Code so that traffickers who traded in people for the purposes of prostitution would be brought to justice. The maximum penalty for this is now set at 16 years (Yael Weisz Rind, Amnesty International Israeli Section, personal communication 2001).

The Pakistan gender programme of the UNDP, recognising the link between violence against women, women's low status, and development, has worked on several concrete areas with the Pakistani government such as women's mobility, social and economic empowerment, access to credit, negative portrayals of women in the media, and enterprise development for rural women. However, none of its projects directly addresses the prevention of violence against women, facilitates women's access to justice, or the improvement of the State's response to violence against women (Human Rights Watch 1999, 98).

The Well-Being Centre in Kenya, which seeks to rehabilitate street children, focuses specifically on young girls who live on the street between the ages of six and 18, by providing them with basic needs, and educational and training opportunities. The Centre recognises that the street girls face additional threats not experienced to the same extent by boys, largely because girls are more vulnerable and face a higher frequency of sexual abuse and physical violence (PASF, Oxfam internal document 1998). In Central Africa, economic crisis, displacement, and insecurity have rendered many women vulnerable to sexual violence and/or in a position of having to resort to prostitution as a means of supporting their families and dependants. In response to this trend, a Reproductive Health Programme in Central Africa has been developed to collect data on Sexually Transmitted Diseases (STDs) with a view to designing a programme to provide access to diagnostic, treatment, and prevention services (Oxfam internal document 1996).

One organisation which has made links between the different dimensions of poverty faced by girls is the Kenya Alliance for the Advocacy of Children's Rights, which aims to increase girls' completion of primary and secondary schooling, and to advocate for the prevention of violence against girls. The Alliance addressed Kenyan girls' vulnerability to forced early marriages and sexual abuse by recognising the complex links between this abuse, girls' secondary status at school, and the excessive workload imposed on them at home. The fact that girls' education may not be accorded as high a value as boys' education, and that girls may be expected to learn how to do domestic chores from an early age, means that girls are often left with no economic alternatives to marriage. The Alliance responded by developing 'child rights clubs' in primary schools, to educate children on their rights through various activities such as creative writing, poems, songs, drama, and debates, and a programme to increase girls' completion of primary and secondary school (PASF, Oxfam internal document 1997).

Poverty also determines women's options to resist violence. A report by a Zambian centre for women victims of violence concludes on the significance of poverty: '… while poverty cannot be said to cause the abuse women face, it does limit the choices women can make around staying in violent relationships.' (YWCA 1994, 37) The political and social dimensions of women's poverty affect their ability to challenge violence against them.

In the home, constraints on women's ability to make independent decisions and control resources, including their own labour, mean that they face severe obstacles to challenging violence from a husband or other family member. Women's economic dependency on men, and the cultural value attributed to women being 'a proper wife', or 'a good mother', and 'loyal' to the family may lead women to decide that the repercussions of contradicting these gender ideologies are worse than those of staying with violent husbands. In Lebanon, staff in a counselling and legal advice centre of the League to Resist Violence Against Women have met women who have endured years of violence by their husbands but have not contacted the police, since they are economically dependent on their husbands. Sometimes the trigger for a woman to come to an advice centre is the husband becoming violent towards her daughter, rather than herself (interview with a programme counsellor 1998).

Women living in poverty tend to have limited access to formal institutions that might offer assistance in resisting violence. These include health, education, social, psychological, legal, and police services. Women and their dependants may be deterred from going to such institutions because of the costs associated with such action. Such costs may be financial, but the costs of facing social disapproval for having made the violence public may also act as a deterrent . This is exacerbated by divisions in social policy that in most countries mean that 'women's issues' such as violence are separated from policy on health, education, housing, and so on.

While it is the case that poverty and racial discrimination on the part of the authorities may decrease poor women's access to the institutions that are supposed to provide protection from violence, it may also be the case that middle-class women have fewer support networks and friends in whom

they can confide when confronted by violence. Ludmila Mikhailovna
Ermakova, the manager of the Domestic Violence Crisis Centre for Women
and Children, 'Ekaterina', in Russia, which offers individual psychological
and legal advice and legal representation in court, has noted that women
from high status households are more constrained by an ideology of
privacy in the home:

> *If the woman victim and the man aggressor occupy some position*
> *[with status], have weight in society, then women rarely turn to*
> *friends for help. They're ashamed. They look after the reputation of*
> *their family, and try to hide [the violence] more. These women more*
> *often come to us [at the crisis centre]. They have a higher developed*
> *knowledge, they understand that they shouldn't live like that*
> *anymore, and that they need to change something in life. Our*
> *statistics show that 50 per cent of the women who come to us have a*
> *higher education. They turn to relatives for help less. But more*
> *ordinary [worker] families turn to relatives for help – the woman can*
> *escape and hide at her sister's or brother's. Relatives can simply*
> *conceal her, they can go to to the husband aggressor and beat him.*
> *Violence for violence.*

(Personal communication 2000)

Of those women who seek support against violence, those from higher
economic strata are more likely than women living in poverty to be shown
respect when they are seeking assistance from the police, health workers,
and legal officials. Following her mission to South Africa to report on
violence against women in the community, the United Nations Special
Rapporteur on violence against women, its causes and consequences,
noted, 'Although white communities in the urban areas boast some
extremely interesting programmes concerning the policing of rape, the
appalling lack of resources, personnel and sensitivity in the black townships
with regard to the crime of rape was deeply disturbing.' (Coomaraswamy
1997b, para.15) Of course, the fact that this example is from South Africa is
significant. Race, as well as poverty and gender, constrained black South
African women's recourse to the law under apartheid. In South Africa, black
women are reluctant to report rape to the police. It has only recently
become possible for black women to have access to police services, and
there remains a general distrust of the police force because of its history
under the previous regime (ibid.).

An obvious solution to male domestic violence would seem to be for a
woman to leave and find another place to live independently, or to live with
a relative. However, women living in acute poverty may be able to do this
only with great difficulty, if at all, while those living in relative poverty are

invariably worse off if they move to form their own household. Women generally earn lower wages than men for commensurate work. However, for some women these difficulties are outweighed by the advantages of living in a household without violence, and where there are more equitable income distribution and consumption patterns.

Although much research still needs to be done on the links between violence against women and poverty, a gender analysis suggests that women who are living in poverty are most exposed to the risk of violence, and least able to remove themselves from violent situations. A range of factors, including material need, makes women vulnerable to violence. In order to secure their livelihood, women may have to take decisions to act in a way deemed 'socially unacceptable', thereby making themselves vulnerable to violence. Discriminatory institutions and beliefs hinder women's access to the tangible and intangible resources that can allow them to challenge violence. The obstacles to women freeing themselves from violent situations or relations are not simply economic, but relate to contractual relations in the family and household, as well as powerful norms sanctioned by community and state institutions. All these factors shape women's control over their options, through constraining their access to resources, and their own actions and behaviour.

1.4 Some useful concepts from gender and development

If violence against women is caused by unequal power relations between women and men, perpetuated by institutions which bolster male privilege, what is the right response for development policy and practice?

While power relations between men and women are unequal, they are not static or monolithic. In fact, they are constantly adapting and responding to social, economic, and political factors. While this constant change and fluidity may seem obvious, it is an important point to stress in relation to evolving strategies to end violence against women. Secondly, the fact that violence against women is a political issue means it is impossible to end it through development interventions that focus narrowly on economic needs. Women face a web of gender-specific social, political, and ideological constraints that prevent them from achieving violence-free lives.

1.4.1 Ending violence against women as a strategic and practical gender issue

Ending violence against women is in women's practical and strategic gender interests. The twin concepts of practical and strategic gender interests were coined by Maxine Molyneux (1985).[4] Practical gender interests are those interests shared by all women that arise from their current position in society and role in the existing sexual division of labour. In contrast, women's strategic gender interests denote those interests shared by all women which, were they met, would enable women to challenge inequality and transform gender relations. The distinction between practical and strategic gender interests helps development policy-makers and practitioners to understand the degree of resistance that is likely to be met by different kinds of interventions addressing violence against women.

Clearly, it is in women's immediate practical gender interests to end violence against women, and responding to violence as a practical gender issue has some value. It is a highly pragmatic approach, which focuses on the ways in which a woman should change her behaviour to placate the abuser and so avoid violence.

In Cambodia, common advice given to victims of domestic violence is:

> *Be a good wife, speak softly, take care of the house, serve your husband;*
> *Don't say bad things when he comes home from work;*
> *It's your karma, you must be patient;*
> *Cook food better. Don't burn the food;*
> *The man is very strong, don't refuse him, give him what he wants.*

(Nelson and Zimmerman 1996, 49)

While offering women practical advice of this kind is very common between family and friends, it is a much less common approach for formal organisations. However, at an advice centre for women victims of violence in Lebanon, psychologists working with women who continue to face violence on an ongoing basis told me how they help women to think of ways in which they could change their own behaviour to lessen the violence they face. This response reflects an awareness on the part of the advice centre workers of the considerable difficulties facing women in challenging the violence against them. Non-confrontational advice may help some women avoid violence on some occasions. However, such advice may also harm women at the level of their strategic gender interests, by exposing them to more incidences of violence.

Contrary to the way in which the practical/strategic distinction is often thought of by development workers, in real life no development intervention actually effects change at only the practical *or* the strategic level. Every practical development intervention has a 'strategic' effect on the power relations in women's lives, whether or not this is intentional. The fact that violence against women has its roots in inequality between women and men means that practical interventions alone are highly unlikely to stop violence for good. However, practical, pragmatic responses may ultimately enable women to challenge violence at the strategic level.

It is also possible that the effects of isolated practical development interventions on women's strategic gender interests will be adverse: unequal gender relations may be perpetuated and rationalised. In the case of the Lebanon advice centre cited above, in the act of advising women to change their behaviour in order to avoid violence, victims are – either directly or by implication – blamed for the violence inflicted against them, while abusers are not being challenged. This is ultimately a disempowering message that harms women's strategic gender interests.

More radical initiatives see violence against women as an abuse of women's human rights that is an outcome of structural inequality. Such initiatives are clearly concerned with women's strategic gender interest in transforming gender relations. Together with other 'strategic' interventions (for example, campaigning for women's suffrage, or provision of para-legals to enable women to gain knowledge of the law and how to use it), they are likely to be met by resistance.

It cannot be assumed that women will identify violence against women as an issue of concern, or one which they wish to challenge. Women's interest in stopping the violence perpetrated against them requires transforming gender relations that are widely perceived as part of the 'natural order'. Awareness that ending violence is in women's 'strategic interests' is likely to emerge only through a process of struggling 'against the grain' of common-sense notions about gender inequality (Kabeer 1994, 299). The exchange of knowledge 'with someone who knows that it is possible to change the natural order' such as an external facilitator or a community member who has experienced another culture or environment (March, Smyth, and Mukhopadhyay 1999, 20) may serve as a catalyst to action against violence.

1.4.2 Power, 'empowerment', and violence against women

Many of the organisations and women's groups that tackle violence against women as an issue of strategic interest to women start from the premise that the most appropriate way to do this is to support the empowerment of women, to enable them to overcome the economic, social, and political barriers to equality with men, to challenge existing power relations, and thereby realise their human rights. At the outset, it is worth stating that development policy-makers and practitioners need to be modest about what their interventions are likely to achieve for women who face violence, for two reasons. Violence against women is the outcome of unequal power between women and men, and is therefore concerned with relationships, rather than with women as individuals. Many development interventions that aim to bring about changes in gender relations still tend to focus most of their attention on women (although there are some notable exceptions, some of which feature in later chapters of this book). Secondly, change brought about by development interventions is only a tiny part of wider social, economic, and political change.

Many of the development interventions that use the term 'women's empowerment' do so very loosely. Around the time of the Third United Nations Women's Conference (held in Nairobi in 1985), the term entered common usage in development organisations of all kinds, regardless of the very wide range of philosophical standpoints that informed their work. Inevitably, this difference in standpoints prevented many of them from adopting the radical agenda of women's empowerment.

Caroline Moser's (1989b) WID/GAD matrix – a loosely historical typology of policy approaches to women and development – includes empowerment as the last of five policy approaches to be developed. Moser distinguishes between five different approaches to development with women:

1. **Welfare**: this approach is characterised by development interventions that further the goal of women's welfare by focusing on the practical needs of women, in their conventional roles as wives and mothers. The approach, which predates the UN Decade for Women (1976-85), is politically conservative, understanding women to be passive beneficiaries of development activities. A project on violence against women informed by this approach might focus on ending violence because of the detrimental impact it has on women's health.

2. **Equity**: this approach is characterised by development interventions that further the goal of equity (fair treatment in the eyes of the law) between women and men. This is a politically radical approach, developed in the UN Decade for Women (1976-85), which has, as a result, not proved popular with mainstream organisations involved in development, including governments. It has also been criticised as a western, 'top-down' approach. Responses to ending violence against women from legal institutions and human rights organisations (discussed in depth in Chapter 2) are informed by this approach.

3. **Anti-poverty**: this approach is characterised by development interventions that understand women to be disproportionately represented among the poor, and aim to move women and their dependants out of poverty by increasing their role in production. This approach focuses on economic poverty, and as such is unlikely to address violence against women directly. An intervention may be based

on the adverse impact of violence on an individual woman's ability to earn money for household survival, or on the impact on women's ability to escape poverty through access to markets or productive assets. It does not address the inequitable gender relations of production within the household.

4. **Efficiency**: this approach is characterised by development interventions that understand economic development to be hampered by inefficient working relations between women and men. In this view, governments and development agencies should create conditions in which women's potential for economic production can be exploited to the full. This approach has been the most popular with mainstream development organisations, including governments. It might result in a development intervention that justifies work to end violence against women in terms of the costs of that violence to the public health system, or in terms of the amount of women's labour lost as a result of violence. This approach is often seen as diametrically opposed to approaches that focus on women's empowerment as an end in its own right.

5. **Empowerment**: this approach is characterised by development interventions that understand human development as concerned with justice, peace, and equality, as well as economic growth. It has been developed by southern women, and critiques the current model of global development from a race, as well as a gender, perspective. It emphasises women's potential for self-reliance, and the importance of grassroots mobilisation to effect changes in power relations in favour of women and the South. Because empowerment is, by definition, self-generated, the role of development organisations is to provide women with support to enable them to transform their own lives. A project that addresses violence against women through an empowerment approach would focus on building women's self-esteem and capacity to protect themselves from violence, and their ability to challenge oppressive gender relations and end violence throughout their community.

1.4.3 Examining power and empowerment

Both power and empowerment are contested terms, understood in different ways by different individuals and institutions. Various theoretical perspectives on power are available to development policy-makers and practitioners (Lukes 1974; Kabeer 1994). These are potentially helpful in understanding how women endure, survive, and overcome violence and abuse, and in considering what social, political, and economic changes are needed to create equality between women and men at all levels of society.

The notion of '*power to*' focuses on the needs of individuals to be at liberty to make decisions, to express themselves, or to earn an income and be economically independent. In contrast, '*power over*' refers to power possessed by some people to the detriment of others. Those who have '*power over*' others may be able to control the actions, thoughts, and beliefs of those others, with the result that those who are being dominated consider the situation as 'natural', or ordained by religion or culture. In this view, power is a scarce resource, and is possessed by some to the detriment of others. Men's power over women emanates from beliefs about gender relations that accord men control over women's bodies, behaviour, mobility, access to material resources, and labour. Men's power over women can be overt – expressed as violence and physical coercion – or may be more subtle, influencing women's psychological processes in such a way as to restrict the range of options that they perceive to be open to them (Rowlands 1998). The power exercised over a woman by a violent man may cause a woman to internalise her oppression. For example, a woman who is subjected to abuse when she expresses her own opinions may start to withhold her opinions, and eventually believe she has none. This restricts women's '*power to*'.

The idea of '*power within*' refers to the power to transform a situation that an individual can gain through becoming aware of how '*power over*' operates, and how oppression is internalised. This awareness reveals that unequal power is not natural and inevitable, and enables individuals to begin to consider how to challenge this. '*Power with*' (Eade and Williams 1995) refers to the power attained by individuals working together in a supportive group, to build awareness of alternative beliefs and ways of life, and their ability to transform society together.[5] Some alternative notions of power do not depend on control over others; for example, 'the power that some people have of stimulating activity in others and raising their morale' (Hartstock 1985, 223). This definition of power sees it as an energising force that acts as a catalyst for change without being dominating.

1.5 Supporting women's empowerment and avoiding violent backlash

Following the discussion in the last section, this section attempts to answer two key questions for development policy-makers and practitioners who wish to support women's empowerment, and end violence against them. What different kinds of power do individual women and women's groups need to enable them to challenge violence against women and transform gender relations? And what is the role for development organisations in supporting women's empowerment?

The three aspects of power – 'power within', 'power to', and 'power with' – are considered separately. However, in real life, they are interconnected, and of equal importance.

Building 'power within' through confidence-building and awareness-raising

Responses from organisations supporting women against violence (both outside and inside the home) have tended to focus on 'power within', stressing the need to support women against the debilitating consequences of violence and to repair the psychological harm and damage to self-esteem that violence causes. In contrast, in mainstream development work with women, development organisations have tended to focus on promoting women's empowerment through supporting group activities in the community. They have made few attempts to measure the impact of women's involvement in such activities on violence against them, in particular within the home. They have tended to assume that women's power within their homes is increased by such work, while the real impact on women's power to negotiate with their partners, fathers, sons, and other family members – and the incidence of violence within the home – goes largely unmeasured. But what is empowerment, if it is not concerned with being able to live free from the fear of violence, and make choices on an equal footing with men, in *all* the sites where power is played out: at home, at school, in the workplace, in community fora, in government offices, and in parliaments? The ultimate goal is that, as women gain self-esteem and freedom from internalised oppression, they will be able to find ways of escaping, resisting, and reducing the violence directed at them.

A range of processes enables women to bring about changes in their personal relations that may have an impact on men's violence toward them within the home. The first stage is the development of 'power within', the development of self-esteem and self-worth. Power from within has been described as 'the spiritual strength and uniqueness that resides in each one of us, and makes us truly human. Its basis is self-acceptance and self-respect that extends, in turn, to respect for and acceptance of others as equals.' (Eade and Williams 1995, 234) The development of 'power within' can enable an individual to maintain a point of view, or continue an activity, in the face of overwhelming opposition; or to take a serious risk (Rowlands 1998). The concept of 'power within' offers an explanation for women's bravery and tenacity in holding on to their gains in the face of increasing threats of violence by men who fear a threat to their position of dominance.

Development interventions may have an express aim of promoting women's sense of themselves as powerful, or may implicitly aim to do this through providing a forum for women to meet and exchange ideas while engaged in other activities. Participation in collective activities informed by a commitment to empowering participants and promoting awareness of 'power within' may help women to become more assertive and able to make their own decisions. They may become better able to discuss issues with their partners, as they evolve an awareness of their own worth, needs, and personal interests, independently of their role within the family. Many forms of training build women's sense of 'power within': for example, some of the most effective training programmes aiming to raise awareness of women's legal rights focus on increasing women's self-esteem as well as their knowledge. An empowerment approach to training raises women's awareness of their oppression, and allows them to identify their own solutions to fighting violence inside and outside the home. It is clear that focusing on 'power within' is about more than simply making a woman feel better within herself. Such strategies need to be grounded in an analysis of gender power relations and a condemnation of male violence. Ultimately, men's 'power over' women must be challenged. The outcome of processes that aim to build women's sense of 'power within' will vary according to the degree to which abusers are able to change themselves. Men may oppose the idea of wives, mothers, or daughters participating in projects and programmes, particularly if these have an explicit aim of promoting women's sense of power and self-worth. Development interventions therefore need to ensure that women are provided with practical options to enable them to escape from future violence. Interventions with an explicit aim of empowering women may therefore focus on supporting women, for example through provision of counselling (face-to-face in information centres, or via telephone hotlines in some contexts), and shelters, where women can take refuge.

The outcome of interventions that build women's sense of 'power within' differs widely. As stated in an earlier section in this chapter, in the absence of a condemnation of violence, some women may adopt conciliatory strategies, in the belief that they can minimise violence and preserve the status quo. Others may successfully bring about changes in their close personal relationships, which lead to a lessening or cessation of violence against them within the home, and enhance their other life chances. Others may choose to leave violent relationships. Women may also experience changes in their relationships with others, including their children.

Building 'power to' through skills training and provision of resources

A second form of power that women may develop is the 'power to' bring about changes in their lives to meet their own interests and needs. Development interventions that promote women's 'power to' enable them 'to participate more effectively in the wider process of socio-political development, to wrest from society the rights, the dignity and the resources to which they were entitled for their own development, through collective action to increase their voice in development decisions that affected their lives.' (Mazumdar 1989, 11) This may involve developing vocational skills, undergoing leadership training, gaining access to economic and social resources, and learning how to use the legal system to challenge men and to assert their rights.

In some contexts, development interventions that provide women with credit have been assessed for their impact on violence against women in the home. The debate over the role of credit in decreasing or increasing violence against women is a complex one. Although some credit programmes do seem to have reduced violence against women in the home, women's increased role in income-generation and their more visible economic contribution to the household livelihood may not always lead to a reduction in violence.

There is no simple way to end violence against women through economic interventions. According to one theory, the participation of abused women in activities and social networks outside the home is an important factor in reducing male violence, because violent men face a greater risk that their activities will be exposed in a public context (Schuler *et al.* 1996). This argument holds that projects aiming at 'economic empowerment'[6] will not in themselves help reduce violence against women, unless they foster networks that offer women long-term support.

Many women's groups have evolved procedures to enable them to intervene quickly in such incidents, and to shame the perpetrator of the violence. If a woman in one income generation project supported by Oxfam Fair Trade in Bangladesh experiences violence, the other women from the project go immediately to her house. Their presence is enough to pressure the husband to stop (Barney, internal Oxfam document 1999).

Building a sense of solidarity: 'power with'

Both the preceding sections have emphasised the ways in which women are able to change the dynamics of their close relationships: directly, and indirectly through involvement in groups and networks. This sense of collective power can be termed 'power with'. It 'involves a sense of the whole being greater than the sum of the individuals, especially when the group tackles problems together' (Eade and Williams 1995, 234). This book provides many examples of this collective notion of power developed through belonging to a group.

One of the consequences of violence against women is what Medica Zenica, a Bosnian women's organisation that was created during the Bosnian war in response to women's need for confidential medical, psychological, and shelter services, has called 'the assassination of the subject self' (Medica Zenica Women's Therapy Centre 1995, 1). The opportunity to participate in women's organisations and to engage in political activity can provide women survivors with a vision of an alternative, new identity: not as victims of violence, or as clients or patients receiving treatment, but as women who have 'power within' and 'power to', working collectively to bring about positive change. Many women's groups that work with women survivors of violence use a 'positive approach to crisis', characterised by an emphasis on mutual learning, to develop solidarity between women from different backgrounds.

In all of these power-building strategies, women's own sense of self-esteem is essential to their being able to take actions and make decisions.

1.5.1 The impact of development interventions on violence against women

Wherever economic and social change – whether planned or unplanned – challenges gender power relations, there is a very real risk that women will be targets of male violence. This is true at least in the short-term, as men attempt to reassert their domination of women. Women working in interventions that address forms of violence against women directly are at particular risk of violent reprisals from men. Similarly, development interventions with the explicit aim of empowering women, and furthering women's strategic interests, are likely to place women at increased risk of male violence.

However, *all* development projects and programmes intentionally or unintentionally trigger changes in existing gender power relations. As argued earlier in this chapter, even development interventions with aims that seem to be wholly practical or technical have an impact on gender power relations. An example often given is that of a water project where women's time for strategising about their marital relationships is taken away when a standpipe relieves them of their journey to the water-hole. If impacts on gender relations are not taken into consideration during the planning of an intervention, it may have negative outcomes for women. The risk of male violence is therefore a concern for all involved in development interventions, including those that have an ostensibly technical aim.

The realisation that development interventions can have a negative impact on levels of violence against women is profoundly disquieting and difficult to tackle. However, development policy-makers and planners should explore all the possible outcomes of a project with the women concerned, and plan for all eventualities. Initiatives to strengthen women's existing networks and their strategies to prevent violence can provide women with support in dealing with risks of increased violence. Backlash may come from individuals, communities, religious groups, or the State. In some cases, men's violent response may be directed to destroying project resources, rather than towards women themselves. In Bangladesh, men brought a women's empowerment programme to an end by burning down mulberry trees, which women were cultivating as food for silk-worms (Bunch, Carrillo, and Shore 1998).

However, in most cases it is women themselves who are placed at risk of increased conflict and violence in the short- to medium-term. At present, we know far too little about the impacts of development projects and programmes on violence against women. It is rare to encounter development workers who consider that development might actually *increase*, rather than decrease, violence. Impact assessments of development interventions should routinely consider changes to the frequency and intensity of violence against women in the community and in households, as a result of the intervention. Indicators of violence against women need to be built into programme planning, review, and monitoring systems.

The fact that fewer women will be willing to participate if increased violence is the immediate result leads some development interventions to fail. For example, the survival of a revolving loan project, run by the Indian NGO Working Women's Forum, was seriously threatened when its most committed participants began dropping out due to increased levels of domestic violence (Carrillo 1992). The scope offered to women to empower themselves through companionship with other women, exchange of ideas, and involvement in activities outside the home, may incite men to violence. In an example from Papua New Guinea, Christine Bradley, the Principal Project Officer for the PNG Law Commission reports: 'some husbands prevent their wives from attending meetings by locking them up in the house, or by pulling them off the vehicle they have boarded to take them to a meeting, or even by pursuing them to the meeting and dragging them home.' (Bradley 1994,16)

Loan and credit programmes

There is a widespread belief that there is a direct correlation between increases in women's earnings and their bargaining power in intra-household decision-making. This is based on considerable evidence, from many contexts (A. Sen 1999). However, this correlation cannot be assumed (Standing 1990), and there is certainly no automatic second link between increased bargaining power and decreased violence against women; on the contrary, some research suggests that increased violence is an outcome of women's attempts to challenge male-dominated decision making.

Credit programmes in two regions of Bangladesh have been the focus of much research into these linkages. Four providers have administered loans,[7] predominantly to poor, rural women. Prior to the loan schemes, violence against women in the home was widespread in all the villages studied, but particularly so among married women. The reasons given by women for this violence were many, including giving birth to daughters, not performing household chores to their husband's satisfaction, talking back when reprimanded, challenging their husband's unemployment or gambling, and asking for money (Hashemi *et al.* 1996).

Evidence about the connection between violence and involvement in loan programmes is complex and sometimes contradictory. One study argues that domestic violence increased as a result of credit programmes in cases where women were unable to retain control over their loan. Disputes arose when men took control of the loan but were unwilling to pay it back, or when men were frustrated at their wives delay or failure to secure a loan (Goetz and Sen Gupta 1996). Other studies suggest that involvement in credit programmes causes violence to decrease, but only when women's contributions to the household income reach high levels (Schuler *et al.* 1996; Schuler *et al.* 1998). According to Schuler *et al.* (1996), the highest rates of male violence after credit programmes began occurred in a village where many women wanted to retain control over their loan and use it to fund their own economic activities, rather than choosing to pass control over it to their male relatives. Male appropriation of women's loans in these villages was reported as 33 per cent, in contrast to ten per cent in the villages where women were most likely to surrender their loans for their husbands to use as they wished (Schuler *et al.* 1998). Husbands became increasingly violent as their wives began to earn independent incomes and to become more mobile and autonomous (op. cit.). Similarly, households in which women have more economic autonomy and decision making power may experience increased conflict, arising from women's refusal to be dominated in decision making. A Bangladeshi woman recipient of credit reported: 'After joining Grameen Bank we learned to speak out. I argue with my husband... my husband gets angry and wants to beat me up.' (op. cit., 153)

Research like this has led to the argument that increased male violence in the short-term is not a sign of a project failing to 'empower' women. Instead, it is actually the opposite – an indicator of positive long-term change to gender relations. 'It would appear that conflict, violence and struggle over resources are most likely to be reported in the context where the transformation of gender relations and challenge to male privilege has gone furthest.' (Kabeer 1998, discussing Schuler *et al.* 1996) Women who have no economic resources of their own, and are completely dependent on their husbands, are rarely beaten. Households where women are dependent on men are characterised by co-operation, because such women are more likely to compromise (Kabeer 1994). Research in Bangladesh showed that women who possessed nothing tended to be so insecure that they went to extremes to avoid provoking their husbands (Schuler *et al.* 1996, 1739). In this context, the absence of conflict and violence against women indicates extreme inequality.

While conflict that arises from negotiation is an indication of a positive shift from unequal bargaining to bargaining that is more equitable, there is clearly a serious problem if this conflict becomes violent. Are all interventions aiming to increase womens bargaining power likely to result in violent backlash against women? Bearing this possibility in mind, what role should development NGOs take to minimise women's vulnerability to violent backlash? These examples show that development interventions that aim to improve women's earning capacity cannot be assumed to result in a smooth, automatic improvement in women's well-being and status, including ensuring women's safety from violence. On the contrary, such interventions may expose women to violent backlash.

The risk of violent backlash is not a justification for development organisations to end interventions that aim to support the empowerment of women. Rather, it is a vindication of the importance of such projects. Increased male violence in the short- to medium-term may be seen as an indicator that a transformation in gender relations is underway. What is clear, though, is that development policy-makers and practitioners need to ensure that all the possible outcomes of a project are explored with the women concerned; that steps are taken in partnership with women to prevent violence; and that structures are put in place to protect them in the event of violent backlash. A key aspect of this is to support women in dealing with the risk of increased violence by strengthening their existing networks and evolving strategies to prevent violence.

Credit programmes in Bangladesh provide an example of this kind of work. They have tried to counteract violent backlash through a number of measures. These include awareness-raising with programme staff and their families; group discussions of domestic violence in communities; separate discussion sessions for couples; and networking with other organisations that work specifically on violence against women. Women who were attending the credit programmes' weekly meetings had access to a network of people to whom they could turn in the event of violence. Such networks can cause men to fear that violence in their families may be exposed by women in the meetings, and as a result may help to lessen violence (Schuler *et al.* 1996). The programmes can also intervene in violence as it occurs, and provide women with temporary safe accommodation (Schuler *et al.* 1998). Oxfam GB has found that women's involvement in networks, and training in gender-awareness and women's rights, have contributed to a reduction in the violence faced by income-generation project participants in Bangladesh (Maria José Barney, personal communication 1999).

Health interventions

In the health sector, programmes that seek to enhance women's control over their reproductive health and sexuality may spark violence from men. Many women are only able to exercise reproductive choice if they conceal their decisions from their partners. In particular, many are reluctant to raise the issue of contraception for fear of abandonment, accusations of infidelity, or violent reprisals, and choose instead to take the risk of using contraception without their partner's knowledge. For example, women in focus groups in Peru and Mexico said they did not discuss birth control with their husbands because they were afraid they would become violent (Population Council 1994). A study of the sexual relationships of Xhosa-speaking women in South Africa revealed that marital violence was often precipitated by contraceptive use (Wood, Maforah, and Jewkes 1998).

HIV/AIDS prevention cannot succeed without challenging power inequalities between women and men. In the context of AIDS prevention programmes, Anke Ehrhardt, director of an AIDS research project at the New York State Psychiatric Clinic explains: 'We have... rushed into prevention efforts aimed at getting women to insist on condom use, but without taking into account that they may risk severe repercussions, such as violence and other serious threats to their economic and social support.' (Freiberg 1991, cited in Heise 1995a, 244)

In the last five years, an increasing number of reproductive health programmes have looked for solutions to these problems. In response to the failure of projects focusing on women alone to achieve widespread acceptance of condoms and other forms of contraception, some have focused on the need to have 'male involvement' in family-planning decision making. In the absence of efforts to raise men's awareness of unequal gender power relations, such programmes risk entrenching inequalities still further. They seek to change men's answer from 'no' to 'yes' regarding contraceptive uptake, rather than challenging men's assumption of the right to be the sole or principal decision maker on contraceptive issues.

The fact that decision making about contraceptive usage often results in violence against women has important implications for family planning strategies that stress the need for couples to 'negotiate' use of contraception or condoms, or the need to 'involve' men (International Planned Parenthood Federation 1996). Such strategies assume a degree of equity of power in relationships that frequently does not exist. If coercion in sexual relations is not accounted for, there is a danger that health interventions will exacerbate existing inequalities between men and women.

More progressive work has aimed to challenge men's views of themselves, and to stimulate their interest in different ways of 'being a man', promoting 'male responsibility' as partners and fathers. The Nicaraguan group, Men Against Violence, aims to combat *machismo* and male violence (Broadbent 1999). CISAS (Centro de Información y Servicios de Asesoría en Salud), a prominent Nicaraguan non-governmental health promotion organisation, began working with groups of men in 1996 to challenge *machismo*, in response to the demands of women from some of the poor communities where it works. The women argued that working with women and girls to promote sexual and reproductive health and empowerment is not enough: if things are to change, men will have to change.

1.5.2 Violence as backlash against women's activism

Many women involved in work that challenges women's subordination become targets of male violence. The threat and use of violence is often employed by men as a last resort to end women's activities. Its intention is to assert male control, and the result renders women vulnerable, isolated, and traumatised.

At the Oxfam international workshop on violence against women held in Sarajevo in 1998, Eunice Sena, Director of the Amazon Women's Forum, a grassroots women's NGO in Brazil, explained how individual women involved in the work of her organisation had been confronted by male violence. One of the organisation's projects is to train women to work as para-legals in police stations, in order to encourage women to report cases of violence to the police. As a result of the project, the number of registered complaints of violence from women increased considerably. However, some of the para-legal workers themselves faced daily threats of violence as a result of their work. One woman who worked as a para-legal in the small town of Juruti, in northern Brazil, was involved in supporting the victim of a rape case. The alleged rapist was the son of a prominent local politician. As a result of her support of the rape victim, she received violent threats, including death threats. The local police chief threatened to put her in prison.

Eventually she had to leave the town and live temporarily in hiding. In this case, the regional women's organisation supported her by exposing the situation to higher authorities, attracting media attention to the case, and disseminating information on her case to other popular movements in the region.

The Women's Centre for Legal Aid and Counselling (WCLAC), an organisation based in Jerusalem, lobbies to improve women's position in relation to existing laws. It initiated a Palestinian Model Parliament (PMP) project that aims to set up symbolic court events in various regions (the Nablus area, Hebron, and Bethlehem) where experts hear cases of violence and discrimination against women. The project's success meant that the organisation faced daily attacks in newspapers from men resistant to the feminists' work. Men used mosques and other religious and educational fora to attack the organisation, asserting that the activists were prostitutes. When the central Model Parliament was convened in April 1998 in Jerusalem, participants received threats that if they continued to meet they would be attacked with acid. The Palestinian women's movement has continued to find it difficult to deal with men's accusations that their work is unethical or dishonourable, and continues to fear violent attack from religious groups (Julie Aslop, personal communication 1998).

Individual women who become public figures as a result of challenging violence against women are particularly vulnerable to violent reprisals. In 1981, the first all-female law firm in Pakistan was founded by four women: Hina Jilani (currently the UN Secretary General's Special Representative on Human Rights Defenders), her sister Asma Jahangir (currently the United Nations Special Rapporteur on Extrajudicial, Summary, and Arbitrary Executions), and two others. In 1987, the firm created a Women's Legal Aid Cell, to respond to the legal needs of women fleeing their abusive husbands. Hina Jilani and Asma Jahangir were under threat of death for providing legal assistance to a 29-year-old woman murdered in their office by her family for trying to obtain a divorce from her abusive husband (Amnesty International 1999b). Members of the local chamber of commerce (of which the deceased woman's father is president), as well as several religious groups, have publicly issued a call to kill the sisters. Fatwas[8] were issued against them because, the groups said, the lawyers were 'misguiding women'. In the Senate in Pakistan, Senator Ilyas Bilour referred to Asma Jahangir and Hina Jilani in the context of the abuse and threats they had received from other senators, and stated: 'We have fought for human rights and civil liberties all our lives, but wonder what sort of human rights are being claimed by these girls in jeans.' (Amnesty International 1999b, 21) To date, no one has been arrested for the killing, and newspaper reports failed to condemn it; they were, in fact, overwhelmingly positive about it.

In 1992, the woman leader of a government-sponsored women's development programme in Rajasthan, India, was gang-raped at home, in front of her husband, by men from the community who were enraged by her efforts to organise against child marriage (Morrow 1995). The Indian women's movement launched a campaign to support her and to bring the rapists to justice. Despite this, the rapists were acquitted.

In these four examples from Brazil, Israel, Pakistan, and India, it is clear that work with the potential to empower women can generate hostility among members of the community, the police, and the judiciary. At times, alliances between these different groups act as a powerful force to oppress women. In all four cases, a regional or international network of women's groups provided some support to women victims of violence, and went on to seek justice on their behalf.

1.6 Summary and implications for development organisations

Over the longer term, men's violent backlash against the gradual process of women's empowerment can actually strengthen women's resolve, making them more determined to continue. In her book, *Questioning Empowerment: Working with Women in Honduras* (1997), Jo Rowlands describes the story of Nelly Suazo, a Honduran woman who was murdered by her sister's partner and his friend. Her participation in the Urraco health promoters' training programme led to a process of growing self-confidence and commitment to fighting violence and exploitation. She was murdered by her sister's ex-partner, having encouraged her sister to leave him when he was violent to her. Her sister was also left for dead. At first, the murder stunned the participants in the health promoters' programme, and the community as a whole, and plunged women into despair. As time passed, the murder, combined with women's subsequent efforts to support Nelly's family and obtain justice, had the catalytic effect of galvanising the group: '[The women's group was able] to move from seeing Nelly's case as an illustration of what happens to women who step out of line, to an example of a woman who had taken on great challenges, who must be remembered with pride, and who provides inspiration to those that remain to continue to push for equality and justice.' (Rowlands 1997, 58)

The approach to violence against women outlined in this chapter is that it is an outcome of unequal power relations between women and men. Men use violence to achieve, and consolidate, power over women. In all societies, there are some men who are violent towards women and some men who are not, but men as a group benefit collectively from women's fear of violence. Even when the intent to harm is not evident, or the perpetrator of violence is herself a women, the victims are nevertheless targeted because they are girls or women, and the implicit aim is the perpetuation of women's subordination.

Much of the work to combat violence against women focuses on supporting the empowerment of individual women or groups of women. This chapter has examined concepts of power and empowerment, using conceptual frameworks developed to help policy-makers and practitioners to understand the relationship between women's immediate needs within existing gender power relations, and their need to challenge those unequal relations. Development workers who use the distinction between 'practical' and 'strategic' gender interests as a planning tool recognise that the linkages between these interests are as important as the differences. An intervention that addresses women's practical interests always has an impact on the power relations between women and men.

It is also imperative that women who may face backlash are protected and supported in cases where development interventions initiate a transition in gender relations. The chapter highlighted the risks of making assumptions that involvement in development interventions will lead smoothly to increased bargaining power within the household, and from there to a decrease in violence against women. The linkages are much more complex than that, and increased violence can be the short- to medium-term effect of a project that is successfully challenging male dominance.

Women are acutely aware of the possibility that their challenges to men's domination of the household, community, market, and State may lead to violent reprisals. They are also aware that challenging violence against women involves a fundamental questioning of the dynamics of power in their societies. The possibility of violent backlash against them further confirms the importance of development interventions being designed in partnership with the women they are intended to benefit. Empowerment cannot be given, but must be generated by the women it is meant to serve.

2 Human rights and development responses to violence against women

Human freedom is a commonplace purpose and common motivation for human rights and human development. The movements for human rights and human development have had distinct traditions and strategies. United in a broader alliance, each can bring a new energy and strength to the other.

(UNDP Human Development Report 2000, 2)

Human rights and development organisations have made great inroads in addressing violence against women. When human rights workers are deciding what issues to prioritise, violations such as rape in the context of armed conflict, or FGM, now figure high on the list. These organisations have also successfully widened state responsibility for human rights violations, to include abuses by 'private actors' as well as agents of the State. Equally, when development policy-makers are deciding where to allocate resources they increasingly acknowledge the need to ensure gender equity. International development organisations have demonstrated that violence against women is a drain on resources, and a barrier to women's participation in development processes. Yet, despite this progress in acknowledging the gravity of violence against women in the human rights and development arenas, there has been little measurable impact on the reality of the prevalence of violence against women.

To understand why this is so, and in order to produce more effective responses to violence against women, this chapter argues that we must acknowledge the links between economic, social, and political subordination. Responses to violence against women must be founded in a rights-based approach to development that challenges women's subordination on all these fronts. We have already noted that many international and national development organisations continue to understand development as an issue of economic growth. Their activities have focused on overcoming women's lack of access to – and control over – economic resources. Despite their rhetoric of 'women's empowerment',

46

such organisations tend to view women in instrumental terms, focusing on overcoming the barriers to women's role in production. In contrast, international and national bodies dealing with human rights from a legal perspective tend to focus on enforcing women's civil rights and political freedoms, and overlook the fact that women's ability to claim these rights and freedoms is constrained by poverty and the denial of their economic and social rights.

2.1 Human rights approaches to violence against women

The concept of human rights provides women and men throughout the world with a universal standard against which to measure the treatment of individuals and groups by governments, NGOs, community institutions, and individuals. Because the concept of human rights provides people with a basis on which to identify abusive behaviour and demand change, it has been described as 'action-demanding' (Freeden 1991, 10). Understanding violence against women as an abuse of human rights potentially provides activists with access to the armoury of international law. This provides a useful set of tools, since it is universally held to have political weight. Using these tools, women can demand both the State's protection, and recourse against the perpetrators of abuse.

Some of the developments in international law pertaining to women were mentioned in the introduction to this book. The collective action of women activists resulted in women's human rights being placed on the agenda of the UN Conference on Human Rights, held in Vienna in 1993. Later that year, the UN General Assembly adopted the Declaration on the Elimination of Violence against Women. A thematic mandate on violence against women was created in early 1994, together with the appointment of a 'Special Rapporteur on violence against women, its causes and consequences'. In 1995, the Fourth UN World Conference on Women was held. Finally, in 1998, the Statute of the ICC codified rape and other sexual violence as war crimes (in armed conflict of international or non-international character), and when committed on a systematic or widespread basis, as crimes against humanity, including genocide.

2.1.1 The 'public' and 'private' spheres

Radhika Coomaraswamy, the UN Special Rapporteur on violence against women, its causes and consequences, has stated: 'The public/private distinction, that has been the root of most legal systems, including human rights law, has created major problems for the vindication of womens rights.' (Coomaraswamy 1995, para. 70) However, women have not, until recently, been strongly protected from violence under international human rights law. Human rights law focused narrowly on violations committed directly by the State, due to the traditional view that the 'public' and 'private' spheres of life are distinct and separate from each other, with events within the private sphere of the home as being beyond its jurisdiction. States have until recently not been obliged under international human rights law to take action against violence that occurs within the household.

The majority of women are most likely to experience violence (including domestic violence, incest, and marital rape) at the hands of parents, husbands, sons, and partners within the home.

The idea that the public and private spheres are clearly distinct from each other, and that the State should only be concerned with what occurs in the public sphere, is connected with a widely-shared vision of the family as a 'natural' unit. Violence that occurs between husband and wife is often also seen as 'natural'. Kay Famm, a Haitian organisation that works with women victims of violence, has argued that judges in Haiti often attribute wife-beating to women's 'disobedience' to their husbands. The practice of beating wives within the home is considered a legitimate punishment for a wife who fails in her marital duties, within a cultural context that values female obedience and deference to men. As a result, judges fail to see such beatings as a violation of women's human rights.[1]

Deference paid to the family as an institution worthy of protection has led to it being placed outside the remit of public action, since it is very difficult to introduce the concept of inalienable rights into intimate relationships. The right to privacy in the family is enshrined – inter alia – in the Universal Declaration of Human Rights (UDHR) and in the International Covenant on Civil and Political Rights (ICCPR).[2]

The way in which the distinction between public and private spheres has been enshrined to women's detriment in human rights law is perhaps nowhere more evident than when we consider torture. Violence routinely faced by women in the home is, in the main, excluded by the definition of torture enshrined in Article 1 of the UN Convention against Torture and other Cruel, Inhuman, or Degrading Treatment or Punishment, which states that torture must be 'inflicted by or at the instigation of or with the consent or acquiescence of a public official or other person acting in an official capacity'. The definition of torture requires that it takes place within the public realm, and that a public official or person acting in an official capacity must be implicated. Amnesty International explained this limited definition by stating that 'private acts (of brutality) would usually be ordinary criminal offences that national law enforcement is expected to repress. International concern with torture arises only when the State itself abandons its function of protecting its citizenry by sanctioning criminal action by law enforcement personnel.' (Rodley 1988, cited in Charlesworth, Chinkin, and Wright 1991, 628)

However, as international feminist legal scholars have pointed out, in so defining torture, human rights law fails to address women's experience. 'The traditional canon of human rights law does not deal in categories that fit the experiences of women. It is cast in terms of discrete violations of rights and offers little redress in cases where there is a pervasive, structural denial of rights.' (Charlesworth, Chinkin, and Wright 1991, 628)

For women victims of domestic violence, this makes no sense. Indeed in India, 'wife torture' is a term used by women and organisations to describe domestic violence (P. Sen 1997b). As Catherine MacKinnon has noted in her critique of this state-centred definition of torture: 'If "the political" is to be defined in terms of men's experiences of being subjugated to power, it makes some sense to centre the definition on the State. But if one is including the unjust power involved in the subjugation of half the human race by the other half – male dominance – it makes no sense whatsoever to define power exclusively in terms of what the State does. The State is only one instrumentality of it. To fail to see this is pure gender bias.' (MacKinnon 1993, 27)

The challenge to scrutinise human rights law from women's perspectives has finally been taken up by some mainstream international human rights organisations. In a recent report on women, published in the context of its Torture Campaign, Amnesty International notes: 'Human rights treaties are "living instruments" that evolve and develop over time. Decisions by inter-governmental bodies that monitor states' compliance with international treaties, as well as national courts, continually refine and develop the interpretation of what constitutes torture. Largely thanks to the efforts of the worldwide women's movement, there is a wider understanding that torture includes acts of violence by private individuals in certain circumstances.'[3]

Thanks largely to the work of the women's movement, some prominent mainstream human rights organisations have been compelled to address violence against women in the home and community as torture. Compare the comment by Nigel Rodley, then director of Amnesty International's Legal Office and now the UN Special Rapporteur on torture, noted above, with the following passage in Amnesty International's report on the torture of women 13 years later: 'Amnesty International considers that acts of violence against women in the home and community constitute torture for which the State is accountable when they are of the nature and severity envisaged by the concept of torture in international standards and the State has failed to fulfil its obligation to provide effective protection.' (Amnesty International 2001, 4)

2.1.2 Recognising state responsibility for human rights abuse in the private sphere

In 1988, a landmark judgement clearly established state responsibility for human rights abuses, even when committed by private persons unconnected to the State. The case, at the Inter-American Court of Human Rights, dealt with the disappearance and presumed killing of Angel Manfredo Velásquez Rodríguez, a Honduran student, by an unidentified party. The court stated: 'An illegal act that violates human rights and that is initially not directly imputable to the State, for example, because it is the act of a private person or because the person responsible has not been identified, can lead to international responsibility of the State, not because of the act itself, but because of the lack of due diligence to prevent the violation or to respond to it as required by the Convention.'[4]

Under the American Convention on Human Rights, the State is not responsible for every attack on individuals, but for its failure to fulfil its obligations to ensure people's rights are enforced. It has a responsibility to put into place a legal and administrative system that will protect rights and ensure access to remedies, should violations occur. In the judgement of the Velásquez Rodríguez case, the Inter-American Court of Human Rights held that, 'The State has a legal duty to take reasonable steps to prevent human rights violations and to use the means at its disposal to carry out a serious investigation of violations committed within its jurisdiction, to identify those responsible, to impose the appropriate punishment and to ensure the victim adequate compensation .... This duty to prevent includes all those means of a legal, political, administrative, and cultural nature that promote the protection of human rights and ensure that any violations are considered and treated as illegal acts, which, as such, may lead to the punishment of those responsible and the obligation to indemnify the victims for damages.'[5]

There is a range of inter-governmental organisations such as the Organisation of African Unity (OAU) in Africa, the Organisation of American States (OAS) in the Americas, and the Council of Europe (CoE), that operate at regional level, and are active in human rights and democratic development work. In Africa, under the auspices of the African

Commission on Human and People's Rights, the drafting of a protocol to the African Charter on Human and People's Rights on women's rights is well underway. In the Americas, the Inter-American Convention on the Prevention, Punishment, and Eradication of Violence Against Women, adopted by the OAS in 1994, was a tremendous achievement. This is the first ever binding human rights instrument whose exclusive focus is violence against women. The treaty binds those states of the OAS region that are parties to it. It states that discrimination against women is one of the fundamental causes of violence, and also includes as a specific right, women's right to a life free of violence (Article 3). The State is held responsible for finding the means to eradicate violence (Article 7). Individuals and organisations can take cases to the Inter-American Commission on Human Rights (Article 12). State parties must inform on the methods they have adopted to prevent and eradicate violence and to assist women affected by violence, through the submission of national reports (Article 10).

2.1.3 Recognising violence against women as discrimination

Violence against women is a serious form of discrimination, and, as such, contravenes the principle of non-discrimination on the basis of sex, which is clearly enshrined in international law. Anti-discrimination provisions are contained in all the major international human rights instruments, including the UDHR(1948), and the ICCPR (1966). According to these provisions, states must ensure that human rights are enjoyed by everyone without discrimination of any kind. However, in practice, these instruments have not been used in relation to violence against women, failing in this regard to call perpetrators to account for a fundamental violation of a wide range of women's rights.

Violence against women was not originally mentioned explicitly in the 1979 Convention on the Elimination of all Forms of Discrimination against Women (CEDAW, or the Women's Convention), adopted by the UN General Assembly. However, in a subsequent recommendation – General Recommendation 19, issued in 1992 – the Committee on the Elimination of Discrimination against Women (the CEDAW Committee) recognised that violence against women is one of the key mechanisms by which women are forced into a subordinate position in relation to men.[6]

General Recommendation 19 incorporates violence against women into the definition of discrimination[7] provided for in the Women's Convention. It notes that gender-based violence impairs or nullifies the following rights:

a. The right to life;

b. The right not to be subject to torture or to cruel, inhuman, or degrading treatment, or punishment;

c. The right to equal protection in situations of armed conflict;

d. The right to liberty and security of the person;

e. The right to equal protection under the law;

f. The right to equality in the family;

g. The right to the highest attainable standard of physical and mental health;

h. The right to just and favourable conditions of work.

General Recommendation 19 states: 'The Convention in article 1 defines discrimination against women. The definition of discrimination includes gender-based violence, that is, violence that is directed against a woman because she is a woman or that affects women disproportionately. It includes acts that inflict physical, mental or sexual harm or suffering, threats of such acts, coercion and other deprivations of liberty. Gender-based violence may breach specific provisions of the Convention, regardless of whether those provisions expressly mention violence.' (para. 6)

General Recommendation 19 emphasises that its prohibition on violence against women is not restricted to acts by the State, but extends to acts by private individuals. It states: 'Traditional attitudes by which women are regarded as subordinate to men or having stereotyped roles perpetuate widespread practices involving violence or coercion, such as family violence or abuse, forced marriage, dowry deaths, acid attacks, and female circumcision. Such prejudices and practices may justify gender-based violence as a form of protection or control of women. The effect of such violence on the physical and mental integrity of women is to deprive them of equal enjoyment, exercise and knowledge of human rights and fundamental freedoms.' (para. 11)

In adopting General Recommendation 19, the CEDAW Committee enshrined the prohibition of violence against women in the Convention, and obliged states to report on the measures they are undertaking to combat violence against women.

2.1.4 Recognising women's rights as human rights

Women activists worldwide have made good use of the opportunities presented by the United Nations Decade for Women (1976-85) and the various United Nations conferences of the past 25 years, to draw attention to violence against women as an abuse of women's human rights on a global scale, and to campaign for international and national laws that will protect women from violence. Local and regional NGOs have played, and continue to play, a crucial role in documenting human rights abuses, monitoring governments' commitments to human rights standards, and campaigning for positive change.

The UN World Conference on Human Rights, held in 1993, ended with the adoption of the Vienna Declaration and Programme of Action that declared women's rights to be human rights. This was to a great extent due to the actions of women's rights activists in the run-up to the conference. They argued that it was no longer sufficient simply to extend existing human rights provisions to women on the basis of their equality with men. They claimed that in order to understand gender-based abuses as human rights abuses, the concept of human rights must reflect the specific nature of women's experience of violence.

In 1994, the UN Commission on Human Rights appointed a Special Rapporteur on violence against women, its causes and consequences, Radhika Coomaraswamy. She is authorised to seek and receive information on violence against women from governments, UN bodies, and inter-governmental and non-governmental organisations. She is to respond to such information and recommend measures to eliminate violence against women. To fulfil her mandate, the Special Rapporteur engages in direct dialogue with governments to seek clarification of allegations of violence against women she has received. In April 2000, her mandate was extended for another three-year term.

In her first report in 1995, the Special Rapporteur dealt with the issues of violence against women generally (Coomaraswamy 1995). Subsequently, her main reports have addressed domestic violence (Coomaraswamy 1996a); rape and sexual violence, including sexual harassment and trafficking and forced prostitution (Coomaraswamy 1997a); violence against women in armed conflict, custodial violence against women, and violence against refugee and internally displaced women (Coomaraswamy 1998); violence in the family (Coomaraswamy 1999d); migration and trafficking in women (Coomaraswamy 2000); and in 2001 on violence against women perpetrated and/or condoned by the State during times of armed conflict. Alongside these, she has also compiled reports following missions to Korea and Japan on the issue of military sexual slavery, to Poland on trafficking in women and forced prostitution, to Brazil on domestic violence, to South Africa on rape in the community, to Rwanda on violence in the situation of armed conflict, to the United States, to Indonesia and East Timor, to Cuba, to Afghanistan and Pakistan, and to Bangladesh, Nepal, and India.

In 1995, the Fourth UN World Conference on Women produced the Beijing Declaration and Platform for Action, which specifically addresses violence against women. The Platform makes specific reference to acts of violence including forced sterilisation and forced abortion, coercive or forced use of contraceptives, female infanticide, and prenatal sex selection leading to abortion of female foetuses. Furthermore, the particular vulnerability to violence of particular groups of women receives attention. Among others, groups discussed are women belonging to minority groups, indigenous women, refugee women, women migrants, and women in detention. The Platform also sets out specific steps that governments must take to end violence against women, including violence against women in the home. Such measures include:

- condemning violence against women and refraining from invoking any custom, tradition, or religious consideration to avoid their obligations as delineated in the Declaration on the Elimination of Violence Against Women;
- refraining from engaging in violence against women and taking active steps to punish and redress such violence;
- adopting, implementing, and reviewing legislation to ensure its effectiveness;
- ratifying international human rights norms and instruments;
- actively mainstreaming a gender perspective in all policies and programmes;
- providing women who are subject to violence with access to mechanisms of justice;
- enacting and enforcing legislation against perpetrators of violence against women;
- formulating plans of action against violence against women;
- raising awareness, creating a safe and accessible environment for reporting, training, and appropriate judicial, legal, medical, social, educational, police, and immigration personnel;
- reporting on measures taken, and co-operating with UN human rights monitoring bodies. (Chapter IV para. 4.9)

2.1.5

Recognising the State's duty to exercise 'due diligence'

In 1993, the adoption of the Declaration on the Elimination of Violence against Women by the UN General Assembly affirmed that states must 'exercise due diligence to prevent, investigate, and, in accordance with national legislation, punish acts of violence against women, whether those acts are perpetrated by the State or by private persons.' (United Nations 1993b, Preamble).[8] Radhika Coomaraswamy has noted that the '… emergence of state responsibility for violence in society plays an absolutely crucial role in efforts to eradicate gender-based violence and is perhaps one of the most important contributions of the women's movement to the issue of human rights.' (Coomaraswamy 1995, para. 107)

Under international human rights law it has now become possible to argue that if the State fails to act with 'due diligence' to prevent, investigate, and punish abuses, including violence against women by non-state actors, then it is responsible under its international legal obligations for failing to take positive action to stop violence from happening. State responsibility under international law requires the State to put into place a system that can protect human rights and ensure that individuals can exercise them. As far as violence against women is concerned, it is clear that the 'due diligence' standard requires a host of initiatives by the State, including the training of state personnel, education, and efforts to demystify violence against women (Coomaraswamy 1996a). Little by little, the obligation of the State to protect women from violence is increasingly being seen as an integral part of fulfilling its human rights obligations.

2.1.6 Protection for women and girls in armed conflict

One branch of international humanitarian law is, in the main, concerned with the conduct of hostilities and warfare methods – that is why it is more aptly referred to as the laws of armed conflict. Another branch, for which the adjective 'humanitarian' is perhaps more suited, is concerned with protecting all those affected by conflict: civilians, combatants, and anyone who has been placed *hors de combat*. Drafted under the auspices of the International Committee of the Red Cross, the Geneva Conventions of 1949 came about as a result of World War II. The aim was to ameliorate the conditions of those members of the armed forces who had been taken out of action as a result of sickness, injury, shipwreck, and capture, as well as to enhance the protection to be afforded to the civilian population in time of war. However, none of these agreements has an effective enforcement mechanism.

With respect to violence against women, it was not until 1949, with the adoption of the Fourth Geneva Convention (relative to the Protection of Civilian Persons in Time of War), that reference was made to rape and sexual assault (Charlesworth and Chinkin 2000, 314).

This Convention offers women limited protection. The first limitation is due to the field of application of the Convention, that is, international armed conflict. Secondly, according to Article 27 of the Convention, women are to be protected 'against any attack on their honour, in particular against rape, enforced prostitution, or any form of indecent assault.' This formulation has been criticised by feminist scholars as it fails to define sexual violence as an attack on the person. Hilary Charlesworth and Christine Chinkin have noted that this provision does not explicitly prohibit these offences, but portrays women as in need of protection from them. In addition, 'by designating rape as a crime against "honour" rather than one of violence the provision presents women as male and family property.' (2000, 314)

The two Additional Protocols to the Geneva Conventions of 8 June 1977 (i.e. relating to the Protection of Victims of International Armed Conflicts, Protocol I, and to the Protection of Victims of Non-International Armed Conflicts, Protocol II) further develop the protection measures to be accorded to civilians in times of conflict. With respect to women, Protocol I forgoes the notion of women's honour but retains the language of special respect and protection to be accorded to them (Article 76). In turn, Protocol II, in a similar vein, prohibits 'outrages upon personal dignity, in particular humiliating and degrading treatment, rape, enforced prostitution and any form of indecent assault' (Article 4), thereby failing to define rape as a violent attack on the person.

The Geneva Conventions and Protocol I provide for universal jurisdiction in national courts for particularly heinous crimes – known as 'grave breaches' of the Conventions. Universal jurisdiction imposes a duty on the High Contracting Parties to the Conventions to investigate, arrest, prosecute, and punish, those responsible for such acts irrespective of whether the acts were committed in the territory of the State, by one of its nationals, or against one of its nationals.

However, rape, enforced prostitution, and sexual assault are not explicitly designated as grave breaches, although some argue that they fit within other categories of grave breaches such as 'wilfully causing grave suffering or serious injury to body or health' and 'torture or inhumane treatment'.

In addition, Common Article 3 to the Geneva Conventions, applicable to internal armed conflict, prohibits violence to life and the person, cruel treatment and torture, and humiliating and degrading treatment. As with the concept of grave breaches, sexual violence is not explicitly mentioned in the list of proscribed acts.

As a result of lobbying by women's groups, activists, and NGOs, governments recognised in the 1990s that the Geneva Conventions had not dealt adequately with crimes of sexual violence. In stressing women's 'honour', the Conventions fail to treat sexual violence as a human rights abuse that violates women's bodily integrity. As noted by Radhika Coomaraswamy, stereotypical concepts of femininity have been enshrined in humanitarian law (Coomaraswamy 1998, 4).

The establishment of the ad hoc *International Tribunals*

In the context of the conflict in the former Yugoslavia and of the genocide in Rwanda, reports of sexual violence appeared regularly in the global media. Women's rights activists were instrumental in ensuring that the definition of crimes against humanity to be codified in the Statutes of the International Criminal Tribunals for the former Yugoslavia (established by Security Council resolution 827 of 25 May 1993) and Rwanda (established by Security Council resolution 955 of 8 November 1994) be framed in terms that would at least begin to take account of the reality of what was happening to women in those countries, by including rape in the definition of crimes against humanity. However, rape was left out in the definition of war crimes enshrined in both Statutes. NGOs and women lawyers played a crucial role in collecting evidence to ensure that the tribunals indicted the alleged perpetrators of sexual violence.

Historically, four international tribunals have been set up specifically to address criminal acts during armed conflict, and to tackle individual criminal liability for – *inter alia* – cases of war crimes and crimes against humanity. The International Military War Crimes Tribunal for Nazi War Criminals took place in Nuremberg, Germany, from 1945-6. The International Military Tribunal for the Far East (IMTTE) was set up in 1946, in Tokyo. Japanese war criminals were tried by a prosecution team from 11 of the allied nations.

The International Criminal Tribunal for the former Yugoslavia (ICTY) has jurisdiction to try people responsible for serious violations of international humanitarian law committed in the territory of the former Yugoslavia since 1991. In accordance with its statute, the Tribunal has the power to prosecute people responsible for grave breaches of the Geneva Conventions of 12 August 1949, persons violating the laws and customs of war, persons who have committed genocide, and those who have perpetrated crimes against humanity against any civilian population in the context of an armed conflict.

The Statute of the International Criminal Tribunal for Rwanda (ICTR) gives it jurisdiction to prosecute persons responsible for serious violations of international humanitarian law committed in the territory of Rwanda, and Rwandan citizens responsible for such acts committed in neighbouring states between 1 January 1994 and 31 December 1994. The Tribunal has the power to try people who have committed genocide, and crimes against humanity when committed as part of a widespread or systematic attack against any civilian population on national, political, ethnic, racial or religious grounds, as well as the power to prosecute violations of Article 3, common to the Geneva Conventions of 12 August 1949 and Additional Protocol II thereto of 8 June 1977.

The Office of the Prosecutor (OTP)[9] for both tribunals pushed the boundaries of international law in bringing charges of rape, sexual assault, and mutilation in public indictments. The OTP has charged specific defendants with sexual violence as a war crime, a crime against humanity, genocide, enslavement, a grave breach, and enforced prostitution (Coomaraswamy 1998, Section C, para. 4).

Despite this breakthrough, most of those charged with sexual violence are not in custody (Women 2000 1998). However, a number of judgements are of particular significance in the recognition of sexual violence during armed conflict as a crime. In the first judgement by an international court for the crime of genocide, in September 1998, the ICTR convicted Jean-Paul Akayesu of genocide and crimes against humanity. This judgement was reaffirmed by the Appeals Chamber of the International Criminal Tribunal in 2000. The judgement was unprecedented at least in three respects. It was the first ever judgement by an international tribunal for the crime of genocide. It was also unprecedented in recognising that rape and sexual violence constitute genocide, if committed with the specific intent of destroying, in whole or in part, a particular targeted group. Lastly, the judgement provides the first ever definition of rape under international law.[10]

In December 1998, the ICTY convicted Anto Furundzija, a former local commander of the Croatian military police unit, of war crimes. The Tribunal found that aiding and abetting in outrages upon personal dignity, including rape, constitutes a war crime (ibid.). The ICTY delivered an unprecedented judgement on 22 February 2001. On that occasion, the ICTY returned the first ever conviction of rape and of enslavement – including in particular for sexual purposes – as a crime against humanity. The trial focused on the Serb campaign in the Foca region of Republika Srpska, where a large number of Muslim civilians, particularly women, were targeted as part of the armed conflict between Serb and Muslim forces from early 1992 to mid-1993.

The violence against Muslim civilians was intended to terrorise them and ultimately achieve their expulsion. Women and girls were rounded up from in and around the Foca region and detained. Once in detention, women and young girls were regularly moved to other locations to be raped. They were sold to other soldiers and were enslaved for months on end. The Trial Chamber found that the Muslim women and girls were 'robbed of the last vestiges of human dignity, women and girls treated like chattels, pieces of property at the arbitrary disposal of the Serb occupation forces, and more specifically at the beck and call of the three accused.' (Summary of the Judgement of Trial Chamber II, The Hague, 22 February 2001)

The International Criminal Court (ICC)

On 17 July 1998, 120 governments adopted the Statute of the International Criminal Court (ICC).[11] The ICC builds on the positive precedents of the Statutes of the ICTY and ICTR. It integrates sexual crimes into international law. As a result of intensive work and lobbying by women lawyers and activists, the definition of 'crimes against humanity'[12] and 'war crimes'[13] now includes rape, sexual slavery, enforced prostitution, forced pregnancy, enforced sterilisation, or any other form of sexual violence of comparable gravity.[14] Seven governments voted against adopting the ICC statute, including the USA, and 21 abstained (Amnesty International 1999a). The process of adoption of the Statutes, and the role of NGOs in lobbying on this, is described in more detail in Chapter 8.

2.1.7 Protection for internally displaced women and girls

According to international refugee law, states have agreed to provide protection to refugee women who have been displaced or who have been forced to flee their own country. States provide this protection on behalf of the international community.

Unlike refugees, internally displaced people have not crossed an international border, and their primary claim to rights remains with their own state. Their state has certain obligations to them under national and international laws. However, the occurrence of displacement may imply a fundamental breakdown in their own state such that the State cannot be relied on to protect them from violence or other human rights violations.

The international community can insist that states respect their citizens' rights. For example, it can insist that states do not forcibly displace citizens. In practice, however, it is clear that in many cases, women who are internally displaced have scant protection, and are in many circumstances subject to violence.

The UN Guiding Principles on Internal Displacement, agreed in 1988, are a useful tool for protecting the rights of internally displaced people, before they are displaced, during displacement, and on return (Deng 1997).[15] The Principles pay heed to efforts to protect women's rights within human rights and humanitarian law. They recognise the needs of displaced women and girls for protection from 'rape, mutilation, torture, cruel, inhuman or degrading treatment or punishment, and other outrages on personal dignity, such as acts of gender specific violence, forced prostitution, and any form of indecent assault; slavery or any form of slavery such as sale into marriage, sexual exploitation, or forced labour of children; and acts of violence intended to spread terror among internally displaced persons.'

(Principle 12, para. 2) In addition, the principles point to the importance of women's participation in the planning and distribution of basic supplies (Principle 18, para. 3); women's special health needs including access to female health care providers and services, such as reproductive health care and counselling for victims of sexual and other abuses (Principle 19, para. 2); and women's full participation in education programmes (Principle 23, paras. 3, 4).

2.1.8 The limitations of a human rights approach

It is clear from the preceding section that women's rights activists have not taken the human rights system at face value. Instead, they have engaged at various points in pushing its boundaries so that it begins to address violence against women adequately. However, some major limitations of the mechanisms and instruments available at international level remain.

The concept of human rights reflects the values and priorities of the male- and western-dominated bodies that created it. The language of human rights and law creates the illusion that everyone is equal before the law, regardless of gender, and masks the reality of unequal gender power relations that affects all societies.[16] In addition, the 'first generation' of human rights reflects the concerns of eighteenth-century Europe and the United States that governments should uphold and respect the civil and political liberties of their citizens. Civil and political rights have continued to receive the lion's share of international concern within human rights discourse up to the present day, despite the fact that the UDHR placed equal emphasis on both sets of rights: social and economic on the one hand, and civil and political on the other. During the Cold War, social and economic rights were largely ignored by western states, which concentrated on criticising the denial of civil and political rights to citizens of Communist countries. The conceptual divide that has been set up between socio-economic and civil-political rights has been reinforced by the fact that different international organisations have been set up to focus on one or the other, and the fact that inter-governmental bodies, including the United Nations, have traditionally given much more prominence to civil and political rights within human rights discourse. The claim that economic and social rights should be addressed on a par with civil and political rights has been attacked in particular by northern states on the basis that the enforcement of social and economic rights is progressive, as opposed to the immediate and direct enforcement of civil and political rights. The neglect of economic and social rights in human rights discourse has been compounded by the claim that they are not justiciable, that is, enforceable by the national courts. The historical emphasis on civil and political rights has been detrimental to women because it ignores how women's enjoyment of their rights is severely restricted by the social and economic power relations in which they are embedded.

A second limitation with the human rights perspective is lodged in its conceptualisation of 'the family'. As the earlier description in this chapter of the public-private division in international human rights law pointed out, the family is considered to be a natural unit of society in need of state protection. The predominant notion of the family is that of a heterosexual married couple with offspring (Peterson and Parisi 1998) that takes for granted traditional power relations and identities within the family. In addition, emphasis on the unity of the family prohibits scrutiny of violations of rights that may take place within it. It has been pointed out that several actors, such as commercial and religious institutions, have an interest in maintaining this differentiation between the human rights scrutiny of private and unregulated 'family' space, and that pertaining to the regulated area of the public sphere (Chinkin and Charlesworth 2000, 233).

A third limitation of traditional human rights approaches is their gender-biased understanding of equality between men and women. This assumes that bringing the treatment of women onto a par with that of men is sufficient. With the exception of the CEDAW Committee's General Recommendation 19, which recognised violence against women as a form of discrimination, anti-discrimination provisions in major international human rights instruments have in practice ignored oppression that occurs within the family and household. Instead, they focus on public life, the economy, the legal system, and education. Our understanding of gender equality needs to be broadened to take on board the structural inequalities and power relations inherent in society, at work, in politics, in development, and in processes of globalisation. 'The concept of equality means much more than treating all persons in the same way. Equal treatment of persons in unequal situations will operate to perpetuate rather than eradicate injustice. True equality can only emerge from efforts directed towards addressing and correcting these situational imbalances. It is this broader view of equality that has become the underlying principle and the final goal in the struggle for recognition and acceptance of the human rights of women.' (United Nations Centre for Human Rights 1994)

Fourthly, human rights have shown themselves to be difficult to enforce. As yet, there is no global civil society through which individual states can effectively be prevented from abusing human rights, though some argue that one is emerging (Desai 1996). Human rights depend for their enforcement on governments, which may be corrupt, unstable, or uncommitted. In recognition of this, women's organisations have played an important role in lobbying the State at the national level to keep its commitments to eradicating violence. In Peru, women's organisations conducted an evaluation of women's status and came up with proposals to be incorporated into the official document at the Fourth UN World Conference on Women at Beijing in 1995, and into the outputs of the Beijing NGO Forum (PASF, Oxfam internal document 1994). Following Beijing, these organisations circulated information about the agreements reached, drafted a national plan for implementation, and fostered the participation of Peruvian women in monitoring progress (PASF, Oxfam internal document 1996). Despite the growth of civil society organisations like those in Peru, and their growing capacity to pressure governments to honour their human rights commitments, reliable enforcement mechanisms through which subordinated groups and individuals can bring claims on their own behalf are still a rarity (Petchesky 1998). In addition, although these organisations are growing, they remain dependent on foreign financial support, and are therefore vulnerable and unsustainable at this point.

Human rights are also difficult to enforce because the very concept of human rights remains unfamiliar to many women. Few women know what their rights are, and fewer still are in a position to claim them. In spite of the 'principle of non-discrimination' found in the major human rights instruments, gender identity is still a significant determinant of access to rights. 'Women face routine violation of their human rights on a massive scale simply because they are female. ... [They cannot] take their rights for granted. They have to be fought for. ... The field of human rights is controversial, where political interests, legal norms and different social and cultural systems conflict. It is often an area dominated by sterile legal debate and alienating abstractions – while in the daily experience of ordinary men, women and children the defence of basic rights can be filled with violence and terror.' (Williams 1995, 9) Reasons for this include the failure of national law to address women's concerns; women's lack of education; women's lack of recourse – through lack of knowledge or poverty – to legal support; and the dominance of customary or religious law over civil law.

In order to reform biased laws, and better enforce laws that do exist to protect women, women need to be informed about the legal framework (Plata 1996). Recognising the significant limits to women's access to their rights, women's organisations play an important role in educating women to ensure that the law becomes a tool of relevance to their lives. The International Federation of Women Lawyers (FIDA) has affiliates in most countries of the world, most of which are involved in legal literacy projects. For example, the Uganda Association of Women Lawyers works to 'take law to the lay people' by assisting poor women to take advantage of the protection available under the law. One of its main activities is the running of free legal aid clinics for poor women. These clinics deal with a wide range of issues, mainly concerning inheritance, succession, and domestic violence (PASF, Oxfam internal document 1993).

This section has argued that in order to address violence against women as an infringement of human rights we need to challenge the belief that human rights provisions adequately address women's rights, which is based on blindness to gender-based inequalities between the sexes. Strategies to re-conceptualise human rights in order to ensure that they provide women with protection against violations have centred on integrating gender issues into human rights concepts and mechanisms, and expanding the role of the State in protecting women. A major part of this project has been to challenge the idea of a division between the 'public' and 'private' spheres, and the notion that the State should not intervene in relations between spouses and their immediate families. This has required asserting and demanding that the State be accountable for abuses against women committed by non-state actors, and emphasising that violence against women is part of a larger societal web of discrimination that oppresses women. Violence against women cannot easily be delineated as exclusively occurring in the civil and political realms, or as solely caused by state actors. The indivisibility of all rights is therefore a vital concern.

This section also emphasised the vital role played by women's organisations and some development organisations in challenging the State and international bodies through documenting abuses, lobbying, and campaigning, and by promoting and supporting legal education and awareness-raising among women about their human rights and the law. These and other ways in which development organisations can become involved in supporting human rights responses to abuses of women's human rights are discussed in more detail in Chapter 8. The involvement of development organisations in making the law available to women is a vital part of transforming the law from a top-down male-biased instrument, into a useful tool to promote women's human rights. The law can only be of practical help to women when it is addressed alongside women's social, economic, and political inequalities with men.

2.2 An integrated response: human rights and development

> *Violence, rape, prostitution, insecurity are issues that have not been touched by Oxfam or other organisations in Darfur. It is an area that 'does not exist'. Oxfam is absolutely not in a position to think of approaching such topics in the foreseeable future … [it] would be meddling and intrusion by amateurs, and likely to add to the problems.*

(Oxfam worker in Sudan, cited in internal Oxfam document 1994)

Over the past 25 years, development organisations have increasingly focused on women in development and gender analysis, and have developed an increasingly sophisticated understanding of the ways in which social and political discrimination and marginalisation are linked to poverty. In spite of this, most development agencies have only very recently begun to consider violence against women as a 'development issue', and many still do not recognise it as a concern for them. In light of the prevalence of violence and abuse of women in all countries throughout the world, and its impact on all aspects of women's lives, why is violence missing from the analysis and agenda of development organisations? The reasons are a complex mixture of prejudice, principle, and pragmatism.

On the face of it, the argument put forward by the Oxfam worker quoted at the start of this section is pragmatic: where development organisations have no experience or expertise in working on violence against women, they may have legitimate concerns that to intervene will make matters worse. However compelling this may sound, however, the fact that the speaker uses the words 'meddling and intrusion' gives a rather different indication of development organisations' profound unease about 'interfering' in an alien culture, and in gender relations in particular.

Cultural sensitivity is frequently advanced by staff in development agencies as a reason for not challenging gender relations in the communities where they work (Smyth 1999). It is striking that while development workers often express reluctance to challenge gender relations, they nonetheless appear willing to challenge other aspects of 'traditional' culture, such as ethnic or caste-based inequality. The latter seldom manifests itself within marriage or the family, but is more commonly played out at community and state level. Do development workers share the anxieties expressed within human rights provisions about venturing into the intimate area of relations between spouses, and asserting women's full and equal humanity with men? 'Cultural sensitivity' can be used as a smoke screen to disguise profound discomfort at the idea of alienating men in grassroots communities and in governments, through 'interfering' in gender relations. This is sometimes expressed as a fear that development organisations may find they are not able to work at all.

Development workers who argue for 'non-interference' in culture ignore the fact that 'culture' is not fixed, coherent, or homogenous. While relationships between men and women are portrayed as fixed by tradition, norms, taboos, kinship, and religion, these are constantly being negotiated and contested by subordinate groups. Cultural beliefs adapt to accommodate new values and understandings that emerge over time or as a result of contact with other cultures. For example, the binding of women's feet in China and the cutting to acquire face marks in Sudan are two 'customs' that have been abolished successfully. Even when cultural practices are justified on grounds of religious texts, and this presents a serious barrier to challenging them, the interpretation of the texts may be open to debate.

Some of the most innovative responses to violence against women involve local women accepting and celebrating those aspects of their culture that are beneficial to them while rejecting aspects that are harmful. For example, in Ethiopia, the National Committee on Traditional Practices (NCTPE) uses popular education – including communications media like radio, posters, and leaflets – to discourage and eliminate harmful practices, particularly female genital mutilation, and to promote traditional practices that have positive benefits for women and children (Spadacini and Nichols 1998). In so doing, local feminists aim to reconceptualise 'tradition' so that it co-exists harmoniously with the values of non-violence and human rights. It is obvious that this is a difficult task that requires constant vigilance.

A further argument that is often advanced as a justification for non-interference in gender relations in developing countries is that to intervene would be to impose a western feminist agenda. However, it is mistaken to assume that ending violence against women is a western agenda. While western women's views have been most often published in popular media and in research and analysis (Mohanty 1991a), this shows an historical bias against publishing the experience of southern and black women, rather than a lack of action on their part. In fact, women everywhere have long been engaged in a struggle to abolish violence against women, and to attain justice and equality.

Women's struggles have taken place on a variety of levels and platforms. Slave testimonies and diaries written throughout the nineteenth century reveal the dynamic of racial and sexual abuse at work within the plantation system in the Americas. They are filled with examples of resistance strategies, such as deliberate acts of induced abortion as an assertion of reproductive control against the plantation masters' 'breeding' policies (Thomas 1997). In Brazil in the 1850s, a rare 'women's rights press' criticised the oppression of women within family relationships (Corcoran-Nantes 1997). In the second half of the nineteenth century, women in the Arab women's liberation movement fought with their pens against all kinds of oppression, including the oppression of women by men inside the family

(El Saadawi 1993). Sex workers have challenged violence and discriminatory laws in non-western settings for many years. The Uruguayan organisation AMEPU claims a history lodged in the struggle of Polish sex workers in Uruguay during the nineteenth century (Kempadoo 1998). In many parts of Africa, the 'wives of the lineage' are an important body in pre-colonial African politics, taking action against men who mistreat their wives or insult women (Moore 1986).

How best can international development agencies and indigenous NGOs support the efforts of women in the countries where they work to challenge the violence against them? What is development, who are the intended beneficiaries, and at what cost? The next section will argue that violence against women has often been framed as a concern for development agencies in narrowly economic terms. This reflects a common focus in international development organisations on economic growth and poverty alleviation that has precluded adequate analysis of power relations between men and women in development processes.

2.2.1 Existing 'efficiency' approaches to violence against women

Existing development approaches recognise violence against women as a barrier to women's full participation in the economic activities of their nation and community. This policy approach stresses that women's 'efficiency' as economic actors is at stake (for more on efficiency approaches to women in development, see Moser 1993). Such approaches emphasise the costs of violence against women to women themselves, to the State, and to communities, rather than emphasising that violence is an abuse of women's humanity. They are based on a vision of development as economic growth, and on the assumption that development will lead to a decrease in violence against women. In this light, initiatives to address violence can be justified by the fact that they help maximise returns on investments in many sectors of national development.

While this approach may seem abhorrent to activists who would prefer to argue that violence is an abuse of human rights, arguing that violence against women must be eradicated because of its cost to society and development is a useful strategy in contexts where more radical arguments may not succeed. Establishing the financial cost of violence against women may lead to donors or governments giving funding to organisations that work on the issue, and it may persuade legislators to act. As Nüket Kardam, a Women In Development (WID) scholar and practitioner, found in a study on the World Bank, 'WID issues have received a more favourable response from the staff members when they were introduced and justified on the basis of economic viability. The more the indispensability of WID components to the economic success of projects can be demonstrated, the more staff members are likely to pay attention.' (Kardam 1991, 80)

Violence against women as a barrier to national development

Development researchers, international organisations, national govern-ments, and many local NGOs are in agreement that women's full participation in all areas of economic, political and social work is paramount if poverty is to be alleviated worldwide. In particular, interventions that focus on areas of life where women have a key reproductive role must have the full participation of women if problems such as high fertility, deforestation, and hunger are to be solved (Heise 1995b). Women's participation is seen here not as an end in itself, but as a means to achieving other development objectives.

Violence against women wastes women's potential to participate in the economy and society, by sapping women's energy, undermining their confidence, and compromising their health. Awareness of the impact of violence against women on women's participation is evident in the World Bank's argument that 'women cannot lend their labour or creative ideas fully, when they are burdened with the physical and psychological scars of abuse.' (Heise *et al.* 1994, 24)

Violence can prevent women's participation in development directly, by detrimentally affecting their health.[17] Attempts to quantify the cost of violence against women to development are likely to be conservative, because of continuing reluctance by many public institutions to recognise violence as a legitimate public concern, and because of under-reporting of the problem by the women involved. However, the World Bank (1993) estimates that rape and domestic violence are significant causes of morbidity and mortality among women aged 15-44 worldwide. According to World Bank estimates, rape and domestic violence account for six per cent of the total disability-adjusted life years (DALYs) of healthy life lost worldwide, for 90 per cent of the morbidity associated with disability from injury worldwide, and for five per cent of the healthy years of life lost to women of reproductive age in developing countries. Such data may prompt governments and businesses to begin to count the losses caused by violence against women systematically.

Violence against women also hampers women's ability to participate in development indirectly, by intimidating them from taking part in development activities, including education. Domestic violence and the fear of it are often key factors in limiting women's participation in development projects. A recent research programme on social participation in Latin America highlighted that domestic violence and marital disapproval were major factors limiting women's participation in development projects in the area of study (PASF, Oxfam internal document 1998).

In all states, violence against women has a vast indirect cost. This includes the costs of purchasing physical and mental health care for victims of violence; the cost of women's lost labour; the cost of the provision of temporary and permanent housing; and the costs of the loss of children's education when their lives are disrupted by violence. In countries where laws against violence exist, and women can gain access to the legal process, costs to the State include those of criminal and civil investigations, and legal proceedings.

In 1992, the National Committee on Violence Against Women in Australia reported that violence against women costs the Australian community hundreds of millions of dollars annually. In New South Wales, the annual costs incurred in relation to violence against women were $1.5 billion; the annual costs in Queensland were $447 million for domestic violence and $63 million for rape and sexual assault (National Committee on Violence Against Women, 1993). Extrapolating from a study of domestic violence in Hackney, an inner city London Borough, the total annual costs of domestic violence to health and social services in Great Britain may exceed £1 billion (Stanko 1998).

Violence against women as a barrier to the development of 'social capital'

Violence against women does not only cause pain, fear, and suffering to individual women, and to women as a group; it also has a negative effect on wider society. It is widely recognised that peace must underpin all attempts to alleviate poverty in the most deprived communities. The World Bank has recognised that violence of all kinds erodes the 'social capital' within communities, which it defines as 'the networks, norms, and trust that facilitate co-ordination and co-operation for mutual benefit. These are the reciprocal exchanges that exist first and foremost, between individuals and households, but which then extend into the social institutions at the community level.' (Holland and Moser 1997, 4)

A recent World Bank study on urban violence and poverty in Jamaica, which was conducted to inform the design of the Jamaican Social Investment Fund[18] project, demonstrates how violence breeds fear and distrust, and deepens the cycles of poverty and violence in which its members live (op. cit.). The World Bank study states: 'At the individual level, violence inhibits the ability of poor men and women to utilise their most important asset, labour, efficiently and productively. At the community level, the society is dominated by fear and distrust. Communities often lack the very basic forms of co-operation or communication, and despite heroic efforts by individuals and organisations, violence in all its forms – political, drug, gang, economic, interpersonal, and domestic – has left communities bereft of the most basic stocks of social capital.' (op. cit., 41)

The Jamaican study used participatory methods to explore local people's perceptions of violence and its impacts on poverty, employment, and local infrastructures.[19] Community groups identified 25 different types of violence. These were then categorised by the researchers as: political violence, drugs-related violence, gang violence (often concerning guns), economic violence including house-breaking and stealing, interpersonal violence, and domestic violence. Overall, gang violence was perceived as the most serious type of violence, while domestic and interpersonal forms of violence were perceived as pervasive in daily life but less serious. Men and women in the study stated that violence was linked to unemployment. Men said that high male unemployment led to frustration and idleness, which in turn led to an increase in gang violence, interpersonal conflict, and domestic violence. Women, in turn, perceived high female unemployment as leading to an increase in domestic violence as women became more dependent on men for an income.

The study posits that the two 'assets'[20] vital for reducing poverty – labour and social capital – are eroded by violence. Violence has this effect because it results in the stigmatising of a community, and instils fear in poor people, which discourages them from venturing far from their homes. As a result, residents of these poor communities cannot access jobs, businesses are deterred from investing in the area, children's education suffers, and communities themselves do not invest in local infrastructure and services. The study concludes that violence is a serious social problem with important economic and social development consequences:

> *The costs of violence include weak investor confidence, higher health and police costs, the disaffection and migration of the urban middle class, higher morbidity and mortality rates, reduced access to social services, dysfunctional families, deeper oppression of women and an overall climate of fear that replaces a spirit of co-operation and participation in community life.*
> (op. cit., 2)

To sum up, this approach to working on violence against women as a develop-ment issue emphasises the importance of preventing crime and violence, including violence against women, because of its negative impact on the social capital of the community. In this view, prevention work should secure existing social capital and enable it to be increased, consequently increasing the resources of the poor and ultimately increasing economic growth.

2.2.2 Towards an 'empowerment' approach to violence against women

'Efficiency' approaches to violence against women are based on a firm foundation: it is quite true that violence against women impedes the effectiveness and efficiency of national development. This emphasis on efficiency and economic growth within the context of economic development strategy may imply that negative impacts on economic development provide the main reason for combating violence against women, and that the effects of violence can be reduced to a price. Consequently, it may appear that violence against women is only of relevance to development agencies because it limits the continued development of emerging economies in low-income countries, not because of the harm done to women. The emphasis is on what development can get from women, rather than what women can get from development (Kabeer 1994).

A more fundamental criticism of efficiency approaches to violence against women is that development policies and programmes that address violence as a brake on economic development misunderstand the cause of violence against women, and hence respond inappropriately. The root cause of violence against women is not poverty or lack of economic development, but the societal structures of inequality between men and women. These structures of inequality also give rise to unsustainable models of development.

Feminists from around the world have criticised the current model of development because of its narrow focus on using women's labour more productively to deliver inequitable economic growth. They argue that the assumption that 'including' women in current economic development will lead to a decrease in violence against women is mistaken. In fact, violence against women plays a role in driving the current unequal and exploitative development model. Proponents of efficiency approaches do not question what stake women might have in the current model of profoundly unequal economic growth, which relies on the exploitation of the South by the North; of poor communities by elites; of black people by white people; and of women by men (Sen and Grown 1987). Efficiency approaches focus on how violence 'excludes' women from national development. Feminist critiques have argued that instead it ensures that they will continue to be included on terms that are profoundly unequal. Male violence against women prevents women from contesting an unequal world, and excludes them from decision making positions where they could begin to transform the world.

The impacts of global industrialisation on violence against women

The rapid incorporation of women into the new export manufacturing sectors from the 1970s onwards illustrates this argument. Women were promoted as the optimal and preferred, 'docile, cheap labour force' in this industrialisation, which has been described as 'female-led as much as it was export-led' (Joekes 1987, 81). Using a female labour force has a commercial logic. Women's lack of formal skills and training obscure the fact that many women acquire a wide range of skills through household or informal sector work. As a result, many women provide skilled labour at unskilled wage-rates (Elson and Pearson 1981). The poverty of populations in southern countries, and of immigrant populations in northern countries, means that many employers are able to recruit workers on very poor terms, and that workers wishing to protest against terms and conditions of employment are in a weak position. In this view, industrialisation has its roots in sexism and racism (Ong 1987).

Violence against women plays a key role in this process. In Chile, for example, women textile workers suffer violence and verbal abuse from male bosses, constant camera surveillance, and restrictions of movement. In response, women have organised training programmes for textile workers, and developed union activities. Far from taking an uncritical, efficiency-based attitude to women working in industry, these programmes concentrate on empowering women workers to combat the exploitative conditions in which they are included in global industry. The programmes provide a work-site cafeteria for women textile workers, and offer training on gender and labour issues, cultural activities, and a communications campaign to help women workers combat unjust and violent working conditions. Women have also helped to develop a methodology to monitor work-site environmental conditions. This enables women to detect problems as they occur, and propose solutions (Oxfam internal document 1999).

The impacts of economic crisis on violence against women

Another example of the way in which gender inequality and violence against women are linked to unequal global development comes from the economic crises that occurred in many developing countries during the 1980s and 1990s. There is a vast and growing body of evidence for the devastating effects that economic crisis has had on households and on gender relations, particularly within low-income communities. The evidence also points to a related increase in violence against women. Women are the usual victims of spousal violence in low-income neighbourhoods, as reported in many studies in Latin America (Benería and Roldán 1987; Schmink 1985; Chant 1991), but this has worsened during the economic crisis. For example, small-scale qualitative studies carried out in Mexico (Chant 1994a) and Ecuador (Moser 1989a), show an escalation in the incidence of domestic violence at the time of the economic crisis in all households where women were not able to continue earning money on a regular basis. Women's income can in some instances allow them to avoid conflict by asking their husbands for money less often (Dwyer and Bruce 1988). Any decline in already low incomes from informal sector earnings can result in women experiencing reduced financial control, lower self-esteem, and increased conflict with their husbands. In female-headed households where older women depend on their relationships with their adult sons, conflict between women and their adult offspring is also exacerbated by structural adjustment policies (Kanji 1995).[21]

Development interventions, efficiency, and violence against women

As discussed earlier in this book, the vision of development that informs the work of many international and national development organisations is of sustainable 'human development' (UNDP 1990), brought about by a combination of economic growth and a commitment to equality and social justice. However, this radically different vision of development does not necessarily adopt a commitment to challenging and changing unequal gender relations. Some development interventions may actually increase violence against women, at least in the short-term.

Currently, as Chapter 1 stated, the impact of credit provision to women on gender relations is a major focus of interest among both academic researchers and development practitioners conducting evaluations and impact assessments (Kabeer 1998). In addition to the discussion in Chapter 1, further material on this subject can be found in Chapters 4 and 5.

Credit provision is seen by many as 'an increasingly important intervention for addressing poverty ... as a result of successful evaluations attesting to their substantial developmental benefits' (op. cit., 5). However, while development projects may use the language of 'women's empowerment', many are in fact working from a concern for efficiency, targeting women for credit provision because of their favourable reputation for prompt repayment of loans. Consequently, the motive for promoting loan and credit programmes for women may be less concerned with the benefits women get from an independent financial resource, than with the efficiency gains to be made from the development of financially self-sustaining rural development institutions (Goetz 1994, 30). Credit programmes that do not account for the impact of loans on household dynamics ignore the possible violence that may result from the struggle for control and repayment of the loan. In some cases, women may avoid domestic tension and violence by handing control of the loan to their spouse or male relative. In such situations, women may typically exert no control over the way the money is used, but retain full responsibility for repaying the loan to the credit programme.

Humanitarian programmes and violence against women

Humanitarian programmes may inadvertently increase violence against women in some contexts. Chapter 5 discusses violence against women in humanitarian emergencies further. When humanitarian organisations fail to address violence against women, this is often as a result of an understanding of relief interventions as predominantly driven by technical problems, requiring technical solutions. As Chapter 5 highlights, the physical planning of refugee settlements is all-important in determining failure or success in protecting women refugees from violence and rape.

However, while good design can help lessen the opportunities for violence and abuse of women in refugee camps, it does not completely solve the problem. This is because violence against women in refugee camps arises not only from spatial factors but also from unequal social relationships between women and men, and between relief workers and the populations with whom they work. There are many documented examples showing how relief workers and support staff have been implicated in acts of violence against women. For example, FIDA carried out research on refugee women in Kenya, in collaboration with the Women Victims of Violence project (WVV).[22] The study revealed gross violations against women in camps. Local government agencies, as well as international relief and development agencies, were identified as perpetuating acts of violence against refugee and displaced women (PASF, Oxfam internal document 1995). Reports in 1992, 1993, and 1994 revealed that UN peacekeeping troops in former Yugoslavia and Somalia were involved in child prostitution and the rape of girls and women (McCollum, Radford, and Kelly 1994). Chapter 8 looks at ways in which this kind of violence against women can be countered.

This section has argued that the focus in international development organisations on economic growth and poverty alleviation has precluded any systematic or clear analysis of power relations between men and women in development processes. The fundamental problem with an efficiency approach to tackling violence against women is that the development structures in which women are being encouraged to participate are left unquestioned. Not only is this true of international economic and political development, but it is also true of many development and humanitarian interventions that critique neo-liberal models of development, instigated by NGOs as well as bilaterals and multilaterals.

2.3 Summary and implications for development organisations

The concept of human rights, as originally conceived, was blind to gender differences and gendered patterns of inequality. The international laws that enshrine the concept of human rights have not therefore included violence against women explicitly. However, successful lobbying and campaigning on the part of feminist human rights activists and organisations has led to significant advances, so that violence against women is now recognised as a core human rights concern. This chapter has shown how recent reconceptualisations of international human rights and humanitarian law articulated by feminist scholars and activists have sought to promote interventionist approaches in international jurisdictions in order to address and promote women's human rights adequately. This is evidenced by women's efforts to have rape and other forms of sexual violence viewed not as crimes against their 'honour', but as acts of cruel, inhuman, or degrading treatment, and under some circumstances as war crimes or crimes against humanity.

However, there is a long way to go before human rights become a practical tool for women's organisations to use in their fight against violence. Although women's rights organisations have done much to widen the scope of human rights to include violence against women, the majority of women have no knowledge of their rights, and no resources with which to claim them. Regardless of the national or international law, the vast majority of women are still totally powerless to defend themselves in the home, when dealing with the police, or in court. In addition, some opponents of women's human rights use notions of religious and cultural diversity to argue that women's human rights are not universal.

The chapter considered the validity of the argument that development organisations should not interfere in 'culture', and suggested that this is actually a smokescreen for the real concern that development work should not actively challenge gender power relationships in intimate relationships between women and men. Paradoxically, development actors have become involved in work to eradicate violence against women: not because of the impact it has on women as human beings, but because violence against women acts as a barrier to women's participation in development, and erodes social capital. Efficiency approaches focus the costs of violence against women. These approaches show how violence places a serious financial burden on the State, through the 'opportunity cost' to women of disability and illness, through the cost of health care and other support for survivors of violence, and through the cost of prosecuting the perpetrators.

While these arguments may prove persuasive in getting mainstream development organisations to allocate resources to violence against women, a more radical commitment to questioning the structural social, economic, and political inequality between women and men at all levels of society is needed. Violence against women is caused by, and perpetuates, this inequality. Not only is an efficiency approach unable by definition to address the structural causes of violence against women, but by encouraging women's participation in gender-blind social and economic processes, it implicitly condones and perpetuates violence against women.

A rights-based approach to development combines the strengths of the human rights and development responses to violence against women. Human rights agreements that assert women's rights to be human rights are invaluable in paving the way for states and international bodies to establish a climate of non-violence towards women, and go some way towards raising awareness that violence against women is a gross violation of their rights. It is not simply a 'cultural' issue, and for those who still need convincing, southern women's critiques of development make it very clear that global action on the part of development organisations to support women's struggles against violence against women is welcome (Longwe 1995). Development responses highlight the links between violence against women and their participation in development, but need to deepen and develop their understanding of this link. Violence is not an apolitical impediment to women's participation in development; rather, it is the ultimate means of enforcing unequal social, economic, and political relations between women and men, at all levels of society and in all countries of the world.

While international institutions have drawn a line between political and civil rights on the one hand and economic and social rights on the other, all these rights are interconnected. There is a pressing need to recognise the synergies between human rights and development work, and this has not been made easy by the division that exists between the international institutions that focus on political rights, and those that are concerned with economic growth and development. However, development NGOs are not hampered by such a history. It is possible for them to develop analyses of human development that stress the indivisibility of political, social, and economic rights. Equally, they are able to work in partnership with women's organisations that are already exploring the linkages between violence against women, poverty, gender relations in the home, women's position in the 'public sphere', and women's ability to claim their rights. Development NGOs need to recognise and challenge analysis, planning, and action that are based on apolitical or technical development approaches. Development interventions need to be founded on an understanding of the linkages between human development, social well-being, and women's struggles to attain their full human rights – not only to economic prosperity, but also to political leadership, and social autonomy.

3 The prevalence, forms, and impacts of violence against women

I was wearing a pinafore. Justice ripped it off with a knife, and stabbed me on my feet. The others joined in assaulting me. My husband was made to watch everything. Every time he attempted to avert his eyes or turn his head, they would hit him. When Justice was finished raping me, they poured water on my vagina. When I attempted to close my legs, they hit me. The youths took turns raping me and pouring water over my vagina. When they hurt me and I cried out they stabbed me and hit me. I eventually lost consciousness. ...When they left they took some chickens. ... When I regained consciousness in hospital I discovered that my womb was stitched and they had had to perform a hysterectomy.

(Survivor of apartheid-era violence in KwaZulu Natal, South Africa, in Padarath 1998, 68)

3.1 Problems in estimating the prevalence of violence against women

As discussed in Chapter 2, the true prevalence of violence against women is still unknown. Mainstream national statistics focus on macro-economic issues, revealing relatively little on accompanying political and social trends. Most of these statistics are, in any case, not disaggregated by gender.[1] Even if governments and international bodies were to commit themselves to centrally collating and publishing the official statistics on violence against women that do exist in some countries, these would be conservative. This is because the true prevalence of violence against women is concealed as a result of under-recording by the police, and under-reporting by the women involved.

Under-recording occurs when violence against women – particularly in the home – is viewed as a 'normal' part of gender relations. Under-recording by state agencies is therefore not just a problem of poor data collection procedures, but also results from the fact that violence against women is not considered to be a priority in many countries. Ignorance and prejudice among police and other state officials means that women survivors of violence risk being blamed for the violence inflicted against them. Women who have been trafficked may experience arrest, harassment, or expulsion if they report their experiences to the police, especially where prostitution is illegal. Where arrests are made, it is often women and not the traffickers who are detained. In Israel, between 1994-97, the government arrested and deported over 1000 women to Eastern Europe and the former Soviet Union (Vandenburg 1997).

Many women opt to remain silent about violence. This under-reporting may be the result of fear of the attacker, of the social taboos surrounding violence against women, or of a lack of support to women survivors of violence. In the Republic of Korea, fewer than two per cent of women rape survivors have ever contacted the police (United Nations 1995a, 158).

Perhaps the most common reason for under-reporting, especially in cases where the attacker is known, is women's fear that their attacker will retaliate and further harm them. A second reason is the cultural stigma attached to violence. Forms of violence that are part of many women's daily lives, such as domestic violence, may be perceived as a result of women's failure to fulfil their roles as wife or mother in some way. Women fear that reporting abuse may bring shame, damaging her own or her family's reputation. In Cambodia, the *Cbab Srey*, a lyric poem known to most Cambodian women, warns wives, 'Never tattle to your parents anything negative about your husband, or this will cause the village to erupt.' The message of the poem is that women should endure beating in order to save their marriage and keep the family together (Zimmerman 1994, 24).

Although women may feel that violence used against them is painful or wrong, they may not necessarily define it as a crime. Many women do not define forced sex as rape, if they are living with or married to the attacker (World Health Organisation 1997). Many different cultures have sayings or proverbs that reflect widespread beliefs about violence against women as a normal aspect of relationships between women and men. In countries as far apart as Russia and Ethiopia, there are sayings along the lines of: 'If he beats you, it means he loves you', reflecting an attitude of tolerance to violence that has existed for centuries. The belief that violence is an indicator of love is a shocking example of how both women and men can be made to believe the unbelievable: that it is actually desirable and acceptable that one human being should cause pain and suffering to another. In a study carried out in Cape Town, South Africa, with pregnant teenagers, all but one of the 24 informants interviewed described assault as a regular feature of their sexual relationships (Wood and Jewkes 1997).

A third reason for women's under-reporting of violence is the failure of formal institutions to provide effective protection for women. In countries where a woman's virginity is associated with family honour, unmarried women who report rape may be forced to marry their attacker (WHO 1997). In countries where there are no legal or social sanctions against violence by an intimate partner, or where such sanctions are ineffective, women may decide that to report the violence is pointless.

Despite these obstacles to uncovering the prevalence of the problem, quantitative and qualitative research that gives a more accurate picture of the problem does exist. This ranges from large-scale sample surveys to participatory research and case studies collected by women's support groups and by individual researchers. This evidence, together with other statistical indicators – for example that of trauma statistics from hospitals – has resulted in a widespread understanding of the scale of violence against women. The previous chapter discussed some estimates from mainstream development institutions, including the World Bank, of the staggering proportions of violence against women. Large-scale surveys and small-scale studies demonstrate that violence is a 'normal' part of being female in all parts of the world.

3.2 Forms of violence against women

> *I fell in love with him because he beat me up.*
>
> (Young woman in South Africa, quoted in Wood and Jewkes 1997, 43)

Some forms of violence against women are known in all countries and regions of the world. These include physical violence against a wife or intimate partner, often known as wife-beating; rape and sexual violence (both in conflict and in non-conflict situations); violence and sexual violence against girls; and the trafficking or bonded labour of women and girls. Other forms of violence discussed here are associated with particular cultures, countries, or regions of the world. The terms 'culture-bound practices', and 'harmful traditional practices', are often used. These terms encompass a huge variety of gross violations of women's bodies and minds, including child marriage; female genital mutilation; widow immolation (*sati*); so-called 'honour' killings of young women who have sexual relationships outside marriage; and the persecution and killing of women accused of witchcraft. They are also used to describe ongoing abuses that may appear to be mild, but have a cumulative weakening effect on women and girls, resulting in a serious threat to health. These include intra-household discrimination against girls in the allocation of food or health care, and taboos around pregnancy.

There are several problems with the use of terms like 'harmful traditional practice'. Firstly, as can be seen from the above discussion, they are catch-all terms, and can be used both for gross violations of women's bodies and minds and more minor issues. Secondly, they may underpin assumptions that these practices are accepted by all those who live within the culture, or imply that all cultures in which a particular form of violence is found will attach the same significance to it. In fact, a particular form of violence against women will have different significance in different settings; it may also differ qualitatively. Female genital mutilation, for example, is believed by many in North Africa to be an Islamic practice – a belief which has no foundation in religious texts (Dorkenoo 1994). In Lesotho, where the community is not Muslim, female genital mutilation is present here as a part of 'female circumcision' rites of adolescent girls, but involves pulling, not cutting, the genitalia.

From the perspective of development policy and practice, perhaps the most important problem to arise from use of the terms 'culture' and 'tradition' in relation to these forms of violence against women is that they encourage beliefs that violence is a sign of a 'backward society', and that economic development and a democratic government will eradicate it. In fact, the situation is much more complex. If unequal economic, political, and social relations between women and men go unchallenged, old forms of violence against women will simply mutate into new forms. For example, in parts of South Asia, preference for sons over daughters has strong roots in poverty as well as cultural norms. This has resulted in female infanticide. As poverty grows and women's status remains secondary to that of men, son preference remains. Technological progress leads, not to the end of violence, but to the development of new methods of avoiding the cost of bringing up daughters. The availability of pre-natal screening to determine foetal sex has resulted in the new phenomenon of sex-selective abortion (George 1997).

Forms of violence are also being exported from their countries of origin into other regions of the world, as migration takes place and ethnic minority communities try to retain their sense of cultural identity in a new setting. For example, the Somali community in London, UK, continues to practise female genital mutilation. Health providers' prejudices about what they perceive to be an alien, backward practice makes it hard for them to respond to the reproductive health care needs of 'circumcised' women. In fact, cutting the perineum in western maternity wards has some similarities with female genital mutilation, both in the result and in the reasons given for doing it (Cameron and Anderson 1998).

In the light of the above, some gender and development policy-makers and researchers argue that the terms 'cultural violence' and 'harmful traditional practice' should be consciously used to denote certain harmful practices that are associated with post-industrialised societies. They point out that the universal basis of violence against women is unequal gender power relations, not lack of development. In line with this, the World Bank report, 'Violence against Women: The Hidden Health Burden', includes eating disorders and cosmetic surgery as examples of violence against women in industrialised countries (Heise, Pitanguy, and Germaine 1994). Women suffering from eating disorders restrict their dietary intake to conform to cultural standards of beauty. In North America and Europe, roughly one in every 150 women suffers from anorexia, a psychological disorder characterised by self-starvation, sometimes leading to death. Bulimia, a similar disorder, involves binge eating and self-induced vomiting. Both these conditions can result in death (op. cit.).

Finally, while it is positive that many development workers no longer assume that the knowledge and practices of Western cultures are superior to those of other cultures, we saw in Chapter 2 that an undiscriminating respect for indigenous culture can derail arguments about the universality of human rights.

Before moving on, the limitations of the list of different forms of violence against women which follows should be made clear. No such list can be complete: readers will be aware of other forms of violence against women that are not mentioned here. The act of categorisation may also create the false impression that this list describes discrete forms of violence that are distinct from each other. The headings used here have been chosen in the hope that they will help to highlight the ways in which different types of violence are linked to social institutions – in particular, marriage and the family. They show how women become vulnerable to different forms of violence at different stages of their lifecycle, and how changing social and economic conditions can result in violence against women mutating into new forms. Both 'old' and 'new' forms of violence are rooted in a constant: unequal power relations between women and men.

3.2.1 Physical violence from an intimate partner ('domestic violence')

Research shows that the vast majority of violence experienced by women occurs in the home, and is instigated by a husband or intimate partner. In some cases, however, other members of the extended family, including co-wives and in-laws, may commit violence. A recent report by the John Hopkins University Population Information Program, based on over 50 population surveys, concluded that domestic violence is a serious human rights threat to women in all societies, and that on average one in three women around the world has experienced violence in an intimate relationship (Heise, Ellsberg, and Gottemoeller 1999, 5).

Forty-two per cent of women in Kenya, 38 per cent of women in Korea, 28 per cent of women in the United States, and 35 per cent of women in Egypt reported being beaten by their husbands or partners (UNICEF 2000, 5). A study on domestic violence in Cambodia found that 74 per cent of respondents were aware of at least one family where domestic violence has occurred (Nelson and Zimmerman 1996, 15).

The World Health Organisation (WHO) estimates that, worldwide, up to 52 per cent of women suffer physical violence from their male partners (World Health Organisation 1997). Data from Latin America and Asia repeatedly shows that up to 60 per cent of women have been physically assaulted by a spouse or male partner in their lifetime. Many of the survivors have been beaten many times, or have been subject to escalating abuse over a substantial period of time (United Nations 1995a, 158). Ethnographic research carried out in six villages in rural Bangladesh found that two-thirds of the women interviewed said they had been beaten at one time or another, and in one village the incidence was as high as 87 per cent. Thirty eight per cent of women said they had been beaten in the previous year, with percentages ranging from 14 to 60 in different villages (Schuler *et al.* 1998, 150). In a study of domestic violence in Calcutta, 79 per cent of women reported that they had experienced either physical or sexual violence, or both, in their marriage (P. Sen 1997a).

The Calcutta study bears witness to the appalling injuries that women sustain through marital abuse. One in five women in the Calcutta study had injuries that may be classified as serious, such as fractured bones, impaired vision, dislocated bones, cuts requiring stitches, poker burns, and internal cuts. Most women said they experienced pain lasting several days. One woman's husband had bitten her breasts and used his toenail to cut around her vagina (op. cit.).

3.2.2 Rape and sexual violence

The WHO estimates that at least one in five women suffer rape or attempted rape during their lifetimes (World Health Organisation 1997). Other studies report a higher figure: one study found that 44 per cent of women in the United States had been the subject of rape or attempted rape at least once in their lives (Russell 1982).

Rape occurs between strangers and between marital partners, friends, and colleagues. Women never 'provoke' rape; their bodies are not the property of men, and they are free to consent or refuse sex, inside as well as outside marriage. Equally, men have the ability to control their sexual urges.

Rape is not usually the result of sexual attraction, but arises from a desire for violent domination. Men do not only rape conventionally attractive, young women, but also babies and elderly women. Raping a woman is a method of asserting control and possession over her body. As a strategy of attacking individual women's bodies in an attempt to attack women as a group and ensure their subordination, rape is often used as a weapon of intimidation not only against an individual woman, but against her spouse and male relatives. During war, rape may be used as a 'weapon' to intimidate an enemy.

Box 3.1 below, 'Myths and Misconceptions about Rape', is from a leaflet designed by People Opposing Women Abuse (POWA), an organisation working with women survivors of violence in South Africa. The leaflet aims to undermine and destroy pervasive myths about rape.

Rape is often believed to be carried out by strangers. However, as the POWA leaflet asserts, the majority of raped women actually know their attackers, and many of them are close relatives, spouses, or acquaintances. The majority of the American women survivors of rape in the US study had been raped by men they knew, and who were in positions of trust or power, including friends and relatives (Russell 1982). This is confirmed by statistics from Malaysia, Peru, Panama, Chile, and Papua New Guinea (Heise, Pitanguy, and Germaine 1994).

Women who experience non-sexual physical abuse in intimate relationships are particularly likely also to experience rape and sexual violence. A household survey on violence against women in Zimbabwe found that one in three women reported some form of sexual violence (37 per cent) within the household. Forty two per cent had experienced psychological abuse, and 32 per cent had experienced physical abuse: most commonly being kicked, bitten, slapped, or hit (Musasa Project 1997). Within intimate relationships, marital rape is extremely common: a survey of 125 women in Georgia, USA found that 42 per cent of women had had a male partner who used physical force, or the threat of such force, to coerce them into having sex (Kalichan, Williams, Cherry, Belcher, and Nachimson 1998).

Rape and sexual violence have now been recognised within international human rights standards as a tactic of repression and torture that has been used by states on many occasions. 'Rape by government agents is a common method of torture inflicted on women. It is both a physical violation and injury, and an assault on a woman's mental and emotional well-being.' (Amnesty International 1991, 18)

The rape and sexual assault of women takes place on a massive scale in war, conflict, and humanitarian disasters. In her path-breaking account of the history of rape as a weapon of war, Susan Brownmiller states that during World War II, Japanese soldiers occupying China raped more than 20,000 women during the 'Rape of Nanking'. In the Bangladeshi war of secession in 1971, between 200,000 and 400,000 Bengali women were raped by Pakistani soldiers as part of a systematic campaign (Brownmiller 1975). The wars in the former Yugoslavia witnessed the rape of tens of thousands of women – estimates range from 20,000 to 60,000 (Stiglmayer 1994). In the genocidal conflict in Rwanda, more than 10,000 Rwandan women became pregnant as a result of rape – of these, 1100 women gave birth and 5200 underwent abortions; the disarray following the conflict made it impossible to track the remaining women. Some Rwandan women had been held and repeatedly raped for up to nine months (Human Rights Watch 1996).

During conflict, rape is used not only to dominate, degrade, and instil fear in women themselves, but also as a 'weapon of war' to subjugate and dominate an enemy community. Such violence against women is intended as an attack on everyone, to violate and demoralise men and to destroy community identity, especially when ethnic or religious purity is at stake (Bennett, Bexley, and Warnock 1995). As the Special Rapporteur states in her first report to the Commission on Human Rights in 1995: 'Violence against women who are seen as being the property of the males in a rival group becomes a means of defiling the honour of that social group. Female sexuality has been a battleground in feudal and in modern vendettas, where male privilege and honour are challenged.' (Coomaraswamy 1995, para. 60)

More discussion of rape and forced impregnation during conflict can be found in Chapter 4.

As stated in Chapter 2, displaced women are at risk of rape and violence, even when they inhabit a refugee or displaced persons camp. Women refugees experience higher rates of violence than women in the general population (Wulf 1994). Refugee women and girls are at risk of physical and sexual abuse at the hands of male refugees, especially refugee leaders, and local relief officials (Lawyers Committee for Human Rights 1995). A recent study by the International Rescue Committee that assessed the prevalence of sexual and gender violence among Burundian refugees in Tanzania reported that since becoming a refugee, 26 per cent of 3803 Burundi women aged 12-49 in the Kanembwa camp had experienced sexual violence (Nduna and Goodyear 1997).

Box 3.1
Myths and misconceptions about rape

Myth: Rape occurs between strangers in dark alleys

Implications:

- Assumes 'nice girls' don't get raped;
- Implies that home is safe;
- Implies that rape can be prevented by avoiding certain places and therefore blames the survivor;
- Assumes a particular survivor profile and therefore stigmatises her;
- Entrenches racial and class prejudices.

Facts:

- More than half of all rapes are committed by persons known to the survivor;
- Date or acquaintance rape is very common;
- Women are often raped in their homes.

Myth: Women provoke rape by the way they dress or act

Implications:

- Attempts to excuse rape and 'blame the survivor';
- Assumes that a woman who draws attention is looking for sex or 'deserves what she gets';
- Stigmatises the survivor.

Facts:

- Dressing attractively and flirting are an invitation for attention and/or admiration, not for rape;
- Only the rapist is responsible for the rape!

Myth: Rape is a crime of passion

Implications:

- Assumes that rape is impulsive and unplanned;
- Assumes men to be incapable of delaying gratification or controlling sexual urges;
- Assumes that rape is about uncontrollable lust;
- Attempts to excuse, minimise, and romanticise rape.

Facts:

- Research and evidence from rapists themselves suggests that most rapes are premeditated and planned;
- Many rapists fail to get an erection or ejaculate;

- Interviews with rapists reveal that they rape to feel powerful and in control, not for sexual pleasure;
- Stereotypically 'unattractive' women are raped, including the elderly and babies;
- Many rapists are involved in sexually satisfying relationships with wives or girlfriends at the time of the rape.

Myth: If she didn't scream, fight, or get injured, it wasn't rape

Implications:

- Disbelieves and re-traumatises the survivor;
- Invalidates her experience;
- Discourages her from seeking help.

Facts:

- Women in rape situations are legitimately afraid of being killed or seriously injured, and so co-operate with the rapist to save their lives;
- Rapists use many manipulative techniques to intimidate and coerce women;
- Women in a rape situation often become physically paralysed with terror or shock and are unable to move or fight;
- Non-consensual intercourse doesn't always leave visible signs on the body or the genitals.

Myth: You can tell if she has 'really' been raped by how she acts

Implications:

- Disbelieves and re-traumatises the survivor;
- Invalidates her experience and individuality;
- Discourages her from seeking help.

Facts:

- Reactions to rape are highly varied and individual;
- Many women experience a form of shock after a rape that leaves them emotionally numb or flat – and apparently calm.

Myth: Husbands cannot rape their wives

Implications:

- Assumes that marriage means perpetual consent;
- Disempowers married women.

Facts:

- It is always rape if the woman does not consent, no matter what her relationship with the man.

(Source: Dunkle and Potter 1997)

3.2.3 Sexual violence against girls

An extraordinarily high percentage of girls experience sexual violence.[2] In national sample surveys from Barbados, Canada, the Netherlands, New Zealand, Norway, and the United States, 27 to 34 per cent of women interviewed reported having experienced sexual abuse during childhood or adolescence (United Nations 1995a, 159). A study from the Netherlands showed that 45 per cent of victims of sexual violence within the domestic sphere were under the age of 18, and of these, victims were far more likely to be girls than boys (Netherlands Department for Justice, cited in UNICEF 2000). In Papua New Guinea, 40 per cent of rape survivors were girls under the age of 15 (Interpress 1999). Between 40 to 60 per cent of known sexual assaults have been found to be committed against girls aged 15 and younger, regardless of region or culture (op. cit.). In a refugee camp in Kasulu in Tanzania, 65 per cent of the reported cases of sexual violence were children of 16 years or younger. The figure rose to 73 per cent when 17 and 18 year olds were included (UNHCR 1998).

The figures on sexually transmitted disease (STD) infection in children are a key indicator of the prevalence of sexual violence against girls. A survey carried out in Zimbabwe in 1990 found that 907 children under 12 years of age were treated for sexually transmitted disease at the Genito-Urinary Centre in Harare. Most of the children had been infected by neighbours or close relatives (Meursing *et al.* 1994). A 1988 study conducted in Zaria, Nigeria, found that 16 per cent of female patients treated for STDs were under the age of five years (cited in Heise, Pitanguy, and Germaine 1994, 11).

In many countries, the risk of HIV infection has led to men coercing young girls into sexual relations. These men consider that they are less likely to be infected with HIV if they have sex with very young women. Many of these men are themselves HIV-positive, with the result that the girls they have sex with are put at risk of the disease. In South Africa, increasingly young girls are being forced to have AIDS tests in order to establish that they are still marriageable (Futhi Zakawala, personal communication, 1998).

In some parts of the world, there is evidence of a connection between rising rates of rape of young girls, and beliefs about HIV infection. Rapists are deliberately targeting increasingly young girls in parts of sub-Saharan Africa, since it is believed that sexual intercourse with a young virgin is a cure for AIDS. In the words of one Oxfam development worker in Kenya, 'men who knew they were HIV-positive were seeking out girls who had barely reached puberty with whom to have sex.' (Bridget Walker 1998)

'Sexual violence against girls' does not only mean rape and abuse outside marriage: it is used here to mean all forms of sexual activity with girls and adolescents, including sex within marriage. In the section below on child marriage, there is further discussion of this issue.

3.2.4 Trafficking in women and girls

The Global Alliance Against Trafficking in Women defines trafficking as: 'All acts involved in the recruitment and/or transportation of a woman within and across national borders for work or services by means of violence or threat of violence, abuse of authority or dominant position, debt bondage, deception or other forms of coercion.' (Wijers and Lap-Chew 1997, 77)

The UN estimates that as many as four million people are smuggled into foreign countries each year, generating up to seven million US dollars annually in illicit profits for criminal syndicates. A significant portion of these people are women, who find themselves trapped in debt bondage contracts. Trafficked women are typically forced to work against their will as sex workers, domestic workers, or in sweatshops (Forced Migration Monitor 1997).

There is evidence to suggest that the number of women and girls being trafficked is rising. Traffickers (that is, those involved in the coerced, illegal movement of persons for work elsewhere) are able to exert control and violence over those women seeking economic or political refuge or security. Since the break up of the Soviet Union, the trafficking of Central and Eastern European women is said to have reached 'epidemic proportions' (Coomaraswamy 1996b, para. 44).

Trafficking can be understood as violence against women in two respects. Firstly, all trafficking can be understood as violence against women in the sense that those trafficked are targeted because they are women. They are trafficked in order to perform 'female' work as domestics or as bonded labour in garment factories and other feminised sectors of industry, or for sex work. They face physical coercion and, often, imprisonment. The second respect in which trafficking constitutes violence against women is that many trafficked women face rape and sexual abuse. This may take place in a formal way as a result of working in the sex industry, or in an informal way as a result of their powerlessness and vulnerability to abuse by male employers in households or sweatshops. It is useful to separate out these issues, not least since the issue of trafficking in women has in some quarters become conflated with sex work. This interest in 'the trade in sexualised services' (Pearson and Theobald 1998, 987) has on occasion overwhelmed discussion of the exploitation and violence that are a feature of other experiences of bonded work.

According to the Report of the Special Rapporteur, submitted to the 56th UN Commission on Human Rights, 'The International Organisation for Migration has been cited as estimating that 500,000 women are trafficked into Western Europe alone. The United Nations has estimated that four million persons are trafficked each year.' Anita Gradin, the European Union's Commissioner for Justice and Immigration, estimates that two-thirds of them come from Eastern Europe (Vandenberg 1997). Thousands of Asian women and girls are trafficked into Thai brothels every year, where they work in conditions tantamount to slavery (Asia Watch and Women's Rights Project 1993). A report on the trafficking of women and girls from Nepal to brothels in Bombay, India, estimates that they constitute up to half of the city's 100,000 brothel workers (Asia Watch and Women's Rights Project1995).[3] Those who have obviously contracted HIV/AIDS are thrown out, and return home, where they are frequently ostracised by their own communities. Some are forced to continue to work as sex workers, in the absence of other opportunities to make a livelihood (Poudel and Carryer 2000).

Certain forms of trafficking in women have emerged from traditional or customary practices. In Pakistan, where blood feuds between clans are resolved by *swarah* (marriage between members of the hostile parties), the weaker clan offers a bride to a man from the stronger clan. The bride is a tribute paid by men of one clan or extended family to another in order to spare the sons of both (Richters 1994). In Nepal, the *deukis* system entails rich families without daughters buying young girls from impoverished rural families, and offering them to the temple as their own daughters. These girls are prohibited from marrying and often become either 'kept wives' or prostitutes. In 1992, 17,000 girls were endowed as *deukis* (Poudel 1994, cited in Richters 1994).

3.2.5 Violence relating to 'son preference'

Preference for sons rather than daughters is a feature of many societies. The cumulative effect of discriminatory practices against girls has led economists to conclude that there are over 60 million missing females worldwide; these 'missing women' are the victims of foeticide, infanticide, selective malnourishment, and lack of investment in women's health (A. Sen 1990).

In some regions – notably South Asia – there is a very clear economic reason for this, namely the high cost to a family of providing a dowry for daughters. In contrast, in cultures where bride-price is paid from the husband's family to that of the bride on marriage (which is the case in many sub-Saharan African countries), sons may still be preferred, but the birth of a daughter does not lead to such severe economic repercussions. In other contexts, national development policies, notably the one-child policy implemented in China from 1979, have interacted with existing preference for sons to result in reports of the re-emergence of female infanticide, which was thought to have been eradicated in China after the communist revolution (Kristof 1993).

In Bihar, the 1991 census recorded a ratio of 820 girls for every 1000 boys aged six and below. A survey carried out by Adithi, an Indian NGO that works with resource-poor women in Bihar, concluded that female infanticide[4] in certain caste groups was the primary factor underlying the low ratio of girls to boys (Strinivasan *et al.* 1995). Infanticide of baby girls may be carried out by family members, or by traditional midwives (Murthy 1996). Some baby girls may die through neglect or lack of food (Dasgupta 1987). In a workshop in 1995 in Bihar, India, four *dais* (traditional midwives) reported that of the eight female babies they had delivered over the past month, four were killed. They mentioned strangulation, giving the baby a large quantity of salt, mixing poisonous seeds with milk, and leaving the infant in a clay pot as common methods (Murthy 1996).

Infanticide is now becoming less common, due to access to modern technologies: ultrasound and amniocentesis have created the possibility for pregnant women to have sex-selective abortions. In Bombay, public hoardings openly advertise the availability of amniocentesis, and the selective termination of female foetuses (Kelkar 1992). For those who are poor and do not have access to this technology, infanticide remains a cheaper option.

Statistics bear witness to the fact that amniocentesis and sex-selective abortions are used to such an extent that they are skewing the 'sex ratio' (ratio of males to females) at birth in some countries. In China, in 1994, 117 boys were born for every 100 girls, a figure significantly higher than the world average of 106 males to every 100 females. Approximately 500,000 more male children than female children are born each year in China (Amnesty International 1995a).

3.2.6 Female genital mutilation

Estimates suggest that between 120 million (UNFPA 1997) and 135 million females worldwide are genitally mutilated (Dorkenoo 1994). Female genital mutilation (sometimes known as female circumcision) is practised in 26 African countries. In a number of countries, such as Djibouti, Mali, Sierra Leone, Somalia, and large areas of Ethiopia and Sudan, nearly all women are affected. It is also practised in some minority communities in some Asian countries, and by some immigrant groups in Europe, Canada, Australia, and the United States (Toubia 1993).

Female genital mutilation is generally carried out on girls of any age from three days old up to puberty. It occurs in a variety of forms, from the removal of the prepuce of the tip of the clitoris (*sunna*), to removal of the clitoris, the labia minora and labia majora, and the sealing of the two sides through stitching, leaving only a small opening at the lower end to allow the passage of urine and menstrual flow (Abdalla 1983). The most common form involves excision of the clitoris and the labia minora. The short- and long-term health impacts of female genital mutilation on women are discussed later in this chapter.

3.2.7 Child Marriage

Article 16(2) of the Women's Convention states: 'The betrothal and the marriage of a child shall have no legal effect, and all necessary action, including legislation, shall be taken to specify a minimum age for marriage and to make the registration of marriages in an official registry compulsory.'

Despite international law's unequivocal rejection of the marriage of very young girls, national law is often at odds with this. The minimum age for marriage in some countries such as Chile, Ecuador, Panama, Paraguay, Sri Lanka, and Venezuela is 12 (Bunch, Carrillo, and Shore 1998). The early marriage of girls is an accepted part of many economic and social systems, and is based on the view that brides must also be virgins. Child marriage has been described as 'the socially legitimised institutionalisation of marital rape – the rape of (sometimes very) young girls' (Ouattara *et al.* 1998, 31). The impact of this on girls' health and well-being is discussed later in this chapter.

It is often the practice to marry very young girls to older men, in order to maximise the girls' years of child-bearing. One study conducted within the Palestinian community in the Gaza Strip (Radwan and Emad 1997) found that 42 per cent of the randomly selected sample of women and girls and just 3 per cent of boys were married between the age of 12 to 17 years. The study found that 62 per cent of the girls had delivered babies within nine to 12 months of marriage, and 40 per cent of 18 and 19 year old women had five children or more. Over 68 per cent of the adolescents had been physically or verbally assaulted or beaten by their husbands (op. cit.).

3.2.8 'Crimes of honour'

So-called 'crimes of honour' are the murder of a woman by a family member or husband, or on behalf of them. The murder is justified by the fact that the murdered woman is suspected of having a pre-marital or extra-marital sexual relationship; that she is seeking divorce; or that she has been raped.

The majority are murdered on the mere suspicion that they have entered illicit sexual relationships. Typically, husbands, fathers, or brothers go unpunished after having murdered their wives, daughters, or sisters in order to defend the 'honour' of the family (Jahangir 1999).[5]

Honour killings have been reported in some countries in the Middle East, Latin America, and South Asia. There is also evidence of them occurring in migrant communities, in countries including the United Kingdom.

Estimating the prevalence of honour killings is very difficult. Such killings are often unreported or disguised as accidental deaths, and since they frequently occur in rural areas, they may escape official scrutiny. There are a few statistics, however. In Yemen, a survey reported more than 400 women killed for reasons of honour during 1997 (Jehl 1999). In Jordan, official crime statistics show that honour killings account for one in every four homicides, or 25 deaths a year. The non-governmental Human Rights Commission of Pakistan (HRCP) reported that in 1999 more than 1000 women were the victims of honour killings in Pakistan. The Sindh Graduates Association reported 132 honour killings in Sindh, Pakistan, during the first three months of 1999 (cited in Amnesty International 1999b).

3.2.9   Dowry-related violence and murder

In Pakistan, India, and Bangladesh, a bride's family traditionally gives a dowry,[6] or gift of money, to the family of her prospective husband before marriage. Women may be violently attacked, and even murdered, by their in-laws, if they do not bring enough money through their dowry. The most common form these attacks take is burning, often claimed to be accidental. A woman may be doused in kerosene, and set on fire. The murder is then disguised as a 'kitchen accident', caused by the bursting of a stove used during cooking.

In India, despite the Dowry Prohibition Law having been passed in 1961, and twice amended since, dowry-related violence and deaths continue (Narasimhan 1994). In urban Maharashtra, one in five deaths among women of reproductive age is due to 'accidental burns' (Karkal 1985). In India, the official dowry death toll rose from 2209 in 1988, to 4835 in 1990, and 5157 in 1991 (Kelkar 1992). According to the statistics compiled by India's National Crimes Bureau, this climbed to 5623 deaths over dowry disputes in 1993 (Gerwertz 1995), and 6929 dowry deaths were reported in 1998 (Amnesty International 2001, 6). The Ahmedabad Women's Action Group estimates the real scale of the problem to be much greater. It estimates that as many as 1000 women may be burned alive each year in Gujarat state alone (Heise *et al.* 1989).

In some countries in South Asia, the terms 'dowry-related violence' and 'dowry death' have become almost synonymous with domestic violence. As Meeta Rani Jha, an activist on domestic violence, immigration, and anti-racism in the United Kingdom has pointed out in relation to India, these terms have become 'a key issue and rallying cry, in practically all movements in which women are active. However, we need to remember that dowry is only an excuse used by patriarchal families to continue to torture and kill women. The unfortunate consequence of using [these] term[s] as a rallying cry is that [they] minimise the regular abuse and killing of women. The result is that dowry-related wife murders and suicides are criticised, but other domestic violence may not be, since it is thought that the wife could have been provoking the abuse.' (Jha 1999, para. 33) With these cautions in mind, there is nevertheless considerable evidence to suggest an increase in violence against women related to dowry. Acid attacks, where sulphuric acid (being cheap and easily obtained) is thrown over women in order to disfigure or kill, are a form of dowry-related violence. In Bangladesh over 200 acid attacks each year are estimated to occur (UNICEF 2000).

3.2.10 Sati

Sati (widow immolation) is the ritual burning of a widow on her husband's funeral pyre. It takes place in Hindu communities in India. *Sati* is a relatively rare form of violence, banned in India by the British colonial government in 1829. However, it persists today.

In 1987, 'Eighteen-year-old Roop Kanwar of Deorala village in Rajasthan State died seven months after marriage. Roop Kanwar walked to the funeral pyre of her husband in broad daylight at 1.40 pm. Her body burned before 4000 people. No one tried to stop her, and the police did not come until 3 pm. The Rajputs believe that no one can intervene when the goddess Sati takes possession of a widow, as the goddess can put a curse on the person. Villagers speculate that Roop Kanwar was given opium or a sedative, or was deeply traumatised by her husband's death, or the thought of being a widow and not re-marrying.' (Quoted in Asian and Pacific Women's Resource Collection Network 1990, 172)

Following Roop Kanwar's death, she was heralded by some as a heroine, willing to die for Indian values, and willing to defy the secular State. In Indian traditionalist discourses, *sati* is viewed as an extreme form of selflessness and self-sacrifice on the part of women. In contrast, Indian feminists renewed their criticisms of *sati* as negating women's right to life, and symbolising the repression and powerlessness of women. They argued that Roop was coerced by in-laws, and those who stood to gain from the revival of the ritual (Kumkum and Vaid 1996).

Despite the fact that it is comparatively rare, *sati* has been the focus of much debate. During the pre-colonial and colonial eras, westerners depicted the practice as a symbol of a savage, backward treatment of women, and proof of the irrationality and unreliability of 'the Orient' (Said 1979). It has been argued that western perceptions of 'Third World women' as victims of bizarre forms of violence, including *sati,* has resulted in racist attitudes that do not acknowledge the diversity of southern women's experience, and contrasts them with liberated, knowledgeable, modern western women (Chowdhry 1995).

3.2.11 Violence against 'witches'

Women who are violating norms of female behaviour by living on their own – often in widowhood – face accusations of witchcraft in many parts of the world. The persecution and killing of 'witches' has a long history. Although exact estimates are difficult, it is believed that some two million people were killed as witches in Europe, between the fifteenth and eighteenth centuries, and around 80 per cent of these were women.

Between 1991 and 1994, 60 women were accused of being witches, and tortured to death, in West Singhbhum district, Bihar, India. In research carried out in the area while she was Project Officer for Oxfam India Trust, Calcutta, Puja Roy (1998) questioned the assumption that the persecution of women accused of witchcraft is a problem restricted to tribal people, and that it is caused by illiteracy and superstition. Her research suggests that violence against 'witches' is better explained against a background of female economic subjugation, sexual exploitation, and the persecution of widows and independent vocal women.

In Bihar, witches are almost always women, while witch-doctors, a symbol of power and good, are always men. These beliefs are exploited by powerful community members with ulterior motives for suggesting that a woman is a witch – to expropriate her, sexually exploit her, or exact vengeance for past grievances or family feuds. The village witch-doctor (*ojha* or *sokha*) is granted power by the community to identify witches. It is in the witch-doctor's interests to charge a woman as a witch, because he can then charge her family a great deal of money in order to exorcise the evil spirits believed to be possessing her. Widows, unmarried women, and women who speak out are targeted; they defy gender stereotypes since they are not controlled by any man (Roy 1988), and also lack protectors. In a village in Hazaribagh, a widow and her daughter-in-law were forced to parade around the village naked. They were branded as witches because they refused to oblige four prominent village men with sexual favours. When they reported this to the police, the villagers responded by burning their house down (op. cit.).

Older women are at increased risk of being accused of witchcraft. In participatory research undertaken by HelpAge International in Tanzania, older widows living alone raised accusations of witchcraft as a key issue of concern for them. 'The solitude of a widow brings additional problems – if she is not seen much about the village, an air of mystery may grow up around her, which contributes strongly to accusations of being a witch... they are alone, so have no support to ward off the accusations, they are weak and vulnerable, they are poor, so do not have resources to fight, they are often seen as being cleverer than older men, they often have physical signs of being a witch, for example red eyes, wrinkles, bags under the eyes, twisted limbs, gnarled hands.' (Beales 2000, 12)

3.2.12   Girls in armed conflict

Children are increasingly being recruited into armies as combatants, in countries such as Angola, Ethiopia, Liberia, Mozambique, Sierra Leone, Sudan, and Uganda. At least 300,000 children under the age of eighteen are taking part in hostilities around the world (Coalition to Stop the Use of Child Soldiers 1998). Girls are recruited – albeit in smaller numbers than boys – and used as cooks or concubines. Graça Machel, the Expert of the United Nations Secretary-General on the Impact of Armed Conflict on Children, recognises in her final report that children, and especially girls, are vulnerable to sexual exploitation in many settings during armed conflict. She states that girls who become child-soldiers are frequently subject to rape and other forms of abuse, as are girls who are refugees or displaced persons. Her report also states that 'children may become the victims of prostitution following the arrival of peacekeeping forces.' (Machel 1996, para. 98) Machel has blamed the increase in the use of children as soldiers on technological developments and the proliferation of arms, especially light and easy-to-use small arms (ibid.). The proliferation of small arms has meant that children who are too slight or young to manipulate heavy and cumbersome weapons become useful fighters.

In Mozambique, a country devastated by 15 years of civil war, an estimated 250,000 boys and girls were separated from their families. Many were kidnapped mainly by RENAMO and pressed into service. Boys younger than eight years old helped in base camps until they were old enough for military training while girls cooked, cleaned, laundered, and provided sexual services for the men (Keller 1994). Children were forced to undergo military training, to commit atrocities, kill, and steal. In some cases they were made to murder their parents or people very close to them, in order to prove their capacity to be good soldiers: 'The bandits gave me a knife and forced me to kill my father by cutting his throat.

They threatened me with being killed in the same way if I did not do it. Then they gave me a heavy bag to carry and took me to the base.' (Carlos, 17 years old, quoted in Castelo-Branco 1997, 494) Boys were frequently forced to inflict sexual acts on girls, who were forced to suffer these in order to avoid being killed or starved.

3.2.13 Gender-specific forms of torture instigated by the State

Many forms of violence are intended not only as an end in themselves, but as a means to another end: to produce psychological harm (Herman 1992). Violence against women is often intended as an attack on women's fundamental perceptions of what it is to be a woman. Testimonies from detainees who gave evidence at the Truth and Reconciliation Commission in South Africa described how women not only experienced constant fear of rape, but also experienced other forms of mental torture that exploited their gender identity. Agents of the State would strip-search them in front of other men, or would tell them that their children were ill or had died (Meintjies 1997). The Security Police would typically search for and exploit these areas of vulnerability in female detainees.

One woman who had been a detainee in the apartheid era in South Africa explained to the Truth and Reconciliation Commission: 'The way women experience detention is totally different from the way men do. I burst into tears when a security policeman said to me, "I really enjoy interrogating women. I can get things out of them and do things with them that I cannot do to a man."' (Meintjies 1997). Another detainee explained: 'You are 30, you are single, therefore there is something wrong with you as a woman and that is why you get involved in politics. They were attacking your identity with their own particular conception of what a woman is.'

In the context of the counter-insurgency operations in Guatemala during the 1980s, many women were raped and axed to death by members of the Guatemalan army. Torture in the form of rape and sexual abuse was a common tactic. Women were raped repeatedly by members of the military. One woman, who was detained for almost a month in an army base in Rabinal, Baja Verapaz, told a human rights organisation how she was raped over 300 times in front of her father who had been tied up in the same room. She stated: 'Night after night, a group of soldiers would enter – sometimes ten, sometimes fifteen – and they would throw me down. One would strip me and would do it over and over, and you can't say anything because they threaten to kill you. I had two nights when they left me alone because the soldiers went to a party to get drunk. But there were nights when I really suffered.' (Americas Watch Report 1984, 111) This testimony demonstrates the way women's sexuality was explicitly used to create mental, as well as physical, suffering.

3.3 The impact of violence upon women

> *On the 8 April, four men from the militia came. On 24 April six*
> *soldiers came. I can't even remember the numbers but those who were*
> *sitting near me tell me that the total who raped me was 12 people.*
> *After this I became unconscious. After this, I got serious sickness and*
> *gynaecological problems. Life was very tough, I was sick and there*
> *was no medication. I was very hungry. The Interahamwe kept*
> *checking my house and threatening to kill me. After the war I*
> *continued in that terrible situation with terrible sickness. Now that*
> *there are medical services, I have been told that I am HIV-positive.*

(Woman from AVEGA-Agahozo, Rwanda, Oxfam internal document 1994)

The impact of violence on women varies widely. It depends on the nature of the particular incident, the woman's relationship with her abuser, and the context in which it took place. Violence against women typically has physical, psychological, and social consequences. For the survivor, these are interconnected.

The aim of this section is to draw attention to some of the long- as well as short-term implications of violence for women, their children, their families, and wider society. It also looks at the impact of violence on the perpetrators themselves. By examining the consequences of violence on individuals other than the women themselves, and on society, this section refutes the assumptions that violence is made up of individual, isolated episodes that have a clear beginning and end, and that its lasting impacts are restricted to affected women.

3.3.1 The impact of violence on women's health

Worldwide, it has been estimated that violence against women is as serious a cause of death and incapacity among women of reproductive age as cancer, and a greater cause of ill-health than traffic accidents and malaria combined (World Bank 1993).

Physical health

Violence against women in the home is widely dismissed as a normal part of life with a male partner. However, this violence can be extreme. In the worst cases, violence can lead to death. In Russia, in 1994, nearly 14,000 women were killed by their husbands, according to statistics from the Prosecutor's Office (Pisklakova 2000).

The savage violence described by the South African woman quoted at the start of this chapter resulted in very severe physical injuries. In 1997, the

Cambodian organisation PADV revealed the severity of the physical injuries sustained by 50 women who faced violence from their husbands in the home. PADV's survey reports:

> *[It] usually began with punching. Once the woman collapsed on the ground, the husband commonly began kicking her. He kicked arms, legs, and into the stomach and back. One woman explained how she vomited blood during one episode while her husband was kicking her in the back. Other women described being kicked in the head or face. In addition women were strangled until they could barely breathe; they were dragged by their hair and their heads pounded against a cement floor, a wooden bed frame, a column of the house, or the dirt ground outside the home; they were intentionally poisoned. Thirty-four of the 50 women interviewed were hit with weapons such as bamboo rods, sugar cane, palm stems, and metal bars. Knives, axes, guns (about one-quarter of the women's husbands owned guns) were also used. Several women were burned using smouldering firewood and burning torches. Many of the women used the word for rape, rumlop, or described how they were physically forced to have sex.*
>
> (Zimmerman 1997, 11)

The physical consequences of rape include the risk of pregnancy and possibly permanent damage to women's health, including their reproductive health. It does not matter whether this rape occurs within marriage, within an economically coercive context, as in the case of women trafficked into sexual slavery, or in wartime. All sex under duress places women at risk of immediate and horrific physical injury, of pregnancy, and of sickness or death through sexually transmitted diseases (STDs) (Coomaraswamy 1999b). Numerous surveys in the United States indicate that up to 30 per cent of women who are raped acquire an STD as a result. Rape survivors are at a higher risk of contracting STDs because of increased likelihood of harming the delicate surface of the reproductive tract, which normally offers some degree of protection from infection. The spread of HIV/AIDS to women in the heterosexual population is closely linked to coerced sex and sexual violence.

For a woman who is impregnated as a result of rape, abortion may be legally denied, practically obstructed, or unacceptable to her on religious or cultural grounds. Abortion, or the lack of it, can compound women's physical and emotional trauma, and may create additional hostility within her community towards her.

The fact that condom use is a form of protection that is controlled by men makes women additionally vulnerable. Within the context of intimate relations, norms of male infidelity and *machismo,* and female fidelity and chastity in marriage make it difficult for women to exercise control over the sexual behaviour of men. Prostitutes, a group often singled out as 'high risk', are not always in a position to enforce the use of condoms by their clients. High rates of HIV among brothel prostitutes in Thailand, for example, have been explained in terms of the refusal of many clients to use condoms, despite the favourable attitude of prostitutes towards their use. Women's lack of mobility (women were often prevented from leaving the brothel) and lack of access to health care services are also contributing factors (Pyne 1995).

The negative health impacts of female genital mutilation on girls are well-known. The use of unhygienic instruments during the operation can lead to infections, abscesses, ulcers, delayed healing, septicaemia, tetanus, and gangrene. Short-term complications can include severe pain and haemorrhage that can lead to shock or even death. Long-term complications can include urine retention, resulting in repeated urinary infections; obstruction of menstrual flow, leading to frequent reproductive tract infections and infertility; and prolonged and obstructed labour (Coomaraswamy 1999b; Panos 1998).

Many girls undergo terrible injuries as a result of experiencing sexual activity, pregnancy, and childbirth before their bodies are fully mature (Anti-Slavery International 1994). Pregnancy-related death is the leading cause of mortality among girls aged 15-19 worldwide. Women in this age-group face an increased risk of dying during pregnancy of between 20-200 per cent compared with women aged between 20-24 (UNICEF 2001). Childbirth in girls whose bodies are not mature can involve many complications. Prolonged or obstructed labour due to underdeveloped pelvic bones can cause the tearing of the walls between the vagina and the bladder or the rectum, resulting in a fistula. If left untreated, this condition can cause leaking of urine and faeces, may result in infertility, and almost always leads to divorce or separation, and sometimes to ostracism by the family or community (Coomaraswamy 1999b).

Psychological impact

Men who rape or sexually violate women not only attack individual women; they also attack women as a group, seeking to dominate and degrade them, and render them powerless. Violence against women in a community instils fear in other women. In this way violence can serve to control all women in a community. Violence against women accused of being witches is one example of this.

Where an attacker is an intimate partner or person in a relation of trust to the victim, violence can lead to feelings of confusion and despair. Women who receive physical violence from their husbands or partners are 12 times more likely than other women to attempt suicide (Heise 1993). A cross-cultural study drawing on data from Africa, South America, and several Melanesian islands, showed marital violence to be a leading cause of female suicide (Counts 1987).

Along with the usual consequences of trauma, such as irritation, experiencing flash-backs, and loneliness, a woman who has survived rape may also have a changed relationship with her body, and with men (Medica Zenica Women's Therapy Centre 1997). This can have long-term effects not only on her psychological and physical health, but also on her fertility and sexuality. In instances of attempted rape, where the attack has not involved penetration, women often do not even realise that their psychological problem originated with violence. However, such sexual violence can result in similar symptoms (op. cit.).

A study conducted by the Medical Foundation for the Care of Victims of Torture on the effects of rape on women of the Luwero Triangle in the sub-counties of Masulita and Wakiso in Uganda found that five years after the event, women were still suffering considerably. The study found that a quarter of the women interviewed now had no relationship at all with a man, because of negative feelings towards men since the rape. For those who were in relationships, half of them had not told their husbands or boyfriends about the rape, and two-thirds no longer enjoyed sexual relationships. Over half of the women had not talked to anyone aside from the interviewers about the rape. Of the remainder, all but one had mentioned it only to their doctor, husband, or parents. Overwhelming feelings of shame and humiliation prevented them from seeking help for their problems because of fear of being further humiliated or derided (Giller and Kabaganda 1990).

Two years into its operation, and after the Croatian 'war within a war' had ended, around half of the women passing through Medica Zenica (a Bosnian women's organisation that was created during the war in response to women's need for confidential medical, psychological, and shelter services) had been subject to rape. The organisation's psychotherapy team analysed the data for these women in 1995. Forty-eight per cent had been raped in group situations. One in three had been gang-raped. Almost half had been raped in front of members of their family or acquaintances. The youngest was 12, and the oldest 52. Half of the women were married. Forty per cent had never experienced sexual intercourse before. Thirty per cent of the women had become pregnant as a result of the rapes, and most of the pregnancies had resulted in live births. Of the women giving birth in Medica Zenica's centre, the great majority kept the child. Only two per cent of the raped women did not need treatment for adverse gynaecological symptoms. Most found it difficult to talk at first about what had happened to them. Many were severely withdrawn, and nearly half attempted suicide or gave signs of being suicidal. Fifty per cent were suffering anxiety and depression. Feelings of shame, fear, repulsion, and aggression were a common reaction (Medica Zenica Women's Therapy Centre 1995). Rape survivors were often ready to find themselves guilty, because of their appearance or behaviour (Medica Zenica Women's Therapy Centre 1997).

According to one of Medica Zenica's psychologists, women survivors of rape arrived 'feeling shame, guilt, and frequently with a mental block against speaking about rape or an unreadiness to receive help. In these instances, they experience stomach pains, loss of appetite, difficulty concentrating, a feeling of indifference, that they cannot make contact with members of their family, that they are aggressive to their children, that they feel separated from their bodies, or that they feel the constant need to bathe themselves.' (Medica Zenica 1997, 9)

Forcing women's husbands, children, or parents to witness sexual violations produces some very specific psychological symptoms in women undergoing violence, related to the shame and stigmatisation the victim feels as a result of what has happened to her. Although the physical symptoms of torture tend to lessen over time, 'the psychological, behavioural, and social problems persist for years... For women in particular, rape and sexual abuse suffered during detention often affects their sexual and emotional well-being for years after the abuse.' (Desjarlais *et al.* 1995, 124)

Women clearly suffer negative psychological consequences as a result of violence inflicted against them. It is difficult or impossible to separate these from the physical impacts of violence. Interventions to support survivors of violence must appreciate the interrelated physical, social, and emotional implications of violence for the women concerned.

Recognition of the psychological consequences of rape, and the physical symptoms that it produces, has led to the development of the term 'Rape Trauma Syndrome', considered to be a form of Post-Traumatic Stress Disorder.[7] Rape Trauma Syndrome does not affect all survivors of rape, but the probability of symptoms associated with it occurring is high. Box 3.2 sets out some of the common symptoms associated with this syndrome.

Box 3.2
Rape Trauma Syndrome

What influences how you react to rape?

A survivor's individual response to rape, including whether and how she experiences Rape Trauma Syndrome, depends on many factors, including:

- Whether she knew or trusted the rapist;
- Whether her family and friends are supportive and patient or blaming and unhelpful;
- How the police and justice system treat her, should she choose to report the rape;
- Her age and previous life experiences;
- Her cultural and religious background;
- The degree of violence used by the rapist;
- Whether any injuries, illnesses, or disabilities result from the rape;
- Whether the rape brings up memories of past trauma she has experienced;
- Her emotional state prior to the rape;
- Her practical and material resources.

Every rape situation is unique and it is thus very important to treat each rape survivor individually.

Physical symptoms of Rape Trauma Syndrome

- Shock: usually an immediate response; may include numbness, chills, faintness, confusion, disorientation, trembling, nausea, and sometimes vomiting;
- Sleeping problems: unable to sleep, sleeping more than usual, or other changes in sleeping patterns;
- Eating problems: no appetite and subsequent weight loss, or compulsive eating and subsequent weight gain;
- No energy or too much energy;
- Physical illness: the stress may weaken her immune system, and make her more vulnerable to sickness, she may have caught a sickness from the rapist, or she may simply feel sick;
- Pain in her body: this may be as a result of injuries inflicted by the rapist, or a physical reaction to her emotional pain;
- Cardiovascular problems: heart palpitations, breathlessness, tightness or pain in the chest, high blood pressure;
- Gastrointestinal problems: loss of appetite, nausea, diarrhoea, constipation, dryness in mouth, butterflies in stomach, feelings of emptiness in stomach;

- Exaggerated startle response: over-reacting to sudden noise or movement;
- Oversensitivity to noise.

Cognitive symptoms of Rape Trauma Syndrome

- 'As if' feelings or flashbacks: re-experiencing sensations that she felt during the rape, or actually reliving parts of the experience in her head;
- Intrusive thoughts: sudden or forceful "intrusive" memories of aspects of the rape, thinking about the rape all the time;
- Memory loss: the survivor may be unable to remember the rape or parts of it; this is usually temporary, although it can last for many years;
- Poor concentration.

Source: People Opposing Women Abuse (1998)

While conceptualising the psychological and physical effects of rape and sexual violence as Rape Trauma Syndrome is useful in raising awareness of the impact of violence on women and ensuring that they receive support, it has also been criticised. Critics argue that use of the term potentially stigmatises women who have been raped or attacked. This stigma may itself cause further suffering to rape survivors. These criticisms are discussed in more detail in chapter 5.

3.3.2 The economic and social impact of violence on women

Violence against women has a serious impact on women's ability to participate with their peers in social and economic activities. At community level, women who have survived violence may face rejection and social stigma. In societies that do not understand marital violence to be an abuse of women's human rights, women who are known to be beaten or abused by their intimate partners are often blamed for 'bringing it on themselves'. Social stigma surrounds women who have been abused; they have been shamed and should remain silent. For example, Sotho customary law in South Africa and Lesotho permits married women to be beaten by their husbands 'to correct a fault'. Women who have been beaten are told to obey the tradition of '*mosali o ngalla motseo*' – which states that when a woman is beaten or abused, she should subjugate herself and remain in her house (personal communication, FIDA, Lesotho).

In societies where unmarried women are not supposed to be sexually active, women who have been raped or sexually attacked may be seen as unclean, 'defiled', or deviant. As we have seen, this justifies appalling violence against them, including 'crimes of honour' in many contexts. This violence affects all kinds of relationship that a woman has with other members of her community. Survivors of rape may be shunned or ostracised from their community, or considered unmarriageable. Women are often treated differently as a result of what has happened to them. Individuals and organisations in the public sphere, because of sexual taboos, often do not provide support to women who have been raped in the same way that they would offer it to other survivors. Women are persecuted, hidden, or become the object of curiosity and voyeuristic interest. 'The woman is blamed for what has happened to her, and sometimes society doesn't even have a feeling of relief that she has survived. Women are considered permanently branded and humiliated. It is as though society thinks it would be better if she had died.' (Medica Zenica Women's Therapy Centre 1997, 8)

The fact that ideologies of fidelity in marriage are present in almost all societies in the world means that married women survivors of rape often face rejection by their husbands, families, and/or communities. Men who view the rape of female relatives as an attack on their status or 'property', have been known to reject their wives, daughters, or sisters (Thomas and Regan 1994). Women who become pregnant as a result of rape, unable to deny that rape has occurred, are placed at greater risk of being rejected or attacked by members of their community, particularly in cultures that emphasise virginity or chastity in women (Center for Reproductive Law and Policy 1996). Underlying this reaction is panic about the breakdown of patriarchal social structures when a woman is impregnated by a man other than her husband. For patriarchy to survive as a social order, any children to whom a woman gives birth must be the biological children of her husband.

Marginalisation of women survivors of rape and sexual violence prevents and delays women from rebuilding their lives following rape and sexual attack. In northern Uganda, Oxfam researchers at the Impevi Refugee Settlement project observed that women who were raped by soldiers in Sudan came to the refugee camp without the alternative means of support that might have supported them through the enormous sense of shame and stigma brought as a result of the rape. Some were afraid to move out of the immediate environment beyond their homes; many were left feeling that they had lost the will to live. They complained of domestic quarrels. Some of the women who had been raped were abandoned by their husbands. Recounting the experience of another woman refugee, one woman explained: 'Her husband left her when he had discovered that she had been raped by three men; it was the shame and fear of AIDS. She returned to Sudan rather than face the shame of living on here.' (Payne 1998, 83)

Ostracism of rape survivors due to a perception of rape as unsanctioned sexual activity rather than as violence against women may also lead to rape survivors finding it extremely difficult to gain support and protection from state institutions. As has been mentioned earlier, women who have been raped often find it difficult to convince the police and judiciary that an offence has taken place. This is particularly the case for women who have a past history of sexual activity outside of marriage. Chapter 8 will discuss this in more detail.

Survivors of rape are also very likely to have an acute fear of future violence. This fear extends beyond the individual survivors of violence, to other women in their communities. Research carried out by Volunteers for Humanity in Indonesia on the rape of ethnic Chinese women during the May riots in 1998 shows that for those who witnessed the rapes, the boundary between 'seeing' and 'experiencing' was obscured. In their report, Volunteers for Humanity quote the sister of a girl who had witnessed rape: 'After accidentally seeing Chinese girls raped by many people, my sister is so frightened and stressed. Her speech is incoherent and her body trembles every time someone comes near her. For two weeks she was in the hospital. I wondered whether my sister only saw someone raped, or she herself was also raped. Why does she react this way?' (Volunteers for Humanity 1998) In Chapter 6, there are more details of the research carried out by this organisation.

Beyond the physical and mental harm caused directly as a result of violence, the experience of rape can drive women into poverty by preventing them from participating in educational and economic activities. By damaging women's and girls' confidence and making them scared to venture into public spaces, it can often curtail their education. The fear of their daughters being subject to sexual harassment, abduction, or rape is also a deterrent to parents sending their daughters to school in some countries (Rose *et al.* 1997). Lack of education can limit women's income-generating opportunities, and this may leave them with few alternatives to marriage. In turn, this makes women more vulnerable to violence, as a woman with an abusive partner cannot leave if she does not have independent access to income or productive resources.

Violence may also have a direct effect on women's power to generate income: a recent study conducted in the United States shows that women who were sexually abused as children achieve an annual income that is 3-20 per cent lower than that of women who have not been abused, depending on the type of abuse experienced and the number of perpetrators (Hyman 1993, cited in Heise *et al.* 1994). Women with formal sector employment may lose their posts due to absenteeism resulting from the impact of violence, the fear that others in the workplace may find out, or the fear that they may be the target of more violence from male employers or colleagues. Similar concerns restrict the income-generating activities of women working in the informal sector. Women traders may decide they cannot travel far from their homes; women farmers in rural settings may decide that it is safer not to go to the fields; and all women who need to collect water, rations, or firewood may feel compelled to restrict these activities. In Ikafe and Imvepi refugee settlements in northern Uganda, women were normally responsible for harvesting, but a series of rapes in 1996-7 meant that married women relied upon their husbands to do this. Single women had no choice but to continue to make the hazardous journey and risk attack (Payne 1998). Finally, as stated in Chapter 1, women may be stopped from participating in economic development projects due to threats of violence.

3.3.3   The impact of violence against women on their dependants

The impact of violence has direct or indirect repercussions on women's children and other dependants. Many babies are born injured because their mother was beaten during pregnancy. In Malaysia, a study revealed that 68 per cent of battered women were pregnant (Abdullah 1997). Clients of the Musasa Project, a grassroots organisation that works with women survivors of violence in Zimbabwe, have reported being beaten while pregnant. Musasa's experience suggests that in some cases violence may be ongoing prior to pregnancy, and increases in intensity during pregnancy. Violence may also start during pregnancy, especially among young unmarried couples, as a result of tensions over who is the father of the child (Meursing *et al.* 1994). A study conducted in León, Nicaragua, found that children of women who were experiencing physical or sexual abuse by their partners were six times more likely than other children to die before reaching five years of age (Asling-Monemi *et al.* 1999).

Studies have confirmed a link between violence against women during pregnancy, and low birth weight (Bullock and McFarlane 1989; Asling-Monemi *et al.* 1999). A Cambodian study showed that a large proportion of women are beaten while pregnant. Thirty-one of the 46 women who replied that they were beaten by their husbands stated that their husbands beat them while they were pregnant. This violence caused a disproportionate number of miscarriages, premature births, and low birth weight babies (Nelson and Zimmerman 1996). The children of girls who undergo child marriage are also vulnerable to being born with low birth weights (Ouattara *et al.* 1998).

Research shows that violence against children is more likely to occur in households where there is domestic violence. In a national survey of over

6000 US families, 50 per cent of the men who frequently assaulted their wives also frequently abused their children (Straus and Gelles 1990).

The effect of growing up in the midst of domestic violence can be devastating for children. Children who witness violence at home display emotional and behavioural disturbances as diverse as withdrawal, low self-esteem, nightmares, self-blame, and aggression against peers, family members, and property (Peled, Jaffe, and Edleson 1995). In addition, a child may perform less well at school and may exhibit behavioural problems, becoming either aggressive or withdrawn (Bradley 1994).

As discussed in Chapter 1, there is on-going debate about the connections between experiencing or witnessing violence as a child, and growing up to be either a perpetrator or a victim of violence.

The impact of violence is also felt indirectly, as the effects of violence compromise survivors' ability to care for any children they may have. In addition to the constraining effect that violence may have on women's livelihood strategies, discussed in the previous section, research in Kenya suggests that the children of women who suffer domestic violence receive less food because men's violence adversely affects women's bargaining position in marriage (Rao and Bloch 1993, cited in Heise 1995a).

Where women conceive as a result of rape, whether it be in the context of a long-term relationship or not, they may develop ambivalent or negative attitudes towards the resulting child. It has been estimated that in 1993, during the war in former Yugoslavia, 20,000-60,000 Bosnian women became pregnant as a result of rape during the conflict (Vulliamy 1993, cited in El Bushra and Piza Lopez 1994). Medica Zenica staff reported how women who gave birth as a result of rape experienced ambivalent feelings towards the child, ranging from aggression to compassion and love. Some women did not want to see the baby after birth, and those children were released for adoption. It was especially difficult for girls who were unmarried and without children before rape; the children of these mothers were noticeably neglected, pale, often sick, poorly fed after leaving Medica, and often left unsupervised. Other women or girls would not cuddle their children born as a result of rape in front of others, although, in private, they would give the child love and care (Medica Zenica Women's Therapy Centre 1997). The future of these children remains uncertain, as their mothers may be emotionally or materially unable to care for them.

3.3.4 The impact of violence on the perpetrators

Men who are violent to their partners may be sanctioned by the community, and may face arrest and imprisonment. They may also face legal restrictions on seeing their families, divorce, or the break up of their families.

Typically, in the context of intimate relations, men who are abusive to their partners tend to 'forget' or minimise the significance of the violence for which they are responsible, to deflect responsibility onto their partner, and to fail to associate it with their relationship (Hearn 1998). Men who are violent within intimate relationships may feel alienated from their families as they lose their love and respect. Violence against women is thus likely to exacerbate tension in the home.

The impact on men of seeing at first-hand the impact of socially-sanctioned violence against girls and women can result in trauma, guilt, and a change in subsequent behaviour (personal communication). For example, female genital mutilation (FGM) is a form of violence against women that is instigated by a girl's parents, based on patriarchal ideas of controlling female sexuality, but is performed by women. Understanding the impacts of FGM on women may result in a desire among men to end the practice. The National Committee on Traditional Practices in Ethiopia has made a video, *Infibulation*. 'When this video is shown, people leave the room. It is very intense for men to see it for the first time and to suddenly become aware of the suffering involved.' (Spadacini and Nichols 1998, 47)

As stated in Chapter 1, women are sometimes involved in certain forms of violence against other women, as part of a 'bargain' with a patriarchal system in which they will be penalised for refusing to conform, and rewarded for conformity (Kandiyoti 1988). In a workshop with traditional midwives (*dais*) in Bihar, India, *dais* reported that their extreme poverty, dependence on upper-caste households for agricultural employment and credit, and the power wielded by some of the village men, forced them to kill female babies. More research is needed into the impact on women of perpetrating, or being complicit in, violence against other women, and on how they can be involved in challenging its perpetuation. It should be recognised that many female perpetrators of violence against women have been abused in the same way themselves.

3.3.5 The impact of violence against women on society

Research from many different contexts indicates that the survival of households is placed in jeopardy by violence against women within marriage. In response to widespread drunkenness, overcrowding, unemployment, and male violence against women, many women eschew marriage completely. In research in South Africa focusing on the households of men who have been made redundant from mining work, women rejected marriage in favour of greater security in female multigenerational or sibling households. Many women wanted no relationships with men, referring to them as violent, unreliable, and irresponsible (Banks and Hobson 1993).

As highlighted in Chapter 1, violence against women creates a huge burden on health and judicial systems, and hinders economic stability and growth through women's lost productivity. Future productivity is also held back as a result of the loss of children's education when girls suffer violence, or when children of either sex have their lives disrupted by violence against their mother or carer. Violence against women hinders women's participation in development processes, and constrains their ability to respond to rapid social, political, or economic change.

A key rationale for stimulating women's income generation, and control of that income, is the belief in 'maternal altruism' (Razavi and Miller 1995). 'Maternal altruism' refers to research findings that show that women spend a larger proportion of their earnings on household welfare than men do. If fear of marital violence means that women are unable to make economic decisions at household level, this rationale for investing resources in women is negated. Case studies of survivors of violence in Peru, and of Mexican *maquiladoras*, have shown that men frequently beat their wives to obtain the income women had earned (Vasquez and Tamayo 1989, cited in Carrillo 1992). Women's potential to contribute to the welfare of their families and the economy is wasted in such situations.

Another, cumulative, effect of marital violence and other forms of violence may be the breakdown of trust in social relationships, and the weakening of support networks on which people's survival strategies depend. Research from Cisne Dos, Ecuador and Angyalfold, Hungary found that while marital separation was found to reduce stress and violence, it also meant that households had fewer social assets to call on (Moser 1996). Women's participation in civil society is profoundly affected by violence and the fear of violence. Violence against women reduces women's self-esteem and their trust in others, both of which are necessary for full engagement in civil society (Dean 1996, 92). It strains and fragments networks that are of vital importance in strengthening the capabilities of communities in times of stress and social upheaval. Research on civil society demonstrates that when women are able to contribute fully to public life, their contribution is often different to that of men. Women often co-operate across ethnic lines, emphasise concrete achievements, have a broader notion of social responsibility, and a greater tendency towards peaceful resolutions of conflict (Hirschmann 1998).

3.4 Summary and implications for development organisations

The chapter began with a discussion of the lack of data on the prevalence and impact of violence. This is due to two related problems of under-recording by state agencies and under-reporting by women survivors. With these points in mind, the collection of information about the prevalence of violence against women is a key strategy for overcoming the silence and taboos surrounding violence. Governments are primarily responsible for producing statistics on the nature and prevalence of violence against women. However, development and human rights organisations, including women's organisations, can play a vital role in data collection, particularly of a qualitative nature. This data can be an important tool in lobbying governments to ensure they are accountable for the way they respond to violence. It can also be used to expose the reluctance of states and state institutions, including the police and judiciary, to address violence against women adequately. This strategy is especially powerful when backed up with research by grassroots women's organisations on the prevalence of violence, its impact on women, and the lack of support provided to them.

This chapter has described the scope of violence against women and its consequences at various levels. The consequences of violence against women for the survivor extend beyond physical harm and injury to include economic, social, and psychological impacts. Interventions to support survivors of violence need to address these different dimensions of harm. Responses should look at women's well-being in the broadest sense and assist women in terms of the immediate physical injury, the impacts on their health, including psychological health, and on their social status.

Different forms of violence vary in terms of their nature, the relative frequency with which they occur, and whether they are associated with particular societies, or are generally acknowledged to be widespread in all societies. They also vary in their association with different economic and social aspects of women's subordination in particular contexts. However, gender analysis reveals that these very different acts not only have a similar outcome of fear and pain for women and girls, but also have a single underlying cause: unequal power between women and men.

Finally, the chapter discussed the impact of violence on women survivors and their dependants, particularly focusing on violence of a sexual nature. This points to the need to address the shame felt by the survivor that prevents her from claiming the support of institutions and networks around her, and to the need to challenge community conceptions of violence as a private taboo rather than a criminal act.

The fact that gender relations are seen as natural and unchanging in many societies ensures that many abused women do not recognise the common causes of violence against them, and do not see such violence as an abuse of their human rights. In the absence of a gender perspective, it may seem to survivors and perpetrators that different forms of violence are driven by very different motives. Women who have suffered different forms of violence may not identify with women who have survived other forms. As will be seen later in this book, when there are opportunities for women to unite across differences, this can result in a realisation of the common causes of violence against women which can be extremely empowering.

4 The contexts in which violence against women occurs

About 11.30 a.m., I saw people among the crowd stopping a car and forcing the passengers to get out, and they dragged two girls out from the car. [They] began to take off their shirts and raped them. The two girls tried to fight back, but it was in vain. ... After the two girls got away from the savage rapists, I came to them and embraced them. They begged me to help them find a secure way to go home. Since I lived in that district, I know well the short-cut to the main road. At the Cengkareng crossroad, I saw some nude female corpses, their faces covered with newspapers. They must have been raped, for I could see the dried blood from their vaginas, on which the flies swarmed. After guiding the two girls, I went home back through the same road, but when I arrived at the crossroad, the corpses had gone. But where to? Who took them?

(An eyewitness of violence against women from the ethnic Chinese community, Jakarta, Indonesia, 14 May 1998, cited in Volunteers for Humanity 1998, 1)

As suggested at the end of the previous chapter, violence against women is not caused in any simple way by unequal power relations between women and men. Women's vulnerability to violence against them is caused by this unequal power, but the precise nature of this vulnerability varies in different contexts. In order to develop responses to violence, development organisations need to start by asking questions about how and why violence against women is manifested in these different locations, and what protection women have against violence. Each woman faces different threats of violence according to where she lives, and depending on whether she is at home, in the street, in the marketplace, the factory, or the office. Her protection from violence in any location depends not only on her individual circumstances, and on custom, but also on the State.

This chapter starts by considering violence against women in the context of social institutions. It goes on to look at violence against women in two contexts of change and crisis that are of paramount concern to development and humanitarian workers: poverty, and armed conflict. Poverty and insecurity, in both peacetime and wartime, vastly increase the incidence of violence against women. Many related factors contribute to an increase in men's violence against women during and following war. However, as argued in Chapter 3, violence has the same roots in conflict as it has in situations of relative stability. Violence against women from intimate partners, friends, neighbours, and 'protectors', is intimately linked to wider violence in society, between communities, armies, countries, and regions.

4.1 Violence and social institutions

Understanding the different contexts in which violence against women occurs is a fundamental step in understanding how we can transform our societies to reflect a commitment to equality, peace, and prosperity. Using Naila Kabeer's Social Relations Framework (Kabeer 1994; March, Smyth, and Mukhopadhyay 1999), we will attempt to gain an understanding of the role of social institutions in producing and reproducing gender inequalities in different contexts. The social institutions examined here are the family, the household, the community,[1] and the State.[2] The patriarchal norms and practices of these institutions overlap and reinforce each other, so that cumulatively, the barriers they construct against women's efforts to resist violence may at times seem insurmountable.

Following North (1990), Kabeer defines institutions as 'distinct frameworks of rules for doing things, and organisations [are] the specific structural forms that institutions take. Thus, the State is the larger institutional framework for a range of legal, military and administrative organisations; the market is the framework for firms, corporations, farming enterprises; the 'moral economy' of the community provides the framework for patron-client relationships, village tribunals, lineage organisations, etc.' (Kabeer 1994, 68)

Kabeer argues that although institutions display cultural differences, they all share five inter-related but distinct characteristics: rules, resources, people, activities, and power. Rules determine 'what is done, how it is done, by whom and who will benefit' (op.cit., 281). Rules may be formal laws, or may be informal agreements, norms, or customs. They generate 'routinised patterns of practice' (op. cit., 282) that shape the rewards and claims that people can make on resources. These are crucial to the reproduction of gender, class, and other inequalities. Because they often go unquestioned, they appear natural, inevitable, and unchangeable. Institutions determine who gets resources: either material (such as money, food, or other assets); human (such as education or skills); or social (such as networks, information, or political status). According to patterns associated with gender, class, and social inequalities, institutions include and exclude people, and assign them specific tasks. Institutions embody hierarchical power relations, even when they profess to accord to egalitarian principles. The distribution of resources and responsibilities within any institution means that some members will have authority over others, and will promote practices that reinforce this privilege. Those with authority are likely to be most resistant to change.

This analysis echoes many earlier feminist analyses, which proved how the contexts in which we live and work are not neutral spaces where all are treated alike. The household, community, State, and market are not neutral social institutions that serve the interests of everyone equally. Instead, they 'provide men of a given group with a greater capacity than women of that group to mobilise institutional rules and resources, to promote and defend their own interests' (Kabeer 1994, 299). The majority of the leaders of institutions at all levels of society – from the household to the international financial institutions – are male. In addition, institutions are not isolated from each another, but inter-relate to reinforce women's subordination. This male bias in institutions may be deliberate, or may be because male leaders treat their own social roles and identities as a proxy for those of the whole population, and thereby fail to develop policies and practices that enable women to compete on an equal footing with men. The result is that women face discrimination in their homes, within community bodies, from governments that fail to advance or protect their interests, and from the 'free market'.

4.1.1 The family and household

As previous chapters have highlighted, conceptions of the family as a harmonious unit, and the household as a private space where outsiders should not intervene, have left millions of women over the centuries with no recourse against the appalling intra-family violence they have experienced from spouses, partners, parents, and other relatives.

Many development workers recognise the need to question the assumption that the household or the family is a homogeneous unit. They acknowledge that households and families are usually characterised by unequal power relations, and the need to attempt to understand the impact that development interventions will have on intra-household relations. As discussed in Chapter 2, most development interventions that seek to increase women's role in production are not only founded on an assumption that this will be beneficial to national development as a whole, but also on a hope that this will increase women's power within their household and family. However, we also saw in Chapter 2 that when it comes to the issue of violence against women, there may be less certainty that this is an appropriate matter for development workers to address.

The family is an institution central to all human life. It is an institution through which human beings give and receive love and affection, care for dependants, and receive care in return. The ideal of 'the family' is of a natural unit characterised by altruism, and free from conflict. However, this ideal is far from reality. In reality, family life is often more of 'a paradoxical mix of love, companionship, and support, combined with friction, domination, and cruelty' (Sweetman 1996, 3). Radhika Coomaraswamy, UN Special Rapporteur on violence against women, its causes and consequences, states in her preliminary report: 'The institution of the family is ... an arena where historical power relations are often played out. On the one hand, the family can be the source of positive nurturing and caring values where individuals bond through mutual self-respect and love. On the other hand, it can be a social institution where labour is exploited, where male sexual power is violently expressed, and where a certain type of socialisation disempowers women.' (Coomaraswamy 1995, para. 54)

Women can experience the family as an institution that subordinates and constrains them, socially, economically, and politically. The social roles ascribed to different family members are invariably gender-specific and form a critical part of everyone's identity. However, in contrast to men, women may not be seen as having a social role beyond the family, due to beliefs that men are head of the household, and represent the household in the public sphere. In such circumstances, women's roles entail them remaining within the family sphere, performing work associated with reproduction: sexual services within marriage, childbearing, and caring for dependants. Women face constraints on their mobility and activity due to childbearing, and the requirement that they perform most of the work of child-rearing, and also because they either have no recognised role in production, or because it is believed that this work is of secondary importance.

In the discussion of 'crimes of honour' in the previous chapter, we saw how the requirement that women be faithful wives and mothers in patrilineal and patrilocal societies can result in extreme methods of control over women's sexuality through norms of virginity, marriage, mothering, and fidelity. For example, the Collectif 95 Maghreb Egalité, a network of women's organisations that lobbies to end violence in the Middle East, describes the obligation of unmarried women in the Maghreb to remain virgins as a 'permanent state of sexual harassment' (Collectif 95 Maghreb Egalité 1998, 33). Girls must be constantly watched and watching themselves. Their bodies are the property of their family, and they underpin the honour of their male relations. From childhood, girls are exposed to all kinds of physical and psychological pressures to keep their virginity. The Collectif notes:

> *The long wait for the wedding night constitutes a real ordeal which ends in a few drops of blood, a source of great joy and happiness for the family. If matters take a different course [the family believes she is not a virgin] the measure of drama which may ensue is indescribable. It may involve the heaping of opprobrium on the family, a justification for the exclusion if not the murder of the shameful bride and the punishment of her accomplices.'*
>
> (ibid.)

In some contexts, the social pressures on women to remain virgins until marriage results in legalistic responses, such as medical checks to see whether women's hymens are intact, and the issuing of 'certificates of virginity'. In contexts where virginity is highly prized, perceived violations of these practices can result in violence against women. In its January 1997 issue, the Moroccan monthly magazine, *Femmes du Maroc*, describes an incident that took place in Morocco in December 1996. A newly married young man forced his way into a doctor's surgery in Agadir, and thrust a pair of scissors into the doctor's head, accusing her of having issued his wife-to-be with a false certificate of virginity. The police investigation later revealed that the woman had still been a virgin (ibid.).

Where a major aspect of women's identity is concerned with bearing children, childlessness can lead to women being 'punished' with violence. A study from Uganda showed how beatings began when a woman failed to conceive, and then subsequently became more brutal when her partner discovered she was using contraception (Banwell 1994). In other contexts, women may be required to have sex with a 'surrogate', if male infertility is suspected. Research from Zimbabwe relates how a husband may ask a male relative to have sex with his wife in order to save his family's reputation. Women's agreement is not required in creating this arrangement, into which women may be forced against their will (Njovana and Watts 1996).

In some circumstances, her natal family may protect a woman from violence she is experiencing as a wife. In particular, natal families may protect married daughters against marital violence or violence from their husband's relations. Young brides are particularly vulnerable to violence, as indicated by the example of physical abuse by mothers-in-law described in Chapter 1. Women who face violence from their husband or his family may appeal to their parents or siblings to intervene with the abuser. However, increasing mobility between generations of families means that in both developing countries and post-industrialised contexts, many women have moved away from their natal areas and have lost these valuable support networks. For example, in Sotho custom in South Africa and Lesotho, a woman being abused by her husband has recourse through return to her parental home. However, increasing rural-urban migration means that it is often impossible to utilise this family support system (Sweetman 1995a).

For many women, it is clear that family is an important part of their identity and status in the community, and crucial to their livelihood. This has implications for the kinds of strategies that it is possible to use with women survivors of violence. Chapter 5 contains many different examples of work – by development organisations and by organisations set up to promote the rights of women – to support women survivors of violence. It is often argued that women's organisations should create a space where women can break away from the restrictions of the family. However, some women prefer not to do so; for them, remaining silent about abuse is a conscious and rational strategy based on a realistic evaluation of their material dependency on men, and/or their status as married women within the community.

For example, in South Asia, the dominant discourse situates women as dependent on men. In her role as wife and mother, '[A woman] is expected to possess the qualities of obedience, patience, endurance and sacrifice – failing which she is liable to reactions amounting to any degree of violence' (Matin 1998, 3). Women may seen as deserving of violent treatment when others perceive that they have failed in their prescribed role in some way. In Lesotho, for example, a history of male migration to the mines of South Africa has meant that wives are largely dependent on the wages of their miner husbands. Some respondents did not identify with other women who faced marital violence, stressing that women who were beaten had disobeyed norms of female virtue, and had therefore brought their troubles on themselves. One respondent said, 'Other women don't have a good attitude, and have affairs and drink. I find this behaviour very stupid.' (Sweetman 1995a, 35)

The shame resulting from being 'punished' with violence, together with a general respect for the family and marriage, can lead women themselves to ignore violence, and to the community and the State denying that it takes place (Matin 1998). Even when an abused woman is able to seek legal redress, she may be criticised as being weak for her intolerance towards a certain degree of domestic friction, and queries may be raised about her emotional disposition and conduct as a wife. See Mehra (1998) for an example of a court case from South Asia where a man who had murdered a woman was given a lenient sentence because his victim was not considered to have behaved as 'an ideal wife'. This cycle of guilt, blame, and denial may lead to difficulties for organisations seeking to support abused women, particularly if they assume that women in communities will easily sympathise and identify with acquaintances and friends who have been abused.

Having highlighted some issues relating to violence against women within the family, it is helpful to turn briefly to look at violence in relation to the household. Both concepts emphasise economic interdependence, but while the family comprises people related by blood or marital ties, the household includes people who are co-habiting. The household often contains family members, but may also include people who are not related either by blood or marriage. The criteria for belonging to a household vary according to different theorists, but a common understanding is that a household consists of people who share food (often expressed as people who 'eat from the same cooking pot').

Like families, households continue to be seen by many development researchers, policy-makers, and practitioners as units, rather than institutions. When 'the household' does receive attention from development workers who understand it as an institution, it may be assumed to be a harmonious place, presided over by benevolent male heads. In fact the household is made up of individuals and groupings with different identities and interests, in much the same way as the family, and is characterised by conflict as well as co-operation (A. Sen 1990). Feminist analyses from numerous different contexts on all five continents have, over the past four decades, demonstrated that the roots of social, economic, and political inequality between women and men are to be found within the household. They argue that relationships between different household members are dynamic and imbued with power, constantly being reproduced and challenged. The outcome of disputes is shaped by differences between members' bargaining power. Bargaining power is determined by the range of options available to individuals. Where individuals have fewer options, they will have to capitulate faster in a dispute (op. cit.). Different members' bargaining positions are shaped not just by economic and political factors, but also by gender ideologies about the worth of the contribution of different individuals, and what they should receive. This is relevant for understanding not just women's frequently unacknowledged domestic responsibilities, but also men's responsibilities as breadwinner, and what happens when men fail in this role and their bargaining position is threatened.

However, this analysis has not tended to be 'mainstreamed' into all development work: 'In numerous donor agencies, "women's issues" [have been] ensconced in a specially defined field of "women in development", whereas households appear as units of analysis and social units addressed within substantive fields, such as rural credit, agricultural development, small scale enterprise, nutrition and so forth.' (Guyer and Peters 1987, 210)

What new issues arise regarding violence against women if we consider the household? Households take many different forms, and vary over time, as well as within different cultures and parts of the world. Initial observations suggest that there is a link between women's vulnerability to violence, and the stage at which the household is in a 'household development cycle' (Murray 1981). For instance, one study in Mexico found that the highest rates of violence were found in households consisting of recently married couples with young children (González de la Rocha 1994). As stated in the previous section, newly married women who have moved into their husband's family's households are often vulnerable to violence. In South Asia, as a bride in the marital home of her husband's kin, women are vulnerable to violence, often inflicted by senior females (P. Sen 1998a). In households where the head is a son or a daughter, on the other hand, a widow may have low status. A study on violence against widows in Jaipur found the most common abuse to be verbal abuse from in-laws, and the denial of access to their husband's assets. Half of the women with adult children reported abusive behaviour from their sons and daughters-in-law (Ahuya 1996). The experience of HelpAge International is that much of the violence faced by older women and men takes place within the domestic environment, and survivors are 'both ashamed and afraid to disclose evidence' (Beales 2000, 15).

A household's internal relations shape the terms on which its members engage with other social institutions, including those of the State. In many parts of the world, the consequences of domestic violence are often not seen as sufficiently serious to warrant modern medical care or even traditional care. In South Asia, some Islamic countries, and parts of sub-Saharan Africa, women may not be able to choose to seek medical care; the decision to seek care may be made by a woman's husband (who may control the money needed for transport and access to health services), her mother or mother-in-law, village elders, or other family or community members (Acsadi and Johnson-Acsadi 1993, cited in Kutzin, no date given).

Despite the evidence of unequal power relations within the household, and the desire to change these through projects and programmes that aim to increase women's income generation, violence against women and girls has not been addressed in a sustained way in development work. As discussed earlier in this book, the shift in rhetoric from women in development (WID) to gender and development (GAD) approaches was supposed to herald development interventions that would start from an analysis of the oppression of women in the family and household (Moser 1993). In fact, this has not led to any real change from the focus on women in production. Perhaps, by focusing their attention on integrating women into production via women-specific projects, development organisations have mistakenly believed they can bypass the thorny issue of relations between men and women in the household.

It is noticeable that while resistance to intervening in relationships within the household exists in relation to violence against women, a very different story can be told about family planning and population control. Over the past 30 years, concern about overpopulation in the Third World has justified many interventions that have persuaded – or coerced – women to use contraception or be sterilised (Hartmann 1987). In this sector, experience shows that questioning assumptions about consensus in the household can have immediate and dramatic effects. For example, when family planning clinics in Ethiopia removed the requirement of spousal consent, clinic use rose by 26 per cent in just a few months (Cook and Maine 1987, cited in Heise 1995a).

4.1.2   The community

Violence against women occurs within communities. We need to understand in more detail how communities perpetuate violence against women, through condoning it within particular community customs, practices, and organisations.

'The community' consists of all individuals living within a particular location, who are members of various informal groupings and associations, and formal organisations. Community organisations may reflect the interests of social, religious, clan, caste, racial, and ethnic groups, that lie outside the control of the family and State. These include religious groups, burial societies, rotating savings and credit associations, and community-based organisations with development objectives, set up either by community members themselves or by the State, to organise labour and distribute resources.

Like households and families, communities are not homogeneous, but contain individuals and interest groups that have the potential to clash with each other as well as to co-operate. It is generally understood that social identities determine people's access to assets and resources, and their ability to win arguments and conflicts.

At community level, as well as family level, women's modesty is often perceived to be critical to men's honour and identity. As discussed in Chapter 3 in the context of rape in armed conflict, where community identities are threatened, women's sexuality may take on heightened symbolic importance. Similar pressure is placed on women in migrant communities, where community identity may be fragile or threatened. For example, research into Pakistani communities in Britain has found that 'men display great concern over "appropriate" female dress and behaviour, because these are taken to signify not only women's honour, but that of their families and the wider community' (Macey 1999, 51). According to a study of the conflict in former Yugoslavia, the rape of women by soldiers, paramilitaries, and male civilians was widely seen as the result of men's failure to protect their homeland. Many informants believed that community honour could only be retrieved by raped women committing suicide (Zajovic 1993).

In theory, women can turn to a wide range of community institutions for assistance, when faced with violence within the family or household. These include friends, neighbours, work colleagues, religious bodies, schools, elders, local leaders, community-based associations (CBOs), and NGOs. Often however, rather than providing women with support, these individuals and groups meet women with disapproval and hostility. Rather than sanctioning against men's violent behaviour, they ignore it – and thereby pardon and condone it.

There are some cases where progressive legislation has been passed by the State to protect women from violence, but this has not been widely enforceable because it runs counter to community norms. Recent legislation banning female genital mutilation in Senegal is a case in point. An amendment, passed by parliament in January 1999, bans anyone from violating 'the integrity of the female genitalia', or 'influencing' others to do so. Some commentators have suggested that the legislation has backfired, as traditional leaders say they will defy the ban. It was reported that in one village in the south, 120 girls were circumcised *en masse* in response to the legislation. The new law has also been criticised for undermining local efforts to stop female circumcision (Hecht 1999).

Many societies in developing countries have retained a system of 'customary law', administered at local level, parallel to western-style 'civil' law, administered by the State. While civil law is used for crimes associated with modernisation, the public sphere, and commerce, in many contexts customary and religious law remains important for matters relating to the private sphere, including family law. In some countries in sub-Saharan Africa, for example, customary law is a written encapsulation of the older system of 'custom', which existed before the colonial era. Custom was an oral system of community regulation. During and after colonialism, codification took place, and some elements of customary law have been incorporated into the 'formal' western-style legal systems in some countries. While customary law may be accorded lower status than civil law in the eyes of the State, for many women it is the more readily available system. This is particularly true for women facing violence in the family in rural societies where traditional structures remain relatively strong, and police and law courts may be distant.

Customary, religious, and civil legal systems may all perpetuate existing unequal power dynamics between women and men. Sometimes, when different legal systems may appear to clash, they actually reinforce each other. The work of Women Against Fundamentalism and Southall Black Sisters, two British women's organisations, demonstrates how the British State has failed to challenge violence against women in Muslim immigrant communities, where male leaders speak and act on behalf of a seemingly monolithic Muslim community, 'so that community and State legitimise and reproduce each other' (Hasan 1994, ix).

Women Against Fundamentalism was formed in 1989 by a group of women from a wide range of faiths. The group includes amongst its numbers Jews, Arab and Asian Muslims, Hindus, white and Afro-Caribbean Protestants, and Irish Catholics. The organisation was set up to fight any kind of religious dogma that justifies violence against women. In newsletters and seminars, Women Against Fundamentalism traces the ways in which more conservative sections of their communities have used the politics of multiculturalism (Katz 1995, 43) to deter the State from championing women's rights within ethnic minority communities. Respect for 'difference' has often resulted in a failure to uphold women's human rights. Political leaders have tended to delegate decisions concerning women from religious minorities to their 'community leaders', who are often the most conservative, religious, and patriarchal forces in their communities (ibid.).

Similarly, Southall Black Sisters, which offers support to women survivors of domestic violence in minority communities, has found that welfare agencies and policy-makers frequently refuse to assist women from minority communities. Lack of assistance usually arises either from a sense that minority communities can solve such problems without external assistance, or from a concern that it is wrong or racist to criticise minority cultural or religious practices. As a result, women from minority communities are made invisible and left unprotected (Siddiqui 1996, 99).

On the positive side, women can and do build on their relationships with other women in their communities to protect themselves from violence perpetrated within the home or within the public sphere. They may also be able to call on particular formal or informal bodies within their communities to protect them against violence in the home. Chapter 7 looks at the strategies that women's groups have employed to create allies within the community.

4.1.3 The State

We have seen already in this book that, both directly (in the form of
violence perpetrated by state officials) and indirectly (in the form of laws
that permit violence, or fail to prevent it), the State can be responsible for
violence against women.

All states have complex institutional structures with specific political and
economic histories. But regardless of their history, all states develop policies
that affect the status of women, and have a direct impact on their daily lives.
These policies are not necessarily designed to oppress women, but are
nevertheless designed according to prevailing ideologies about gender
relations and the role of the family in society. The State reflects prevalent
societal assumptions about gender identities, and reinforces these within
the construction of laws (Showstack-Sassoon 1987) and through the
behaviour of state agents. For example, the fact that police forces in most
countries are ineffective at dealing with violence against women legitimises
and encourages violence to continue. In the case of one refugee camp in
Tanzania, young men would rape girls so they could take them as wives,
since they could not afford the high bridewealth that men must pay to a
woman's family on marriage. It was understood that a man could 'own' a
woman once he had sex with her. Since the police never arrested anyone,
and the community tribunals levied fines that were a tenth of the cost of
bridewealth, young men felt that the practice had been tacitly permitted to
increase (UNHCR 1998).

There is evidence from many different contexts of public service officials
using their position of authority and public trust to abuse women. A recent
report by the Latin American and Caribbean Committee for the Defence of
Women's Rights (CLADEM) documents numerous cases in Peru of
physical and psychological violence against women who use public
reproductive health services, including rape, assault, and numerous forms
of verbal abuse. In the relatively few cases in which women were willing to
file formal complaints, health officials and the judicial system failed to
provide adequate recompense to victims.

One woman in the report testified:

> *The doctor made me enter and didn't let my sister or my father come
> in and told the nurse to stay outside. Then he told me to take off my
> clothes, my pants and blouse, and to lay down on the table. There I
> was without clothes. Then the doctor told me: "So you are pregnant?
> Who could you have been with?" I felt him put his fingers in my
> private parts. He was hurting me a lot, and then I realised that both
> his hands were on my waist and he was thrusting himself into me and*

hurting me. He was abusing me. I was scared and he told me that "that is how it is." Then I pushed him away and started to cry, he told me that I had nothing wrong with me and to put on my clothes.

(Center for Reproductive Law and Policy and CLADEM 1999, cited in Coomaraswamy 1999b, para. 77)

Women in custody are particularly vulnerable to violence by state agents acting under the cover of authority and public trust. Human Rights Watch reports that in the United States, the sexual and other abuse of women incarcerated in local jails, state and federal prisons, and immigration detention centres is a serious problem. In one report on the United States, the organisation provides evidence that prison guards, most of whom were men, subject women to verbal harassment, unwarranted visual surveillance, sexually abusive body searches, and sexual assault (Collins 1998). Adequate and transparent mechanisms rarely exist whereby victims of assault could safely and confidentially report abuse, and seek an investigation without fear of reprisals (ibid.).

State institutions and policies do not relate to all women in the same way. They differentiate between women according to their race, ethnicity, class, religion, and sexual orientation. In some countries, physical and psychological violence against women of low socio-economic status occurs in public health facilities. So-called 'medical violence' includes forced sterilisation of poor, minority, or mentally disabled women. This has occurred in developing and post-industrialised countries as diverse as the United States, Puerto Rico, and India (Petchesky 1990). Sometimes women choose sterilisation despite the fact that other forms of birth control better suit their needs, because government policies severely limit access to reversible contraceptives. This is the case in Puerto Rico and Brazil, where respectively 60 per cent and 41 per cent of women contraceptive users have been sterilised (Jacobson 1991).[3]

Legal systems: legislation, structure, and culture

In principle, the legal system should protect and uphold the rights of all. It therefore has potential to offer women solutions for ending violence. In practice, legal systems tend to reflect the male bias of the State, and often fail to protect women from violence. Margaret Schuler has usefully distinguished between three levels at which the law operates to oppress women, and which need to be addressed if the law is to be transformed to support women. She identifies a 'substantive' level (the actual laws themselves), a 'structural' level (the organisations and structures that enforce the law), and a 'cultural' level (the beliefs and attitudes held by wider society, including women and men who work as lawyers and within the legal system) (Stewart 1995b).

Laws themselves may actually protect male perpetrators, legitimising violence against women. Laws defining rape in narrow terms to exclude rape that takes place within marriage would fall into this category. Similarly, some laws hinder prosecution of the perpetrators of violence. In Pakistan, according to the Zina Ordinance passed in 1979, a woman's testimony is only relevant to the lesser forms of punishment imposed for *zina* – the 'crime' of sex outside marriage. Her testimony does not count as evidence for more severe forms of punishment, even if she is a rape victim. A woman who has been raped may herself be prosecuted for *zina* if she cannot prove that she was raped. Conversely, men who kill their partners are often excused, or their sentences mitigated, as a result of defendants claiming provocation or a need to protect their honour (Amnesty International 1995c).

At the structural level of the legal system, the administration of the law by law courts, law enforcers, and the administrative bodies of the State may all result in problems for women. These organisations typically show a predominantly male leadership in most countries. Women who reach positions of leadership have frequently succeeded in a system that rewards conformity, and may either share societal biases about proper ways in which women should behave, or be in too much of a minority to be able to represent women effectively. Consequently, legal administrative systems may not offer support to women survivors of violence, either inside the court, or before the case is brought. Women's and human rights groups have documented many cases in which social biases, attitudes, and gender-stereotyping have affected court judgements. Judgements about the 'appropriateness' of women's sexual behaviour have often become the focus of rape cases, with the result that men who attack women who display independence, or evidence of sexual behaviour that is deemed to be improper, are less likely to face conviction (Coomaraswamy 1997a).

Women survivors of violence may face cultural difficulties when a lack of legal awareness means they do not, or cannot, use the law. A study conducted by Grupo Apoyo Pedagogico (GAP) in Colombia found that, in addition to a lack of knowledge of their rights and a fear of exacerbating the aggression by their abusers, the main reason women gave for not reporting violence to formal institutions was the institutions' inefficiency in dealing with cases of violence. Women commented that officials were cold, distant, and sometimes hostile towards them. No guidance was given to them concerning their rights, or how to cope with judicial procedures. Travel to formal institutions was viewed as intimidating, costly, and time-consuming. When women succeeded in lodging a complaint, they discovered that there was no mechanism to enforce the law, for example, to make men obey a summons, or to ensure investigation of their complaint (Gonzalez-Sanchez 1998).

The problems encountered by women who try to access the law for support against violence relate to the intimidating nature of its enforcers and their trivialisation of women's experiences, coupled with women's lack of support and knowledge about their rights. Schuler's framework can also be used to analyse customary or religious law, which is particularly important for women in societies where western-style legal systems overlay or co-exist with an older system (Stewart 1995b).

It is possible to challenge state reinforcement of women's subordination, and to use opportunities created by the State to change gender relations. As has been noted in the South American context, 'Feminists should not dismiss the State as the ultimate mechanism of male social control nor embrace it as the ultimate vehicle for gender-based social change. Rather, under different political regimes and at distinct historical junctures, the State is potentially a mechanism either for social change or social control in women's lives.' (Alvarez 1990, 273) Chapter 7 will consider strategies that women's groups have employed to negotiate with the State on the issue of violence against women.

In summary, for women to challenge violence, the culture and structure of institutions at all levels must be transformed. Transformation must occur in all these institutions, since where one is altered to reflect women's interests, another may still be working in opposition. As the work of Women Against Fundamentalism and Southall Black Sisters with ethnic minorities in Britain shows, negative reactions of community organisations to the egalitarian policies instigated by the State can have detrimental consequences for women.

4.2 Violence against women in times of change and crisis

In this section, we consider violence against women in two contexts of change and insecurity: worsening poverty, and militarisation or armed conflict. In conditions of economic hardship, scarcity, conflict, and post-conflict, social relationships are strained and challenged. Gender roles may be changing under external pressures. In such situations, men may experience threats to their identity, where women are forced through necessity to challenge existing gender power relations and roles, or when a third party or social situation challenges men's idea of themselves as powerful.

4.2.1 Violence and increasing poverty

As highlighted in Chapter 1, there is considerable evidence that poverty and deprivation are contexts in which violence against women increases. This section examines the links between poverty and physical violence from an intimate partner (domestic violence), and between poverty, sexual violence, and exploitation.

Poverty and domestic violence

In our discussion of the household, we described how relationships between spouses are characterised by confrontation and negotiation over the distribution and allocation of resources. Where violence is viewed in the context of beliefs about women's and men's roles and status within the family, a complex picture emerges of the relationships between poverty, frustrated masculine identities, and violence in intimate relationships. Various studies have noted that a typical effect of macro-social changes on poor urban households is men's loss of the position of sole breadwinner. This may undermine their status and their authority within the household and outside it. This may in turn lead to men using violence to try to impose their authority on the family.

Conflicts over decisions about money and food are a source of violence within poor households. In contexts where violence against women is permitted or condoned, it is often exacerbated as a result of unstable working conditions, unemployment, financial insecurity, and the resulting difficulty of providing household necessities. Conflict intensifies in situations of acute poverty. The UN has recognised that conditions of underdevelopment, poverty, and poor housing produce stress that results in high levels of domestic violence (Connors 1989). Much of this violence has been linked to the challenges that economic difficulties pose to men's role as household head, and their control over women.

While prevailing ideologies create expectations that men should head households and make household decisions, household survival in times of escalating poverty may depend on women assuming control of more of the income. Research from various contexts has indicated that when women control income, this correlates to improved nutritional status and family health (Bruce 1989), since women as a group prioritise spending on household welfare more highly than men do (Razavi and Miller 1995). Men opt to keep more income for personal use in social settings beyond the household, which can '...claim a sometimes substantial portion of their earnings, and may loosen their personal and social contracts to provide materially and emotionally for their immediate families' (Bruce 1989, 982). While most women accept their husband's right to personal spending, in the context of declining incomes conflict can arise about the amount of money available for collective needs. In contexts where men are – tacitly or overtly – able to resolve such disputes with violence, violence will increase. A study in Ecuador found that domestic violence increased as a result of a reduced family income. Forty-eight per cent of the women interviewed claimed that violence occurred when they had to ask for more money to maintain the household (Moser 1989).

During social upheaval, normative gender roles and relations are challenged by new circumstances. When money is in short supply because inflation means households can no longer survive on existing levels of earnings, or where men lose their means of livelihood, the security of the household comes under threat, putting all its members under pressure. Worsening social conditions, poverty, and unemployment oblige families to create multiple strategies for survival, including increasing economic activity on the part of women and children. Men who perceive that they have failed as sole providers can take their frustration out on women. 'Male social exclusion' is a term enjoying popular currency that offers some scope for understanding the processes by which an increase in violence against women comes about. When '…the means with which to attain at least a partial sense of achievement of "maleness" is lost, the confusion and dysfunction that results can be termed "male exclusion"' (Porter with Smyth 1998, 9). This male crisis in gender identity contributes to a breakdown in social structures, associated with rising crime, aggressive behaviour, and an increase in male violence against women (ibid.). For example, in South Africa it has been argued that black men's sense of political and economic disempowerment under apartheid resulted in increased efforts to assert dominance within the household, marked by escalating domestic violence (Segel and Labe 1990, cited in Sweetman 1997, 5).

Male violence against intimate partners may occur at the point where men see their gender identity within the household breaking down (Moore 1994). Men invest their resources and energy in a particular masculine identity, whether it be as breadwinner, as virile, as wealthy, or as a husband whose wife stays at home. These identities are imbued with power and prestige. Men may use violence against women when their identity – and thus their power and status and control of women's mobility – is threatened. Men's violence and domination of their partners reconfirms their masculine identity, and re-asserts control. For example, in Mexico and other Latin American countries, higher levels of male violence towards women and children have been associated with women's increased labour force activity. Women's increased income-earning threatens men's position as chief providers for the household (Chant 1994b, 211). Their activities in the public sphere challenge the traditional 'privacy' of feminine roles (González de la Rocha 1991).

In Papua New Guinea, many wives have observed that their husband's violence towards them increases when the men are out of work, and in the period around the start of new year when school fees are due, and couples argue about how money is to be found. At these times, 'It appears that working wives suffer more wife-beating than unemployed wives, because husbands feel threatened by their wives' potential independence and attempt to retain their control through physical dominance.' (Bradley 1994, 19) In the East Sepik region, women in a rubber development scheme reported that a fall in rubber prices caused an intensification of violence when men beat them as a way of venting their frustration (ibid.).

In Cisne Dos, Ecuador, women have observed a direct link between declining male earnings and increasing domestic violence, often associated with alcohol abuse. Violence frequently occurred when women asked for cash. Women attributed men's anger to feelings of frustration stemming from insufficient earnings, or to defensiveness when challenged about retaining earnings to spend on other women or alcohol (Moser 1996).[4]

Some investigations into the impact of credit provision to women on household welfare and women's empowerment support the argument that economic hardship is linked with intensified domestic violence because of a crisis in relations between women and men. In one study on the impact of credit on violence against women in Bangladesh, women gave two distinct answers explaining the domestic violence they experienced. Some women characterised their marriages in terms of 'exceptional violence', while others saw the violence within their marriage as linked to scarcity. These latter understood why the violence occurred, and did not regard it as exceptional. The study concludes that in both types of relationship, credit mitigated against violence. In the latter, it did so by reducing shared tensions and suffering around scarcity, and in the former by allowing women in 'exceptionally' abusive relationships greater economic and personal autonomy (Kabeer 1998, 44). The interesting suggestion here is that, for some, poverty can lead to violence within what would otherwise be co-operative relationships.

Some research into credit provision in Bangladesh suggests that violence against women can diminish when women bring home a resource, in this case money, regardless of who actually uses the money (Schuler *et al.* 1996). However, other research suggests that women's independent income, not simply extra resources, reduces violence (Hashemi *et al.* 1996). As noted in Chapter 1, there are complex and sometimes contradictory findings on the impact of credit provision to women on gender relations and violence against women. What is clear is that income-generation and credit provision cannot in themselves be assumed to reduce violence.

Not all men who are poor are violent, and not all violent men are poor. More research is needed to find out why increased economic hardship may lead in some instances to greater co-operation between household members and in others, to greater conflict and violence. While scarcity in some contexts leads to intra-household conflict, it seems that it may also lead to increased co-operation and interdependence. For example, a local-level study conducted in Mexico during the period of economic restructuring from 1982-1992, when incomes in poor urban households fell, found that there was less conflict in male-headed households during this period. Domestic violence was less apparent, and men seemed to be investing their earnings in consolidating housing and making living conditions more comfortable for their families (Chant 1994b).

Equally, the arguments should not be read as implying that men at the bottom of the socio-economic hierarchy are necessarily more violent towards women than wealthier men. Men and women in middle-income and high-income households also disagree over the allocation of resources. However, it may be more difficult for men of lower-income groups and low social status to maintain their view of themselves as the sole or main breadwinner than it is for wealthier men. Living in conditions of poverty can create an awkward disparity between normative ideals about gender roles, and the reality of men's unemployment, or women's income contribution to the household.

Men from lower income groups may feel particularly threatened in contexts where there has been a restructuring of the economy with the result that industrial blue-collar jobs have been destroyed. The transformation of the workplace in Russia and other post-Soviet countries shows how central wage work can be to men's identity. Massive downsizing and closures of workplaces in the 1990s have led to men venting their frustration angrily and violently within the family sphere (Kibitskaya 2000, 99). However, it should be noted that these factories also employ large numbers of women, who also have to deal with wage arrears and redundancy.

Challenges to men's view of themselves as main or sole earners are particularly intense in homes where male resentment of women's participation in earning income vies with economic need, which renders women more likely to have to defy male opposition. One study from the United States reported that the rate of violence between husbands and wives was twice as high in blue-collar, low-income families than in white-collar, middle-income families (Straus, Gelles, and Steinmetz 1980).

Poverty, sexual violence, and exploitation

Escalating poverty can lead women into dangerous situations as they try to maintain their livelihood. It also shapes the opportunities for escape or assistance available to women. Poor or displaced women may resort to prostitution as a strategy for supporting their families – a strategy that makes them vulnerable to sexual violence. The coercion applied to women who use their bodies to carry drugs is a further form of abuse. In many cases, Colombian women imprisoned in the UK for drug-carrying offences agreed to undertake the work because of poverty and fear of violent reprisals (Fisher 1994). The Association for the Defence of Women's Rights in Azerbaijan runs a prison visiting project. They have found that some of the longest sentences given to women are for drugs smuggling. Often, women are pressured into this work by their families, who are approached by drug trafficking groups and offered considerable financial rewards for carrying out this work. One of the project's aims is to have the sentences for women charged for drugs trafficking reviewed to account for coercion by families and traffickers (Elmira Aleksperova, personal communication 1998).

Poverty, unemployment, and homelessness may cause women to seek unequal marriages in which their husbands will provide for them. In post-Soviet Russia, marriage agencies have mushroomed, and many women are looking for husbands overseas. Three-quarters of these women are single mothers (Olesya Chudinova, Ekaterinburg Marriage Agency, personal communication 2000) and are motivated by the wish to provide stability and an education for their children. Women who undertake such marriages often migrate to a country where they may be unable to speak the language. Frequently, they lack friends or knowledge of institutions where they can gain support or employment. Their resulting economic dependency and isolation may mean that they are particularly vulnerable to violence.

Extreme poverty can result in women and girls taking work that places them in sexually exploitative situations. A study of the factors leading to child prostitution and other child labour in Chile found that it was extremely difficult for young girls in poverty to change their situation. Girls who came from violent or poor families, and who had often received limited education, were confronted by tremendous difficulties in finding work. Prostitution was one of the few options for survival, providing a salary far greater than most other forms of paid work (Castelli 1998).

This research also found that pressure from within the family could easily lead to early prostitution and exploitation. Girls wanted to comply with familial expectations for fear of punishment and rejection, and to gain affection. The study found that when girls started to bring money home, their mistreatment within the family lessened and there was less conflict.

From this finding, the study concluded that family relationships could encourage and reward child prostitution (ibid.).

This section on the links between poverty and violence against women concludes with a cautionary point on the links between them. It is often the case that violence is likely to become more visible during periods of stress. What was hidden and taboo is often brought into the open at these times. Poverty is sometimes offered as a satisfactory explanation for violence against women in a turbulent context where what are perceived as 'normal' gender relations are disturbed by 'external' forces. Such explanations may even be offered by women themselves. For example, in Lesotho, some wives of unemployed miners explained the violence they experienced as an understandable reaction to unemployment. One said, 'He is frustrated because he is no longer working and gets fed-up for almost anything, to the extent of beating me for minor things. He is an unhappy man, you see, but he is basically good.' (Sweetman 1995a, 35).

If violent male behaviour during periods of instability is presumed to be an aberration that can be explained in socio-economic terms, the converse assumption is that communities can be returned to some state of 'normality', when women will not suffer violence. However, the fact that violence against women is a global phenomenon, taking place in wealthier households as well as those in poverty, shows that 'normality' is violent too. By themselves, poverty-reduction and political stability will not eradicate violence against women.

4.2.2 Violence and armed conflict

During armed conflict, as in peacetime, communities, national governments, and state actors – including those in military organisations – may jointly or severally be involved in violence against women. These institutions may fail to protect women from violence during conflict, or in some cases may be responsible for perpetrating it. This section explores and analyses violence against women during and after armed conflict, highlighting the different roles of armies, paramilitaries, police, liberation fighters, occupying troops, peacekeeping forces, and demobilised soldiers. These different players are governed by different sets of rules of engagement, have differing expectations of impunity, and may or may not be held accountable for violence against women in different ways.

Finally, the section discusses the role and motivations of the perpetrators of violence against women during armed conflict. It highlights the fact that while some men and children are coerced into participating in conflict, through legal means or through violence, others choose to join the military, often as a result of poverty or a perceived lack of alternative options.

The socialisation of young men into the military

In almost all societies, it is men who are tasked with the responsibility of doing battle. Hence, military organisations, and states at war, are deeply 'gendered', in the sense that they are heavily male-dominated, and imbued with masculine values (Cock 1989). A nation at war is encouraged to stand solid against an external aggressor. Ideas about nationhood involve 'specific notions of "manhood" and "womanhood"' (Yuval-Davis 1997, 1). Men are not necessarily predisposed to fight. Evidence of the intimidation and coercion involved in securing participation in armed conflict, such as the use of drugs, deprivation of sleep, or compulsory viewing of violent war videos (Large 1997), suggests that military masculinity is a fragile trait that has to be continually reproduced. Men's private stories of the military and of participation in fighting during armed conflict suggest their ambivalence or unease about conformity to military masculinity. This ambivalence suggests that the prescribed ideal masculinity is a 'precarious or artificial state that boys must win against powerful odds' (Gilmore 1990, 11).

What motivates men to join the military? To understand men's violence against women during and after armed conflict, we need first to understand how and why men become involved in war and the armed forces. Many have no choice; in many countries, conscription into the army is compulsory. Others are driven by a desire to avenge atrocities against their families or communities, or to ensure their own survival. Research conducted by the Quaker UN Office in Geneva showed that the majority of children who volunteered to join armed opposition forces did so as a result of ill-treatment of themselves or their families by government troops (Brett and McCallin 1996, 96). But while violent coercion is used in forcible recruitment of adults and children to fight, others have at least a semblance of choice. For them powerful social, economic, and political incentives exist for participating in generalised violence. In armed conflict, 'a hierarchy of interests and power operates within the framework of masculinity. Men may be unwilling to participate in acts of violence, yet the social relationships in which they are caught up pressurise them into complicity.' (Large 1997, 25)

Some analyses connect entry into the army with a context of poverty and lack of employment alternatives for young men. A lack of economic options available to boys and men leads many to become soldiers. For young men who are denied traditional paths to manhood because of rapid economic and social change and a lack of educational and employment opportunities, the use and threat of violence can represent a way of coming of age. Young men's violence is a medium of empowerment for men who have little else (Richards 1995). Many governments exploit groups of marginalised boys and young men when they undertake recruitment drives to bolster numbers in the armed forces. The United Kingdom recruits 16-year-olds (the lowest legal school-leaving age), and encourages young people to embark on their applications for recruitment earlier than this, while they are still at school (Hetherington 1998). British soldiers under the age of 18 fought and died in the Falklands and Gulf wars. The Ministry of Defence has recently embarked on recruitment drives of unemployed youth. In 1998, young people without jobs were urged to join the armed forces as part of the government programme that cuts benefits from those who refuse work or training. It was thought that the move would increase the numbers of recruits from ethnic minorities (Castle 1998).

Research into the motives of soldiers in Bosnia highlights the importance of economic incentives in fuelling men's decision to fight in armed conflict. Borislav Herak, a Serbian soldier, was recruited into one of the Serb nationalist militias in 1992. Before the war, he had done poorly in school, and grumbled about his dead-end job pushing a cart in the one of the city's textile factories. He drank heavily, and physically intimidated his father. However, he had not thought of the Muslims in his extended family as the source of his unhappiness, and had in fact been close to his Muslim brother-in-law. He had wished for girlfriends, but had no history of sexual assault on women, or of using pornography. In research after the conflict, Herak recalled what a revelation it had been to him when older Serbian men in his militia explained to him and other new recruits how Muslims, since the Ottoman Empire, had been the cause of Serbian misfortune (Burns 1992, quoted in Enloe 1993).

While Herak was serving as a fighter in the militia, he became a multiple rapist and murderer of women civilians. He did not question his commander's order to rape the Muslim women whom his militia was holding captive in a motel outside the Bosnian town of Vogosca. His commander's explanation made sense to Borislav Herak: raping Muslim women was, he was told, 'good for raising the fighters' morale'. And he presumed that his commander meant him and his colleagues to murder each one of the women after he had raped her. He followed these implicit orders (op. cit.).

In the army, for the first time in his life, Herak was able to acquire things that had previously been beyond his reach: videos, television sets, and women. He was an ordinary man who felt cheated by the way life had treated him. And he was given a scapegoat, in the form of Muslims, to blame for his failure to succeed in life. He learned in the military that raping women was part and parcel of fighting a war, and decided not to question this.

Women's role in armed conflict: mothers of the nation

What of women in militarised societies? The portrayal of women as passive and weak, while men are strong defenders of 'their' women and children, is central to the military's claim that its function is to protect civilians (Enloe 1988). However, in reality, military organisations are instruments of the State, and their activities may in fact increase women's vulnerability to violence. Propaganda about nationhood typically promoted at times of crisis and conflict incorporates stereotypical notions of men as warriors and women as nurturers (Cockburn 1998). In particular, women's role in reproduction is often emphasised. Prevailing views stress the importance of bearing and nurturing children, to ensure that the rival group is outnumbered and that the culture of the nation is perpetuated. In Israel, demographic competition between the Jewish majority and the Palestinian Arab minority led the Israeli government to channel free contraception to Palestinian Arab women and subsidies to encourage a high birth rate among Jewish women (Yuval-Davis 1987).

As discussed in Chapter 3, male desire to control women's sexuality and potential for childbearing can cause extreme atrocities against women during armed conflict. Examples of this kind of violence have arisen from the conflicts in Indonesia, Bosnia, Rwanda, Peru, Liberia, Somalia, Cambodia, Haiti, and Uganda.[5] In contexts of war, women may be forcibly impregnated as a weapon of nationalist ethnic cleansing. In giving birth to the children of the 'enemy', women's role as wives and mothers in a patrilineal society is destroyed, and the genetic inheritance of children altered forever. In the campaign of violence against women during the war in the former Yugoslavia, Serb soldiers and paramilitary troops who raped Croat and Muslim women told them that they would give birth to 'little Chetniks' (Serb soldiers), who would grow up to kill their mothers. In Bosnia, rapists were former colleagues, neighbours, and friends (Copelon 1995, 202). Croat and Muslim women were told by soldiers that when a woman was impregnated by a Serb, then both she and the foetus became Serbian (State Commission for Gathering Facts on War Crimes in the Republic of Bosnia and Herzegovina 1992). Some women were held in 'rape camps' in Bosnia until their pregnancies were so advanced that they would not be able to obtain an abortion (Tresnjevka Women's Group 1992).

Violence against women by 'official' armies

Many people assume that armies controlled by civilian governments and international bodies can be trusted to uphold the human rights of women, as well as men. However, violence against women is often an integral part of military strategy. It has been argued that the military establishment is inherently male-biased and misogynist, and inimical to the notion of women's rights (Gardam 1993), and that military institutions are intrinsically anti-female (Adams 1993). The military as an institution often fails to protect women during conflict, and preserves a male-dominated social order (Enloe 1988). When professional armies that are accountable to civilian governments and international bodes perpetrate violence against women, it is likely to be construed as legitimate behaviour.

One example of this is the forced drafting of women to provide sexual services for soldiers as an integral part of Japan's wartime policy and strategy (Sancho 1997). 'Comfort women' is the euphemistic name given to women who, before and during the Second World War, were prostituted to the Japanese army. Up to 200,000 women are estimated to have been forced to serve as 'comfort women' in military brothels (Hicks 1995), 80 per cent of whom are believed to have been Korean, although Japanese women and women from other occupied territories such as Taiwan, the Philippines, Indonesia, Burma, and the Pacific islands were also used (Soh 2000). The Japanese rationale for the 'comfort system' before the war was to reduce the number of rapes around army bases. This became even more of a concern following the infamous 'Rape of Nanking' in 1937, during which it is estimated that up to 20,000 women were raped. Later the 'comfort system' became a strategy for enhancing the morale of the military by providing an institution for recreational sex.

Women were captured and otherwise forced to enter the brothels, and imprisoned there. Those who tried to escape were tortured and often murdered. Those who stayed were also tortured – the sex was brutal and violent and often accompanied by slashing with swords, and chopping off parts of women's bodies. The only Japanese women involved were women who had already been in other brothels. There is a view that this institutionalisation of rape made the behaviour of the Japanese soldiers even worse when they marched into villages, by encouraging them to see women as slaves and sexual fodder. As the war went on, they became more terrible in their treatment of women, as well as enemy soldiers and POWs.

The Women's International War Crimes Tribunal on Japan's Military Sexual Slavery took place in December 2000 in Tokyo. It was established by activists to seek redress against the Japanese government for acts of sexual violence perpetrated against the 'comfort women' during the Asia-Pacific War.[6] Women from North and South Korea, China, Taiwan, Indonesia, the Philippines, and East Timor demanded an official apology and compensation from the Japanese government. Prosecutors indicted

Emperor Hirohito and other high-ranking Japanese officials during the war for crimes against humanity and sued the Japanese government for state responsibility in the commission of these atrocities (Asia Pacific Forum on Women, Law, and Development 2000).

More recently, the fight of the 'comfort women' to have the Japanese Government admit legal responsibility has received a setback. In March 2001, a Japanese court overturned the first, and so far only, compensation award made to a World War II 'comfort woman'. Hiroshima's High Court reversed a 1998 district court ruling that ordered the Japanese government to pay damages to three South Korean women. The judge said that the abduction of the women to use them as forced labourers and sex slaves was not a serious constitutional violation.

In Guatemala, 200,000 people were killed, or have disappeared, as a result of political violence since 1962. Repression through an illegal and underground punitive system directed by military intelligence became a substitute for the law, and constituted the State's main form of social control; state forces and related paramilitary groups were responsible for an estimated 93 per cent of the violations committed (Commission for Historical Clarification 1999). Over the decades since 1962, human rights organisations have documented thousands of atrocities against Guatemalan women by the army and police. Women were killed, tortured, and raped, because of their political beliefs or participation, or indiscriminately massacred. Women were also targeted because they defended and protected their relatives: wives, mothers, daughters, and sisters have all 'disappeared' at the hands of Guatemalan death squads, because their male relatives were suspected of being guerrillas or guerrilla sympathisers (Amnesty International 1998). The Guatemalan legal and judicial system facilitated the violence, protecting the perpetrators of state violence with impunity.

A central element of human rights work in Guatemala has been to uncover the truth about the atrocities that took place and the ways that individuals, families, and entire communities experienced them. This has involved collecting factual information that can be used in judicial proceedings, and taking testimonies to record the psychological impact that the violence has had on its victims. Guatemala's truth commission, the Historical Clarification Commission, has the task of recovering people's experiences of the violence in order to 'help build a Guatemala that can form a collective judgement about its past' (Lira 1997, 396).

Violence by international peacekeeping forces

Women may also be vulnerable to violence inflicted by international 'protectors'. The National Campaign for Eradication of Crime by US troops in Korea has brought attention to the case of a young girl, who was battered to death with a drinks bottle, which was then placed in her vagina. The accused, Kenneth Marle, a private in the United States Army stationed in Korea, proceeded to put an umbrella up her anus. In order to eliminate evidence of the murder, he spread soap powder over her body and stuffed matches into her mouth. The Korean Supreme Court sentenced him to 15 years' imprisonment (Jeong 1997).

Cases such as this, committed by foreign military personnel or international peacekeeping forces, raise questions about whether national or international courts should try the men involved, and whether humanitarian law applies. As explained in Chapter 2, the Statute for the ICC, drawn up in 1998, defines sexual violence as war crimes and crimes against humanity. The US Government voted against the adoption of the Treaty establishing the ICC, in part because it did not want its servicemen abroad to be prosecuted. Kenneth Roth, the Director of Human Rights Watch, wrote in a commentary, 'The territorial hook might catch American troops, or their commanders, for alleged crimes committed while they were abroad. If the country where US troops are present has ratified the treaty, the ICC could pursue a case against them even though the United States had not joined the court.' (Roth 1998, 45)

International human rights standards recognise that rape and the threat of rape of women detainees by prison, security, or military officials always amounts to torture,[7] even when the officials are not acting on orders or policies dictated by their commanders. The Statute of the ICTY states that persons other than the physical perpetrators have personal criminal responsibility for rape.

United Nations protection and peacekeeping forces have been connected with prostitution and trafficking rings. Medica Zenica, a centre that works with women victims of violence in Bosnia, has appealed to the forces, international agencies, and NGOs to discipline their male employees about the use of prostitutes who are under the legal age of consent, some of them as young as 14 (Cockburn 1998, 205). In Cambodia, the presence of UN peacekeeping forces has led to a large increase in prostitution, in part involving children. The International Children's Rights Monitor has reported that the deployment of UN peacekeeping troops has resulted in a 'breath taking increase in prostitution, in part involving children'. One health official estimated that the increase in women and girls involved in prostitution in Phnom Penh leapt from 6000 in 1991 to 20,000 in 1992

(Arnig 1993, cited in McCollum, Kelly, and Radford 1994, 14). In Liberia, for many women without employment or financial security, selling sex to international forces presents the only source of income (Bennett, Bexley, and Warnock 1995).

Examples of violence and sexual exploitation by UN peacekeeping forces lead us to question whether soldiering for the State calls forth different notions of masculinity than does soldiering for a non-state international agency. As Cynthia Enloe points out,

> *United Nations peacekeeping forces remain as overwhelmingly male as most state militaries. With such a composition, it must have the same sort of policies around masculinity as other more conventional forces do. … Are the blue-helmeted men on duty in Cambodia explicitly ordered not to patronise prostitutes? What steps are being taken to prevent AIDS and other forms of STDs among UN peacekeepers? Each of these policies will be informed by ideas about women, about roles women must play if a male soldier is to be able to do his job.*

(Enloe 1993, 35)

Violence against women from armies of 'national liberation'

Women's position in relation to political movements that stress national, religious, or ethnic identity is an ambiguous one. The fact that liberation struggles are armed and militaristic indicates that they have much in common with other conflicts that glorify aggression and the use of force, yet some argue that these movements are 'different'. The rhetoric of many national liberation movements is that women and men are equal partners in fighting the enemy, and women's active participation is often encouraged. Women have fought in national liberation wars in countries including Lebanon, Vietnam, Sri Lanka, Ethiopia, Eritrea, and South Africa. Are national liberation armies really different from other military organisations in their stance towards violence against women?

Strict rules against sex within liberation movements, for example in the Tigrayan People's Liberation Front in Ethiopia (Bennett, Bexley, and Warnock 1995), and the South West Africa People's Organisation (SWAPO) in Namibia (Shikola 1998), have to a certain extent protected women fighters from sexual violence and abuse. However, sexual abuse has been documented, and may be masked for security reasons. It is also painful for ex-fighters to acknowledge that violence against women is part of the revolutionary movement; in particular, women ex-combatants may be reluctant to acknowledge acts of violence. A woman SWAPO guerrilla army combatant stated:

*I didn't see any rape cases as such, but you know, sometimes,
when you are coming from home, you are new, and they train you
in the army to say yes… You feel scared of saying no, you cannot
talk directly to a commander. Sometimes the chiefs would call out
these poor young girls fresh from home. The chiefs made love to
them, and the women became pregnant without knowing the
person who impregnated them, sometimes they didn't even know
his name. Some commanders had fifteen or eighteen kids.
It's not really rape in a direct way as such, but just the way the
chiefs were.*

(Shikola 1998, 143)

Violence against women from armed opposition groups

Despite their rhetoric of representing 'the people', some armed opposition groups cannot be represented here as forces for national liberation. Beyond the jurisdiction of the State and with no popular support, they have been responsible for widespread violence against women.

Women and girls in many contexts are abducted by armed opposition groups and rebels to supply sexual services to fighters. In Uganda, testimonies have been taken from girls and boys who were abducted and forced to become child soldiers by the Lord's Resistance Army, an armed opposition group fighting government forces in the north of the country. The testimonies describe a macabre re-ordering of children's experiences of the family, which takes place as a means of gaining children's allegiance to the organisation. Children under the age of 13, known as 'siblings', are abducted and allocated a 'family'within the army (Amnesty International 1997). Abducted girls become 'wives' to soldiers, and are forced to provide sexual services to their 'husbands'. Soldiers may transfer girls to other 'husbands', and within a year, a girl may have been 'wife' to several different men (op. cit.). Girls carry out domestic tasks under life-threatening conditions, and are policed through fear of violence. Some girls explained how allowing smoke from the cooking fires to be seen carried a life sentence (op. cit., 17).

Also in Uganda, a study carried out by the Medical Foundation for the Care of Victims of Torture, a London-based organisation that works with victims of torture, conducted research on rape in the war-ravaged Luwero Triangle in Uganda. The report concluded, 'Tens of thousands of women died at the hands of the soldiers, often following rape. These were not acts of sexually starved men, but expressions of violence, aggression, anger, hatred and revenge: the need to demonstrate power by soldiers in an army that was being defeated.' (Giller and Kabaganda 1990)

In Liberia, a study of women rape survivors conducted by The Association of Female Lawyers found that soldiers forced women to watch the murder of fellow Liberians, and required them to laugh or applaud. They were shot if they did not comply. Women who showed any emotion when they were forced to watch the murder of their own or other people's children were shot (Association of Female Lawyers of Liberia 1998).

In Chad, a recent history of 'warlordism' (the rise of regional centres of power based on personalised rule and military force) has resulted in a state of lawlessness, where women are often raped by state security forces, for suspected collusion with the opposition. If they live in an area where armed groups are active, they may automatically be considered supporters of the rebels (Women's Commission of the Human Rights League of Chad *et al.* 1998).

In Chad in September 1996, four young women were raped by three members of the armed opposition group, the *Forces armées pour la République fédérale* (FARF), who intercepted them as they returned on foot to their village. One of the victims gave the following account:

> *They asked where we were from and we said we were from Tilo.*
> *They asked us if the chief was there. They said they had been to him*
> *and asked him to give them and their comrades food but he had run*
> *away. They said that if we had been men they'd have killed us...*
> *they insulted us and said we were dirty. Then they went with us one*
> *by one. One of us resisted, but they put a knife against her neck and*
> *she had to give in.*

(Amnesty International 1996b, 14)

In Chad, in addition to having undergone rape by state agents, women have also been raped by opposition groups on the assumption that they have denounced the rebels to the government authorities. Research by Amnesty International in southern Chad demonstrates that local political and military authorities, along with armed opposition group leaders, are often aware of the systematic abuses committed against women and girls, or have condoned such violations as part of war tactics. As a result, effective measures have rarely, if ever, been taken against perpetrators responsible for the rape and sexual abuse of women and girls (ibid.).

Violence by armed forces can be a reason for women fleeing during conflict, as this example of violence against women by paramilitary forces in Bangladesh shows. Amina fled to Bangladesh with her children when the paramilitary force 'Lone Htein' started raiding the villages to collect able-bodied people as forced labourers, including women for household work.

They targeted women-headed households in their search for young girls. In the first days they took Amina's life savings of 500 kyats, two goats, and her gold earrings. The second time, when she had nothing to offer, they wanted her 12-year-old daughter for two or three days. Amina explained, 'I refused and cried and then they took me to their camp and kept me there for the whole night. Next day they released me, but took me again on the following day for another two nights.' It was then that she decided to cross the river Naf to protect her children. Lone Htein confiscated all her money, national registration cards, and possessions as she crossed the border and she then spent eight months going from one camp to another. On one occasion her son was caught by the camp guards selling pulses to buy dried fish and he was taken into custody. The *Manjhi* (male community leaders) gave Amina two alternatives – either to face her son's imprisonment, or to agree to be voluntarily repatriated within the week. She chose the latter (Wahra and Goldring 1993).

During armed conflict, the death and disappearance of husbands, partners, fathers, and sons, means many women are left on their own with children and elderly dependants. They need to find a way to ensure the survival of themselves and their families. Bartering sexual services for food or money may be the best, or only, strategy women possess for supporting themselves and their families. In this context, the line between coerced and consensual sex is even more blurred than in the contexts of extreme poverty and lack of livelihood opportunities open to many girls and women in peacetime. During the civil war in Rwanda, displaced women were forced to cohabit with security officers, and wives whose husbands are in prison have been bribed by soldiers to give sex in return for seeing their husbands (Twagiramariya and Turshen 1998).

At a symposium co-hosted by CSVR and the South African office of Oxfam GB in June 1996, it was noted that the gender dimensions of war, recovery, and reconstruction are often ignored, 'What happens, for example, to the women who are abducted by militias and forced into sexual slavery? In Mozambique and Angola as elsewhere, women's specific needs have seldom been considered during the demobilisation process. If they leave (or are abandoned by) their abductors, they lack the means of survival. Yet if they stay, they are not recognised as dependants in the demobilisation packages.' (Eade and Williams 1997, 437)

Linking state-level violence to violence within the household

Wars that manipulate identity, ethnic, religious, racial, or otherwise, can put women at greater risk to violence within the family and household; from intimate partners, or from other men known to them.

Escalation in domestic violence, rape, and sexual assault has been linked to armed conflict and its aftermath in many countries – among them, South Africa (Wood and Jewkes 1997; Goldblatt and Meintjes 1998), Mozambique (Abreu 1998), Serbia (Mladjenovic and Matijašević 1996), Guatemala (Zur 1996), and Cambodia (Zimmerman 1994). We have seen that the family and household are not necessarily safe locations for women either in peacetime or in war. During war and armed conflict, violence against women in intimate relationships may increase, as sanctions against men's violence break down, and women's social and economic vulnerability increases. There may be fewer opportunities for women to escape from violent relationships, or they may be targets of violence from the 'enemy' side. Abusive partners are likely to be in a more powerful position within the communities in armed conflict, because they know that women cannot look for help through the normal channels. Increased general availability of weapons such as small arms may lead to them being held and used within the home.

The SOS Hotline, a telephone hotline for women victims of violence based in Belgrade, Serbia, received calls from women refugees who had been raped when they arrived in Belgrade. While some women had been raped by strangers as an act of war, others found that displacement and societal breakdown had made them vulnerable to violence from men they knew.

> *Mira and her children are refugees. They came to stay at her*
> *godfather's house in Belgrade. During the first week of their stay,*
> *the godfather raped Mira. She was too frightened to give her address*
> *when she called the SOS Hotline.*
>
> (Mrševic and Hughes 1997, 124).

Methods of goading men to fight may result in increased violent assaults on women. In Serbia, media propaganda evident from 1992 played an essential role in generating ethnic hatred of the 'other'. At this time, SOS Hotline reported receiving calls from women who were battered after men watched special TV news broadcasts in which pictures of dead bodies were shown (Mrševic and Hughes 1997). Women said that men became enraged after watching the nationalist propaganda, and beat their wives and partners as a way to avenge their wounded national pride. Some women reported that they were beaten for the first time after men watched TV reports on Serb victims of war. Serbian women coined the term 'post-TV news syndrome' to describe men who are violent towards their partners after watching television coverage of the war (Mladjenovic and Matijašević 1996). Evidence from SOS Hotline in Belgrade suggests that 'more and more women are attacked after news broadcasts; some women take their children and hide before the broadcast begins.' (Mladjenovic 1996)

A similar pattern has been noted elsewhere. In Croatia and Northern Ireland, domestic violence during armed conflict involved many more incidents with weapons. The effects are not limited to combat zones. Canadian refuge workers reported that during the Gulf War, women told of their husbands dressing in army uniforms before beating them after watching the news on television (Kelly 1996).

SOS Hotline in Belgrade, found that there were increased reports of rape from girls aged 16–18 after the start of the war in the former Yugoslavia (Mladjenovic and Matijašević 1996, 122). As the war intensified, the hotline received a noticeable increase in calls made by women about their sons (Mrševic and Hughes 1997). This trend continued after the war ended (Mladjenovic and Matijšević 1996). The women linked conflict with a marked increase in rape and military behaviour in civilian life on the part of boys and male adolescents (Mladjenovic and Matijašević 1996).

Women who contacted the SOS Hotline in Belgrade reported during the war that their partners threatened them with weapons in 40 per cent of cases. The police claim that inhabitants of Belgrade possess 200,000 weapons legally, and up to three times that number illegally, in a city of half a million inhabitants (Mladjenovic and Matijašević 1996). One woman explained to Women in Black, a feminist and pacifist organisation in Serbia, 'Guns are an obligatory part of the apparel of local boys. They never leave home without them. They don't even make love [sic] too far from them. Violence is a part of everyday life.' (Zajovic ed. 1993, 96)

In Northern Ireland, most of the women who were killed or assaulted with legally held guns in the home during the armed conflict in Northern Ireland in the 1980s and 1990s were married to members of the security forces (McWilliams 1998). These security forces can apply for 'personal protection weapons' to keep at home (op. cit.). In 1992, a 12-month study on domestic violence in Northern Ireland showed that the increased availability of guns meant that more dangerous forms of violence were used against women in the home (McWilliams and McKiernan 1993). Women's shelter workers saw women with circular bruising on their necks caused by the nozzle of the gun, and some women said they had been subject to this kind of abuse for long periods of time. The physical marks of violence were sometimes difficult to detect, making convincing those from whom they sought help even more problematic. Because the men in question were part of the security forces, even if their guns were confiscated following a report of domestic violence, they were nonetheless able to retrieve them from the workplace the next day (op. cit.).

Recognising the role of guns in intensifying violence against women during conflict, several projects in Albania aim to remove guns from the community and home. One such project assists children to get away from violence in Shkoder district, and raises awareness of the need to return weapons through posters, radio, and TV broadcasts (PASF, Oxfam internal document 1998). Another project in Albania runs a network that campaigns on disarmament through the process of voluntary weapons collection. It raises public awareness on the dangers of uncontrolled weapons in civilian hands (PASF, Oxfam internal document 1999).

The links between armed conflict at the level of the community and State, and violence within the family and household, require further research. While violent behaviour may be learned through a variety of contexts, the exact processes by which these patterns of behaviour are learned are unclear, as are the interactions between internal psychological processes and their external contexts. While violence against women can be seen as part of a pattern of violence during and after war, it is qualitatively different from aggression between men who do not know each other. Not all men who have fought in wars perpetrate violence towards women in their homes.

For individual women, to see violence against women as a consequence of armed conflict may be a less painful way to explain the violent behaviour of male acquaintances. For example, when Medica Zenica in Bosnia initiated a new project on post-war domestic violence, they were sending out the message that attackers may be one of 'your own', not an enemy fighter. This required the painful acknowledgement that 'normal' gender relations can be violent (Cockburn 1998), or that violent gender relations can in some circumstances be considered 'normal'.

The aftermath: 'cultures of violence'

The official end of an armed conflict signals a change from war to peace at a political level. However, the impact of conflict on society alters it profoundly, and no political settlement can solve the social problems that this causes. 'Culture of violence' is a term used to describe how during and after armed conflict, violence can permeate the symbols, attitudes, values, and beliefs that constitute culture (Campbell 1992). A culture of violence evolves during long armed struggles, when the influence and power of the military permeates into arenas of society and the state where it previously had little or none.

The period immediately after the end of armed conflict is an 'ambiguous moment' (Enloe 1993, 252). Conflict causes an upheaval in society that forces individuals, households, and communities to change their ways of doing things, and challenges their beliefs about who they are and what their role is in the world. Part of this upheaval is a state of flux in gender relations. After a conflict is over, there may be a return to, or increase in, patriarchal control over women. Alternatively, the possibility of a positive transformation in gender relations may arise.

After war has ended, the effects of militarisation often continue to be manifested in relations between men and women. Women may be targets of militarised violence by soldiers who continue to act with impunity, and by peacekeeping forces, as well as by men in the community and home. For example, in Haiti, despite the return of the popularly elected leadership in 1994, very little has been done to break the impunity enjoyed by the armed forces and semi-official death squads. Lise Marie Dejon from Kay Famm, an organisation working with victims of violence in Haiti, explained, 'All the women who had been raped, tortured and mistreated are still hiding because they sometimes meet their aggressors in the street. This means impunity is going on.' (Personal communication 1998) Intimidation of women continues as each March 8th, Women's Day, is marked by the military through raping women (ibid.).

Violence within the family and household may be worse after a war than before. In Cambodia, following the period of Khmer Rouge rule, women reported that on returning from fighting in the war, domestic violence from their husbands increased in scope and intensity. Many women blamed this on the psychological impact of fighting in the armed conflict. One woman explained, 'My husband was a Khmer Rouge soldier. He joined in 1973. I think this has made him broken in some important way. I married him in 1982. I didn't know his character was so damaged.' (Zimmerman 1994, 17) One of the founders of SOS Hotline in Belgrade notes of the conflict in Serbia, 'Some of the men who come back from the front... abuse women, beat their children, sleep with machine guns under their pillows, rape their wives while they are sleeping, destroy the furniture, scream, swear, spit, accuse.' (Mladjenovic 1992, 54)

In South Africa, the number of violent crimes against women and children has risen dramatically since the African National Congress (ANC) came into power in 1994, ending apartheid and bringing peace to the country. Studies undertaken since then in South African townships contribute to the mounting evidence of widespread and increasing violence within sexual relationships (Wood and Jewkes 1997). The number of rapes in South Africa increased by 23 per cent in the three years prior to 1998 (ECN 1998).

Children who have been involved in armed conflict can become the perpetrators of violence in the aftermath of conflict, both directly and in their later roles as spouses and parents. Children may have been socialised into considering conflict positive. SOS Hotline in Belgrade noted that, during the war, parents more often addressed boys as 'my general', 'my soldier', or 'my commander', and boys played war games and dressed in war uniforms (Mladjenovic and Matijašević 1996).

South African boy rapists have spoken about boredom as a reason for raping. Adolescent boys explained that they raped their sisters, cousins, or brothers because they wanted to see what sex was like. One 15 year-old told his eight-year-old cousin after he had raped her that he was going to be a rapist when he grew up (Huber, Donaldson, Robertson, and Hlongweni 1997).

In post-apartheid South Africa, raping sprees, commonly known as 'jack-rolling', emerged as a practice in the 1990s, conducted by organised gangs of township youths. One such group is the South African Rapist Association. This 'association' targets women who are regarded as 'getting above themselves'. Interviews published by the South African Centre for the Study of Violence and Reconciliation quote one man as saying, 'They walk in the street wearing minis. You get aroused. They snub you. We can't stand this shit.' Another says, 'They think themselves better than us; they prefer men with money and big cars. When these women get jackrolled, it's OK.' (Swift 1998)

A study by the South African Centre for the Study of Violence and Reconciliation cites an informant who explains, 'When you leave your child alone in the home, she is not safe. And in the street, she is not safe. And in the school she is not safe. There is nowhere that she can walk and be safe. Girls are afraid somebody in a car will stop them and say, "Get in." When they walk in the street they are raped by men with guns. Sexual abuse happens so much that some students stop going to school.' (Simpson 1992, 10)

In an international study on firearms regulation, the Centre for International Crime Prevention notes a correlation between South Africa's high reported firearm homicide rates (one of the three highest in the world) and its high rate of sexual assault, as compared with countries that report no illegal imports of firearms.[8] The KwaZulu Natal Project for the Survivors of Violence in South Africa works with young men involved in the political violence. In a meeting it held with a youth group, boys said that girls prefer men who have guns. However, the girls said that boys used guns to coerce them into sexual relations (Suzanne Williams, personal communication 1998).

The idea of a culture of violence offers an explanation of aspects of men's behaviour, emphasising that violence is neither an innate quality of individuals, nor a permanent state of societies, but a learned response encouraged by war, and which continues in the form of abusive relationships. This suggests that the levels and intensity of violence against women that exist in some post-conflict societies today are at least partly attributable to the acquired responses that were adopted in order to survive during periods of conflict. However, it is important to emphasise that while individuals internalise norms of violent behaviour in cultures of violence, they can also re-interpret and dispute these norms. The idea of a culture of violence is not meant to underplay men's responsibility for acting in a violent way. Cultures can be and are changed.

Demobilised soldiers and violence against women

Research by SOS Hotline reveals an increase in domestic and street violence against women as men return from the fighting (Mladjenovic and Matijašević 1996). Callers reported that their husbands cursed the Croats and the Muslims in Croatia and Bosnia-Herzegovina while beating them. One of the sharpest increases has been young men's violence against their mothers. The percentage of calls from women who were battered by sons almost doubled between 1991-3 (Mrševic and Hughes 1997).

Taking part in organised or random violence against women is one way in which demobilised soldiers can compensate for loss of identity as a fighter following demobilisation. Demobilised soldiers may be emotionally harmed by the conflict. In addition, the economic options for demobilised soldiers are likely to be reduced with the breakdown of social and economic infrastructure. Without schools or jobs to go to, they vent their frustration and anger on women. As argued in Chapter 1, when masculinity is severely threatened, violence is one of the compensatory responses used by men.

In Russia, crisis centres that work with women victims of domestic violence note how many young men who fought in Afghanistan and Chechnya have learned to resolve conflicts through force (personal communication 2000). They expected to return from war as heroes, promised jobs and privileges. Instead they come back as amputees, with psychological problems, drug addictions, and without jobs. Testimonies from the wives of Afghanistan war veterans show how veterans survived their return to civilian life by replicating the rules and relations that structured their lives while fighting. The wives of these veteran soldiers notice that their husbands are more agitated, suspicious, quick to criticise, and violent. Their training to fight and possession of weapons means they are also recruited into organised crime groups and private security firms. One of the original powerful groups that provided protection in Ekaterinburg in the Russian Urals region includes veterans of the wars in Afghanistan and in Chechnya. As one wife of a veteran of the war in Afghanistan explained:

> *What is war? War is the destruction of all human laws. At war, the laws of human society do not operate. And for some of the old Afghantsi[9] it is easier to again violate law than find your place as a normal citizen in a law-abiding society. It is just difficult for them to survive in this society.*

(Personal communication 2000)

NGOs in Cambodia, Bosnia, and South Africa report that after war, men who were in the military are increasingly violent towards women, abuse alcohol, join criminal gangs in the community, and exhibit other signs of frustration stemming from the disappointment of not being treated as 'war heroes'. A former comrade active in the South African Self Defence Units, and part of the South African Rapist Association (see p. 146), explained:

> *I was a comrade before joining this organisation. I joined it because we were no longer given political tasks. Most of the tasks were given to senior people. I felt that we had been used by these senior comrades because I do not understand why they dumped us like this. Myself and six other guys decided to form our own organisation that will keep these senior comrades busy all the time. That is why we formed the South African Rapist Association. We rape women who need to be disciplined (those women who behave like snobs), they just do not want to talk to most people, they think they know better than most of us and when we struggle, they simply do not want to join us.*

(Vetten 1998, 3)

The stated purpose of the South African Rapist Association is to teach women a lesson and to put them in their place. But the former soldier's explanation also describes the trigger to setting up the organisation as being the anger and feeling of betrayal that he felt when he failed to receive the material rewards or status he expected as a result of participating in the armed struggle. His explanation echoes the idea that violence results from men's masculine identity being threatened – in this case by superiors in the military defence units. The demobilised soldier feels a need to reassert power over someone – in this case, women in the community.

4.3 Summary and implications for development organisations

As the second part of this book will show, development and humanitarian work can be planned and implemented in a way that incorporates an awareness of the existence of violence against women in peacetime and in war, and within different social institutions. This chapter began by looking at violence against women in four institutional contexts of family, household, community, and the State. It went on to show how social, economic, and political change and crisis can lead to an increase or intensification of violence against women in these different contexts. It argued that men – and male-dominated institutions – may use violence to restore or reinforce their power. This happens when women are considered to be challenging gender relations, or when a third party or social situation challenges men's idea of themselves as powerful. In this sense, increased violence against women is an indicator of dramatic change in society. In times of social upheaval, such as economic crisis, or following armed conflict, power relations are in a state of flux. The same crises in masculinity that contribute to increasing violence in times of rapid change can also expose the 'fault lines' of society, pointing up expressions of injustice and indicating needs for transformation (El-Bushra and Piza-Lopez 1994, 181).

It is possible for development and humanitarian policy and practice to oppose violence against women through trying to understand the political, economic, and social dynamics that underlie violence against women, and by identifying openings where the legitimacy of violence can be challenged, and support to women given. Development agencies can take measures to ensure that both emergency and post-conflict rehabilitation programmes address women's experiences of violence. They can play an important role during and after crisis, acting as facilitators in the debate between men and women on gender relations, and the meaning of peace in the family, household, community, and at state level. Gender-sensitive development workers are alert to the signs that women may be facing violence, and aware of the situations that can make women more vulnerable to violence. When working in situations of armed conflict, it is important to recognise that women experience heightened levels of violence within the home, in addition to the violence that they experience outside.

PART 2

Strategies for challenging violence
against women

5 Direct support to the survivors of violence

For 20 years, I lived with every kind of maltreatment from my husband. I did not understand why he treated me like this when if he was in a good mood he would tell me he loved me. But he used to become like an animal and the worst thing was when he came home drunk, late at night. He used to start by knocking down the door of the house shouting, then he would beat me and often throw me of the house. It didn't matter if it was raining or if I was chilled to the bone.

When I went to one of the workshops that one of my friends who worked in the Women's Centre told me about I started to realise that he had no right to treat me like that. And that I was worth something and there were laws to protect me. So I went and spoke to the lawyer and she asked me what I wanted. Then I went to the Family Court and the judge told us that we should have a reconciliation as we should think about the children. Just as we were going to sign the agreement I saw everything very clearly and realised that he was not going to change, that I did not love him, and that I was not prepared to continue living with his abuse and insults. So I told the judge and my ex-husband that I wanted a separation. Both of them became very angry. The judge reproached me for wasting his time as he had taken care of all the formalities relating to the reconciliation agreement and now he would have to change it. But I remained firm and the lawyer insisted that I was within my rights. That night I went to stay with my sister and it was the first night in 20 years that I was able to sleep the whole night without feeling afraid.

(Survivor of violence, quoted in Gonzalez-Sanchez 1998)

This woman lived with domestic violence for 20 years, and then managed to put a stop to it. What processes enabled her to attain a life free of violence? How did different kinds of organisation support her, and what can development policy and practice learn from this?

Many women decide not turn to others for help, for reasons discussed in this chapter. Instead, they develop complex strategies for coping with violence. The services of a development agency or women's group are likely to be used only after a survivor has turned to friends, relatives, traditional leaders, the police, or a health centre. This chapter draws on case study experience to consider the different possible responses that can be made by women's organisations and development agencies to individual women who survive violence.

It should be noted at the outset that, as in the rest of this book, the real-life experiences featured here come in the main from women's organisations that have pioneered service provision to women survivors of violence. Development and humanitarian workers can learn much from this rich experience. Rather than assuming that our own work should duplicate this experience, it is better to consider how these activities can be supported and extended. This may mean providing financial and other support to existing women's organisations and networks, in addition to considering the adoption of similar strategies as part of development or humanitarian interventions.

The chapter looks at each of the possible responses in relation to the contexts in which it might be considered. The scope for different responses will vary according to whether the context is one of rapid change or crisis, or one of relative stability. Context will also shape the nature of women's needs, and their ability to seek assistance.

Interventions that plan to support women survivors of violence need to address women's emotional and material needs in an integrated way. Material needs may be immediate and obvious, and may include immediate access to shelter, legal advice, and health treatment. However, throughout the process of seeking help with material needs, many women need emotional support as well. In the longer term, they may place more emphasis on activities that offer explicit emotional support. Women's other long-term needs include permanent housing, and support in ensuring an independent livelihood for themselves and any dependants. This might involve vocational training, income-generating opportunities, or the opportunity to continue education.

The forms of possible intervention are discussed below from the point of view of the user of the service, and are ordered roughly according to the chronology of the experience as lived by women.

5.1 What are the options available to women?

In instances of violence by known men (or women), such as intimate partners, family and kin, or household members, women are faced with difficult decisions on how to proceed in stopping the violence. Although immediate support and intervention by kin, friends, and neighbours often stops a single event of violence, in the longer term formal agencies may be an important contributing factor in resolving the problem (P. Sen 1998).

Women seeking help from organisations outside the family may face enormous social pressures opposing their actions. In many societies where there is a strong ideology of the family and women's role within it, women who seek professional help outside the extended family network are seen to be betraying their family and community. A woman who files a complaint with the police or who runs away from a violent man may be ostracised from the networks on which she depends.

A Cambodian study on domestic violence (Nelson and Zimmerman 1996) asked women where they sought help after an episode of abuse. The majority of women said they did not seek help, a finding that highlights the constraints on women's ability to act and a lack of any sense of community responsibility. Where women did seek help, they were most likely to seek it from a neighbour rather than a parent or relative. Neighbours were especially important when the victims were not able to contact their parents for help. Women were more likely to seek assistance from the village chief, because of his respected and widely understood role in conflict resolution, than to go to the police. Ironically, however, most women eventually decided not to go to village chiefs, perhaps because they felt that a chief would not necessarily offer them neutrality and support. In terms of the kind of support given by others, the same study found that the majority of abused women were encouraged to remain with their abusers.

5.1.1 The role of family and community structures

Relatives, friends, and neighbours are usually the first to intervene in violence within the home, and many do provide immediate and useful support to women survivors of violence. Levinson's study of domestic violence in over 90 societies has shown that, 'Immediate intervention designed to stop the beating or to prevent it from ever starting is a key first line of defence in controlling wife-beating.' (Levinson 1989, 98) Individuals and community-level institutions can potentially play a crucial role in intervening to stop violent events.

However, even when the commitment to support survivors is there, the ability of friends and relatives to do so will vary according to many factors, such as the proximity of parents and friends, and the legitimacy of offering assistance. Women who support their relatives or friends against violence may be faced with serious reprisals, including violence directed at themselves. As discussed in the previous chapter, male bias inherent in the family, the household, and the community can mitigate against women who speak out against abuse.

If responses from family and community (including neighbours, traditional leaders, and official sources of authority) are inadequate, this can increase women's sense of helplessness, lack of control, and fear. The Cambodian study cited above, which focused specifically on domestic violence, shows that women cannot always rely on the support of traditional structures. Women who report instances of domestic violence may not be believed, or may be blamed for the violence. Women are often advised by family members or community leaders to reconcile with their husbands, regardless of continuing danger to their safety. In instances of rape or abduction of unmarried girls or women, tradition may dictate that the raped or abducted woman should restore the 'honour' of herself and her family by marrying the perpetrator. In addition, community-level responses tend to aim at the outset for reconciliation. Reconciliation-based approaches tend to assume that violence is caused by conflict, and that the disputing parties have equal power. Such approaches are unlikely to be able to be sympathetic to the weaker party where there are power inequalities between the two parties, such as those between men and women (Nelson and Zimmerman 1996).

Violence against women does not necessarily arise from conflict. Perpetrators may inflict violence in order to acquire or reinforce power and control. A woman may not want to be reconciled with a violent man, particularly in cases where she receives no assurance that his behaviour is going to change for the better. It is often assumed that reconciliation is in the best interests of all, but it may actually put women, children, and other female kin at risk of further violence.

In the light of inadequate responses from family, household, and community, what are the barriers to women seeking assistance from official organisations, including the police, women's organisations, or development agencies? The tiny number of women that reported going to the police in the Cambodian study suggests either that they did not believe wife abuse was a crime, that they preferred to keep the issue within the household or community, or that they did not expect the police to take any action.

5.1.2 The role of women's organisations

If and when a woman seeks assistance from a women's organisation, she is aware of the trade-offs she has to make and the risks she is taking. She is openly acknowledging her experience of violence, and the fact that she is challenging it. Women do this in awareness that it may lead to alienation from their husbands or partners, family, and community.

A woman's decision to seek assistance has to be weighed up against the prospect of one or more of the following fears:

- fear of breaking up the family;
- fear of losing her children;
- fear of sacrificing her economic means of support and finding herself destitute without alternative livelihood options;
- fear of isolation from kin and neighbourhood networks;
- fear of the lack of accessible sanctuary;
- fear of a legal system that fails to support her and that tolerates violence against women;
- fear of a criminal justice system that does not effectively challenge violent men;
- fear of social tolerance of violent behaviour by men;
- fear of stigmatisation by society for her failure to live up to circumscribed ideals of womanhood;
- fear of losing her home and jeopardising her right to future housing.

Women may come to women's organisations of their own volition, having heard about them from a number of possible sources. Women's organisations may publicise their services on the radio or television, and on posters and leaflets placed in public places. Information may travel by word of mouth. Some organisations, in contrast, do not wait for women to seek support, but proactively engage women and keep in touch with them, in order to accelerate change in their situation. The Domestic Violence Matters Project in the UK has adopted this approach (see Chapter 8 for a description of this project) (Kelly *et al.* 1999). In some contexts, restrictions to women's mobility outside the household hinder their ability to reach organisations that might be able to help them. Where women have no money of their own and are highly visible and vulnerable to further abuse while travelling alone, their ability to flee violence is severely curtailed.

Women's organisations may offer a range of support services, addressing women's physical and emotional health, their needs for temporary and possibly long-term shelter, access to the legal system, or a means of making a living. By providing these services in a friendly, unassuming, and supportive environment, women's organisations aim to create conditions where women feel empowered to take responsibility for their own lives.

Box 5.1
Supporting victims of violence: some practical guidelines

In a document prepared for the Council of Europe, the principles that guide the practice of organisations geared to supporting women victims of violence are summarised as follows:

- Begin from a climate of belief, rather than one of scepticism.

- Ask explicitly about abuse – this gives women and girls permission, and the opportunity, to talk.

- Create a welcoming environment in which some privacy is possible.

- Do not question or judge a woman's behaviour – she may interpret this as blame.

- Reassure her that she was right to tell, that what happened was not her fault, and encourage her not to blame herself.

- Develop a policy on confidentiality and tell her what the limits – if any – are.

- Check about her current safety, and find out if there is anyone in her kin and friendship network who might be supportive, and offer sanctuary if necessary.

- Document what she has told you, in case she may need this later, and so that other staff members will be aware of the situation if they see her in the future.

- What you offer should be a combination of emotional and practical support. Women often have many practical questions and issues that they want to discuss and resolve.

- Provide her with information about her options.

- Be prepared to move at her pace – just beginning to talk can be a huge step.

- Encourage her to make contacts with community support groups.

Source: Council of Europe 1997

Chapter 1 showed how women's efforts to improve their situation or to challenge gender relations can result in intensified violence against them. Staff working for organisations that support women survivors of violence need to be very clear that their commitment to giving such support may make them, and their organisations, vulnerable to violence directed against them and their work.

Women's organisations operate in rapidly changing contexts, and are constantly challenged to adapt to the way that rapid change alters women's survival strategies. Rapid urbanisation, the breakdown of extended family systems, armed conflict, and rising tensions between traditional and formal legal systems may all create new vulnerabilities to violence against women.

For example, SINAGA, a Kenyan women's organisation, has had to change the focus of its work in order to meet the needs of increasing numbers of girls who are taken to urban areas as domestic workers. More information on its response appears later in this chapter.

The following case illustrates the many different ways in which women's organisations and individuals from the family or community can support a woman facing violence. The case comes from research by Maha Abu-Dayyeh Shamas, Director of the Women's Centre for Legal Aid and Counselling (WCLAC). It illustrates the work of WCLAC, in Israeli-occupied territories in the Gaza Strip and the West Bank.

X dated a person who promised to marry her, but declined taking responsibility when she became pregnant. Fearing violence from her family, she tried hard to abort, but doctors refused to help her. In order to protect herself and the baby, she had no alternative but to go to the police and give birth in prison. The police did not know how to handle the case, and there were no legal grounds to retain X and her baby in prison. Members of the family camped outside the prison walls with the intention of killing her and the baby.

When the case came to the attention of WCLAC, the baby was already several months old. X insisted on keeping the child although according to existing law, single mothers may not keep their children, who must instead be given to an institution. X was living in an occupied area under Palestinian authority, and to bring her to a safe place required the co-operation of the Israeli authorities. Contact was made with both the Palestinian and Israeli authorities, who co-operated in getting her out of prison and moving her. They escorted her to the border, handed her over to the Israeli police who let her through, after which she was met by a WCLAC social worker.

X is currently in a safe place earning an income, and her child remains with her. However, the lives of X and her child are still not free from danger. X is determined to take the case to court, to force the father to recognise his paternity. While staying in prison she filed a complaint against him, but her case was not considered because she could not prove his involvement in the relationship, and because she had lost any support from her father. X is still supported by her mother who secretly visited her in prison and in her new hiding place. These visits are co-ordinated by WCLAC staff. No permanent solution has yet been found as the place where X is now staying cannot accommodate her indefinitely. In addition, WCLAC has conclusive evidence that her family still want to kill her and her son because they 'bring shame and dishonour to the family'.

X's mother and sisters were also threatened with death by male members of the family. Her mother was blamed by the family and community for having failed to bring up her daughter to respect the social and moral values of society. She was physically and verbally abused by the family. X's sisters were stigmatised as immoral; such stigmatisation typically has negative impacts on women's opportunities to marry (Abu-Dayyeh 1998).

In addition to the provision of a safe space, legal support, and support to earn a livelihood, X's story also shows the important mediation role that a woman's organisation can play, negotiating where possible with different agencies and members of the family. Ensuring the safety and protection of X and her child was especially difficult because there are no shelters in the area under Palestinian authority (op. cit.). The lack of support for X was so great that she had to flee to prison for her own protection. Her allies – her mother, sisters, and WCLAC – were severely constrained in what they could do to help. Constraining factors included the legal system, patriarchal values within the family and community supporting the use of violence when women's 'honour' is breached, and women's lack of economic independence. In helping her, family members and WCLAC were putting themselves at risk.

This example illustrates that solutions to violence are often complex, and the resolution of individual cases may take a considerable time and involve many different actors. A strategy to combat violence should ideally include support by women's organisations in addition to, rather than instead of, other actors within the family, the household, and the community.

5.2 Creating a safe space

A place of safety is a vital support to women who have experienced violence. This section starts by discussing the short-term safe spaces provided in situations of stability by traditional bodies and by other organisations. It then looks at the provision of short-term safe space to women refugees. Finally, it considers provision of safe spaces for the longer term.

5.2.1 Short-term safe spaces

Traditional 'safe' spaces
There are various forms of informal shelters, the use of which can enable women to free themselves from a violent situation. These include taking refuge with family members or friends, or sheltering within a religious house or convent, an orphanage, or with a traditional leader.

As stated above, a major obstacle to women seeking help and shelter is the stigma associated with turning to 'outsiders' for help on issues related to the family. In some contexts, less stigma is attached to resorting to 'traditional' solutions, which are not seen as being at odds with the cultural context. However, by definition, if the strategies a woman adopts are non-threatening to those who are abusing her, they are equally unlikely to solve the root of the problem. At most, they may provide a respite from the immediate physical danger that a woman is fleeing. They will not challenge the context which has placed her at risk of violence, and any solutions that are offered may themselves be potentially abusive.

For example, the places where women in Pakistan can traditionally seek refuge from the threat of being killed for allegations of breaches of societal norms of honour are the homes of the tribal chief (*Sadar*) or holy man (*Pir*), or at a religious shrine. If a woman seeking refuge is unmarried, the chief should find her a husband. If she is married, he should ensure that she gets a divorce and remarries in a distant community. In some places, a woman in this situation remains an unpaid servant in the home of the *Sadar*. Another alternative, if the woman cannot be married, is for her to be auctioned at a cattle fair (Amnesty International 1999b).

Safe spaces in state institutions

In some countries, particularly in the Middle East, women are forced to seek safety from violence in prison. In the women's prison in Amman, Jordan, 40 of the 153 inmates are in 'protective custody'. Many have been in prison for years. In several cases the women were victims of rape, and were considered by their families as a source of dishonour. They are at risk of being murdered as a result of their family's attempts to redeem their honour (Borger 1997). Women in this situation may be in an even more precarious position if they decide to leave the prison than when they arrived: by choosing to enter protective custody they may have been perceived as deserting the family and exposing its private affairs to outsiders. In addition, as Chapter 4 showed, state institutions such as prisons may not be entirely safe spaces for women actors. Where prison officials are sympathetic to women, it is unlikely that they will be able to meet the wide range of women's specific needs.

Shelters run by women's organisations

For victims of violence by intimate partners, shelters provide a temporary place of safety and assistance. Women's shelters are central to assistance programmes in western industrialised countries, and increasingly in developing countries as well. Shelters are usually run by non-profit NGOs that sometimes receive financial support from governments. They protect women from violence by providing them with somewhere to stay for a limited period of time. They often combine this with legal and therapeutic/psychological counselling centres and hotlines, child-care provision, and advice for women about state benefits and employment.

Shelters and day centres not only provide a place of refuge, but also an opportunity to meet other women. This is extremely important. Shelters aim to provide women with immediate and friendly support, a space to discuss their options and make sense of what has happened, and by increasing women's access to resources to strengthen their capacity to resist future violence. POWA (People Opposing Women Abuse) in South Africa provides a shelter as one element in its strategy to support women survivors of violence. Details of its work are given in Box 5.2.

Providing immediate safety to women in need of such protection is vital. However, temporary shelters are often restricted to addressing the consequences of domestic violence, and thus do not address other forms of violence women may face. There are exceptions, however, such as shelters for trafficked and migrant women (see for example, the Laksetha Centre, discussed in Box 5.3) and rape victims.

Box 5.2
Shelter provision in South Africa

POWA (People Opposing Women Abuse) was established by a group of volunteers in 1979, in response to high levels of violence against women in South Africa. Between April 1997 and March 1998 the main office in Johannesburg reached 3262 clients by telephone, dealing with issues including rape, abuse, and sexual harassment, and reached 1054 women face-to-face. The Soweto project opened in July 1997 in a local hospital, and by March 1998 it had reached 347 clients. In October 1997, an office was opened in Sebokeng, which is made up of peri-urban, informal settlement, hostel, and township communities. Most of the organisation's clients are black and come from the poorest inner city areas.

POWA's direct support to women includes a shelter, face-to-face counselling, and a crisis telephone helpline. Legal advice and support for women in court is also a crucial part of its work, although it does not have sufficient resources to provide this service on a regular basis.

Source: People Opposing Women Abuse, Annual Report 1997-8

Box 5.3
Laksetha: centre for Sri Lankan migrant workers in Lebanon

Laksetha (in Sinhali, 'well-being') is the only centre for Sri Lankan and other migrant workers, mostly women, in Lebanon. Many of the women who come to the centre have come to Lebanon as part of an international trade in domestic workers. The trade in Sri Lankan domestic workers is maintained by several Lebanese agencies who have contacts in Sri Lanka. Often the women have to buy their contracts, accruing long-term debts that they are unable to repay. Having travelled with forged passports, they are excluded from protection by local labour laws, which makes them very vulnerable to exploitative employers. Employers may typically confiscate women workers' passports, withhold payment of their salaries, prevent them from practising their faith, demand long working hours in bad conditions, and provide poor food. In addition, migrant domestic workers frequently suffer from sexual violence and abuse at the hands of their employers. Many Sri Lankan domestic workers have fled their employers and have taken refuge at Laksetha, the only refuge in Lebanon. The organisation acts as mediator to sort out workers' legal problems while providing them with immediate medical assistance and shelter.

Source: Abou-Habib 1998

Disadvantages to shelter provision

There are potential disadvantages in providing shelters, when compared with other strategies for providing support to women. The high costs attached to creating and maintaining shelters have led some NGOs to choose, instead, to concentrate their limited resources on providing facilities for use by self-help support groups. Related to this are the objections of some women's organisations in countries where state social service provision is low. Some organisations – notably in Latin America – have questioned whether women's organisations should provide shelters for victims of domestic violence. They argue that this allows the State to ignore its responsibility to make such provision. Lugar de Mujer, a violence prevention programme in Argentina, took a political decision not to open a shelter, believing that it is the responsibility of the communities and governments themselves to take steps to end the violence (Oller 1994).

Shelters have been criticised by some for promoting dependency, and failing to address the root causes of violence. In Vietnam, the Woman's Union has rejected shelters in favour of intervening directly in abusive situations, thereby focusing attention on men's behaviour (Asian and Pacific Women's Resource Collection Network 1990).

Shelters can sometimes jeopardise women's safety still further, due to the stigma attached to women who leave their homes and seek external assistance. For example, this has been said in relation to some Islamic societies (Abu-Dayyeh 1998). Counter to such arguments, WCLAC believes that there is a need for a shelter in Palestine, where currently there are none. It believes that provision of a shelter will be critical in preventing the murder of other women like X (op. cit.).

The stigmatisation associated with seeking help from 'outsiders' has led experts to argue that alternative shelter is only feasible in cities with at least 10,000 inhabitants (Carrillo 1992), where shelters can be well disguised and secrecy maintained around their location. A woman will not go to a shelter in a place where she will be recognised and stigmatised, and where her abuser can find her. In Bangladesh, it has been suggested that a woman will always prefer the socially acceptable shelter of a friend's house to a battered woman's home run by strangers (Jahan 1988) for this reason. In the case of the Sri Lankan migrant workers in Lebanon who used the shelter provided by Laksetha, shelter-provision was an appropriate strategy because the women's families were in Sri Lanka, and not present either to support or to stigmatise the women.

Finally, why should a woman have to leave her home and family when she is the victim, not the perpetrator, of a human rights abuse? The fact that she faces stigmatisation for doing so, in addition to numerous other practical problems, means that ideally, alternative shelter should be provided for the perpetrators of violence, not their victims. The 'Men's Houses' programme in Victoria, Australia, recognises that there is a need for shelter or housing for abusers, rather than for women survivors and their children. It provides 'Men's Houses' as a community development response to violence against women in the home. Men are encouraged to move out of the home and live in a men's house while attending an attitude/behaviour change group. This allows women to stay in their home and retain their networks of support. It may also increase the likelihood that blame for the violence is shifted from the victim to the perpetrator. The success of these men's houses is attributed to the voluntary nature of participation and to the fact that the residential facility is one component of a package of services in which the men are involved (Francis 1995).

Whatever women may decide to do ultimately, the knowledge that a safe space exists, whether with relatives, friends, or at a women's centre, can serve to increase women's bargaining power within a violent relationship. The fact that a woman has an institution outside marriage to support her in the event that she decides to leave may encourage couples to negotiate acceptable terms free of violence on which to continue their relationship.

5.2.2 Short-term shelter for women in conflict: the role of refugee camps

Women caught up in the midst of an armed conflict or other emergency often look for shelter and protection in refugee or displaced people's camps. This section discusses the extent to which camps offer women protection from violence.

Earlier chapters have highlighted the link between war, other crises, and increased violence against women, including not only rape and sexual violence as a weapon of war, but also the forms of violence and abuse that are known in peacetime. Chapter 4 discussed violence against refugee women during flight, at borders, and in refugee camps. It highlighted the fact that, far from being safe spaces for women, refugee camps are sites in which violence against women can and does occur.

Conditions of insecurity together with the breakdown of social norms and networks in refugee camps increase women and girls' vulnerability to violence. One woman refugee in a camp in Uganda explained:

> *In Sudan, parents could keep control of young girls; they were often kept inside. Even before the insecurity in Ikafe, if someone played with another person's daughter, she was given to him in marriage. Now, because of hunger, anyone resorts to anything. ... Parents have no power over soldiers. How can we quarrel for goats when a man is holding a gun; we are only refugees here. Which authority could we turn to?*

(Payne 1998, 79)

For refugee women, the harm caused by sexual violence is exacerbated by other health problems, including infections of the reproductive organs, anaemia, and diarrhoea. For women who are malnourished, the consequences may be even more severe. For those who have undergone FGM, sexual violence may be fatal as a result of associated haemorrhage (Fischbach and Donnelly 1996). Data suggests that in refugee families, the loss of previously established family and societal roles, forced dependency, high levels of physical and psychological pain, impotence, and frustration may lead to significant levels of domestic violence and non-consensual sex following resettlement (Kusnir 1993).

Humanitarian protection and its limitations

Despite the wealth of evidence showing women's vulnerability to violence in situations of conflict, humanitarian responses, like humanitarian law, do not always protect women from violence.

The ways in which international humanitarian law addresses women's rights in times of armed conflict were discussed in Chapter 2. To summarise, the Geneva Conventions of 1949 and the Additional Protocols of 1977 contain provisions applying specifically to women. However, there are a number of limitations to the Conventions. For example, the Fourth Geneva Convention treats rape as an attack on women's honour rather than as a form of torture. It has also been argued that the fact that rape is mentioned specifically here, and not in other articles of the Conventions that define 'grave breaches', adds weight to the assertion that rape is not considered as a 'grave breach'. This greatly weakens the power of the Conventions with regard to sexual violence because 'grave breaches' in the laws of armed conflict are the 'infractions of the rules which impose obligations on contracting parties to enact legislation to repress such breaches and in respect of which jurisdiction is conferred on all State Parties to seek out and persecute persons who commit such offences' (Gardam 1997, 75). In addition, there are situations where rape occurs in war which are not covered by the Conventions (ibid.).

In 1998, a major development was the agreement of the ICC's Statute definition of 'crimes against humanity'[1] and 'war crimes'.[2] The definitions include rape, sexual slavery, enforced prostitution, forced pregnancy, enforced sterilisation, or any other form of sexual violence of comparable gravity.[3]

The United Nations High Commission for Refugees (UNHCR) is responsible for ensuring the protection of refugees from violence. The Executive Committee of the UN High Commission for Refugees (EXCOM) states in its Conclusion no. 73 that it 'strongly condemns persecution through sexual violence, which not only constitutes a gross violation of human rights, as well as, when committed in the context of armed conflict, a grave breach of humanitarian law, but is also a particularly serious offence to human dignity'.

EXCOM Conclusion no. 64 urges that agencies should 'integrate considerations specific to the protection of refugee women into assistance activities from their inception, including when planning refugee camps and settlements, in order to be able to deter, detect and redress instances of physical and sexual abuse as well as other protection concerns at the earliest possible moment.' Agencies should also 'identify and prosecute persons who have committed crimes against refugee women and protect the victims of such crimes from reprisals'.

EXCOM Conclusion no. 73 recommends that 'refugee victims of sexual violence and their families be provided with adequate medical and psycho-social care, including culturally appropriate counselling facilities, and generally be considered as persons of special concern to States and to UNHCR with respect to assistance and the search for durable solutions'.

Further to this, EXCOM Conclusion no. 54 'recognised that with regard to international protection, there are situations in which refugee women face particular hazards, especially threats to their physical safety and sexual exploitation'. It called for the 'reinforcement of the preventive measures initiated by the Office and concerned agencies to enhance the physical security of refugee women'. However, despite the existence of such recommendations, responses are rarely planned in such a way as to offer women protection from gender-specific forms of violence.

One reason for not addressing the protection of women from violence is what has been called 'the myth of speed' (Anderson and Woodrow 1989). Humanitarian and development agencies are compelled to respond immediately to a disaster, creating a risk that they will attempt to implement their programme through the quickest and most readily available channels rather than investigate those that may be more appropriate to the social composition of the affected population.

Identifying and responding to the needs of rape survivors in refugee or displaced populations cannot be treated in the same way as rapid diagnosis of other problems facing them, such as the need for safe drinking water, food, or shelter. The nature of violence against women dictates that sensitivity, time, and patience need to be shown by humanitarian workers attempting to tackle the problem.

Where speed of implementation is stressed at the expense of a social analysis of the needs of populations according to their gender, age, and other aspects of their identity, this can lead to a failure to protect women refugees from violence. In a recent Oxfam assessment of the protection of refugee women in Macedonian refugee camps during the Kosovo crisis, it was reported that humanitarian programmes failed both in supporting victims of sexual violence, and in protecting women from violence in the refugee camps (Williams 1999b, c). Standards fell far short of those outlined by UNHCR. The basis of planning for the needs of a refugee population was not in place. For example, the registration and documentation process did not release figures disaggregated by gender and age. There was no information on the numbers of people with particular protection needs, such as unaccompanied women and young girls; women and girls who had already suffered violent attacks and sexual violence; women heads of household; and pregnant women. As a result, the planning of the camp exacerbated rather than reduced women's vulnerability to violence. Box 5.4 gives an extract from the report on this case.

What are the reasons for such failures? Relief programme planning is often carried out by specially recruited, short-term, predominantly male, personnel who may have little understanding of complex gender-related issues (Eade and Williams 1995). Short-term, fast-turnover contract employment does not allow staff to feed their learning into the organisation. When humanitarian organisations learn from their own experience of the impact of their work on refugee women, and from the expertise of other organisations, future responses will be able to ask the right questions in new contexts, and get answers more quickly to inform their planning. Bridget Walker points out the need to ensure not only that women's needs are addressed, but also their representation in programming. 'Awareness of their needs is not enough. As in development work, women should be incorporated in the emergency work from the beginning.' (Walker 1991, 1)

Many of the problems outlined above can be overcome through staff awareness of measures outlined in UNHCR's *Policy on Refugee Women* (1990), in the *Guidelines on the Protection of Refugee Women* (UNHCR 1991), in *Sexual Violence against Refugees: Guidelines on Prevention and Response* (UNHCR 1995), and the EXCOM Conclusions on the subject (nos. 73 and 64).[4]

If humanitarian work is to respond adequately to women's need for shelter from violence, a prerequisite for this is that women and social and community workers should be routinely included in the teams that plan, implement, and assess the impact of emergency responses. Women form a minority within the teams of technical specialists involved in the planning and implementation of humanitarian work. The majority of the skills deemed necessary to emergency work are technical, and male-gendered (Regmi and Fawcett 1999, 68). In an emergency situation, biases towards employing men in these technical jobs are increased since working in a non-traditional role in an emergency is often not seen as appropriate employment for a woman. This is compounded by the fact that gender bias within educational systems may result in the proportion of the working population possessing the relevant technical training for humanitarian work, such as engineering, being predominantly male. Where women are present, they are likely to be there as social scientists or health workers, and their roles may be seen as secondary to the roles of technicians setting up water or sanitation systems, or shelter.

Box 5.4
Protecting Kosovan women from violence in Macedonia: the problems with camp design

Upon arrival I was struck by the stark gendered division of space. First, amongst the throngs of people at the bottom of the hill, clustering around the agency tents and wandering up and down the access roads, there were almost no women. If the majority of refugees in this crisis are women and girls, where were they? Secondly, in the nursery at the top of the hill, run by Oxfam and the ICRC, 90 per cent of the little children were boys. Where were the little girls? The gendered use of public and private spaces, and the gender division of roles and tasks was particularly obvious in this camp. As we walked through the camp, the women were in and around the water points, collecting water and carrying it back to the tents, washing clothes and children; and in and around the tents, attending to small children, hanging up washing, sweeping out the tents, cooking over small fires in the few spaces available between the closely-packed tents.

Source: Williams 1999b

Protection issues in the assistance programme

Safe areas: There are no specific areas for women on their own with children, or for young girls separated from their families, neither is it known how many they are. We have reports of girls alone in Stankovec 2. There have been reports of young girls taken out of the camp overnight by Macedonian officials. Twenty-four-hour patrolling was not in place. There have also been reports of men procuring women from Cegrane for prostitution.

Overcrowding: The camps are very overcrowded, with little space between tents, and little privacy. The largest tents have a capacity for 70 people – unrelated families share these tents. These are situations in which women on their own can be at risk.

Lighting: Since my visit, some lighting has been installed in the camps – but there was none around the latrines or the water points, or on the access roads and paths through the camps. These are very unsafe areas for women, and there have been reports of harassment by soldiers in the camps.

Food distribution: In Stankovec 1, food is distributed from distribution points, three times a day. My observation was that the food queues are composed predominantly of men. Experience in many refugee situations shows that food is easily diverted if not distributed directly to women, and women may have to trade sex for food if the food is not getting to them and their families.

Sanitation in both camps at the time visited was appalling, with little privacy and no protection. Bathing areas were not yet installed.

Fencing: The new camp at Cegrane is not fenced. This could have serious implications for the safety of refugee women and girls.

Source: Williams 1999c

Women also tend to be poorly represented in the committees set up in refugee camps to participate in humanitarian relief efforts, since traditional leaders tend to be male, and humanitarian staff do not always see it as their role to challenge gender power relations. As Bridget Walker, former Oxfam GB Gender and Emergencies Adviser, has noted, 'Women especially lack access to discussions about their needs and are rarely involved in the planning or policy-making. Yet the majority of those affected by emergencies, for example, refugees or displaced, are likely to be women and children. It is therefore essential to understand the gender dimension of an emergency and to find ways of working with women.' (Walker 1991, 1)

Work to protect women from violence, and to support survivors of violence, cannot be done without a commitment to medium- and long-term support. Women's groups in Croatia have criticised the response of relief workers to raped women during the Bosnian conflict, and in particular their emphasis on finding 'instant solutions'. 'The atmosphere of heavy time pressure, produced by domestic and international media, demanding *ad hoc* centres for help to raped women, is counter-productive. Raped women will feel the consequences of the crime during their lives and deserve appropriate help – not instant solutions. Developing of serious women-support projects needs understanding of the problem, patience and time. Otherwise, the good intentions could turn out to be useless or even harmful, bringing some relief only to the conscience of support-givers.' (Women's Global Network for Reproductive Rights)

Creating a safe space in refugee camps can be particularly difficult; space is often extremely limited, and most public space is dominated by men. This can be seen from the case of the Macedonian refugee camp, discussed in Box 5.4. A positive response from Oxfam GB in the Macedonian camp was to set up two café tents: one for men, and one for women. The café tents provided tea and coffee, and accommodated up to 60 people. They were located close to the nursery, so that parents could be close to their children, while finding time for themselves. They were always full. The women's tent provided a much-needed collective and safe space for women, who were otherwise more or less confined to the tents and immediate surroundings. Plans for the women's tent included developing informal, but structured, opportunities for women to discuss issues of concern to them, to establish relationships of mutual support, and to begin to address the traumatic events they had experienced. Oxfam was planning to offer direct psycho-social support, in the form of counselling, to be implemented by exiled NGOs and women's groups (Williams 1999b).

As stated in the earlier section on shelters in peacetime, shelters provide a space for women to meet each other and discuss their problems. In situations of conflict and displacement, where governments, international peacekeeping forces, and humanitarian agencies fail in practice to ensure women's safety, creating a safe, women-only space where they can always come for assistance is vital. In the Burmese refugee camps in Bangladesh, prominent men resisted the creation of a space specifically for women. By developing a health programme that reached out to women, Gonoshastya Kendra, a grassroots health organisation, was indirectly able to support women who had been abused (see Box 5.5).

In both the Macedonian and Bangladesh examples, physical space is a resource of huge social value. Women have to struggle to get their own space, to meet their emotional needs, and for the opportunity to be with other women. The examples show that even in the most adverse circumstances, it is possible to create a space where women can organise to help themselves. The Macedonian and Bangladesh experiences show that there is scope to develop actions that support women's interests, including as part of actions with only limited responsibilities, such as supplying coffee, or water and health provision. The Bangladesh case highlights men's resistance to women's efforts to meet together. It also shows how, even in adverse and transitory conditions, women are eager to organise around their own and their children's needs. Neither the Macedonia nor the Bangladesh intervention explicitly addressed questions of sexual violence experienced by the refugee women. However, they provided conditions that were as conducive as possible for the issue to be raised, should the women so wish.

Despite providing shelter and protection in the short term as emergency responses, both the interventions did this in a way that accommodated a longer-term vision, and strategies for future recovery. Despite the very poor conditions in which refugees are often forced to live, the interventions provided opportunities for communities and humanitarian workers to identify and build upon the strengths and capacities of the women, men, and children. In so doing, they contributed to the long and difficult process of rebuilding the social and institutional fabric of the displaced people within the camps. It can be seen from this that working with women in situations of flux provides opportunities to effect a longer-term positive transformation in gender relations.

Box 5.5
Creating a safe space for Burmese women refugees in Bangladesh

Around 300,000 Rohingya refugees from Arakan, a north-west province of Myanmar (Burma), took shelter in south-east Bangladesh from late 1991. In this situation, Oxfam began by funding Gonoshastya Kendra, the only local NGO working with the refugees, to provide health services particularly to women victims of assault and rape. With UNHCR support, Oxfam then instigated a water programme that initially did not have a gender component. As the Country Representative and Disaster Management Officer explained, 'It was very difficult to work in a gender-blind situation where every decision is taken and implemented by male officials living in the bachelors' dormitory far from their families, with no positive motivation to work with the distressed people.'

Oxfam made an effort to recruit female engineers and health educators. Tap stands were moved to locations where women were less likely to be threatened by security forces and water was supplied at times to suit women's work routines. Health educators arranged women's groups so women could benefit from the health education programme. This became more difficult when camp officials banned all group meetings to prevent any anti-repatriation movement. A new initiative of women's centres in the camp, known as 'health education centres', was set up. These centres were managed by refugee women and became a place of refuge for women. Health educators benefited from them as a place of contact and discussion, giving rise to new ideas about garbage disposal, women-only bathing areas, and the protection of common spaces. Refugee women proposed that the centres be used as children's health education centres in the morning while they were busy with other domestic tasks, as there were no schools.

As it became increasingly evident that the health education centres were women's centres, male refugees and officials began to feel increasingly threatened. It became commonplace for camp officials to order the closing down of the centres claiming that they were a breeding ground for conspiracy against repatriation and other anti law and order activities. Over Ramadan, a group of *Manjhi* (male community leaders) sought permission to use the centre as a praying place, converting the centre into a mosque and thereby preventing the entry of women. The Manjhi sought permission to use the centre for just one month but as one refugee woman explained, 'We will never be able to change the status of the mosque into a women's centre no matter what the agreement was.'

Source: Wahra and Goldring 1994, 6

5.2.3 Providing long-term shelter

Once the immediate short-term crisis is past, women need to ensure their future safety from violence. For women refugees, violence related to conflict may end when peace comes. However, as discussed in previous chapters, violence in conflict is not qualitatively different to that in times of political stability. All women who fear that returning to their own homes will place them at renewed risk of violence are faced with a dilemma. Should they continue living in insecurity and fear at home, or should they move away? As stated in the previous section, an abused woman should have the choice to remain in the marital home, while her abuser leaves. In practice, this rarely happens.

A study conducted by the Young Women's Christian Association (YWCA) of Zambia focused on the action taken by women who were abused by their intimate partners after they left the shelter provided by the YWCA. It revealed that on leaving the centre, around as many women return to their husbands as permanently leave. The most common decision was to stay with relatives immediately after leaving the centre, and this was often followed by a decision to return home. Just over half of those who returned to their husbands took up the opportunity to have counselling together with their husbands at the YWCA. A small number – though still a significant proportion of the shelter's users – set up their own home. This was often with help from the YWCA (YWCA 1994).

There are many reasons why a woman may decide to stay in an abusive relationship. First, a woman may have invested a lot in her relationship with her husband or partner, and she may retain emotional attachments to him and to his family. She may hope for a change in his behaviour, with or without counselling from family, friends, traditional leaders, or organisations.

Even when a woman is convinced that her marriage is over, she may feel unable to leave. Cultural constraints against divorce may have very tangible effects on a woman's options to end her relationship. For example, in Lesotho, customary law does not allow a woman to take her children with her if she leaves her husband, since they are seen as the 'children of the house' (Sweetman 1995a). Lack of property rights, discriminatory laws governing marriage and divorce, and lack of economic options for an independent livelihood may lead a woman to dismiss the idea of leaving. When no safe alternative can be ensured, leaving can be dangerous. Finishing a relationship does not necessarily mean an end to violence, and may make a woman vulnerable to new forms of abuse. Women are at particular risk once they have announced their intentions to leave, but remain within the household.

In Britain, the Housing (Homeless Persons) Act 1977 in England and Wales, and subsequent legislation in Northern Ireland, identifies domestic violence as a cause of homelessness. Some women survivors of violence (for example, those with children) are identified as 'in priority need' of re-housing (Barron *et al.* 1994, 49). However, in other countries, governments may not acknowledge the need to provide survivors of violence with alternative housing, consequently legislation is lacking.

The Collectif 95 Maghreb Egalité has noted that in Morocco, Algeria, and Tunisia, a woman fleeing domestic violence is considered in law to have abandoned her home. If a woman asks for a divorce because of her husband's violent behaviour, she is obliged to live with him until the divorce ruling is pronounced by the Court of Justice. Failing this, she will be judged to have abandoned her marital home. The organisation states, 'In cases of domestic violence, the protection of private life and the integrity of the family takes precedence over the protection needed by the victim of such a situation.' (Collectif 95 Maghreb Egalité 1998, 17) This example of the vulnerability of women before the law when fleeing violence has resonance around the world.

National laws relating to land and property ownership may discriminate against women, and play a significant part in preventing women from overcoming the suffering caused by violence inflicted against them. Until recently, women in Rwanda could not inherit land, property, houses, or cattle and were not eligible for credits and loans (Human Rights Watch 1996). Survivors whose houses were destroyed and burnt down during the genocide were not being rehoused. The Ministry of Rehabilitation and Social Integration, whose responsibility it is to house women without homes, had no funds to meet this need. Government policy dictates that individuals have to vacate houses when the rightful owners return. However, many widows have not been able to reclaim their family home. Many women have had to 'give' sex in exchange for claiming their family property, whilst others have been coerced into the role of 'concubine' for the occupier in their own home. Others who pursued their claims were raped and threatened with death (Twagiramariya and Turshen 1998).

AVEGA-Agahozo is a grassroots organisation in Rwanda, formed by the widows of the genocide, to respond to the needs of survivors. The organisation sees the lack of long-term shelter for women survivors of violence as a major factor in slowing or halting their recovery from the effects of the violence. AVEGA-Agahozo promotes women's legal rights, and contributed to the preparation of new legislation on land and property rights in Rwanda allowing women to inherit land and other property. It also provides practical support, assisting groups of women survivors who are building their own houses, but need materials. AVEGA-Agahozo provides them with windows, doors, iron sheets, and nails. It also runs a vigorous campaign to alert people to the problems of homelessness faced by many survivors. One widow, a member of AVEGA-Agahozo, explained: 'There are some of us who have the problem of lack of shelter. We had occupied houses of people who left after the war, but now the owners have come back and we have to give them their houses back. In some cases some of us are going mad because we don't have anywhere to go. Walking in the street we even meet those people who destroyed our houses.' (Oxfam internal document 1994)

5.3 Supporting women's access to law and justice

After ensuring immediate physical safety through reaching a safe space, one of the first forms of support sought by many women is advice on how the law protects them.

There are many barriers to justice for women. Chapter 1 discussed barriers raised by women's lack of knowledge of their rights, and their fear of exacerbating the aggression directed towards them. Chapter 3 pointed to the failure of police to recognise some forms of violence against women as a crime, and record it accordingly. Chapter 4 described the different levels at which the law operates to oppress rather than support women.

Many of the women's organisations that work with victims of violence recognise the problematic relationship between women and the law, and aim to make the law work *for* individual women survivors of violence, rather than against them. They do this by providing legal advice on women's rights, and assisting women in the legal processes of separation or divorce, and maintenance or custody of children. For example, Profamilia, a grassroots organisation in Colombia, offers legal information and aid to those in need of advice about family law, and help for victims of violence (Plata 1996).

Women's organisations and NGOs play an important role in explaining the legal options available to women. A well known example is the Musasa Project, a Zimbabwean NGO that was set up in 1988 to take action against violence against women.[5] In addition to providing counselling, shelter, and legal support, Musasa has also been involved in training the police. According to Sheelagh Stewart, one of the co-founders of Musasa, the organisation targeted the legal system to empower women to use it to their advantage (Stewart 1992). The Project applied a framework for thinking about the law that breaks the legal system down into three components: the substantive (the content of the law); the structural (the courts, and the enforcement and administrative agencies of the State); and the cultural (shared attitudes and behaviours towards the law). Using this framework, Musasa was able to identify the root of problems relating to domestic violence and the law as being based in entrenched attitudes and behaviours towards the law, held both by police and by women (op. cit.).

The YWCA of Zambia runs a drop-in centre that encourages every woman member of the organisation to know her legal rights. Box 5.6 outlines their suggestions for the steps that women can take to seek legal sanctions against men's violent behaviour.

Box 5.6

Tips from the YWCA of Zambia on seeking police protection in the event of domestic violence

Beaten or threatened?

- Violence in the home is a crime and you have a legal right to be protected by the police and the courts.
- In an emergency, run to the police and insist that they help you find a safe space – it is not a favour, but their duty to protect you.
- If you have been hurt, insist that the police arrest the suspect immediately – there is no need to wait for a medical report. Once the suspect is behind bars, your safety is guaranteed.

Scared of having the suspect arrested?

- You can get an injunction restraining him from harming you or a 'protection order' from the courts.
- You can request that a drop-in counsellor speaks to him, if you feel he is capable of reforming as a peaceful person.
- You can file for a divorce or separation.

Source: YWCA 1997, 10

Another strategy has been for women from local community-based organisations to train para-legal workers to work in police stations, in order to encourage women victims to report their experiences. This strategy is examined further in Box 5.7.

Access to legal systems following conflict

Following war and conflict, a country's legal and judicial institutions are often in tatters. Facilitating women's access to the legal system is a substantial, but important, challenge in these situations. The Rwandan organisation AVEGA-Agahozo works in this area. It is motivated by frustration at the inaction on the part of the authorities in bringing justice to women, and a belief in the ability of women survivors to help and support each other.

Box 5.7
Installing women as para-legals in police stations in Brazil

In the state of Pará in Amazonia, the Association of Women Workers in the Lower Amazon, a network of 25 women's organisations of the Lower Amazon valley, has been active in 14 municipalities in pressing local government to install their members as para-legal workers in local police stations, to deal specifically with cases of violence against women. The unpaid para-legal workers are well-respected, and make significant contributions to public security. As a result of appointing and training them, there was a large increase in the number of registered complaints of violence against women, especially involving the rape of girls. However, the Brazilian legal system is very slow and as a result it can take years to bring perpetrators to justice. During this time the women are often as much at risk of abuse as they were before reporting it, if not more so.[6]

Source: Sena 1998

Esperance, a member of AVEGA-Agahozo, stated, 'I feel that justice should be done, so that other people should not have similar experiences. Those who did these things should be punished for what they have done so that society can learn from the punishments these people get. It is true justice is there but it has been delayed ... to victims it seems as if nothing is being done. We see people walking around who did things to us and we don't even know if anything is going to be done to them. Most of the members of AVEGA don't have anything left, they don't have the means to fight for justice. Some of them have been thrown out of their homes, others are incapacitated, they are disabled.' (Oxfam internal document 1994) AVEGA-Agahozo provides support to women in court over issues including compensation for their dead relatives, and social security funds owed to families whose relatives or husbands died. AVEGA-Agahozo was also involved in lobbying to get sexual violence onto the agenda of the ICTR.

A network of organisations in Belgrade founded on feminist grassroots principles works towards addressing the needs of refugee women of any ethnic or national identity who have lived through rape and other sexual violence. The network is made up of organisations including Women In Black, Autonomous Women's Centre against Sexual Violence, and Group for Women Raped in War. The network helps women in centres and private homes throughout Serbia. The Autonomous Women's Centre helps by buying women clothes, helps establish contact with relatives, finances the journey back home, and pays for hotel rooms or private accommodation, should women either wish not to return home, or have nowhere to go. It also documents the treatment of women refugees.

Ensuring access for all

Ensuring access to legal support for all women who seek it has been a key challenge for organisations working with women survivors of violence. As stated earlier in this book, women's power and resources are defined not only by their sex, but by other factors, including their ethnicity, economic status, caste, class, and disability. Women's identity shapes their decision whether or not to seek help, as well as the nature and quality of the assistance they receive. For instance, black women in a predominantly white society who make public the violence inflicted against them by a man of their own racial group risk exacerbating racism directed at both men and women in their communities (Razack 1994). In a context of ethnic or religious conflict, women from one religious or ethnic community may be less likely to appeal to the law for assistance where the State represents the 'other'.

In the UK, the Refugee Women's Legal Group, established in 1996, has co-operated with Refugee Action and the Immigration Law Practitioners Association to publish a legal handbook for women asylum seekers, aimed primarily as a tool for lawyers and community legal advice workers. The handbook provides information on the legal support to which women asylum seekers in the UK are entitled, and is intended to assist women survivors of violence whose marginal status as asylum seekers makes it harder for them to appeal to the British State for assistance. In seeking asylum, women who have been subjected to rape or sexual abuse are reluctant to talk about their experiences in front of immigration officials. Without this crucial information to support their application (currently, UK law recognises sexual violence as grounds for asylum), women may be refused asylum.

Grassroots organisations in India have pressed for compensation for low-caste (*Dalit*) women who have been abused by police and landlords (see Box 5.8).

5.4 Supporting women to overcome the mental and physical impacts of violence

The physical and medical consequences of violence against women are immense. Women survivors of violence require free and easily accessible treatment for their injuries. Many women's organisations have developed medical interventions such as mobile ambulances for refugee women, the provision of free and easily accessible medical treatment in specialised centres, and the training of local health care workers.

Box 5.8
Mobilisation for legal reform to protect low-caste women in India

In a rural area in eastern Madhya Pradesh, India, the Chhattisgarh Women's Organisation (CWO) has, since 1983, been working with tribal and Dalit women who face discrimination and marginalisation from society. It has been organising against bonded labour and against rape and violence by police, landlords, and individual men in the home and community. Together with Jan Jagriti Kendra, its sister organisation, CWO has helped over 5000 bonded labourers to free themselves, has run centres where women can learn new skills and trades, and has fought for and won financial compensation to help former bonded labourers to make a fresh start. The organisations inform villagers in isolated rural areas of their rights, and have helped set up women's farming and weaving co-operatives in order that villagers will be better able to avoid bonded labour.

Source: Oxfam internal document 1996

It is necessary for medical and therapeutic responses to be co-ordinated if women are to be helped both in the short- and longer term. Most of the physical injuries sustained by women survivors of violence are linked to psychological and emotional effects, as discussed in Chapter 3. The psychological harm caused by violence against women may take much longer to heal than physical wounds. As one woman at the Bombay Women's Centre explained:

> *In fact, the body mends soon enough. Only the scars remain ....*
> *But the wounds inflicted upon the soul take much longer to heal.*
> *And each time I re-live these moments, they start bleeding all over*
> *again. The broken spirit has taken the longest to mend; the damage*
> *to the personality the most difficult to overcome.*

(Asian and Pacific Women's Resource Collection Network 1990, 176).

5.4.1 Psycho-social approaches

The momentum generated over the last decade around the issue of violence against women in the international human rights and development arenas has released more funds for work on violence against women. For example, reports that Kosovan women had been raped following the Serb violence in 1999 led to the international funding of a number of emergency psycho-social interventions. International organisations such as the UNDP, the SOROS Foundation, and Novib funded a number of programmes to counsel 'women who are suffering from post-traumatic stress disorder' (PASF, Oxfam internal document 1999). The unprecedented amount of external funding that has been made available to organisations dealing with the Kosovo crisis, and the value accorded by international organisations to western ways of understanding the effects of violence, have led to few opportunities to capture local understandings in the course of the intervention. At present, the majority of approaches to supporting individual women survivors of violence reflect western responses to trauma.

In Uganda, the Medical Foundation for the Care of the Victims of Torture has provided medical treatment and psychiatric counselling to women and girls who have suffered rape, sexual abuse, and other forms of torture in war-affected areas (PASF, Oxfam internal document 1995). In Tanzania, responding to the influx of Burundi refugees, local health services have participated in training to provide support, medical care, and counselling for women who have been sexually abused (PASF, Oxfam internal document 1993). Medica Zenica, a Bosnian organisation that was set up with the onset of the war in the former Yugoslavia, was one of the few organisations providing such treatment for women. In 1996, approximately 50 women went to Medica each day for treatment and nearly twice as many went to the mobile gynaecological clinic, 'Martha', when it went out into the field twice weekly (Medica Zenica Women's Therapy Centre 1996).

Many programmes to assist women include counselling and therapy to address the psychological consequences of violence. Medica Zenica recognises the role of therapeutic work in addressing the traumatic effects of violence.[7]

> The word 'trauma' is one of the newest words that has found a place in our daily language and communication. Some say it was 'brought' into this place by foreigners (humanitarian and others). However, truthfully, it unfortunately is here among us, and installed in us ... in this country and her people, especially civilians ... And the true word trauma... reflects all survived horrors, living wounds, which we carry ... with all the extreme experiences of hate and abuse, painful violations and powerlessness to endure ... to prevent and prepare ... Many did not know that their own trauma, like their own cross or smothered cries within themselves, does not need to be carried alone, that it is possible to share it with someone, to search for (professional) help.

(Medica Zenica Women's Therapy Centre 1997, 7)

One of the fundamental working principles of the Medica Zenica Women's Therapy Centre is that it treats each woman who walks through its doors as an individual with unique problems and experiences. The starting point of Medica Zenica's therapeutic work with women and girls is that the effects of the violence against them are as emotional as they are physical.

According to Medica Zenica, most of the women who walk into the centre are traumatised. Women recall violent experiences, and at the same time try to disassociate themselves from them, or block them out. Over time, symptoms of mental paralysis increase (Herman 1992). This response suggests that the traumatic event does not just violate women's bodily integrity, but also affects the ways in which she perceives herself in relation to her community. It destroys her sense of attachment to others, including intimate partners, friends, and family. Such a diagnosis of traumatic stress is considered useful by Medica Zenica because it links the psychological and physical effects of violence. It also allows support workers to identify the symptoms of trauma in a woman, rather than mistake them for enduring characteristics of her personality.

Medica Zenica holds that it is very important to establish a relationship between the 'helper' (trained therapist/psychologist) and the 'client' (survivor of violence), in which the 'client' knows she is trusted. At Medica Zenica, the first session is made up of three components (Medica Zenica Women's Therapy Centre 1997):

1. Validation of the experience: the helper must accept what the woman has said, without trying to immediately solve, help, or lessen the problem. The helper tries to reassure the woman that her feelings do not mean that she is weak, and that what she has survived is not insignificant, and to understand and accept that all these events have the power to hurt her psychologically.

2. Validation of her symptoms as 'normal': a woman needs to accept that hers are normal reactions to the abnormal experiences she has survived. This acceptance helps to ease her fear of her symptoms.

3. The chance to vent her emotions: the woman needs to retain contact with her pain, in order to understand and accept it.

Throughout her contact with the client, the helper is engaged in 'active' and 'empathetic' listening. The therapy is conceptualised as falling into two periods: 'crisis counselling' immediately after the rape, and delayed 'non-recent counselling' for women who have suffered violence less recently.

Critiques of psycho-social approaches

The interventions discussed above are broadly in tune with western ideas about the effects of trauma on mental and physical health and well-being, and the best ways to treat these. There is an ongoing debate among professionals in the field about the nature of human responses to extreme stress, and how to address them. This debate points not only to fundamental tensions in responses to violence against women, but to very different ideas about the extent to which human health and well-being can be considered as universal issues that do not vary in fundamental ways in different cultural contexts.

On the one hand, those who advocate a universal model, like Medica Zenica's model of 'trauma' detailed above, argue that it is possible to generalise about the effects of distress and suffering on people because essential human psychological functioning does not vary across cultures. They argue that on the basis of knowledge gained in particular contexts about trauma, it is possible to develop a blueprint for response. Others disagree. Some are highly critical of the idea that women who have been raped are seen as sufferers of a mental disorder, who need to be returned to 'normal'. In the view of Deborah Clifton, a gender specialist who has worked with Oxfam GB's Humanitarian Department, 'Whatever else it might be, the experience of rape is not a "disease", and yet Rape Trauma Syndrome clearly places efforts to understand rape in a medical and psychiatric model.' (Personal communication December 1999)

In both western and non-western societies, there are likely to be limitations to working with an approach that focuses only on individuals, from a psychological perspective. Derek Summerfield points out that since not all societies understand the relationship between individual people and society in the same way, there may be differences in the way in which people understand, and survive, a traumatic experience (Summerfield 1992).

In a critique of western responses to violence, Derek Summerfield argues that every culture has its own constructions of violent events and recipes for recovery. Interventions aimed at alleviating psychological distress may be simplistic and ignorant of local culture, and risk being experienced as insensitive or imposed. He favours a 'community-based' approach, which, it is argued, is based on the specific needs that communities themselves prioritise (Summerfield 1995). This approach emphasises the need to pay attention to the ways in which particular people understand their situation. This would suggest that the ways in which a woman and those around her think about the violence she has survived (including the ways in which they perceive women survivors themselves) will have a significant effect on the woman's recovery and adjustment.

However, this approach rings warning bells for those who are aware of the ways in which the myth of 'community' can obscure women's interests, and who doubt that communities that ostracise women who have survived violence can offer solutions that will benefit them. Community healing rituals are not a mechanism that women can necessarily rely on to act in their interests. A Nigerian witness to the Biafran war (1967-70) has recounted how married women who survived rape often could not return to their husbands. She discusses how traditional cleansing or healing rituals further stigmatised and oppressed women survivors of rape:

> *These doomed women were paraded through the community, accused of infidelity, the worst of crimes. They went through a cleansing ritual, entailing sacrificing chickens and goats to appease the gods, to seek forgiveness and reacceptance into the community. I was told that even if the woman's pleas were accepted, they were nonetheless stigmatised for the rest of their lives, and their children and children's children were stained by it.*

(Ugwu-Oju 1995, 192)

The emphasis on healing an individual survivor of violence in post-traumatic stress models may also lead funding organisations to think that the problem is the suffering of particular (unfortunate) individuals. Certainly, during the past decade, considerable funds have been made available by the international community for the therapeutic rehabilitation of victims of violence in conflict in Eastern Europe and other regions, yet there has been little recognition or discussion of the overwhelming, systematic nature of violence against women. A narrow focus on providing trauma-recovery services to individual women, and thinking of trauma as a psychiatric illness, obscures the need to change the social, cultural, and institutional values that perpetuate the acceptance of violence against women. Until this happens there can be no true healing for individuals. As discussed in Chapter 3, the individuals who perpetrate and suffer violence are both influenced by, and shape, the society in which they live. For example, a study of El Salvador has suggested that the psychological effects of the civil war on women are caused by their traumatised awareness of the fact that social relationships between individuals and groups have become 'inhuman', as well as by their individual traumatic experiences (Jenkins 1991).

Both the western approach to healing trauma which sees it as universal and individual, and the community-based alternative, share the disadvantage of ignoring the structural inequalities between women and men that enable violence against women to flourish. Psychological remedies as a response to violence against women do not strike at the social causes of the abuse, since they focus on healing individual survivors and do not begin to address structural inequalities. Community-based approaches can only be useful if, as Chapter 4 showed, they integrate an awareness that the community is not a benign institution where everyone's interests are equally served.

A final question is whether developing countries can afford the luxury of therapy or counselling, which demands large numbers of skilled mental health workers who can offer individual debriefing and counselling to trauma victims. It should be noted that in relation to work with AIDS patients and victims of torture in developing countries, it has been argued that local resources can be used creatively by integrating counselling into routine duties of nurses and social workers in hospitals, or through training with existing networks of community health workers (Schopper, van Praag, and Kalibala 1996).

In conclusion, there is a strong argument for providing psycho-social models of counselling, based on ideas about trauma and mental health; however, these should be adapted to suit local mechanisms for supporting women victims of violence. Approaches to supporting the survivors of violence need to begin from a thorough analysis of the context. It is important to build on intact, supportive, social structures, and provide therapeutic interventions when the mechanisms of support available to women in their communities have been shown to leave women's psychological needs unmet.

5.4.2 Promoting mental health through 'naming' violence

'Naming' an activity means acknowledging it. Understanding a relationship or an event as abusive is extremely important in enabling women survivors of violence to evaluate their lives and, potentially, to recognise ways to end the violence against them.[8] However, as Chapter 1 showed, there are many different understandings of violence against women. It is also sometimes extremely difficult for women to acknowledge that the harm they have suffered is violence. Liz Kelly and Jill Radford analysed reports of sexual harassment of women in the United Kingdom. While the experience was deeply frightening for the women, many of them played down the event, or dismissed it entirely. The women in the study did this largely because their experiences were dismissed by legal officials, who only recognised acts that caused physical harm (Kelly and Radford 1996).

Acknowledging violence in one's own thoughts often (although not always) leads to a desire to speak about it. Survivors do not necessarily have to talk about the violence they experienced in order to heal, but in some cases this may help. In her research in India, Purna Sen found that women wanted to speak about their experiences of violence. One woman said this made her feel 'lighter' (P. Sen 1998b, 134). Speaking out can validate women's experiences, and end their isolation. Organisations that want to support women survivors of violence can play a useful role in providing an opportunity for women to do this. According to Chantal Kayitesi, the

Director of AVEGA-Agahozo, the Rwandan self-help organisation mentioned earlier, one of the consequences of widespread sexual violence against women in Rwanda was that many people did not want to listen to women's stories. So many people had experienced abuse that all were confronting similar experiences constantly, and many wanted to try to forget, rather than talk or listen (interview with Chantal Kayitesi 1998). In this context, the role of the counsellors in listening to women who needed to share their stories was invaluable.

In the context of organised violence in Latin America, Aron (1992) describes how '*testimonio*' (the act of testifying in public) allows women to recover the pieces of their personal and social identity that have been slowly shattered by persistent repression. This can have a therapeutic effect on their mental health. Testifying does not make the violence go away, but it does contribute to sustaining women's own view of the 'truth' about what happened.

Naming can be extremely powerful, in weakening and finally destroying abusers' power (Aron *et al.* 1991). When women face up to violence against them collectively, their mutual support may be a powerful source of assistance for each individual woman. However, the fact that they name violence as a group may also result in public attention, and therefore the risk of stigmatisation or violent backlash.

In post-conflict contexts, the process of naming violence can mean defying the will of the State or community. In Guatemala, the State has waged 'a war on memory' (Zur 1996), concerning events between 1978–85. Thousands of people were killed in widespread political violence, and over 440 villages were destroyed in the government's counter-insurgency campaign, commonly known as *la Violencia*. Guatemalan army commanders were quoted as saying that killing Indian women and children was part of a deliberate strategy of counter-insurgency. Whole families had to be murdered or intimidated, if the insurgency was to be crushed (McClintock 1985). A widespread objective of such conflict is to wipe out ethnic identity and alternative views of history. As discussed in Chapters 3 and 4, this is a key reason why women are targeted for rape and forced impregnation.

The work of Tierra Viva (living earth), a grassroots organisation aiming to support the survivors of violence in Guatemala, is described in Box 5.9.

Box 5.9
Naming violence: Tierra Viva in Guatemala

Since 1988, the organisation Tierra Viva has been challenging the Guatemalan State to tell the truth about *la Violencia*, and supporting women who suffered violence during this time. During *la Violencia*, rape and other gender-specific forms of torture of women were seen as a legitimate part of the military operations of the civilian patrols, the police, and the armed forces. Tierra Viva uses a broad definition of violence: '[Violence is] everything that causes loss of value in our mental and physical integrity and affects our dignity.' (Pellecer 1998) Its response has been to 'get back our own spiritual will... and develop solidarity between women' (op. cit.).

At all levels of society, the Guatemalan State, army, and paramilitary have fabricated stories about *la Violencia* that depict the thousands of deaths as part of a positive process of national cleansing of 'impure elements'. They vilify the dead as communists. They have tried to control society through cultivating an 'historical amnesia', suppressing the stories of the dead. In turn, this suppresses the responses of human rights groups (Williams 1977, cited in Zur 1996). Negating people's personal history and identity weakens their ability to come together and organise (Zur 1996).

As Carmen Lucia Pellecer, the director of Tierra Viva explained at the Oxfam international workshop on violence against women, held in Sarajevo in 1998, 'At the beginning of Tierra Viva in 1988, Guatemala was a country with an internal conflict of 34 years, in which the violation of human rights was very systematic. It was hard to start again and break the silence, talk about what was taking place and approach the causes and effects of women's problems during the war.' (Pellecer 1998)

Tierra Viva's approach centres on the needs of women who have internalised the violence they have suffered. The organisation meets women's need to talk about their memories. The organisation's health and counselling work emphasises that women need to come to terms with their bodily experience of being violated. Carmen Lucia Pellecer notes that 'all of us died a little' (interview with Carmen Lucia Pellecer 1998).

Tierra Viva promotes spiritual and physical health, via the sharing and provision of information. Health is not defined by Tierra Viva in a narrow sense as the absence of disease, but is understood also as a sense of fulfilment or well-being. This perspective on health is consistent with the Maya[9] conceptualisation of shock as the 'loss of soul', when a Maya feels 'spiritually' ill (Wearne 1994, 9). Health has provided an appropriate entry point for women to make sense of *la Violencia*. This traditional, all-pervasive view of health as linked to the religious and supernatural has enabled some women to begin to make sense of their experiences.

Women have used naming in public arenas, as well as within women's organisations, as a strategy to help them overcome the effects of violence. They have appeared in real courts of law, and those set up to symbolise justice, with their personal testimonies of violence.

On 25 October 1996, a women's hearing organised by the South African Truth and Reconciliation Commission was held in KwaZulu Natal, South Africa, to uncover the causes, extent, and nature of gross human rights violations, to grant amnesty to the perpetrators, and to recommend reparations with respect to the victims. Ashnie Padarath, regional director of Black Sash, a women's human rights organisation in KwaZulu Natal, recounts the testimony of one of the women at the hearing. She was returning home with her two sons and fled after having been an eyewitness to the killing of their neighbours by a group of Inkatha Freedom Party supporters. On entering her home, she was surrounded by a group of men whom she identified as a group allied to the Inkatha Freedom Party. The men gang-raped and stabbed her until she was unconscious (Padarath 1998).

At the Global Tribunal on Violations of Women's Human Rights, which was organised by NGOs and took place during the Vienna United Nations Conference on Human Rights in June 1993, women from all parts of the world testified on aspects of violence. The Global Tribunal sought to highlight failure on the part of governments to recognise women as full citizens with human rights, and to afford them protection under national and international laws and procedures. The tribunal did not aim to produce a legally binding resolution, but rather to demonstrate the situation of thousands of women around the world, and to raise awareness in order that similar cases would be handled better in the future (Bunch and Reilly 1994). It challenged the silence of the international community on questions of violence against women (Shallat 1993), and transformed the experiences of individual women into the collective knowledge of all who heard them.

As stated earlier, not all women wish to speak about the violence they have experienced. Speaking about it may not help all women, or it may be too difficult or painful to do so. The act of speaking out can place women in danger. In speaking publicly about their abuse, some women may face stigma that leads to further violence. Interventions to support victims of violence should be based on what individual women themselves want. Many of the examples of support highlighted in this chapter organised in a collective setting, on the premise that women can provide support to each other. At the same time, organisations need to focus on providing alternative means of support for women who need, or wish, to seek assistance on a one-to-one basis.

187

Occupational therapy

Occupational therapy is another strategy used by organisations seeking to provide support to survivors of violence. This approach was adopted by Oxfam GB as part of its work in Bosnia (see Box 5.10). While other agencies were setting up trauma-counselling projects specifically for women victims of violence, Oxfam aimed to create a more informal space where women could talk about their experiences and problems in a less structured way (Hastie 1996). Oxfam had learnt from its previous experience in other conflict areas that – rather than providing medical treatment for trauma – the organisation could best support people who had experienced conflict and violence by creating an environment that would enable them to rebuild their communities and draw on their own coping mechanisms.

Interventions such as Bosfam are valuable in the short term if they can generate a sense of solidarity and bolster local networks. Instead of being passive recipients of aid, women can begin to generate an income. Such projects can 'help people to generate a social meaning for events, to recognise, contain, and manage grief and its social face, mourning; to stimulate and organise active means of coping and problem-solving, individual and collective, in the face of continuing adversity' (Summerfield 1995, 88). This is especially the case in refugee camps and centres for internally-displaced people, which typically confine people and control their movements, and which rarely involve them in decision making.

By making women their focus, such projects are a step towards recognising the key role of women as providers and protectors of children in camps and collective centres, as well as in the setting up of new homes when they leave the camps. These projects illustrate the importance of recognising women's capacities and creating a space where women can organise on the basis of self-help within camps. They provide some immediate relief from the distress of violence that women may have experienced, and encourage long-term recovery defined and maintained by women themselves.

5.5 Long-term strategies: creating a livelihood

Addressing women's psychological needs and their need for short-term shelter, is only part of the story when women are additionally battling against material hardship. Women need, above all, to ensure that they have a long-term future free from violence.

Income-generation

One distinct set of justifications for promoting women's participation in income-generation as a way of lessening violence against them hinges on the perception that women's increased role in income-generation changes

Box 5.10
Knitting as 'occupational therapy' among refugees in Bosnia

Bosfam, now an independent Bosnian women's organisation, originated as an Oxfam rehabilitation programme. Originally, the project was conceived when Oxfam had received funding from UNHCR that was used to distribute wool, an expensive commodity, to collective centres for displaced people. The Bosfam knitting project organised knitting corners in 57 collective centres in Tuzla.[10] The knitting corners were designed to provide 'occupational therapy' to disadvantaged and displaced women, who would receive wool, occupation, contact with other women, and an increased sense of well-being. By 1994, 3500 women were involved in over 55 different centres. In the knitting corners, women would come together around an activity traditionally carried out in their homes. They would knit for their families, but also 'earn' wool for any knitting they did for others outside the family.

Source: Kar 1999

their status within the household. A second, compelling argument for promoting women's income-generation is that, when violence against women continues, women's ability to make an independent income can enable them to leave their abusers.

The argument for using income-generation projects as a strategy for combating violence is based on a belief that if women earn money, this will lead to a shift in patterns of household decision making. In short, economic empowerment is widely believed to lead to a change in gender relations within the household, including women's raised status within the household, and particularly in their relationship with their husbands. This premise is to some extent supported by evidence (discussed in Chapters 1 and 4) of the impact of credit programmes on gender relations in Bangladesh, which suggests that when women are given access to credit, levels of domestic violence are reduced.

An independent livelihood does not in itself increase women's ability to resist individual incidents of violence. However, participation in a project with albeit purely economic aims may result in women gaining access to wider social and political resources. Such outcomes may be unplanned, but are still extremely important. They may be just as important as the credit or income that is the focus of the project, in women's struggles to end violence.

However, development interventions that focus narrowly on promoting women's financial independence will not necessarily result in a cessation of violence against women. In fact, as discussed in Chapters 1 and 4, such projects may place women at risk of increased violence. While violence against women remains a private matter, condoned by the State, and tolerated by communities, women will continue to be abused and to be discouraged from seeking help. Social, ideological, and cultural factors contribute to violence against women, and these can exist independently of the economic obstacles to women challenging violence in their lives. Because of this, income-generation, credit, and employment training initiatives described in this section tend to be combined with initiatives to enhance women's access to networks, information, counselling, and other social resources in order to address their interests and needs more holistically. For example, the Rwandan NGO AVEGA-Agahozo, uses income-generating activities as only one element of its current long-term work to support women, which includes health services, trauma counselling, social assistance, legal assistance, and assistance with the building of housing.

However, economic independence is without doubt a critical factor in enabling women to live away from abusive men. For this reason, all development projects and programmes that focus on promoting women's income-generation, access to credit, skills training, or education have the potential to support women wishing to move away from violence. This section focuses on a few case studies where this aim was explicit in the work of organisations working with women survivors of violence.

Women who have survived violence are – either by choice or necessity – often new heads of household. AVEGA-Agahozo's experience of the needs of survivors of violence in Rwanda shows that, prior to the genocide, most women looked after their children and their husbands, and undertook some occasional farming work. As widows, they have become household heads, assuming full responsibility for the management of the household. This includes securing income for survival, school fees for children, and providing health care and shelter for their families.

In the past, AVEGA-Agahozo has worked with a large number of income-generation groups, but at a time when the organisation was still relatively new and lacking in experience and human resources. When it began, it had only two full-time staff, with a membership of over 8000 women. A further 5000 women, all over the country, participated in local income-generation groups co-ordinated and advised by AVEGA-Agahozo. Many of these groups were given credit without careful consideration of the viability of their projects, consistent follow-up, or training. Although a large number of women who received credit have defaulted,[11] the majority of women have paid back their loans. AVEGA-Agahozo now plans to train some of its helpers in basic accounting and running and managing credit schemes.

Although AVEGA-Agahozo does not currently have adequate funds to provide credit to its members, it is anticipated that with the training, it will be able to contact different organisations in Rwanda that can provide its members with credit (Kayitesi, internal AVEGA-Agahozo document 1996).

While supporting women to make an income is necessary in ensuring a livelihood, it is not sufficient. Livelihoods are only sustained by women's being able to mobilise all available resources and opportunities, including those that arise from social relationships. In societies where women are seen as unequal to men, assistance in the development of women's livelihoods may involve providing women with tools to acquire the necessary skills to survive without being dependent on men. For example, at the Women's Aid Organisation in Malaysia, women who are not used to being alone in public spaces are encouraged to go out alone. They are taught bus routes and required to do their own shopping, or visits to hospitals or other institutions. A companion is provided if necessary. They are taught how to make police reports, obtain identity cards for their children, and how to transfer children from one school to another (Dairiam 1992; Kabeer 1994).

In an external evaluation of the South African organisation People Opposing Women Abuse (POWA) carried out by the Dutch Embassy, some of the recommendations focused on specific measures to support abused women's economic autonomy. The evaluation suggested that within the first month of being at the shelter, women should draw up their *Curriculum vitae* as a step towards job-seeking. It recommended that greater time be spent on assisting women's access to literacy classes, raising bursaries from training institutions, and encouraging employment agencies to find job placements for the women. It suggested the setting up of a 'sheltered employment project' run on business lines providing income-generating opportunities, work experience, and teaching vocational skills (Royal Netherlands Embassy 1995).

In Bosnia, since the start of its Medica II residential project in 1993, Medica Zenica has provided crafts classes. These have included four-month job training courses in sewing, hairstyling, furniture upholstery, knitting, weaving, and more recently, in computing and languages. Women who graduated from the courses wanted to use the skills they had learned, and a Medica Zenica workshop was launched to put their newly acquired knowledge into practice. The workshop, two rooms equipped with sewing and knitting equipment, employs a maximum of 18 women on a permanent basis. These women are often the sole breadwinners of their families (Medica Zenica Women's Therapy Centre 1999). The Medica Zenica sewing workshop provides women with a minimum income and is intended to act as the first step to their employment and financial autonomy. Until April 1996 the women from the workshop had a shop in town where they sold clothes. However, this was closed when they could not afford to pay the taxes. Productivity is dependent on the fabric available each month, for which the women are to a large extent dependent on humanitarian organisations. This, together with high monthly overheads, means that the project cannot make a profit. Each month, between 25 and 75 per cent of costs are covered. Nevertheless, the women receive a fixed sum of money for each item they produce, regardless of whether it is sold (Medica Zenica Women's Therapy Centre 1996).

Addressing women's need to maintain a livelihood in the midst of a humanitarian crisis is just as important as it is in times of relative stability or peace. Women's vulnerability to violence may be heightened, but their experiences of violence should still be addressed in tandem with their other needs. Esther Mujawayo, Project Officer for Oxfam GB in Rwanda, reiterates this point. She alludes to the need to address the links between poverty, rape, and in this case, war. 'There are such basic needs which are not met and contribute to retraumatise again, and you find yourself in a vicious circle.' (Mujawayo, Oxfam internal document 1997)

In Serbia, most of the refugees who came from Bosnia, Croatia, Slovenia, and Macedonia were women and children. Often the women were depressed, some were suicidal, alcoholic, and in many cases had experienced rape and subsequent abortions. The majority were living with friends or in private accommodation. A smaller proportion lived in collective centres, essentially refugee camps. The conditions for refugees in the collective centres, which were designed for use as military barracks or schools, were poor. They were situated in areas isolated from necessary institutions such as health care centres, hospitals, schools, and refugee organisations, and were not connected by good transportation facilities. Dormitories were overcrowded, hygiene poor, and food and medicine in short supply (Bozic, internal Oxfam document 1994).

Few women succeeded in finding a job and were constantly targets of sexual and nationalist abuse if they tried. Women were often afraid to speak fearing that their Bosnian dialect will bring more abuse. Given this situation, the obstacles to women's creating a livelihood were considerable. Some women resorted to prostitution in order to provide clothing, footwear, and better food for their children, or to improve their accommodation.

In Serbia, the organisation Women In Black ran a project, 'Let's be Creative Together', that aimed to support refugee women in income-generating self-help activities involving the making and selling of handicrafts. One sub-project was 'I Remember'. 'I Remember' had several phases – from 'occupational therapy' to a project focusing on livelihoods. First, participants produced a small cardboard booklet. On one side, she would record of her memories of life before the war, and on the other side she would attach an illustration – a photo, drawing, or sketch, of her home town. The text was then translated into English and the project promoted on postcards. The second phase was to create and publish an anthology of the writings, and print the postcards and a poster. The aim was to stimulate creative potential, encourage independence, develop skills, and foster a sense of belonging. A further phase of the project encouraged women to create their alternative history through writing about their experiences and memories. Women showed a great interest in this project, confirming their need to speak out and have their stories documented (Bozic, internal Oxfam document 1994).

Supporting women's education and training

Supporting women's education and training is a key part of promoting livelihoods strategies. Education can contribute to women's and girls' confidence and self-worth, and make their bargaining position within the family and household stronger. The focus here is not on the many development interventions that seek to promote girls' education and training for women without a particular focus on violence against women, but on some projects which start from a specific commitment to education and training for women survivors of violence.

In an Indian study, literacy and numeracy were found to contribute to a bundle of life skills that women could use in their quest for support, were they to experience domestic violence (P. Sen 1997a). Education can also raise women's awareness of oppression, and increase their ability to question norms of male violence. In the study, women who had been educated were able to access written publicity materials from women's and legal aid organisations, and to read media coverage of relevant issues. Paradoxically, Sen found this could sometimes place women at increased risk of violence from men seeking to reassert their dominance over them, as well as increasing women's ability to resist violence. Overall, however, her study found that education beyond the elementary level was positively correlated with deceasing physical violence (op. cit.).

The SINAGA Women and Child Labour Centre in Nairobi is an NGO that responds to the problems faced by child domestic workers. At the Oxfam international workshop on violence against women, held in Sarajevo in 1998, Mary Mzungu from the SINAGA Centre presented a paper on the educational support that the centre provides to girl domestic workers.

The Centre provides girls with the basic schooling that they are missing, during set periods in the day that are negotiated with the girls' employees. The centre also provides opportunities for the girls to socialise with peers, and to receive counselling in cases of abuse (Mzungu 1998).

SINAGA started as an organisation offering legal advice to women and girls suffering battering, violence, and general neglect. It changed its focus towards girls in domestic service on the basis of a study that found that, typically, girl domestic workers were not paid and received no free time. Because of their young age, they were very unlikely to know their rights and were especially vulnerable to abuse. Girl domestic workers were not perceived as a disadvantaged group because their labour was viewed as part of socialisation – providing them with the training needed to take family responsibilities in the future (SINAGA Women and Child Labour Resource Centre 1997). The organisation realised that there was a large population of girls out of school, because their families could not afford school fees or because they preferred to educate boys. 'We found that very large numbers of girls were working in people's houses or on the street, hawking and fending for themselves or supplementing the family income.' (Jane Origolo, the Director of SINAGA, Clayton 1998)

Prolonged periods of conflict can also lead to girls being deprived of education. At Medica II, one of the Medica Zenica housing facilities, young women receive support while they complete their secondary education. Many of the women were unable to attend school during the war, and are now able to re-enrol (Medica Zenica Women's Therapy Centre 1996).

These interventions provide opportunities for girls who have experienced – or are vulnerable to – violence, to continue their education. Education is valuable because it provides girls with resources that increase their ability to challenge violence. The examples described here do this in a social setting that provides opportunities for interaction with peers.

5.6 The right to individual petition under the Women's Convention

The Optional Protocol to the Women's Convention entered into force in December 2000. The Optional Protocol allows the CEDAW Committee[12] to receive and consider complaints of violations of the rights enshrined in the Women's Convention submitted by or on behalf of individuals or groups under the jurisdiction of a State Party.

In welcoming the entry into force of this instrument, Mary Robinson, the UN High Commissioner, stated:

> *It will act as an incentive for Governments to take a fresh look at the means of redress that are currently available to women at the domestic level. This is perhaps the most important contribution of the Optional Protocol. It is action at the national level which will create the environment in which women and girls are able to enjoy all their human rights fully and where their grievances will be addressed with the efficiency and speed they deserve.*[13]

NGOs are now able to use international law to support individual women who have faced violence and whose needs have not been met by the State. Women who have exhausted their options in national law, or who have found that 'the application of such remedies is unreasonably prolonged or unlikely to bring effective relief' (Article 4, Optional Protocol to the Convention on the Elimination of All Forms of Discrimination against Women), are able to seek redress at the international level for violations of their internationally recognised rights.

The Optional Protocol to the Women's Convention empowers the CEDAW Committee to receive individual complaints by women against their governments, where their governments fail to protect them from violence. The NGOs that were lobbying for the adoption of the Protocol fought to ensure that the Optional Protocol would enable NGOs and associations to use it. Article 2 of the Protocol allows them to do this, stating: 'Where a communication is submitted on behalf of individuals or groups of individuals, this shall be with their consent unless the author can justify acting on their behalf without such consent.' This means that NGOs have been granted the right to petition, and are now able to file a complaint with the CEDAW Committee on behalf of a victim.

In addition, the CEDAW Committee can undertake enquiries when it 'receives reliable information indicating grave or systematic violations by a State Party of rights set forth in the Convention' (Article 8). NGOs will be able to submit information alleging violations of this nature (personal communication 1999).

It is now up to international NGOs and civil society at large to promote understanding of how to use the Optional Protocol to protect women's rights.

5.7 Planning support interventions for women survivors of violence

This chapter has discussed some of the many different actions that development and humanitarian policy-makers and practitioners can take to support women victims of violence. However, as with all development and humanitarian responses, the effectiveness of support is directly linked to the degree to which women survivors of violence have themselves been involved in the planning process. An intervention that is helpful to women is one that provides conditions that allow them to empower themselves and challenge the violence in their lives.

Women activists working in refugee camps in Croatia have suggested some basic principles for support:

- Support has to be given by women, because only women can understand a raped woman's feelings of crisis.

- NGOs must be careful to avoid possible misuse of raped women for political aims.

- Support should be given to women's NGOs on the basis of detailed project proposals and clear selection criteria.

- A network of centres should be decentralised and run by women only.

- Exchanges of experience between women working with rape victims in different countries, as well as direct support, are necessary to build a network of volunteers and institutions as quickly as possible. Help should be planned and organised on a long-term basis.

(Women's Global Network for Reproductive Rights 1993, 30-1)

We can identify three key elements of development planning as follows:

1. Identification of the potential barriers to support

   In what aspects of their lives are women most vulnerable? What aspects of the wider environment, such as law, public opinion, or social norms further inhibit women? What aspects of their own situation inhibit women? Do they experience low self-esteem, lack of education, illiteracy, economic dependence, absence of kin in close proximity, or absence of social networks?

2. Identification of the available support

   Where can women find support? What kind of support is available? Does this provide long- or short-term solutions for women? Does it give women realistic protection?

3. Identification of factors that increase women's power

What kinds of intervention will increase women's self-confidence and at the same time ensure that they do not lead to an increase in the violence committed against them? What kinds of intervention encourage women to recognise the oppression that they have internalised, and yet at the same time do not impose their own agenda?

For the most part, the organisations discussed here work directly with women victims of violence. However, initiatives working to combat violence against women may also include legal actions, individual and group protests against violence, self-help initiatives, education, and health or micro-credit programmes that increase women's control over resources. Women can also be supported though development projects that do not focus specifically on violence against women but which are informed by a gender perspective and designed with an awareness of violence against women.

Adapting 'blueprint' approaches to specific contexts

Where women are involved in planning interventions that are intended to assist them, the dangers of 'blueprint' approaches to violence against women can be avoided.

For an individual woman or a group acting to eliminate violence, the shape and character of their strategy emerges out of a specific cultural, ethnic, historical, and political context. Women themselves are best placed to shape interventions that address their concerns as they see them. This is not to contradict the sense, promoted by this chapter, that there are some common elements which are useful in interventions that seek to support individual women survivors of violence. Where women are involved in the design of interventions, the virtues of models developed elsewhere can be identified and these elements retained, while other elements which are not applicable can be recognised and avoided. In this way, preconceived ideas on the part of project workers about how to 'treat' women victims of violence can be challenged, resulting in flexible programmes that are very different from the ones envisaged by development organisations. For example, the Bosfam project in Bosnia was largely planned by women themselves, and resulted in a very different type of intervention from that visualised by some within Oxfam GB (Kar 1999).

The need for modesty and responsibility

Development policy-makers and practitioners should retain a sense of modesty about what they think their organisations can do to support individual survivors of violence. Development and humanitarian interventions are always limited in terms of the scope of what they offer, and the number of women they can support. They are one element in a much larger picture of social institutions, and economic, social, and political change. The fact that violence against women is an issue which affects women on a personal level, that it is often a taboo subject, and that women's close relationships are all shaped by it, means that women are less likely to turn to outside organisations for support to combat violence than they are to participate in 'conventional' development interventions. Development and humanitarian responses also need to be designed in awareness that if handled clumsily, they may hinder more than they help.

Understanding the links between short-term and long-term support

The experience of violence decreases women's motivation and self-confidence. Interventions to support women may focus on short-term and long-term strategies, but these are not very useful distinctions to the extent that short-term protection from violence and the long-term work of strengthening women's self-esteem and helping to build their resources are intimately related. For example, we have seen in this chapter that short-term provision of a 'safe space' may lead to opportunities for women to begin to develop their personal and social resources to challenge violence. This process resembles the development of 'empowerment within', described in Chapter 1, in which women's 'experiential recognition and analysis' of their subordinate position as women or girls is a critical part of the process (Kabeer 1994, 229)

Working to strengthen existing community sanctions on violence

As highlighted earlier in this chapter, a gender perspective leads us to question the kind of support provided by traditional structures made up of family, kin, and neighbours. Family- and community-based protection and support are often flawed or inadequate, since, tacitly or overtly, violence against women is a part of the way in which male-dominated social structures maintain and renew themselves. Women's suffering may thus be exacerbated rather than ended through these forms of support.

Community sanctions against violence can be important, however. For example, in its report on responding to sexual violence in Tanzania, UNHCR noted the importance of supporting local sanctions against the perpetrators of violence. Both Congolese and Burundian communities have their own methods for dealing with a rapist – often ostracising him from the community, not allowing him to drink beer in the bar or trade in the market, and sometimes not allowing him to marry. These activities to deter crime should be supported in a refugee community as anywhere else (UNHCR 1998), when they are accompanied by information or alternative strategies to re-educate men in non-violent behaviour.

In conclusion, an effective response to violence should be based on an approach that is planned according to women's prioritised needs. In particular, having a supportive social network can help victims resist violence. Through participating in networks or groups that are sensitive to their needs, women have access to support from others, and become aware of alternatives to their oppressive situation. Effective responses address women's material and psychological needs in a holistic way by building on existing support mechanisms, as well as introducing new ones where necessary. Informal networks and women's organisations are a form of 'social capital'[14] for women, and a key factor in enabling women to end violence in their lives. Other resources that can increase women's bargaining power include, but are not restricted to, controlling economic assets such as income or property. In addition, education and literacy increase women's ability to find support and to claim their legal rights.

5.8 Summary and implications for development organisations

There is no set path that a survivor of violence will follow as she seeks support. The kinds of help she seeks out will depend on her personal circumstances, and the relationships in which she is involved.

The chapter charted the different short-term and long-term support needs of women who have experienced violence. It discussed women's immediate need for a refuge from violence, looking critically at traditional 'safe spaces' offered by the community and family, and assessing the effectiveness of purpose-built 'shelters' that have been developed in western contexts and which are now increasingly forming a part of the strategies of feminist organisations in developing countries. The chapter then moved on to consider the needs of survivors for legal redress and protection. Depending on the nature of the violence and the identity of the perpetrator, and the degree to which a woman can depend on civil law in a particular context, she may want to seek out information on her rights. The final element in short-term support is the provision of health care. The section on health care focused in particular on the debate about the usefulness of western understandings of mental and physical health, which have led to post-traumatic stress models of the effects of violence becoming popular among international development and humanitarian donor agencies. Finally, the chapter turned to look relatively briefly at possible strategies for long-term support to women survivors of violence. It emphasised that preventing future violence is made easier if women have livelihood strategies grounded firmly in financial, educational, and social resources. For many women, their ability to resist and recover from violence is linked with the struggle to maintain a livelihood. The chapter discussed the various income generation, training, and education projects offered by organisations with a specific commitment to countering violence against women and supporting survivors. It also flagged up the scope for supporting individual women survivors offered by the Optional Protocol to the Women's Convention. Using this, individual women can potentially benefit from the protection of international law, when their own governments fail to protect them. Finally, the chapter discussed aspects of planning support interventions for women survivors of violence, and the best ways to involve women themselves in this.

6 Challenges to violent men

From 1979 to 1993, there was a lot of violence in the family, almost every
night and every day. Men had just emerged from the forest from the Pol
Pot regime, and there were so many pressures. Men tried to forget and
become happy by seeing prostitutes and drinking wine. They forgot their
origins. … Men then came back home and made problems with their
wives and hit them.

(A village chief speaking to PADV Cambodia, in Zimmerman 1994)

The previous chapter discussed some of the ways in which women's
organisations, and development and humanitarian agencies, can support
women in their efforts to resist, survive, and overcome violence. This
chapter turns the focus on to the male perpetrators of that violence. If
women are to live lives free from violence, men must change too. Where
women continue to be the victims of violent conflict due to men's desire to
hold onto power in the household, the community, or the State, they
cannot be said to be fully 'empowered', regardless of whether they attain any
other development goal – for example, financial independence. Directly
challenging the behaviour of violent men, and ensuring that boys and men
are encouraged to reject violence, can be a powerful means of ensuring
women's safety. The interventions to challenge men that are discussed in
this chapter are linked to the interventions to support women described in
the last chapter. Actions to support women and actions to challenge men
exist in tandem and may in practice be difficult to distinguish.

Previous chapters in this book have argued that to understand men's
violence towards women, their individual motivations must be considered
together with surrounding societal pressures. Seen in isolation, neither
provides sufficient explanation of violence against women. Both must be
taken together if we are to form an idea of why, in a particular context,
particular men are violent to women. Chapter 1 argued that while violence
against women is a strategy used by individual men to control women's
bodies and minds, this apparently individual action is justified by social

mores that fail to condemn violence against women unequivocally. This failure is due to the fact that, far from indicating a breakdown in the fabric of society, such violence may be an important tool in ensuring the perpetuation of a society that is based on a vision of inequality between women and men. Chapter 4 built on this analysis to argue that violence against women often increases when societies come under strain. When rapid social, economic, or political change occurs, a rise in the incidence of violence against women may signify a challenge to existing gender relations. Violence is an attempt on the part of individual men to shore up their sense of identity in a context in which a gap becomes apparent between the reality of men's lives, and predominant stereotypes of masculine power, success, and control.

This chapter begins by asking why it is necessary to work with the perpetrators of violence against women. Until recently, men have not taken it upon themselves to question their own, or other men's, violent behaviour to women. Gender and development policy and practice have not focused on working directly with men either. Examples of men's work with men are explored, in the context of a discussion as to why supporting such work is a very recent development in the gender strategies of development and humanitarian organisations. Learning from, and collaborating with, women's organisations is relatively novel to many. Now, extending their partnerships to men's organisations that work from a feminist perspective presents a new challenge in a holistic strategy to eradicate violence against women.

The chapter then focuses on the ways in which women engage with violent men to change their behaviour, as individuals, and supported by women's and development organisations. Many strategies used by women, both individually and collectively, result in effective sanctions against violent men.

Next, we examine how various development and humanitarian organisations, as well as women's organisations, have worked to end violence against women by challenging men's behaviour directly, rather than waiting for this behaviour to be challenged by changes in gender relations brought about by women, feminist men, or by wider social, economic, or political change. We examine four different models for addressing violent male behaviour: traditional healing and reconciliation mechanisms, developed in Mozambique; psycho-social therapy, a technique used with demobilised child soldiers; individual treatment programmes; and education to transform 'cultures of violence', pioneered in South Africa.

Throughout the chapter, development and humanitarian contexts are discussed. Some of the issues and cases are most relevant for policy-makers and practitioners involved in situations of conflict, while others have most resonance for those working in contexts of relative peace and stability. That said, most are relevant for both.

6.1 Why work with male perpetrators?

Why is it necessary to work with men to end male violence against women? The answer to this question may seem so self-evident that some readers may wonder why it is posed in this book. However, it needs to be asked because of the way in which the fields of women in development (WID) and gender and development (GAD) have evolved. Since International Women's Year in 1975, the focus of both WID and GAD policy and programming has been on ensuring that women receive a fair share of the resources and benefits of development. Despite the shift in GAD programmes to problematising the unequal power relations between women and men, most development agencies have retained a focus on working with women (Chant and Gutmann 2000). The term 'gender' is often used interchangeably with 'women'. As argued in Chapter 1, this continuing focus on women rather than on working with both women and men to effect changes in power relations between the two not only results in development work which is doomed to failure – or limited success at best – but also places women at risk of male violence where they are perceived as threatening gender relations as a result of participation in development projects.

A clear reason to focus on men who abuse women is that most forms of violence against women will not end until men change. Women cannot actively avoid every form of violence. Poverty and lack of opportunities for economic independence are key reasons why women stay with abusive men. As discussed in Chapter 5, there are several reasons for promoting women's participation in income-generation as a means of reducing violence against women. It is clear that an independent livelihood is a necessary – although insufficient – requirement for a woman who wishes to leave an abusive family situation. It is also clear that the first strategy in combating violence should be to enable women to have the freedom to choose to leave. However, as one Oxfam worker states, 'I have sometimes wondered why gender and development interventions seem to aim to render women not only economically able to cut men out of their lives (which is good news), but to offer them no other alternative. Social policy is needed which respects the need – and wish – of most women to live alongside men in their private lives as well as outside the house, free of the fear of violence.' (Sweetman 1998, 7)

Most women in developing countries (as well as many in post-industrialised countries) have reasons for preferring to find a way of ending domestic violence without leaving their husband or partner. Many of these reasons are not related to poverty, and therefore cannot be met by organisations offering income-generating projects, credit provision, or training. Some of these non-economic reasons for wanting to stay were listed in Chapter 5's discussion of barriers to women seeking assistance. A woman may have to leave her children behind if she leaves, unless she defies powerful norms of custom and tradition. Her social status in the community may be determined by her position in the family. If she leaves a relationship, she may have to sacrifice important social networks and sources of psychological support, as well as an important part of her sense of belonging and cultural identity. Leaving may lead to her losing her identity and position in society. For these reasons, it is important to look at strategies that allow women to stay in relationships and to terminate the violence.

Why have mainstream development and humanitarian organisations not tended to work with men to alter their behaviour, in line with their critique of unequal power relations? Reasons for resisting working with men are complex. Women activists, and gender and development policy-makers and planners, have fought hard to gain slender resources for their work. Since their goal is to transform the daily lives and status of women, many are – understandably – reluctant to risk diluting the political power of their focus on women, not to mention risking losing resources to men who already have far greater access to them. The starting point for focusing on men's need to change involves showing how men, like women, are constrained by gender stereotypes. However, pointing this out poses a real risk that we lose awareness of the inequalities between women and men worldwide. If we forget this, we risk 'undermining any project for change in gender relations, and so reinforcing existing limitations faced by men and women' (White 1997, 18). Men's position in the structural relations of society means that they have a lot to gain from gender relations as they stand.

A second barrier to working with men to challenge stereotypes of masculinity and male behaviour is that development agencies have traditionally tended to prefer to focus on working with those who are subordinated by unequal power, rather than the powerful: people living in poverty, rather than those who are well-off; people living in developing countries, rather than those who benefit from exploiting those countries. As one worker in Oxfam pointed out at a meeting in 1996, 'would we work with the landlords on the issue of landlessness?'

In their work with disempowered groups, development organisations tend to focus on understandings of power as infinite – as 'power to' and 'power with' – and not to conceptualise it as a limited commodity, access to which is contested. As a result, they are not well-equipped to support women to deal with the potential threat that women's empowerment presents to men, whose conception of power may differ dramatically. Research into men's ideas of their masculinity and the nature of their power in rural areas of Bangladesh, for example, has indicated that men do not feel confident that power is infinite. Rather, their status as leaders within the household and community is constantly under threat, and needs to be continually reasserted. It rests primarily on their control over women in their family and household being seen and acknowledged by the community, including – critically – by other men (White 1997). It seems that men's own 'power to' command respect at community level is determined by the extent to which they have 'power over' women and children in the household. In the context of widespread conflict, it is clear that male identity is also constructed and reconstructed continuously. Many men and boys would prefer to reject violence, but conform under enormous societal pressure and leadership or coercion from men more powerful than themselves.

In addition, as we have seen earlier in this book, reluctance on the part of development policy-makers and practitioners to take on the difficult work of supporting women in intra-marital and intra-household conflict has often been justified by the idea that interpersonal relationships within the household are a private or personal issue, in which organisations should not play a role. Even when this idea is rejected, from a pragmatic perspective, it is much more difficult to work on changing gender relations within households, supporting women's empowerment in their intimate relationships, than it is to work at a community level on supporting the empowerment of women as individuals and as a group.

6.2 Direct challenges to violent men

This section looks at some of the strategies used by women – either individually or collectively – to cope with, and challenge, violence in the household and family. The notion of 'coping' denotes women's strategies to manage or control violence inflicted against them. These strategies are likely to involve various expressions of disapproval of the violence, but not outward condemnation. The term 'resistance' signifies overt challenges to male violence, which often take place within the context of a group (P. Sen 1997a).

6.2.1 Individual women's strategies

Women may use a range of individual strategies to challenge men's violent behaviour. These vary immensely, and can include:

- Avoidance: leaving the abuser and returning to one's natal kin;

- Self-protection: inviting relatives to come and stay; complaining to the abuser's relations or employer; concentrating on household tasks that can be performed outside or near the door to enable running away;

- Shaming: for example, publicly denouncing the abuser, or flaunting a relationship with a lover;

- Retaliation: with violence; drugging or poisoning the abuser; withholding consent to sexual relations; carrying out domestic tasks to a lower standard; invoking supernatural revenge.

Challenges to violence against women are much more likely to have a lasting effect when community members intervene and condemn the violence. This vastly increases the social cost to men of violent behaviour. Men's sense of masculinity often depends 'on the estimation of others', and 'is highly vulnerable to attack by ridicule, shaming, subordination, or "dishonourable" female action' (White 1997, 17). Among the Garífuna, an Afro-Amerindian community in Belize, when a man begins to hit his wife, a female neighbour or kinswoman alerts other kinswomen and neighbours. Often, women's presence as witnesses to the act is enough to shame the man and stop the violence. In particularly severe cases, the community will provide an alternative place of safety for the woman until the conflict is resolved or she can find another place to live permanently (Kerns 1992, 132).

Of course, such shaming is only effective in situations where there is general public disapproval of violent behaviour towards women, or of particular forms of violence. Community strategies to challenge violence depend on strong social bonding between affected individuals and others in the community. They imply an attachment or commitment on the part of the violent individual to the local community, and a willingness to be held accountable to those around him. In contexts where violence against women is not strongly sanctioned by the community, women may not be able to count on others – women or men – to support them.

Informal collective strategies can include gossip about the abuser, open expressions of disdain by his neighbours, retaliation by nearby family and kin (Brown 1992, 14), and threats of retribution from the spirits of the victim's ancestors (as among the Wape of Papua New Guinea – see Mitchell 1992). In Chapter 3, we saw how accusations of witchcraft can instigate violence against older women. In some situations, older women can subvert these ideas to protect themselves from violence. On Ujelang Atoll, part of the Marshall Islands in the Pacific, young male warriors are seen as perpetrators of physical violence, while older women are believed to be capable of perpetrating supernatural violence. This is considered more threatening than physical violence because it is often lethal. Young men's physical violence is quickly contained by family members (Carucci 1992, 112). The male aggressor's 'special mother' (his father's younger sister) pleads with him, and is understood to have the power to summon his spirit, reunite it with his body, and thereby stabilise the situation. In this society, women's magic 'violence' has the power to reimpose moral order within social relationships and to bring violent situations under control (op. cit., 120).

Formal methods of collective action include various methods of public shaming and ostracism from places of worship. Sometimes, women will use traditional forms of protest to challenge violence in a very public manner. For example, in Kenya, as in many other places, it is taboo for an elderly woman or mother to expose her body. In March 1995, the General Services Unit, a Kenyan paramilitary force, attacked a camp where women had been holding a hunger strike to campaign for the release of some political prisoners. In response to the violence, some of the women stripped naked (Amnesty International 1995b, 5). The women's actions were considered to constitute a curse on the officials who had attacked the camp.

On the coast of West Africa, women's solidarity groups based on kinship, residential, market, or ritual associations respond collectively to shame men who have assaulted women. A woman who has experienced violence ululates (screams in a distinctive and ritualised way). When they hear a cry, the women of her solidarity group come to her. They listen to her complaint and if they agree that she has been assaulted, they consider the offence to be a collective assault against the solidarity group. The women of the group then dress in vines, smear themselves in mud, and approach the abuser. They sing obscene songs, cover the abuser with excrement, humiliate him, and demand that he admits his guilt and pays a fine to the women's group (March and Taqqu 1986, 83, cited in Richters 1994). In her discussion of women's collective strategies against violence, Richters points out that these tactics have been described by women themselves as 'making war on a man' or 'sitting on a man' (Richters 1994).

Similar strategies have been successful in urban neighbourhoods. In Mira de Flores, a shanty town in Lima, women have organised themselves into a neighbourhood watch committee. They wear whistles with which to summon other women if they should be attacked (Heise *et al.* 1989). In some neighbourhoods in big cities in Argentina, women organised in local groups surround a house where a woman is suffering violence, and begin to shout and call for the police (Chiarotti 1998).

A range of strategies for consideration by communities who wish to end men's violence against women is suggested in the Stepping Stones material in Box 6.1. The aim is to encourage participants to think of different ways in which members of the community could be activated to support a woman who is facing violence. Stepping Stones is a training method developed by the UK-based international development agency Action Aid. It sets out a participatory approach to working with communities on issues of HIV, gender, communication, and relationship skills. This material is taken from a new module of the Stepping Stones project, which was developed in South Africa, and focuses on gender violence. Over 1500 organisations in 103 countries now use Stepping Stones. A survey of users carried out in 1997 noted findings of interest to the current discussion – namely, that users often reported a decline in domestic violence and alcohol consumption, and improved negotiation between girls and boys over condom use.

Are strategies such as those outlined in Box 6.1 realistic, or do they form an impracticable wish list? They include several that depend on men to intervene, and others that demand that men allow women to intervene – for example, beating pots to publicise violence occurring in a neighbour's house. If these strategies are to work, they depend on men as a group refusing to support individual male abusers. Is it really the case that men will police individual men? And if so, why? Is it simply that – as highlighted earlier in this chapter – men's sense of masculinity is easily undermined by loss of face in the community, and that certain kinds of abuse of women, in certain communities, are not openly condoned (even while they remain tacitly acceptable)? In situations where there are strong ideologies about the private nature of violence against women within the household and family, intervention will be more difficult.

Another important factor in the success or failure of mobilising communities to take action against abusers is the presence of women (and men) who are supportive of the survivor of violence. Such support is most likely to come from relatives and long-standing friends and neighbours. These relationships can be seen as a very important resource to women facing violence. For women who live far from their natal kin, or who have moved away from long-standing friends and neighbours, support may not be so readily available.

Making allies of local religious leaders, local judicial authorities, community elders, and influential local residents may be crucial in severe cases of violence.

Box 6.1
The Stepping Stones module on gender violence[1]

Participants are asked to act out a role-play. This will start with a man hitting a woman. The group agrees where this is taking place, at what time of day, and positions neighbours and other family members. When the woman is hit, what does she do? What do the neighbours and family members do? The group considers what the woman, neighbours, and family members could do to help the woman. Can they get the actors to act this out?

Recommendations that arise from this exercise can include the following:

- When neighbours hear that a woman is being beaten they could pick up some wood and start beating a cooking pot. When others hear this they could do so as well until the beatings stop. In this way the man will know that the community knows that he is beating his wife.

- A child could summon some older men who could come and beat at the door to break up the violence. The older men could take the man away to the headman's home for the night.

- The neighbours could try to take the woman and children to their home for the night to protect them.

- The neighbours could call the police.

- The situation could be that men are drinking together when a man arrives and says that he has just raped a woman. The other men might take him to the police or headman. They could also ostracise him thereafter.

- Usually, men who abuse or even kill women try to find other lovers and are successful. Women could refuse to go with a man who is known to beat women.

Some communities have developed their own legal systems, intended to protect victims. In Cajamarca in central Peru, the *Rondas Campesinas* (peasant patrols) have developed their own system of justice that considers the possibility of applying public sanctions in cases of robbery and abuse. This system is recognised by the state constitution. The punitive measures against the aggressors that are exercised by the Rondas Campesinas include loss of liberty, public exhibition in the central square of the village, public humiliation, and physical punishment (Chiarotti 1998). In Northern Ireland, women have begun to name men who have systematically abused women and children. In some cases, they have approached the perpetrators to issue them with unofficial 'exclusion' orders. These have time limits attached stating when men should leave the area and when they may return (McWilliams 1998).

Women workers can use industrial strikes as a strategy to combat violence. For example, in Morocco, the women workers of a private transport company in Sale went on strike to protest against their boss, who had raped one of their co-workers. The victim denounced him, and was backed by the subsequent testimonies of other women who had been sexually harassed by the same man in the workplace. The women organised a sit-in at the company's site. The *Confederation Democratique du Travail*, a Moroccan NGO, supported their action by making their boss declare all his workers to the social security authorities, and made him recognise their rights as stipulated in existing legal texts (Collectif 95 Maghreb Egalité 1998).

6.3 Ending violence through fostering women's empowerment

This section asks how individual women can be supported by organisations to end violence in close relationships without ending the relationships themselves. It examines the experience of women's organisations and of development and humanitarian agencies in supporting these efforts. Appropriate interventions and services can enable women to develop their self-confidence and sense of their rights in their personal relationships, to control resources, to hold opinions, and ultimately to bring about change in their most intimate relationships with men.

Experiences of women's organisations such as CMV, outlined in Box 6.2, show how their work can support the creation of more equitable relations between men and women.

In her research into women's empowerment in Honduras, Jo Rowlands argues that to develop a sense of power in their close relationships, women need self-confidence, self-esteem, and a sense of agency (Rowlands 1997, 119). That Munnawar Jahan, discussed in the case study in Box 6.3, attended a women's training event in defiance of her family and could express her opinions on her marriage and intention to earn her own income, is evidence that she was well aware of the issues she faced and already had sufficient power to attend the meeting.

However, empowerment in close relationships also depends on the development of an individual's ability to negotiate, communicate, and defend herself and her rights (op. cit.). Here, the support of other women can play a critical part. In Munnawar Jahan's case, the co-ordinated back-up and protection of a group of women brought about the conditions whereby negotiation could take place with her relatives over her future. It is difficult to see how, in the absence of the support of the women's group, Munnawar Jahan would have been able to resolve the conflict in her own

---

Box 6.2
Empowering women to reduce violence within the home: the experience of CMV

Colectivo Mujer Vida (CMV) is a Brazilian community-based organisation. Since 1991, it has been involved in projects for poor women suffering domestic and sexual violence in the north-eastern Brazilian towns of Olinda, Pualista, and Recife. CMV's programmes are based on the notion that by increasing a woman's self-esteem or 'power within', she is in a stronger position to change and equalise her relationships with others. CMV tries to help women to make a transition to a life free of violence by developing their self-esteem, teaching them their legal rights, and training them in skills that will enable them to find employment. CMV works with young girls and women from the *bairros* (slums) who suffer domestic violence. Abuse in the family can cause girls to leave home, often to live on the street and work in prostitution, drugs trafficking, and sex tourism. At the Oxfam international workshop on violence against women held in Sarajevo in 1998, Tertuliana de Oliveira of CMV reported that there are indications that women have more power in their intimate relationships as a result of participation in CMV's projects. The women who meet in community groups often become more assertive, and feel they are better able to make their own decisions, and to discuss issues with their partners. They think this stems from their growing awareness of their own worth, needs, and personal interests. Overall, there seemed to be fewer assumptions about gender roles in the families of these women. In the long term, CMV has found that as women gain psychological and financial independence, they begin to set limits to men's behaviour, and domestic and sexual violence decreases.

Source: de Oliveira 1998

---

interests. Having contact with the women's group may also have encouraged her over the longer term, evident in her ability to negotiate autonomy in her marital relationship several years later.

Participation in development projects with no specific aim of improving relationships between women and men in the household may be very positive for women who face violence in the home. Women can be provided with a useful combination of resources that support them in their individual attempts to equalise the balance of power between themselves and their male partners.

For example, women participants in an Oxfam fair trade income-generation project in Bangladesh noted a decrease in domestic violence following their participation in the project. In an evaluation of the project, women identified a number of factors that had contributed to this decrease.

Box 6.3

A workshop for women in India: encouraging women's empowerment in their intimate relationships

Munnawar Jehan is a Muslim woman who lives with her widowed mother in Sultanpur village in north-west Uttar Pradesh. Her family and the local community wished to prevent her from working in the public sphere, but she was very keen to work with DISHA, a grassroots women's organisation working on issues of health and rights. She decided to attend a ten-day training camp that required her to reside at the voluntary organisation. The objective of the training session was to enable the women participants to identify gender discrimination in their families, communities, and society, to enable them to make connections with one another, and to recognise their common voice in protest against oppression. Slowly, women started talking about their experiences of violence, and the behaviour of their husbands, brothers, in-laws, parents, landlords, and government officials. Munnawar talked about her fears of retaliation from her family and local community for defying their wishes by coming to the training. On the second night of the training, Munnawar's maternal uncle, her sister's husband, and a local Muslim boy came to take her away, announcing that they had organised her wedding in a neighbouring village. The women formed a protective ring around Munnawar who was determined not to go with them. For two hours the men argued and threatened the women.

The women set up a meeting for the following day. They invited Munnawar's relatives and some male members of the Muslim community to discuss the issue with the women's group, the voluntary organisation, and the trainer group. The aim of this process was to solicit everyone's opinion and to develop a strategy for resolving the conflict in Munnawar's favour. The women's group emphasised the positive aspects of Munnawar's working to support herself and her mother, since they had no regular source of income. To increase the social pressure, the group sought the support of an influential local Muslim leader and his daughter. It was decided that Munnawar could continue the training but would go home in the evenings. Her mother attended the training in order to lessen her anxiety about it, and on one day her uncles were invited to a discussion to reduce antagonistic feelings. Her family agreed to Munnawar's employment, and agreed not to force her into marriage.

Four-and-a-half years later, Munnawar was married with one child. She married only on condition that she would not leave work, she would not wear the veil (purdah), and she would continue to live in Sultanpur where she works.

Source: Mahajan 1994

The principal factor they identified was the training they received in women's rights. The women said that this training made them come to realise that they had their own identity, that their husbands could not 'torture' them, and that they had equal rights with men (Barney, Oxfam internal document 1999).

A very significant second reason given by the participants in the income-generation project as an explanation for the decrease in violence was the group pressure provided by fellow project participants. On hearing that a husband was being abusive towards one of the participants, women would go directly to the participant's home to ensure that the man stopped his violent behaviour. This method of shaming men was effective in part because the women had worked together in the project for many years. Participation in the group provided women with the resources to achieve social and political action on a collective basis.

Finally, the women attributed some – relatively minor – significance to the steady income that participation in the project provides, suggesting that women's income was contributing to increasing their bargaining position within the household (Maria José Barney, personal communication 1999).

6.4 'Healing the abuser': working with male perpetrators

Interventions for healing may focus on the recovery of individual men, or on reconciling entire communities in which violence has ceased to be widely sanctioned.

6.4.1 Traditional healing and reconciliation strategies

In contexts in which violence has become a way of life, a key strategy is to encourage community members to recall age-old community sanctions against violence. Box 6.4 shows how women in native Canadian ('First Nation') communities are addressing domestic violence by reclaiming traditional methods of conflict resolution.

Indigenous methods of healing have played an important part in rebuilding the social fabric of some societies which have developed entrenched 'cultures of violence' as the result of several years of armed conflict. These interventions are of particular interest to the concerns of this book since, as Chapter 4 showed, during and after conflict violence against women is often more widespread, and may take more extreme forms, than during peacetime.

At a symposium on 'Building Bridges in Southern Africa: Reconstruction and Reconciliation in Times of Change', co-hosted by the Centre for the

Study of Violence and Reconciliation and Oxfam, and held in Johannesburg in June 1996, Noel Muchenga Chicuecue, who works with the UNESCO Culture of Peace Programme in Maputo, explained how in Mozambique, community institutions, traditional healers, community leaders, and extended families have developed procedures to assist in healing those who have been damaged by war.

Box 6.4
Tackling domestic violence through circles of healing in First Nation communities in Canada

In Manitoba, Canada, native Canadian women from the Hollow Water Reserve have begun to use the traditional 'Circle of Healing' to end violence against women in the community.

There are two possible Circle of Healing approaches. One involves intensive therapy given to a violent man over five days. The other has 13 steps, which take between two and five years to complete. The Circle insists that an offender should admit his guilt before it will work with him.

The power of the Circle is attributed to a special convocation where members of the community come together with the victim, the abuser, and their family members to confront the crime. In so doing, the community members confront the abuser, requiring him to acknowledge his crime publicly. At the heart of the meeting is the testimony of people who tell the abuser how they feel about what has happened. They then offer their support in healing both the victim and perpetrator. They also speak to the victims and the family or families involved.

The abuser is given a 'healing contract' setting out the punishment, which is usually community work. Arrangements are made to protect the victim. When the contract expires, a cleansing ceremony takes place to symbolise the return of balance to the abuser, the family, and the community. At this point healing is considered complete and the crime is forgotten. The healing process can be slow – it may take years – but usually it proves effective.

Source: Match International 1990, 11-14

People in Mozambique believe that purification rituals can heal the negative effects of bad spirits and war traumas. Ex-soldiers, returning refugees, child-soldiers, sexually abused women, and internally displaced people have all passed through cleansing rituals upon returning to their communities and families. These cleansing rituals date back to the pre-colonial period when warriors underwent purification rituals in order to free themselves from revenge by the spirits of their victims. Without these healing rituals, the spirit of the victim can bring bad luck or death not only to the killer but also to his extended family or community. The Red Cross,

UNICEF, and local NGOs are collaborating with local communities in the re-integration of child soldiers back into their communities, using healing rituals. This involves a child soldier going to his relatives, the traditional healer, or community elders and confessing any wrongful deeds. The chief acts as judge and is assisted by a woman adviser who acts as mediator between the living and dead. The boy may have to pay a fine to victims' families, and may have to swear an oath that he will no longer undertake violent actions (Muchenga Chicuecue 1997).

Such traditional purification and healing rituals offer perpetrators of violence a means of reintegrating themselves into their community, provided that they subsequently adhere to certain punishments or conditions. Where an offender fails to comply with the rules he may face strong sanctions, including exclusion from the community. These methods of healing have legitimacy and political weight, because they are rooted in existing cultural traditions. The strength of the Circle of Healing example from Canada is that women have mobilised the whole community to condemn violence against women, and to back their initiative.

Despite these positive examples, traditional strategies to 'heal' perpetrators and victims of violence should be adopted with great caution. Firstly, healing and reconciliation strategies may not always provide the solutions to contemporary problems of violence. Communities may feel that their traditional methods are simply inadequate to respond to the effects of certain forms of extreme violence. As a Mozambican traditional healer explained:

> Some of these kids have wounds because they see things they shouldn't see, that no child should have to see – like their parents being killed. They change their behaviour. This is not like being mad. That we can treat. No, this is from what they have seen – it is a social problem, a behavioural problem, not a mental problem. They beat each other, they are disrespectful, they tell harsh jokes and are delinquent. You can see it in their behaviour towards each other: more violence, more harshness, less respect – more breaking down of tradition. There is no medicine for this.

(Nordstrom 1992, 270)

Secondly, as discussed in the previous chapter, traditional methods of law, order, and reconciliation employed by communities do not always provide solutions that respect the equal rights of all in the community. Since social institutions are often founded in beliefs of women's subordination to male leaders, this is particularly true for women. Survivors of violence against women may find that community 'solutions' do not offer them justice.

An example comes from post-apartheid South Africa. Here, extremely high rape statistics bear witness to the failure of the judiciary and police to protect women against violence both inside and outside the home. Traditional, community-led forms of justice and reconciliation have been harnessed as part of an initiative that aims to rebuild trust and a sense of community responsibility. This initiative is supported by the Peace and Development Project (PDP), a project funded by a European development agency that aims to stabilise some of the most neglected squatter camps, training community workers in conflict resolution, community liaison, and street patrols (Bateman 1998).

The methods of resolution used by the PDP can sometimes appear to be unsatisfactory. In one case, a man from rural Transkei went to an urban area to find a wife. He abducted an unwilling 18-year-old woman, took her back to his home, locked her in his shack and raped her intermittently for two days. One of the rapes was allegedly committed with the help of a male friend, who held the woman down. She escaped by forcing open the bars of the toilet window, and went to the police. However, police officers did not take up her case. A PDP worker took up and settled the case 'amicably, and in the best interests of all', with no charges being laid. The rape victim did not want to press charges. At a community meeting, the rapist agreed to pay the cost of medical tests and treatment, and associated costs including bus fares and food for the journey home. This way of 'resolving' the incident was seen by the community as successful because the rape victim was spared the ordeal of testifying in a lengthy trial. In addition, the report of the case states that the rapist 'has not been sent at the taxpayers' expense to learn the criminal ropes from fellow prison inmates, to emerge resentful for what he sees as exercising a Xhosa man's rights' (Bateman 1998, 3).

Such strategies illustrate the double-edged nature of customary or community reconciliation. Community efforts to administer justice are usually presided over by men, and operate within a very traditional patriarchal framework. The reconciliation process in this case did not challenge the attacker to revise his view of a Xhosa man's right to marry a woman after abducting and raping her. As a result, although the woman was allowed to go home, rather than be forced to stay with her abductor, the rape was simply treated as an offence that could be paid for. The fact that the case was declared resolved by a relatively small financial penalty – the 'price' of the attack – fails to challenge this view adequately.

Community healing rituals may not only fail to address the physical and psychological harm caused by violence, and fail to protect women from future violence; they may also perpetuate the social and moral harm that results from taboos surrounding violence against women, and sexual violence in particular. It cannot be assumed that traditional healing strategies for reintegration into the community can treat the many different effects of sexual violence on women.

Is the answer to reject community justice systems that fail to offer adequate justice to women survivors of violence, or to examine ways of narrowing the scope of responsibility of such systems? In Pakistan, for example, there is debate as to whether the *karo-kiri* system of community justice should or can be reformed to offer women better protection from crimes of 'honour'.

The *karo-kari* is a system of belief in which a family's honour can be defiled as a result of a woman being perceived to behave in ways that are considered unacceptable. Within this system, women may be killed for a range of different forms of assertive behaviour. They can be killed for supposed 'illicit' relationships, for marrying men of their choice, for divorcing abusive husbands, or even for being raped. the Allegations alone may be enough to justify the killing of a woman, regardless of whether the accusations are true.

Women are seen to embody the honour of the men to whom they 'belong', and as such they must guard their virginity and chastity. By being perceived to enter an 'illicit' sexual relationship, a woman defiles the honour of her guardian and his family. She becomes *kari* – literally, a 'black woman' – and forfeits her right to life. The man involved in the relationship becomes *karo* – a 'black man'. In cases of real or alleged sexual misdemeanour, he may escape with his life because the woman is killed first and he has the chance to flee. Once he has fled the *karo* can pay the defiled male kin member compensation, which may take the form of money or of women, and have his own name cleared.

Local chiefs in areas where this is happening have recently been considering initiating reforms to provide women with better protection from fake 'honour-killings'. It is suggested that cases could be checked, by demanding that accusations be made under oath or by taking the monetary incentive out of 'honour-killings' – putting a limit to the fine demanded from the family of the accused, and challenging the practice of using women to pay compensation (Amnesty International 1999b). However, the belief remains that a genuine *karo* or *kari* should not be spared, and even if local chiefs succeed in weeding out false allegations, women's lives are still in danger.

One possible strategy for women's rights activists and other organisations to use in this situation would be to expose the contradictions between the chiefs' national and local responsibilities. Many hold office in the country's legislature, a democratic system based on the notion of equal rights for all. Despite this, chiefs clearly use separate norms and standards in their community capacity. Suggesting possible reform moves (alongside legal, preventive, and protective measures), Amnesty states, 'Tribal leaders, familiar with the constitution of Pakistan and statutory law … should use their influence in society to introduce the rights and freedoms they swear to uphold as parliamentarians into a society bound by tradition.' (Amnesty International 1999b) In addition, well-known men and women in Pakistan could be involved in public campaigns demonstrating that the practice is not condoned by Islam.

In general, there is a need for caution in assuming that traditional leaders will support and protect women who face male violence. However, traditional community institutions are powerful, and where possible should be motivated to protect women from violence.

6.4.2 Rehabilitating ex-combatant men and boys

Development and humanitarian agencies have relatively recently begun to consider ways in which they can mitigate the psychological impacts of participation in armed conflict on the men and boys who have fought in them. This is not often explicitly connected to an aim to reduce violence against women, but rather is seen as a means of ensuring the general recovery and reintegration of individuals into society. However, many of the programmes that exist focus on helping young adolescents and children to 'unlearn' violent ways of resolving conflict, and to develop peaceful ways of negotiating with others, including women and girls. The aim is to foster the ability to express emotions in constructive and non-violent ways. Boys and men who have fought in wars are addressed both as the perpetrators and victims of violence. A major focus is on developing men's and boys' self-esteem.

Some programmes have taken explicitly psycho-social approaches. An example of this is work in Mozambique which has taken place after demobilisation of child soldiers, following the end of the 16-year Mozambique civil war in 1992. The government supports a programme, run by the Mozambican Association for Public Health, that aims to reintegrate former boy soldiers into their communities. Efforts are made to reunite the children with their families. Therapy is offered individually, and in groups, to children and their families. This includes play, art, dance, and counselling. Material support and training for livelihoods has also been provided to participants (Castelo-Branco 1997).

In December 1997, Rädda Bärnen (Save the Children Sweden) launched a project to demobilise, rehabilitate, and reintegrate child soldiers in southern Sudan. The project aimed to demobilise several hundred youngsters, and to provide them with psycho-social support services. On their return home, the children were provided with kits including school stationery, mosquito nets, and soap. Community workers and teachers received training in preparation for the children's return, and undertook subsequent follow-up and monitoring of the children's progress. The project, which was set up after two rebel movements in the area asked for NGO assistance, seeks to prevent further military recruitment of children, through a range of strategies including engaging in dialogue with local commanders and community leaders (Coalition to Stop the Use of Child Soldiers 1998, 18).

Such projects provide boys and girls who have been perpetrators and victims of atrocities with an opportunity to contemplate their lives and experiences in a controlled setting. This affords them the mental and physical 'space' that they need in order to prepare them to re-enter society. Easing children and youth back into community life is also aided by bringing parents into the programmes at the later stages, to help rebuild damaged relations.

In Chapter 5, we discussed the limitations of western-based psycho-social interventions. That said, the growing interest in the effects of armed conflict and militarisation on the mental health and well-being of boys and men of all ages is to be welcomed. The need for such a focus is illustrated by the descriptions of violence by boys who have participated or lived through armed conflict, as described in Chapter 4. The participation of a generation of boys and young men in armed conflict can lead to the emergence of a 'culture of violence' that remains even after the conflict has formally come to an end. However, it is not enough to hope that such interventions will end male violence towards women. An emphasis on 'returning' to a pre-conflict social setting will not encourage boys and men to be critical of the fact that, even in so-called peacetime, violence and abuse occurs. Changing the norms and values of relationships between women and men from those of control and dominance to those based on mutual respect and equity requires long-term education. It also requires change at a structural as well as an individual level.

Demilitarisation and demobilisation programmes for ex-combatants are most useful when they include an exploration of unequal gender power relations in both peace and war, and stimulate discussion about stereotypes of men and women's roles, and how these differ from reality – before, during, and after conflict. Reintegrating boys into their communities necessitates helping them to find alternative non-violent ways to become men. This is likely to require the challenging of traditional patriarchal gender identities, and not simply those specific to times of war.

Some interventions, like the KwaZulu Natal Programme for the Survivors of Violence (KZN PSV) in South Africa, move beyond psycho-social approaches to challenge gender stereotypes and unequal gender relations.

KZN PSV is a project set up by a group of psychologists from the University of Natal, Pietermaritzburg, South Africa. They were concerned about a lack of official response to the needs of the thousands of people affected by the civil conflict that occurred in KwaZulu Natal from the mid-1980s.

Violence had been escalating in KwaZulu Natal since the early 1980s, and finally erupted into an 'unofficial war' in 1987. Following South Africa's first democratic election, the unofficial war continued within KwaZulu Natal. In 1995, there were 75 deaths per month, making up 70 per cent of the national figure, and many more cases of non-fatal political violence (KwaZulu Natal Program for the Survivors of Violence 1997b).

The programme aims to assist individuals, families, and communities through providing services that are both healing and empowering. The organisation addresses mental health issues, but has questioned the applicability of narrow and individualistic models of the psychological effects of war and violence (see Chapter 5 for the organisation's critique of the psychological trauma model). It opts instead for community-based approaches, working particularly with young people who are not attending school. KZN PSV shares its experiences with other organisations. Topics on which learning is disseminated include 'models' for working with survivors of violence, mental health issues in low-intensity conflict, linking mental health with development, and training lay people as mental health agents.

KZN PSV addresses the need to change relations between men within a community, as well as those between men and women. It recognises that a mass of norms and institutions need to be addressed in order to do this. It conceptualises the effects of violence, and the programme's interventions, in terms of human relationships at all levels of society. Events at different levels impact on those at other levels in the system. Broadly, at each level 'civil violence'[2] acts in two ways – to 'disempower', and to 'fragment'. The most effective approaches to 'undoing' the effects of violence may be through linking and empowerment strategies (see Appendix 2 for a diagram of this model). In encouraging the perpetrators of violence to understand their behaviour, understandings of 'civil violence' are linked to violence against women, which is, in turn, viewed in terms of unequal gender relations. Participants are encouraged to question dominant ideologies of masculinity in terms of power and control, and not to just see them as an outcome of armed conflict.

KZN PSV's youth project sets up youth groups with the aim of re-integrating former combatants into society. There, boys can come to terms with their experiences and participate in skills-training programmes for employment. For example, the creative writing programme tries to encourage political tolerance by allowing for contact and shared experiences between youth of different backgrounds and histories. This programme recently produced a publication made up of testimonies of violence by participants (Malange, McKay, and Zhlengetwa eds 1996). Leadership training programmes aim to foster the youth movement in KwaZulu Natal so that ongoing youth structures become more effective (PASF, Oxfam internal document 1997).

Gender issues, such as the changing role of women, what men and women want from intimate relationships, and experiences of sexual violence and rape, are dealt with in the PSV project's groups as they are raised.

6.4.3 Psycho-social therapy for individual male abusers

In the UK, Canada, and the USA, there has been increasing interest in rehabilitation programmes that aim to end the violent behaviour of individual men through psycho-social therapy. These programmes are based on the premise that violence is behaviour learned through socialisation, a behaviour that can be changed through educating men about the power dynamics of violence. Treatment focuses on improving men's ability to control their emotions. Some programmes go further, by challenging men's perceptions that they have the right to control women through violence.

One UK initiative, developed by Probation Service staff, has created a treatment programme for men in prison, which aims to reduce future crime. The programme works with groups of men who have been convicted of serious violent offences. It aims to enable them to change their attitudes, to recognise the impact of their behaviour on victims, and to take responsibility for changing their future behaviour (Potts 1996). Batterer Intervention Programmes also aim to change men's violent behaviour. Initiated in the 1970s, they too focus on group treatment. Batterer Intervention Programmes have become mandatory in the USA, where they are used in place of incarceration. The length of these programmes varies, but they are often short (around 20-30 weeks) (García-Moreno 1999).

Many women favour their husbands, partners, or fathers getting this kind of help, and may prefer it to more traditional interventions. However, evidence of the effectiveness of these programmes is, at best, mixed. Court-ordered treatment has been found to have no positive effects on rates of physical violence or threats of violence, or on men's key beliefs about violence (Harrel 1991, cited in Heise, Pitanguy, and Germaine 1994). One study compared men who had been ordered to attend treatment with a control group of men who had not. It also compared rates of men's violence before court involvement with rates following court involvement but before treatment, and with rates following treatment, in order to identify whether any effects were the result of the justice system's involvement or of the treatment (or both). The study found that rates of violence decreased following men's arrest and court hearing, but that subsequent psycho-social treatment had no added benefit (op. cit.).

Criticisms of men's consciousness-raising groups focus on the fact that men do not necessarily have anything to gain by challenging unequal gender power relations. These criticisms are also relevant in the context of psycho-social therapy for offenders.

An additional, and critical, weakness of therapy for male perpetrators of violence is that most treatment is not voluntary (Hearn 1998). One programme which *is* voluntary is located in Victoria, Australia. Residential facilities, called 'Men's Houses', (mentioned in Chapter 5) are a community development initiative to provide alternative housing for male abusers, enabling their wives or partners and children to remain within the family home. Men are encouraged to stay in the housing provided, while attending a behaviour change group. The majority of violent men and their partners have agreed that the groups have had a positive effect, with violence altogether ceasing, or the rate significantly diminished (Francis 1995).

In addition, further criticism of psycho-social therapy programmes arises from the fact that many such perpetrator programmes are based on the view that a man's background and upbringing are in some way to blame for his violent behaviour. Critics consider that this approach may enable men to avoid taking full responsibility for their violent actions. The National Committee on Violence against Women in Australia has noted, 'Psychological therapies, such as anger control, and insight management and relationship therapies, such as conflict management and communication training, are counterproductive if they provide the perpetrator with an opportunity to search endlessly for the cause of his violence without ever actually taking full responsibility for it.' (National Committee on Violence Against Women 1994, 12)

Finally, unlike traditional healing strategies and collective action to shame violent men, therapy programmes for individual abusers do not usually involve the wider community. Such programmes do not offer any possibility of ensuring that a perpetrator's community sanctions him, should he use violence again. Women's future safety may therefore be compromised by reliance on such strategies.

Box 6.4
Principles for programmes educating violent men

A Council of Europe report lays down the following principles with which programmes educating violent men should comply:

- Women and children's safety should be the guiding priority and principle.
- Violence should be responded to as a crime.
- Criminal proceedings and penalties against perpetrators of violence should continue.
- Men's programmes should never be used as alternatives to criminal proceedings.
- A man must be held totally responsible for his violence and the aim of the programme should be the absolute and permanent cessation of violence.
- Joint sessions with women should never be undertaken.
- Linked but autonomous support services for women should be available to ensure they get accurate information about the programme, can feed back information about men's behaviour if they wish to, and have access to independent support to assess their own choices and options.
- Work with men should be educational (rather than psycho-dynamic) in focus, challenging beliefs and attitudes that support gender inequality and justify violence.
- Programmes should be properly and externally evaluated.
- The funding for perpetrator programmes should never take money from resources for victims of violence.

Source: Council of Europe 1997, 85-6, adapted from National Committee on Violence against Women 1994

6.4.4 Men's work with men: awareness-raising on alternative ways of 'being a man'

As Chapter 1 noted, despite the association of masculine identity with dominance, power, and violence, men in all societies are able to find ways of being 'masculine' that do not conform to this stereotype. There may be positive inducements to encourage alternatives to violence against women (Counts, Brown, and Campbell eds 1992), and these can be identified and promoted. For example, a community may express admiration for a man who commands domestic respect without having to impose it with the threat of violence (op. cit.). Of course, an intervention like this does nothing to undermine an overall structure of patriarchal dominance.

Recently, many researchers have explored positive aspects of male socialisation, and suggested the fostering of aspects of masculinity that do not depend on violence. One piece of research focused on the Kosovan Albanian blood feuds. It looked at the possibility of resurrecting the idea that 'honour' may be maintained just as well through forgiveness as it is through killing (Jani 1995).

There are a growing number of examples of men working to address their own violence as a part of a negative notion of masculinity, which harms women and children, destroys and impoverishes family life, and ultimately impacts negatively on men themselves. This work has taken place alongside the activities of development and humanitarian organisations, in much the same way as the work of women's organisations.

At an Oxfam workshop in 1998 that compared experiences of conflict and democratisation in South Africa with those in Latin America, staff asserted that in both regions, men did very little to change their violent behaviour following the ending of armed conflict. One participant explained:

> *The masculine gender identity does not help much to change culture. … In the transition men want to provide, but they do it wrong. They do not go deep into the problematic situation... and they act in a paternalistic way. Men in Central America, Mexico, and South Africa have not yet entered the re-education process with regard to the problems between the genders, and even less to the role that they play in the reproduction of the prominent culture.*

(Oxfam GB 1998a)

However, much of the work considered in this section does not support this analysis. It is essential for development organisations to develop awareness of the interesting work carried out by men's organisations to challenge male gender identity and end violence against women.

An example comes from the Nicaraguan organisation CISAS (Centro de Información y Servicios de Asesoría en Salud), a prominent Nicaraguan health promotion NGO. CISAS began working with groups of men in late 1996, mainly in response to demands from women in some of the poor communities where it works. CISAS and other Nicaraguan NGOs have been at the forefront of championing human rights. NGOs have had some notable successes, for example the passing of a law that made intra-familial violence a crime punishable by imprisonment, and the establishment of several pilot projects of a new police service staffed by officers who are especially trained to deal with crimes against women and children. Overall, however, levels of intra-familial violence perpetuated by men against women and children are increasing in Nicaragua (Ellsberg *et al.* 1996).

CISAS's work began with a participatory research process into men's ideas of *machismo* in Nicaraguan society (see Box 6.5), and the impact of their views of gender relations on their sexual behaviour, and their attitudes to their partners and children. CISAS bases its work on the philosophy of empowerment of the Brazilian educator, Paulo Freire. Freire stresses the importance of the development of 'critical consciousness', or the ability to critique the social and political situation in such a way that it becomes possible to see why change is necessary and how change may be brought about (Freire 1973).

CISAS's work is based on the idea that, in order for men to develop critical consciousness of the effects of their behaviour and attitudes, they must be able to identify the societal norms that legitimate and actually promote risky behaviour. To do this, men need to view their behaviour and attitudes through two 'lenses'. One lens is the social and cultural norms defined by *machismo*, which give rise to a certain model of 'acceptable' male sexual behaviour and a particular set of attitudes. Men should consider the extent to which the hegemonic model resembles their actual behaviour and attitudes; if they are different, why are they different? The second 'lens' acts to encourage men to scrutinise the effects of their sexual behaviour on themselves and on others. This kind of critical questioning will not happen spontaneously, as feminists and pro-feminist men have shown. CISAS aims to make it happen (Sternberg 2000).

Further experience of men working with men comes from examples of gender awareness training with male development workers (Chapter 7) and with male police officials (Chapter 8). These case studies highlight the clear role men have in working with their peers to question perceptions of violent behaviour as a legitimate part of being a man.

Box 6.5

CISAS's work to build men's critical consciousness of their responsibilities in sex and fatherhood

CISAS's research process involved 90 men from five urban and three rural Nicaraguan communities. The men were aged from 15–70 and had an average of 4.7 children each. Thirty per cent of the men were single.

Field work began with a workshop at which 38 men who had participated in activities facilitated by CISAS discussed sexuality, fatherhood, and reproduction with CISAS health educators. During the workshop, participants completed a biographical questionnaire which included questions about their values and practical experience of contraception and fatherhood. Using the results of this, a small team put together a guide for in-depth interviews and focus groups. The research examined men's knowledge, attitudes, and behaviour in three areas fundamental to the social construction of masculinity: sexuality, reproduction, and fatherhood.

Source: Sternberg 2000

The work described above is informed by an explicit commitment to feminist ideals on the part of the men who have formed the organisations and groups. This approach involves acknowledging that individual men are responsible for their violent behaviour, but recognising, in addition, that individuals are socialised into the values they hold, and that certain behaviours are rewarded by society. Men involved in this work emphasise that not all men are violent: there are ways of 'being a man' that retain positive aspects of masculine identity and reject negative aspects. They emphasise that it is important to guard against negative and alienating stereotypes. Dichotomised thinking about men as the perpetrators of violence and women as the victims is likely to overlook the fact that identities are culturally and temporally variable, rather than having a generic or fixed nature. As one commentator on gender and development policy and practice has observed, the way forward for men is to reject 'good girl/bad boy stereotypes, [that] present women as resourceful and caring mothers, with men as relatively autonomous individualists, putting their own desires for drink and cigarettes before their family's needs' (White 1997, 16). Gender roles and relations are socially constructed, and can change and be changed.

Criticisms of men's consciousness-raising groups in western countries focus on the fact that the approach ignores the fact that men have a vested interest in the status quo(Hearn 1998). Because men, unlike women, do not have an obvious mutual interest in changing gender relations, men's therapy groups are seen by many as inherently unstable. They are certainly often short-lived. They tend to retreat from the political into the personal, and can easily shift from being pro-feminist to quite hostile, as men become defensive at having to shoulder all the blame for patriarchy (Connell 1995).

It is necessary to be aware that some men's organisations do not hold a feminist perspective; rather, they are part of a backlash against gender equality. In 1999, in South Africa, an advertising campaign condemning the extremely high rates of rape in the country was condemned by men's groups. The groups alleged that the campaign was sexist and inflammatory because it implied that all South African men were actual or potential rapists. In a ruling, the Supreme Court ruled that the advertisement was in fact acceptable. The reason given was that the advertisement did not imply that all men were violent, but that there are three groups of men – abusers, men who are complicit through non-action, and 'real men' who combat violence (*Weekly Mail and Guardian* 1999).

6.5 Summary and implications for development organisations

This chapter has argued that improving services for victims of violence or enabling women to gain access to resources in the hope that this will challenge inequality cannot by themselves end violence against women. States, communities, and NGOs alike have undertaken very little work to challenge men's violent behaviour towards women directly. If we are serious about ending violence against women, we need to do more of this work. Working to end gender violence involves both supporting women and challenging men. Above all, it means transforming relations between men and women – an enterprise in which everyone should be involved. Working with men to problematise violence against women, and to set it in a context of masculine gender identity, will lead to new ways of understanding how unequal power relations cause, and are in turn perpetuated by, violence against women.

The chapter began by looking at the ways in which women themselves can offer challenges to violent partners in the sphere of the family and household. It went on to describe different kinds of interventions that challenge and work with violent men directly in the public sphere, rather than waiting for changes to come about through other means. The chapter described the role of traditional and community-based methods of publicly shaming violent men. Further strategies explored in this chapter were traditional healing methods, psycho-social therapy, individual treatment programmes, and education. It is too early to draw conclusions about which of these approaches are most effective in bringing about change in men's violent behaviour.

Men informed by commitments to equality and feminist goals are forming organisations to work with male abusers. Interventions that encourage men to understand the role of violence against women, and to take responsibility for challenging social norms and values, have an important role to play in combating violence against women. However, it is important to ensure that resources are not diverted away from the initiatives of women's organisations. It is critical to resource the work of men's organisations, but equally critical that the scant funds for working with women are not re-routed to this new area of concern. It is also very important to be aware that not all men's organisations are feminist in their agenda, and that some are part of a backlash against equality.

7 Challenging attitudes and beliefs

On 25 November 1992 [the UN International Day of No Violence against Women], *the women marched through their community with placards saying, 'Here you don't beat women.' About 300 women joined them. Their husbands threatened them, men stood aside and jeered. The men justified beating their wives because they didn't put their food on the table or they answered back. The march was like a bomb. In 1996, they marched again. This time, men followed the march. The men said they were there because, 'Thanks to Filomena Pacsi, we have learned not to treat our women this way, because it affects all of us.'*

Esther Ricaldi, Peru, participant at Oxfam international workshop on violence against women, Sarajevo 1998

Esther Ricaldi, the woman who recounted the story above, is a member of Filomena Pacsi, an organisation of miner women in the Peruvian Andes. Their struggle to break the widespread silence in their society surrounding violence against women eventually led to a growing intolerance of violence on the part of the community. During the first march in protest against violence held by the organisation, men jeered and threatened the women. But, after four years of local development work by women's groups, men began to condemn violence and to advocate for an improvement in women's status within the community (interview with Esther Ricaldi 1998).

In this chapter and the one that follows, the focus shifts from considering strategies for working with the survivors and perpetrators of violence as individuals, to a consideration of how development and humanitarian work can help transform attitudes in the societies in which violence occurs. As we have seen throughout this book, 'the community' plays a vital role in perpetuating, condoning, and even promoting, violence against women. However, it can also play a crucial role in ending it. Until widespread change in social attitudes occurs, state-level action to support women victims of violence – for example, legal reform – will have only limited success. In extreme cases, where reform is introduced in the absence of popular support, violent backlash against women can result.

A second aim of awareness-raising and popular education is to destroy the stigma experienced by survivors of violence. Taboos associated with violence against women at the community level mean that women often keep silent about the violence they endure, rather than seeking help. The way that individuals and community groups stigmatise women victims of violence can intensify the harm caused by violence, and may increase other women's fear of violence. Support is only likely to be available to women in contexts where challenging male violence is perceived as everyone's responsibility, and sanctions are put in place to reduce incentives for men to be violent. As Chapter 3 emphasised, the consequences of violence for women are social, as much as they are physical and psychological.

This chapter considers ways of working to challenge patriarchal values and attitudes to violence against women at the local, national, and international levels. It begins by tracing the rationale for changing community attitudes to violence against women, through challenging 'common sense' ideas of male superiority and domination, and of the nature and impact of violence. To end all forms of violence against women, we need to challenge everyone's tolerance of it – including our own. As the National Committee on Violence against Women, a government committee in Australia, has stated, 'Members of the community have a collective responsibility to condemn the use of violence against women and to give paramount importance to the safety of victims of violence. Everyone, everywhere, must become intolerant of violence against women and uphold the belief that no woman deserves violence.' (National Committee on Violence Against Women 1994, 15)

Ways of doing this include recording statistics and information, in ways that respect the sensitivities of women survivors, and disseminating the resulting material in a sensitive manner. The chapter goes on to describe national and local interventions that aim to harness the media's influence for good, and challenge negative stereotypes of women and positive images of violence against women.

After that, consideration is given to strategies tried by women's organisations and development NGOs to raise awareness of violence against women, and to end the stigma that surrounds it. Methods of awareness-raising at community level discussed in this chapter include 'cascade' training of members of the community to sensitise others, and the training of development workers to work with the community. Finally, the chapter considers the role of training community leaders, and fostering networks as a strategy for sensitising communities about the true nature of violence against women. Consideration of ways to transform the attitudes of state officials is omitted from this chapter, since this will receive particular attention in Chapter 8.

7.1 Raising awareness and ending stigma

As discussed in Chapters 2 and 5, the drafting and implementation of laws prohibiting violence against women have had a major role in raising awareness of the issue as a human rights abuse. At both international and national levels, the drafting of the Women's Convention, and regional human rights instruments such as the Inter-American Convention on Human Rights, have catalysed attitudinal change on the issue. However, without community-level public awareness of the extent of violence, its impact, and its unacceptability, the scale of violence against women will continue to be perceived as insignificant, and its consequences short-term and inconsequential. As this book has argued, violence is a tangible manifestation of male domination of women, considered by many to be natural and unchanging. Men's superiority and power over women is part of 'common sense' – that is, it is part of an 'uncritical and partly unconscious way in which people perceive the world' (Simon 1991, 26).

There is often a lack of consensus within communities that violence against women is wrong (Lackey and Williams 1995). In particular, violence between intimate partners within the home is commonly seen as the fault of the woman involved rather than the man. This is an example of a 'common sense' understanding of violence against women. A Zambian study found that 24 per cent of respondents said that a woman is to blame if her husband or partner beats her, while 31 per cent said that both the man and the woman were to blame if he beat her. Those who blamed the woman most commonly cited women's disobedience, lack of respect, failure to take care of her husband's relatives, and alcohol consumption as reasons for the beating (YWCA 1994).[1] A study carried out in Armenia found, similarly, that 26 per cent of those interviewed believed that physical violence against women in the domestic context was justified. The most commonly given justifications were a wife betraying her husband, and a wife contradicting her husband (Aleksanyan 1998).

These findings illustrate how, in order to end violence against women, 'common sense' ideas that societies and communities maintain about the scope and nature of violence against women must be analysed and challenged. The political activist and thinker Antonio Gramsci has stressed how information and the media can play a key role in stimulating people to begin this process of questioning. Dominant groups in society use information and the media to attain or consolidate power and domination[2] through ensuring that the ideas they favour pass, via popular culture, into people's shared 'common sense' (Simon 1991, 26).

The starting point in awareness-raising on violence against women is to 'map' it. Women's organisations have a particularly rich tradition of documenting women's stories, and disseminating women's understandings of reality. Having documented and attempted to describe the violence within a community, the next step is to ensure that it is 'named' as violence by society at large. To do this, strategies are required that challenge the 'common sense' attitudes and beliefs, where these ignore or condone violence. This can be achieved through influencing the media, or through public education campaigns.

The UN Special Rapporteur on the protection and promotion of the right to freedom of opinion and expression, Abid Hussain, points out that, 'In order to break the silence and taboos surrounding violence, public awareness campaigns on the impact of violence are essential. These campaigns must be devised with women as full participants, and must proceed on the understanding that most women do not seem to seek help from crisis services or the police, because of ignorance, fear or shame.' (Hussain 1999, para. 40)

In the UN Resource Manual on 'Strategies for Confronting Domestic Violence' (United Nations 1993a, 87), the goals of public education and awareness-raising campaigns are listed as the following:

- raising public awareness of the existence and prevalence of violence;
- providing specific information on where to go for help;
- changing public attitudes towards the problem;
- promoting action to solve the problem;
- making victims and offenders aware of the role of the criminal justice system and providing other relevant information such as on rights under family law.

7.2 Challenging attitudes by recording violence against women

7.2.1 Collecting information

As explained in Chapter 3, there is a lack of official statistical data in most countries on the prevalence of violence against women, and its impacts on economic and social well-being. Reasons for this include a lack of awareness of violence against women as an issue of relevance to national development. The collection of national-level statistical quantitative data is in most cases only feasible for central government to handle. In Chapter 8, there is a discussion on how co-operation between the State and experts on violence against women within the community can ensure data collection on the prevalence and nature of violence against women at a national level.

In turn, legal and judicial institutions that should complile data on cases of violence do not always produce accurate statistics due to widespread lack of acknowledgement of violence against women as a crime, reflected in under-recording by police, health workers, and other officials. Another, related, reason for under-recording is women's own reluctance to report incidents of violence.

NGOs can play a vital role in furnishing much-needed information on the extent and nature of violence against women. As the United Nations has noted, the lack of official statistics means that, 'It is only through the development of creative means of information collection and analysis that a more comprehensive range of violations will be identified. Locating broader sources of information, expertise and materials is an important first step.' (United Nations Centre for Human Rights 1995, 10) Much of the data on which this book draws for its analysis has come out of such work. In particular, we owe a debt to women's organisations at local and national level, whose research has played a key role in raising awareness of the extent and impact of violence on individual women and on wider society.

For example, the YWCA in Zambia has compiled a Femicide Register, details of which are found in Box 7.1. The Zambian YWCA has been working on violence against women since 1987, when it was mandated at a meeting of women's NGOs to spearhead a programme of action specific to violence against women. By 1990 the YWCA had formed an Advisory Committee to address issues around 'women in need', an action that formalised the beginning of its anti-violence work. The initial objectives of this programme were to respond to the huge gap in support services for women through establishment of a drop-in centre; to establish an expert committee made up of lawyers, the media, researchers, and social workers to guide the 'women in need' programme; to undertake awareness-raising through workshops and public education campaigns; and to lobby police, policy-makers, and health care providers for effective formal protection and provision for women.

7.2.2 The collection of testimonies from survivors and witnesses of violence

In the face of official denial and unofficial intimidation, investigators must rely on the collection of information by word of mouth and through informal networks. The collection of testimonies from women who have survived violence, and from witnesses, is a very valuable tool for use in

Box 7.1
The Femicide Register, Zambia

The YWCA's Zambian branch was founded in 1957. Today it has 27 branches and over 3000 members. At first, the work of the YWCA addressed issues of multi-racial understanding and Christian fellowship. Today the work of the organisation includes the provision of skills training, income-generating projects, primary health care, and appropriate technology, as well as women's rights programmes.

The YWCA in Zambia has been cataloguing cases of killings of women in Zambia, including details of the typical penalties handed down by the courts, and the government's reaction to the deaths of women. In the register, the YWCA has developed a powerful tool for highlighting the number of murders of women in Zambia, and the inadequacy of the judiciary's response to this. The idea came from women in Canada, who started a similar list following the Montreal Massacre in December 1989, when a lone gunman killed 14 female university students, shouting that he did not like feminists. Other countries in Southern Africa are now also compiling their own lists. The information is gathered from newspaper accounts, police files, and personal stories.

The types of cases documented in the register range from women killed by boyfriends or husbands in so called 'domestic disputes', through to killings of women due to accusations of witchcraft. More than a simple enumeration of the murders, the register challenges assumptions on the part of the public about the nature of violence in domestic settings. Such a register is a powerful and relatively cheap tool to hold government departments accountable for the way they address violence, and to raise awareness of the extent of the problem.

Some of the killings detailed in the Zambian register were carried out by men who were 'in a rage', and included extreme cruelty and mutilation. The register reports that some women were 'overkilled', reflecting 'the hatred in the murders'. Some women were beheaded, had their breasts cut off, had their faces slashed repeatedly with a knife, or had nails driven into their eye sockets. The perpetrators of violence are the husbands or live-in partners of the women in over one-third of all cases. In other cases it is unclear whether the victim knew the attacker or not.

The register provides a powerful critique of the assumption that women are to blame for provoking men. Some of the reasons given in the register to 'explain' the attack include comments such as, 'She did not cook dinner properly', and, 'She quarrelled with him about where his shoes were.' The register also reveals that, sometimes, lighter sentences were given to men who had children to look after, men who were widely considered to be responsible citizens, or men who did not use a weapon. One judge is quoted as sentencing a husband to ten years' hard labour because he had 'used the blunt end of the axe, indicating that he did not mean to kill her'.

One limitation of this method of data collection is that the information collected is often incomplete and the details available vary from case to case.

Such a register may, in the medium-term, affect the attitudes of the courts to the killing of women. At present, Zambian men who kill women often receive short prison sentences. A typical penalty is a year or two on a charge of manslaughter. Frequently, judges rule that a woman 'provoked' a man to attack her, especially if the two were married or had a relationship. The YWCA of Zambia has noted that there has been more coverage of women's human rights in the Zambian media, following its public criticisms of media portrayals of violence against women.

Source: YWCA 1995

lobbying national governments. Such testimonies can force the State to acknowledge that atrocities have taken place, and to provide support for the victims. At the international level, such research can be used to lobby for states to be forced to take action.

Volunteers for Humanity is a coalition of NGOs in Indonesia. The coalition was established following attacks on the opposition Indonesian Democratic Party (PDI) by government-backed vigilante groups in July 1996. One week prior to the student uprising and resignation of General Suharto from the Indonesian presidency on 21 May, riots took place in the Indonesian capital, Jakarta. During the May 1998 riots, which lasted two days, Volunteers for Humanity opened aid centres throughout Jakarta, to provide emergency help to those in distress. Almost two weeks after the riots began, the coalition began to receive reports of women of Chinese descent having been raped. Volunteers for Humanity undertook the task of uncovering the mass rape of Chinese women in Indonesia through collecting women's testimonies.

Ruth Rahayu of Kayanamitra, a women's NGO in Indonesia, presented the research at the international Oxfam workshop on violence against women, held in Sarajevo in November 1998. Ruth Rahayu explained that the findings of the investigation revealed that most of the victims of the mass rape were ethnic Chinese women. Not a single official report of rape was made, indicating the victims' lack of trust in government authorities. In addition, the rape victims' identity cards were taken from them in many cases, making it difficult to make reports. After the riots, official statements were made denying that the rapes ever took place.

However, the evidence of testimonies and eye-witnesses collected by Volunteers for Humanity indicated the systematic and organised nature of the rape and sexual assault of hundreds of women. Their report on the findings of the investigation detailed where the violence took place and who the victims were. It described intimidation of the investigators, the victims' families, hospital staff, and witnesses.

In Box 7.2, the methodology used by the researchers is explained.

The testimonies collected by Volunteers for Humanity provided valuable evidence that the crimes were organised, and ethnically motivated. In their report, Volunteers for Humanity demanded that the government acknowledge that the rapes had occurred, and conduct a full investigation. At the international level, the research was used to lobby the government to take action (Volunteers for Humanity 1998). In a report by the UN Special Rapporteur on violence against women, its causes and consequences in 1999, it was clear that there had been a positive impact on government policy. Government initiatives undertaken since the violence included a forum, *Kata Bunga*, established by the Ministry for Women's Affairs, aiming to suggest ways to provide assistance to victims of these incidents. In July 1998, the Government formed a task force for the provision of post-traumatic care. Also in July 1998, a National Committee for the Prevention of Violence against Women was created to implement the National Programme on the Elimination of Violence against Women. Finally, a fact-finding team investigated the May riots (Coomaraswamy 1999a).

7.2.3 Researching institutional responses

Secondary research conducted through interviewing formal organisations whose mandates include action on violence against women is important in holding governmental, non-governmental, and international organisations accountable. Such research has been carried out by development and humanitarian agencies as well as by women's organisations. For example, Oxfam GB carried out a study on institutional responses to domestic violence in the Balkans. In drawing up the methodology, particular attention was paid to the ways in which existing laws are used or not used to protect women, or to prosecute the perpetrators of violence. The research also scrutinised the agencies that were responsible for providing support to women. Interviews were conducted with representatives of the police, social workers, judges, health service staff, lawyers and representatives of the international community. Women's NGOs had carried out a great deal of primary research providing essential evidence for lobbying at national, regional, and international levels (Maguire 1998).

However, the research revealed a common reluctance on the part of institutions in the Balkans to acknowledge the problem of violence against women as an issue to be publicly addressed. Typically, it was viewed as a private issue. The police felt little responsibility to act in such cases and didn't believe such violence constituted a criminal act. Representatives of international agencies did not generally recognise violence against women as a human rights issue, nor did they see it as part of inter-ethnic conflict and therefore part of their remit.

The Balkans research highlights the need for alliances and joint work between women's organisations, national, and international agencies on the less-publicised effects of war. The research process served to raise awareness of violence amongst officials through raising the issue, and obliging them to consider how their work was or was not addressing it. International agencies are well-placed to use the findings of research to lobby for change. The Balkans research was additionally useful in that it could be used within Oxfam GB, to place the issue on the agendas of those staff who had either not previously recognised the links between violence against women and conflict or who were unsure as to Oxfam's role and remit.

Box 7.2
The investigation of the rape of ethnic Chinese women during the May riots in Indonesia

The Volunteers for Humanity Group in Indonesia was made up of volunteers who undertook to gather testimonies and to provide protection and treatment for women who were victims of violence during the riots of May 1998. This role included ensuring the victims' safety from threats, confrontation, and intimidation. Volunteers included doctors and psychologists, who were able to contribute their skills to bolster networks of support to the women and their families. Assistance to the survivors of violence included medical and psychological treatment, and spiritual counselling.

By 2 July 1998, Volunteers for Humanity had documented 168 rapes in Jakarta, Solo, Medan, Palembang, and Surabaya. Twenty of the raped women died during or after the incident, and many also suffered other forms of torture or became trapped in fires started by the rioters (Wandita 1998).

Data was collected in a way that would protect the anonymity of the women, their families, and others involved, as far as possible. Women were often unwilling to acknowledge that they had been attacked, due to fears about stigmatisation and rejection by others. The investigators would begin by visiting women and their families, through the assistance of a contact person, in order to express their anger at the attack. The investigators would then explain that it was important for the women to document their experience and their losses in order to demand that the government be accountable for the violence. Finally, the investigators would enquire about women's immediate needs (Rahayu and McAvoy 1998).

7.2.4 The difficulties and dangers of investigating violence against women

The investigation conducted by Volunteers for Humanity in Indonesia, discussed above, exemplifies a key obstacle to uncovering the nature and scale of violence against women. The taboos surrounding violence against women mean that investigating it requires an awareness on the part of the researcher of the difficulties and dangers for the respondent. Women may not want to report the violence inflicted on them. The rape victims in Indonesia were reluctant to talk about the event because of the risk of stigma and scorn by others, who they feared would blame them for their misfortunes.

Conducting interviews with survivors of violence

There are several steps that an interviewer can take. Above all, the wish of a woman not to talk of her experiences must be respected. Where a woman does agree to be interviewed, it is important to follow-up the interview with a later meeting to offer support. The woman may be facing personal as well as social repercussions for speaking out. It is helpful to take a list of addresses of local contacts or organisations from which a woman can seek support should she need it.

Fear of offending sensibilities by trespassing on restricted areas of knowledge often has a constraining effect on research (Lee 1993, 20). However, there is potentially some therapeutic value for survivors in talking about violence, as discussed in the section on 'naming' violence in Chapter 5. This point is raised in the New York City/Balkans Rape Crisis Response Team training manual: 'Victims need to talk about their trauma again and again and the sooner they can do it, the better the chances of healthy recovery.' (New York City/Balkans Rape Crisis Response Team 1993, 15) The manual notes that the victim of assault experiences a tremendous loss of self-esteem, and that by telling others about it she may begin to restore her self-esteem and sense of acceptance (op. cit., 6).

Researchers' own cultural biases about violence and sex may also prevent them from properly investigating certain issues. It may be difficult to accept the truth of allegations of extraordinary cruelty or bizarre behaviour, because of what has been called the 'incredibility' factor (Welsh 1992). An interviewer should not show judgement or fear, and should be keen to investigate all issues brought up by an interviewee. Survivors of torture may appear unreliable or dishonest because they may experience extraordinary difficulty in recalling episodes of their experiences, confuse the location and timing of various events, or add details as they come to mind as they feel more trusting of the interviewer. They may put themselves under considerable pressure to ensure that their story makes an impression and is believed (ibid.).

The difficulty that a researcher may face in listening and confronting a story of violence against women is illustrated by the case of Joan Ringelheim, a researcher on violence against Jewish women during World War II. In a discussion of the research, Ringelheim focuses on an interview she conducted in 1979 with a woman survivor of the Holocaust. The woman had talked about women using sex with men in Auschwitz, the Nazi concentration camp, as a strategy in order to survive, but had not spoken of other forms of violence against women. Three years after the first interview, the survivor revealed to Joan that she had been raped in Auschwitz. Joan Ringelheim recalled: 'I don't remember saying anything right away; I just looked at her. She immediately added that she wasn't gang-raped, and that it was her fault anyway. I began to counsel her. I told her that this was often what rape victims said and tried to convince her that it wasn't her fault... I then said,"When you are ready to speak about this, perhaps in six months, I would like to hear about it."' (Ringelheim 1996, 26) The response displayed her own unreadiness and unease about talking about violence against women. Reluctance due to fear or ignorance on the part of an interviewer is immediately felt by an interviewee. The interviewee in this case did not say anything more about the rape. A better response from Joan to the interviewee's revelation of violence would have been to ask simply, 'What happened?'

Respecting confidentiality

Following an investigation, difficult questions arise related to what to do with the information collected. For example, where information is made publicly available, what should be done to minimise the risk of adverse consequences for victims, their families, and the organisation concerned? This was a dilemma facing the Volunteers for Humanity group in Indonesia. The church and monastery-based groups who had come up with the initial reports requested assistance from the coalition in supporting rape survivors; however, they did not wish the issues to be published the media. Volunteers for Humanity was torn between the urge to campaign publicly against these acts, and the desire to protect the survivors from the effects of publicity. In the end the reports got out through other sources. Consequently, Volunteers for Humanity was inundated with requests by the media for the names and contact details of survivors, and for their full testimonies. Volunteers for Humanity decided to respond with information on the rapes and patterns of violence that had emerged from their research, but refused to divulge names, thereby retaining the informants' confidentiality (Wandita 1998).

As a result of the research, intimidation and threats were directed at Volunteers for Humanity's investigators, informants and witnesses, the medical and hospital staff who spoke on behalf of the victims, and the victims and their families. Human rights and women's groups received telephone threats to stop their investigations and assistance to the rape victims (Volunteers for Humanity 1998). Some threats led to fatalities: Ita Martadinata Haryono was murdered in her home in Jakarta on 9 October 1998. Haryono had taken part in many of the coalition's activities, and had been preparing to travel to the USA with some of the rape victims, to testify before a human rights body. The murder was meant as a warning, and represented an escalation of the campaign to terrorise persons and organisations investigating the May riots (Coomaraswamy 1999a).

Some precautions to ensure the anonymity and safety of those interviewed include picking a topic for investigation that does not appear threatening, such as health, to indirectly broach violence against women (Swiss *et al.* 1998, in the context of war). A random selection process protects participants from the perception that they have been chosen to report a specific experience.

Researchers should inform the contacts or witnesses of the use that will be made of the information provided, of the reasons for gathering information, and of the actions that may be taken. It is important that the woman understands the implications of giving her testimony, and the basis upon which she shares information. Information should become confidential when the source asks for it to be so, or when the researcher decides that given its possible consequences it should remain so. Researchers should inform the woman that she may remain anonymous, or that her testimony will be confidential – that her name, location, and any other factor which reveals her identity – may be withheld. Ideally, testimonies should be taken privately on a one-to-one basis, unless the interviewee agrees to the presence of family members or friends.

Investigating violence against women in the context of conflict

Documenting violence against women in a context of war or conflict presents many additional challenges. These include the personal safety of researchers and participants, the confidentiality of the data, and the logistics of the research design and data collection. The researcher should avoid questions relating to identities of fighting factions, or details about where and when violent events occurred. Researchers may need to keep a low profile, and use inconspicuous vehicles. It may help if researchers are already known and respected by members of the community (Swiss *et al.* 1998).

Where possible, researchers should ensure that women are made aware of local contacts to whom they can continue to talk and report problems. The Medical Foundation for the Care of Victims of Torture, a London-based organisation that provides care and rehabilitation for individuals who have been subjected to torture and other forms of organised violence, followed up its research on rape and its effects on women in Uganda with assistance in seeking medical and legal advice, and a teaching programme with women health workers to promote discussion about rape as an effect of war and violence. In this way, it hoped that the women interviewed would find at least one person in the community to whom they could speak freely about their ordeal (Giller and Kabaganda 1990). More examples of this kind of post-research support can be found in Chapter 5.

7.3 Challenging attitudes by harnessing the media

Surveys conducted by women's organisations have shown that the media portray gender stereotypes that are detrimental to women and that can impact negatively on attitudes towards violence against women. However, because mass media communications reach and influence large numbers of people, they also have the potential to play a positive role in the struggle against violence against women. Communications technologies present new opportunities for the exploitation and abuse of women on an international scale, but also present unprecedented opportunities for individuals and organisations to present a different vision of gender relations and violence against women.

Challenging detrimental portrayals of women in the media

The media and development organisation, Isis International, conducted a survey in 1998 in ten countries in Asia and the Pacific region. Their survey, entitled 'The State of Women and Media: Focus on Violence against Women', examined media codes of conduct on the fair and objective representation of women and gender relations in media including newspapers, magazines and books, television, radio, advertising, film, and the internet. Their findings confirmed that current practices tend to reinforce traditional and cultural values that undermine the status of women. Ten years before the Isis research, another survey was conducted by the Tanzania Media Women's Association, which showed that the media in Tanzania were playing a major role in undermining women's images of themselves, as well as society's images of women (Tanzania Media Women's Association 1994).

Recent research conducted in Honduras examined the way in which the print media were treating the issue of violence against women. When the news made reference to violence against women, it tended to suggest that the violence was the result of the abnormal character of the abuser, or of the treachery of the attacked woman. Incidents of violence were depicted as rare and isolated events taking place mainly in public places, when in reality most violence occurs within the home (Rowlands 1997). Another example is of a television 'soap opera'[3] in Peru. *Leonela* has, as part of its storyline, a passionate relationship between a rapist (played by a well-known and very handsome Peruvian actor) and his victim. This conveys a clear message that rape is a legitimate part of a sexual relationship (Chiarotti 1998).

Women's organisations and local NGOs have valuable experience in encouraging the media to develop balanced and non-stereotyped portrayals of women. In turn, international media organisations are beginning to make efforts to ensure that their own materials contribute towards transforming gender power relations rather than perpetuating inequality. For example, Interpress News Service, a not-for-profit information and communications service for journalists, offers gender training and awareness-raising for media professionals. It is currently developing a specialised training manual, *How to Report on Gender Violence*, which is being field-tested in Southern Africa (Made 2000).

National-level women's organisations working on violence against women are also developing innovative ways of influencing the media. In Cambodia, the Women's Media Centre in Phnom Penh implemented a policy of writing to individual editors regularly, thanking them for positive stories portraying empowering female role models, and praising them for useful information on preventing violence against women (Pandian 1999). This strategy involved identifying possible allies in the media, meeting with them regularly, and enabling them to envisage how they could become part of the solution to the problem of violence against women.

International development and humanitarian organisations can also encourage the participation of media policy-makers, such as editors and publishers, as part of the development and human rights-focused agenda of the Beijing Platform for Action, which includes a section on women and media.

In countries of the former Soviet Union, while some of the barriers to freedom of expression that were in place under Communist rule have been lifted, new obstacles to working on violence against women have emerged. Despite the mass media's new-found freedoms, they have failed to inform the population about violence against women (Zabelina 1996). Instead, the currently predominant tendency amongst the media is to exploit instances of rape as a 'hot subject' that will titillate readers (Khodyreva 1996, 35). In fact, state broadcasting institutions that have continued from the Soviet era have turned out to be the most effective medium for raising awareness of violence against women. They offer a way forward for getting the issue into the public arena for discussion.

In this context of sensationalist media reporting, the work of newly emerging NGOs is especially important. For example, the Information and Consultative Centre, a local development organisation based in Georgia, used the state media to support and develop its work with women survivors of violence (see Box 7.3). Staff of the Centre realised that until the silence surrounding violence against women was broken, the issue could not be placed firmly in the public arena. Until this happened, outreach work with abused women would achieve only minimal success. The strategy of using the state media was a successful way of reaching a large audience, encouraging women to seek help and start using the telephone hotline, and collecting information to inform the development of the Centre's programme of work.

Using new communications technologies to challenge violence against women

The Janus-faced character of the media is illustrated by events surrounding the rapes of the Chinese women in Indonesia, documented by Volunteers for Humanity. The national and international media coverage that the rapes received to some extent reflected the priorities of male-dominated media companies that view rape cases as sensational or titillating. On the other hand, the readiness on the part of the mainstream press to publicise the plight of women victims of violence meant that national and international pressure obliged the new premier, President Habibie, to engage in dialogue with women's groups and to condemn the rapes (see for example Coomaraswamy 1999a). In addition, feminists in Indonesia were able to use electronic technologies to provide more serious coverage of the rapes from a feminist perspective. They used email and the Internet to mobilise networks of feminists, both internationally and nationally.

Some parts of the media carried misinformation and intimidation campaigns against the NGOs that had reported the rapes in Indonesia. In particular, the Internet was used to spread rumours, and to incite further rioting and raping. Bogus pictures of raped women were posted on the Internet in order to discredit the work of organisations aiming to document the rapes accurately. One worker for Volunteers for Humanity, Galuh Wandita, explained the intimidating effect of seeing these downloaded pictures: 'It makes me feel shocked, personally violated, and

---

Box 7.3
Using state television to raise awareness on violence against women in Georgia

With the help of an Oxfam GB-appointed social worker, staff from the Information and Consultative Centre, a local development organisation based in Georgia, went to camps where displaced people were staying, and asked women what they needed. The workers were met with great suspicion, based on people's past experiences of similar organisations acting as a mouthpiece for the State. Grassroots NGOs have no historical basis in Georgia, and for most people, the idea of working with such organisations on their problems was unknown. Gradually, through supporting small business activity, and after receiving phone calls from abused women, the workers began to discover the existence of domestic violence.

The best avenue to bring domestic violence out into the open for discussion seemed to be the strong institutions of state broadcasting. The Centre used a variety of media channels open to it to raise awareness around domestic violence. It publicised its activities through announcements in leading newspapers, on the radio, and, most importantly, through three 20-minute television programmes on violence against women, which were broadcast on March 8th – International Women's Day – in 1998. The first programme showed women victims of violence talking about their experiences; the second programme looked at the difficulties in relationships between men and women; and the third was about divorce.

This resulted in an immediate and marked increase in the number of calls to the Centre's telephone helpline. As a result, the Centre gained greater knowledge of the nature and extent of the problem of violence against women in the area, and was able to consider ways of expanding its activities.

Source: Getiashvili 1998

---

disempowered. Can you imagine the effect that they would have on a survivor? The images suggest, "Dare you speak, we will do this again."' (Wandita 1998, 40)

The Internet has become the latest vehicle for promoting the global trafficking and sexual exploitation of women (Hughes 1997). International media organisations and development agencies may play a role in supporting the policing of the Internet. The Internet Watch Foundation in the UK takes referrals from Internet users about content that is harmful or derogatory towards women and children, such as pornography. They investigate such instances, and where they suspect illegal activity has taken place, they report this to the police (Kerr 1997). In Sweden, the development organisation Rädda Bärnen (Save The Children Sweden) has employed 14 experienced computer hackers to search for child pornography and networking between sexual abusers on the Internet.

It reports findings to the police and Interpol (Kelly 1997).

International development agencies also have the potential to play a very important role in relation to electronic media and communications – that of supporting NGOs in developing countries to gain access to expensive new communications technologies as tools to end violence against women. For example, UNIFEM organised a video conference, entitled 'A World Free of Violence Against Women', which took place on 24 November 1998. This, together with UNIFEM's 'End Violence' electronic mail working groups, demonstrates the power of new technologies in communicating and linking on issues of violence against women. The video conference was held on the eve of the internationally-celebrated '16 Days of Activism Against Violence Against Women'. It aimed to bring together civil society, governments, and UN agencies to address violence against women. It highlighted innovative actions that had emerged from regional awareness-raising campaigns which UNIFEM had undertaken during 1998, and also described examples of innovative initiatives supported by the UNIFEM Trust Fund for violence against women (Heyzer 1998).

7.4 Challenging attitudes through public education and information campaigns

Popular education can be used to challenge assumptions about violence. Such campaigns might use comics, brochures, posters, videos, theatre productions, newsletters, information leaflets, and radio and television programmes.

Innovative methods of disseminating information to women and men must account for their different daily workloads, and the spaces they inhabit. Reaching women will require a presence at places such as market squares, health centres, and water-collection sites. Community-based education campaigns have used some novel methods to disseminate information at the grassroots level. Typically, such campaigns can use a wide range of media and can be more participatory. Community-based communications have included videos, story books, informal theatre, and puppet shows. Box 7.4 gives an example of a campaign that used a combination of media.

Radio programmes may be a particularly appropriate medium in contexts where literacy rates are low, distances from urban to rural areas are large, and where few people own televisions. However, radio has its limitations. In many communities, radios are predominantly owned by men, who control their use. Purchasing batteries may pose a problem for women, where they

Box 7.4

A popular education campaign to eradicate female genital mutilation in Ethiopia

This public education campaign, run by the National Committee for Traditional Practices of Ethiopia (NCTPE), has used a variety of audio-visual and print materials, including newsletters, stickers, slide shows, radio, and video. The mass information campaign is based on a long-term, integrated communications strategy that uses both mass media and interpersonal media to disseminate mutually-reinforcing messages.

A group of communications tools has been specially developed for use in workshop training for the general public. During training, participants learn about the health consequences of FGM, the origins and the prevalence of the practice, and learn to distinguish between the facts and the myths that surround it. Participants are encouraged to discuss the issue at length, to become engaged, and to join the campaign to eradicate harmful practices. Videos and slide shows are accompanied by story books for the participants to keep, once they have completed the workshop. One slide show recounts the married life of Alia, an infibulated woman who loses her child in childbirth, and later loses her husband when it becomes clear that she cannot have any more children. In contrast, another slide show presents a positive story about a couple who decide to resist social pressure to circumcise their baby girl.

In collaboration with UNHCR, NCTPE produced a video about infibulation, which is commonly used during the training sessions. Trainers find the video to be particularly effective with men, who are usually very much removed from the practice of female genital mutilation despite being connected with its root causes.

With the help of a graphic artist, posters on FGM were designed. Once completed, each poster was tested with a group of people representing the target audience, who gave feedback to the artists on their interpretation of the message. One such experiment carried out in Addis Ababa proved to be extremely valuable. The poster depicted a baby girl undergoing female genital mutilation, accompanied by a written message in Amharic saying, 'Female genital mutilation can increase the chances of getting AIDS.' Two members of the NCTPE staff – a man and woman – took the poster to one of the liveliest intersections in central Addis Ababa, to examine the effect of the poster on passers-by. The image showed a situation in which a baby was clearly suffering, but it was not offering a further action-oriented message: was it right or wrong to make the baby suffer, and why? What was the message of the poster? The pre-test showed that the image was ambiguous and the transmitted message unclear, and highlighted the need to develop the posters further.

Adolescents and primary school children are an important target group. In 1996, the NCTPE agreed with the Educational Media Agency (EMA), a government media agency, a series of 28 radio spots dealing with the need to eradicate female genital mutilation and early marriage. In Ethiopia, radio is the communications medium that reaches the largest number of people. The programmes were broadcast to 96 per cent of the school community in the country, in nine local languages. Two further ten-minute radio programmes for general audiences were aired each weekend, to expand on the brief messages highlighted during the radio spots. A set of supporting information leaflets in English and Amharic were sent to all school teachers.

Source: Spadacini and Nichols 1998

do not have control over the household income. In addition, the cost of buying radio time can be very expensive for organisations with limited resources.

Women's organisations and national- or local-level NGOs have played an important role in placing violence against women in the public arena through public education campaigns. They can ensure that messages about violence can be tailored to local realities. Community members can be actively involved in the dissemination and awareness-raising work, and campaigners can get direct feedback from the public about the strategy's effectiveness.

Like NCTPE, the Cambodian organisation Project Against Domestic Violence (PADV) uses a range of media in different contexts in order to reach the widest possible public audience. Research by the organisation demonstrated the importance of using a variety of tools to disseminate information about violence against women generally, and about the services that the programme offers to women in particular. Many clients came to the centre after a neighbour saw a television advertisement for PADV, a friend saw the sign for the organisation on the street, someone met a staff member putting a poster on a wall, or a hospital staff member told them about the project. The research revealed the need to find better ways of providing access for specific groups such as rural women, ethnic minority women, and women in internally displaced communities.

An important component of PADV's public awareness programme is to relate the message that violence is not only morally wrong, but that it is against the law. Through a range of media channels, including posters on public transport, in police stations, markets, government offices, NGOs, and schools, and broadcasts on TV and radio, the organisation raises awareness of domestic violence. Box 7.5 illustrates the process of developing a poster about violence against women. In addition, in co-operation with the Women's Media Centre, PADV has produced a video, with T-shirts and leaflets to help reinforce the message. Further plans for public education include theatre, a story book, and public discussions in villages (Project Against Domestic Violence 1996).

Box 7.5
PADV's poster development process

The Cambodian organisation PADV developed a poster campaign to communicate with both literate and non-literate people on the issue of violence against women.

Initially, PADV collected and archived sample drawings from several artists and cartoonists to identify a suitable designer for the poster. Working in collaboration with the Ministry of Women's Affairs and the Women's Media Centre, PADV conducted 14 focus groups in three provinces and Phnom Penh. The groups included literate and illiterate adults, children, villagers, journalists, and government staff. The focus groups investigated current attitudes about domestic violence, providing baseline indicators for future research. In addition, the groups decided on the message to be used in the first campaign.

After analysing and discussing the information from the focus groups, the three agencies commissioned poster illustrations and market-tested them with nearly 100 randomly selected individuals in local markets, government offices, and private homes, in Phnom Penh and selected provincial villages. Changes and adaptations were made in response to the research. Two thousand posters were produced for a limited release in one province (Kampong Speu) and Phnom Penh as a pilot campaign. Follow-up research and interviews were conducted and the poster was redesigned and reproduced in full colour and laminated for national distribution. The poster was first distributed on Domestic Violence Awareness Day.

Source: Project Against Domestic Violence 1996

Well-drawn images that stimulate discussion are likely to work well at community level. They can promote reflection on issues such as the causes of a specific form of violence and ways of overcoming it. The Karsa Kreatif Foundation in Indonesia focuses on the education and production of alternative media to support NGOs working with women victims of violence. Following requests from many other NGOs for creatively designed books, and exhibition and training material, the project published a cartoon book aimed at raising awareness of violence against women (PASF, Oxfam internal document 1996).

Role play and theatrical representations can also be effective tools for communication. Theatre has the power to raise public awareness of violence against women in a vivid, thought-provoking, and participatory way. Theatre is often effective when discussing sensitive topics, particularly in contexts where there is a strong oral tradition. The Sistren Theatre Collective, discussed in Box 7.6, is committed to using drama to

Box 7.6
Using theatre to say 'No!' to sexual violence in Jamaica

The Sistren Theatre Collective was set up in 1977, when a group of 13 women from the very poorest parts of Kingston, Jamaica, met as part of a government initiative for unemployed women. Sistren's members did not have a background in drama, but used their own lives as a starting point for their work. The plays arise from many hours of research, storytelling, and listening to the communities in which they work. From this, a theme emerges, improvisation starts, and gradually the play develops. Domestic violence, unemployment, teenage pregnancy, and sexual violence are all themes of their plays. The plays are taken all over Jamaica, to schools, community centres, the street, and to Sistren's headquarters (Sistren, no date given).

Sistren Theatre Collective's first play was presented at the annual Workers' Week Celebrations in Jamaica in 1977. The Sistren Collective created the play with the assistance of a drama teacher. After many hours of group discussion and personal storytelling, the theme of garment workers forming a union to defend their rights emerged.

In one play about women sugar workers, Sistren reminded the country's poor women that although Jamaican politics have been dominated by men since Independence in 1962, women also work for national development. However, the fact that their labour is invisible continues to obstruct Jamaican women's entry into the nation's political life (Bolles 1983).

The position of women is the starting point for the organisation's work, but it is set within the context of wider national and international issues such as external debt and militarisation. One of Sistren's newsletters shows how the organisation links class, poverty, and violence: 'The impact of the IMF's stringent measures and decline of the sugar market are linked to day-to-day health hazards and stresses, the urge to emigrate and increasing male violence; the fly-away factories of the free trade zones and exploitative employment are placed alongside rising unemployment and poverty.' (op. cit., 5) Sistren aims to create a critical attitude to violence, an understanding that women are not naturally required to submit to men, and an understanding that the blame for violence does not lie with women.

In 1984, Sistren published a leaflet, 'No to Sexual Violence' and staged a play that stimulated a discussion between the Collective and their audiences on domestic violence, male and female sexuality, and birth control. The play attempted to get the audience to define what they understood to be expressions of violence against women, as opposed to affectionate sexual experiences. It did this through scenes that showed acts of violence between men, women, and children. After each scene, the action halted while actors and audience explored what the problem was, and how it could be solved without violence. This allowed women to give their own interpretation of positive solutions. After each discussion, the Collective would continue the play, incorporating the audience's suggestions (Ford-Smith 1994).

> **Box 7.7**
> ## Using drama to educate men in the UK about violence and changing gender relations
>
> The Red Ladder Theatre Company in the UK has written and toured with a play called 'Wise Guys', a hard-hitting urban drama. The play was developed with young men, and focuses on male identity and the reasons for – and results of – criminal and violent behaviour in particular. Many young men from working class communities in the UK face long-term unemployment, with little or no support to cope with the changing nature of work, and other challenges to traditional male roles. The play presents the idea that young men and boys do have choices, and can use opportunities, such as fatherhood, to consider their behaviour and change it.
>
> The theatre company employs actors who are at ease with mixing with young people. The actors engage with the audience before and after the performance. The production package includes the preparation of materials for follow-up work. The play is a starting point for audience discussion of the changes in gender roles that are affecting their communities.
>
> The focus on men is not a substitute for, and will not divert resources from, ongoing work on women's subordination. It is an exploratory approach that examines the effects of the globalisation of labour, trade, and capital on gender roles at household level. The play will reach 4000 young people.
>
> *Source: Smith 1998, 10*

explore women's oppression. Using personal testimonies as a critique of a system that discriminates against women on the basis of their gender, class, and colour, Sistren confronts issues of sexual and domestic violence. Through theatre and drama-in-education techniques, it encourages the development of grassroots cultural expression on the issue (Sistren 1998).

The UK-based Red Ladder Theatre Company (see Box 7.7) uses an innovative approach, making men's behaviour the focus of its work. As with the Sistren productions, one of its main strengths is in linking global processes with gender relations at the local level.

In drama, as in other forms of popular communication, caution should be exercised when deciding how to present messages about violence against women. Condemnations of violence may be flatly rejected if they are presented in the wrong way. Alternatively, biases in society may be such that violence against women is perceived by an audience – or elements of an audience – as amusing. For example, in South Africa, a play geared to raising awareness about gender and HIV/AIDS depicted a scene where the boy and girl were negotiating condom use. The boy became violent, refused to use a condom, and raped the girl. At this, the boys in the crowd cheered (Nankunda Katangaza, The Law Society, London, personal communication 1999).

Sistren, the Jamaican women's theatre collective, works to overcome this problem:

> *We had to find ways of representing sexual violence that distanced it in such a way that the audience felt uncomfortable. In 1978, we presented an incident of rape where we used stocking faced characters. We elevated the woman who was being raped, and had the rapist use his fists to pummel the woman's vagina. The audience was absolutely hushed.*

(Ford-Smith 1994, 227)

This example suggests, in line with the discussion in the earlier section on printed media, that a symbolic representation of violence against women can sometimes be more powerful than a naturalistic one.

7.5 Group work to build 'critical consciousness' of violence against women

Although mass popular education and training do not by themselves offer a sustainable solution to changing attitudes towards violence against women, there are many cases in which these activities are an important first step.

Changing society's 'common sense' views involves challenging people's assumptions of what is a 'given' in society, and what can be changed. In order to do this, many development and humanitarian agencies have taken up elements of Paulo Freire's approach to 'education for liberation'. Paulo Freire's work on popular education programmes for slum dwellers in Brazil involved groups of people identifying problems and their causes, in order to develop strategies to bring about changes in their lives.

Popular education and training based on these principles is experiential and participatory, and involves starting from the level of awareness of trainees and the communities in which they live. In Freire's approach, people teach themselves through dialogue with each other, and trainers act as facilitators rather than teachers (Freire 1973). The training process stresses exchange of theoretical and experiential knowledge between different actors – community workers, project co-ordinators, advisers, families, professionals, and personnel from institutional services. NGOs and development funders that implement or support development work informed by this approach are making a very significant shift from service provision to supporting groups of poor people in making their own decisions about how social change should be implemented (Eade and Williams 1995, 359).

The process of developing 'critical consciousness' starts from a recognition that women's experience of violence comes about because of their inequality with men, and a recognition of the consequences of violence and inequality both for women themselves, and for society in general. Groups move from a 'common sense' idea of violence against women as a feature of society that is condoned or tolerated, to a 'critical consciousness' of violence against women as an abuse of human rights.

7.5.1 Training community members

Community-level training for attitudinal change on violence against women can take many forms. It aims to make particular powerful groups in society more sensitive to the problems faced by women survivors of violence, and to provide skills to enable these groups to protect women from future violence and support them in recovering from past violence. It is unlikely to work if the participants are not committed to the process of questioning their assumptions about violence, and acknowledging that it is the result of unequal power relations between men and women.

Training on violence against women is often underpinned by gender training, a process that aims to transform attitudes to gender roles and power relations in society. Gender training aims to increase people's knowledge about the distinctions between biological sex and socially constructed gender identities, which are reflected in women's and men's roles in society and the value attributed to these roles. Such an analysis is likely to provide the tools for understanding the causes of violence against women and to enable participants to develop strategies to eliminate violence. There are many sources of information on gender training, for example the *Oxfam Gender Training Manual*, Williams, Mwau, and Seed 1994.

A handbook on gender and popular education workshops, *On Our Feet, Taking Steps to Challenge Women's Oppression*, developed in South Africa, outlines some of the principles of transformatory training for increased community awareness on women's rights.

The handbook states that good training should:
- take place within a democratic framework;
- be based on subjects of concern to learners;
- pose questions and problems;
- examine unequal power relations in society;
- encourage everyone to learn and everyone to teach;
- involve high levels of participation;
- involve people's emotions, actions, intellects, and creativity;
- use varied activities.

The handbook also shows how training follows a cycle of stages; accordingly, training:

- begins with people's own experiences;
- moves from experience to analysis;
- moves from analysis to encouraging collective action to change oppressive systems;
- reflects on and evaluates its own processes.

(Davies 1994)

Often, awareness-raising about inequality is combined with training in applying these new forms of skills and knowledge to the identified needs of the trainee group. This can include self-help counselling for women, 'cascade training' of community workers, or training of traditional midwives in health and hygiene.

The Grupo Apoyo Pedagogico (GAP) in Colombia has used cascade training in its work to combat violence against women during Colombia's continuing civil war. GAP's initiative has been founded on the premise that individuals in the community, when acting as community workers, fuel processes of social change. Cascade training seeks to effect widespread change in attitudes and behaviour by training a relatively small number of women, and encouraging them to share what they have learned with other women and particular groups who can influence society, such as community leaders and school teachers.

GAP's cascade training programme was organised in conjunction with CEDMUJER (Centro de Desarollo para la Defensa de los Derechos de la Mujer – Development Centre for the Defence of Women's Rights), an organisation in Bosa in south-west Bogota. GAP and CEDMUJER set up a chain of informal women's groups to offer individual women assistance in learning to use various conceptual tools which would enable them to challenge the violence against women that they encountered in their daily lives. Paulina Gonzalez Sanchez made a presentation on GAP's experience at the international Oxfam workshop on violence against women which was held in Bosnia in November 1998. Her presentation is outlined in Box 7.8.

It is clear from GAP's experience that an important factor in the success of the cascade approach to raising awareness of violence in the community is the selection of trainees with experience, knowledge, and status, who are well trusted within the community. This increases the likelihood that they will be well received when they themselves adopt the role of trainer.

Many of the GAP trainees were daunted by the task ahead. Creating a safe atmosphere of trust and openness was important for enabling trainees to share their anxieties and to make better use of the exercises introduced. One community worker explained that she gained confidence when, in Stage Two, she started to empathise with the women she was training:

> *When I realised how difficult it was for them to talk, I remembered what*
> *I had gone through with the psychologist when I started, and I told them*
> *how I blushed and my mind went fuzzy, about being afraid and how*
> *I thought "What does she want me to say?" I told them that we aren't used*
> *to speaking in public and it is hard to believe at first that we have anything*
> *useful to say. After I had said this, their eyes lit up and the tension turned*
> *to laughter. One person began to talk which encouraged the others.*
> *I became more at ease, and thought that perhaps I would be able to*
> *co-ordinate my group after all.*

The need to respond to the emotional reactions of those involved in the cascade training, including addressing their fears and doubts, did not form a separate topic of training, but was built into the process of the training course.

In a discussion of such work, Jane Shackman and Jill Reynolds suggest that, 'Addressing participants' own concerns and anxieties is a good way to start such a training course. It will enable you to identify more clearly their training requirements, and increase their confidence in expressing and asserting their needs.' (Shackman and Reynolds 1996, 69) They also advise that, 'You need to build in opportunities for participants to reflect on and talk about the work, and about the training exercises you have asked them to do, and the feelings they may stir up.' (op. cit., 70) In addition, the establishment of on-going support networks for community workers can counteract some of the burn-out that happens in community-level work on violence, where after a while, workers find themselves depressed, bored, or discouraged.

In contexts where there are powerful mechanisms of social and cultural control, gender training with women and girls may be unrealistic. In a society where women are highly secluded, for example, training for women and girls may be seen as threatening to family or community 'honour'. In such situations, local women's organisations are the best-placed to advise on the realities of gender inequality in their particular context, and the best way forward for work to challenge women's oppression (Eade and Williams 1995, 215).

Gender training of community members may not be enough to end violent behaviour. For example, an older woman present in one NGO training workshop was known to harass her daughter-in-law. As a young bride, she had faced deprivation and humiliation at the hands of her own mother-in-law, and she had internalised these patterns of domination. Her only source of security was through her married son, and the only way in which she could exercise authority was through dominating her daughter-in-law and controlling her labour. The woman was unlikely to alter the strategies she had developed to optimise her life options on the basis of a single workshop experience (Murthy 1996).

Box 7.8
GAP's cascade training of women to challenge domestic violence in a displaced community in Colombia
Stage 1

Ten women were selected for initial training as community workers. They all possessed a minimum of ten years of education, personal charisma, and leadership capacity. With the support of psychologists, group members discussed aspects of their backgrounds and daily lives. They visited other communities where they heard women's testimonies of domestic violence. One aim at this stage was for the group to study and become familiar with legislation relating to women, their sexual and reproductive rights, children's rights, and international human rights. The women found some of the work at this stage very difficult, particularly the legal training, the requirement to move from one city to another, and listening to many sad personal stories.

Stage 2

After the group of ten community workers had formed, the next stage was for each of them to create their own groups. To begin with, the community workers could not find enough participants. However, when they thought about their different social networks, they were able to begin to create groups of friends, family members, and colleagues. In the first session, the community workers felt inhibited about talking about their experience in an informal, relaxed way, but they soon realised that the others in the group were much more afraid and unsure about speaking out than they were. When they thought about how they had been when they first started on the training programme, they could empathise with the rest of the group.

At this stage, the ten trained community workers in each group contacted heads of local schools, and organised workshops with parents. Throughout this process, the adviser supported the community workers by creating opportunities for them to meet and reflect on their experiences. The community workers voiced their feelings about leading the groups, the responsibility of having such huge numbers of people in their communities confide in them, and the difficulty of being in situations that involved confronting their own experiences of violence. They also talked about practical issues, such as what mechanisms were needed to support women who had experienced abuse and to sanction the men responsible, and requests for protection. The community workers began to recognise the importance of the academic and legal dimension to their training, which gave them the skills and confidence to carry out their work.

> ## Stage 3
>
> The final stage of the project focused on the provision of legal advice and
> support for women, children, and young people in violent situations.
> As a result of the organised workshops, many women came forward
> seeking protection from long-term domestic and sexual violence.
> Women also wanted to change their own violent behaviour towards their
> children, and to get food assistance where men were unable to provide for
> their families. When a woman in an abusive situation asked for assistance,
> she was directed to institutions where she could lodge a complaint.
> The community worker supported her in doing this, and helped her to
> handle the bureaucratic formalities.
>
> *Source: Gonzalez-Sanchez 1998*

7.5.2 Training workers in the health sector

A number of NGOs have been involved in activities that aim to help health
workers to understand and eradicate different forms of violence against
women. Many workers in these areas are well-aware of the existence of
forms of violence, and, as could be seen from the discussion of female
infanticide in Chapter 3, some may be involved in perpetuating it. However,
health workers may be unaware of the root causes of violence, and may
lack ideas about how best to end it. In the main, awareness-raising and
training tend to focus on changing health workers' behaviour. For example,
training that aims to end female infanticide may encourage midwives and
other health workers to report specific incidents of female infanticide to the
police, and to offer counselling to expectant mothers, in order to prevent
these killings.

However, in order to be effective in ending violence, interventions need to
be rooted in a clear analysis of the unequal power relations between women
and men that result in violence. They also need to contribute to awareness-
raising among the wider community, many members of which may
condone the continuation of violent practices (George 1997). A strategy
that meets these criteria is described in Box 7.9.

In addition to running popular education campaigns, described earlier in
this chapter, the NCTPE also runs training of trainers courses to change
attitudes to genital mutilation. The training of trainers course is held in
different regions of the country, and the training packages are adapted and
translated so that they are appropriate for people living in each region. The
training packages present female genital mutilation primarily as a health
issue, but also explore the social, cultural, and religious aspects in a sensitive
manner. Training packages are adapted according to the target group.

The youth package for male and female secondary school students provides information on puberty, sexual responsibility, and the prevention of STDs.

Box 7.9

Tackling female infanticide: training midwives in Bihar

A workshop with *dais* (traditional midwives) in Bihar, India, explored the underlying power structures within families and communities that lead to son-preference and the practice of female infanticide. The workshop aimed to explore gender discrimination among different caste and religious groups; to understand the history and extent of female infanticide in the region; and to identify strategies to combat the problem. The workshop utilised participatory methods, such as drawing pictures and role-play. Role-play was effective because the sensitivity of the issue made it easier for participants to act rather than talk about their experience directly.

Several innovative strategies were suggested by the dais for tackling female infanticide:

1. Making the prevalence of female infanticide visible to state officials

A further workshop was planned with government departments, district court officials, commercial and co-operative banks, and NGOs to discuss a joint survey that would collect information on the female infants who had died. A campaign for compulsory registration of births and deaths would also be launched.

2. Setting up watchdog committees at village level

Watchdog committees could be set up by NGOs and would be made up of sarpanchs (leaders of local self-governance institutions), school teachers, religious leaders, and government officials. Staff from local NGOs would keep track of the prevalence of infanticide, ensure registration of births and deaths, raise awareness of the problem, exert social pressure to prevent female infanticide, and resort to legal action where necessary.

3. Promotion of anti-poverty programmes with dais and other women from vulnerable groups

Strategies to raise the incomes of all women and not just dais are necessary because otherwise parents will hire other poor women to kill female infants.

4. Raising awareness using dais as agents of change

Carried out by NGOs, such a programme could be directed at men and women from all communities. Awareness could be raised by holding *shivirs* (awareness-raising camps) at village level and organising a *padayatra* (march) of parents who were proud and happy to have daughters.

Source: Murthy 1996

The package for health workers is more scientifically detailed, and, along with the package for community leaders, emphasises the social implications of female genital mutilation, and contains a section on human rights. The trainees themselves then become trainers of community leaders, conducting training seminars with groups that are selected for the influence they command over others in the community. A separate guide for trainers, containing technical and teaching suggestions to help the trainers prepare, conduct, and evaluate the workshops, has also been developed (Spadacini and Nichols 1998).

The examples of work with midwives on infanticide, and work with community leaders and particular sectoral workers on FGM, raise many questions about whether it is possible to create allies amongst those who may condone, or even perpetrate, forms of violence against women. Participatory methods are useful in indicating the complexity of power relations, and are an effective way of capturing the factors that lead to female infanticide and identifying appropriate strategies. In addition, many people involved in perpetuating violence are not actually faced with the reality of that violence; use of video and drama can be effective in bringing violence to their attention – an example is NCTPE's use of video to educate men in particular about FGM.

7.5.3 Training of development workers

NGOs, like other institutions, reflect unequal power relations in society. Their ideologies, resource allocation patterns, rules, and practices can overtly or covertly act in the interests of the men within the NGOs themselves, and the communities in which they work (Goetz 1992). There are countless examples of the ways in which NGOs can reinforce unequal gender relations through their interventions. However, NGOs are often set up by women or men who are conscious of inequality within society, and seek to combat it (Murthy 1998). Their objectives are often based on an understanding of how the subordination of specific groups is reflected by social institutions and by organisations. Staff in such organisations may be more than usually receptive to sharing awareness of the causes of violence against women, and challenging the communities in which they work to end it.

Ranjani Murthy, a gender and development consultant based in India, has identified three objectives that underpin gender training in grassroots NGOs:

1. The aim of 'gender-aware institutional change', to make NGOs more gender sensitive through creating spaces to reflect upon objectives, programmes, and internal functioning from a gender perspective;

2. The aim of empowering women in NGOs in the context of their personal lives, and in their interactions with other NGOs and with the community;

3. The aim of redefining the power of men in NGOs, motivating male staff to redefine their relations within their families, the NGOs, and the community from a gender perspective (Murthy 1998, 203).

Challenging and renegotiating gender power relations is central to these three objectives. Women need to recognise and develop a sense of power within themselves, and men to recognise the injustice of their retaining power over women through institutions.

In NGOs, training is not an end in itself, but one of a portfolio of tools in a wider process of institutionalising competence on gender and violence. While training of NGO staff may go some way to raising awareness of inequality and the role of violence against women in perpetuating it, it cannot be relied on to transform attitudes either as a single strategy, or in the short-term. Rather, it should be regarded as just one element in 'mainstreaming' gender issues into NGOs (Smyth and Porter 1999). Training alone is unlikely to bring about widespread change in people's attitudes towards violence. In this sense, it is best viewed as part of a wider strategy to change behaviour at the community level.

As discussed in Chapter 6, there is growing interest in overcoming the difficulty of working with men to secure women's human rights. In a discussion of her experiences of running gender training sessions with men from NGOs in Bangladesh, trainer and activist Kamla Bhasin argues that male staff tend to find it hard to make links between specific examples of gender inequality in daily life, and an understanding of systemic inequality between women and men throughout society. Men can be resistant to accepting that women are systematically subordinated.

As an example of this point, Kamla Bhasin describes a session in a workshop that focused on the position of men and women in the family. She asked the participants to put on the blackboard the oppressions that men and women may suffer within the family. The women's column was quickly filled with items such as female foeticide, female infanticide, sexual assault, psychological harassment, sexual assault, and so on. The participants were pushed to suggest oppression men face in the family. They suggested, 'They find it hard to cry', and, 'They have to submit to stereotypes.' When Bhasin pointed out the many injustices faced by women in the family, the participants became upset, accusing her of 'wanting to break up peaceful families' and 'attacking local culture' (Bhasin 1997).

If training is linked to other organisational processes, systems, and procedures, attitudinal and behavioural changes are more likely to occur. There is a vast and continuously growing literature on 'mainstreaming' gender issues into organisations, which deserves attention from all development policy-makers and practitioners who are committed to ensuring that their organisations build the capacity of staff to understand and address violence against women.[4]

7.6 Summary and implications for development organisations

This chapter has examined the role of women's organisations and development projects in influencing the values and beliefs that condone violence. Challenging and changing attitudes and beliefs is an important task in creating a climate that refuses to tolerate men's violence. The strategies discussed do not 'target' women survivors of violence, or the individual men or groups of men who perpetrate violence. Rather, they attempt to promote attitudinal change within wider society. Different strategies may be directed at very different target groups, including parents, school pupils, family members, young unemployed men, midwives, health workers, development workers, and so on.

The chapter began by discussing the role that women's groups and development organisations can play in generating and bringing together information on violence against women. This information provides the basis for awareness-raising and campaigning around issues of violence. The chapter discussed the difficulties of researching violence against women, stressing the need for sensitivity and an awareness of the possible repercussions of research, when interviewing survivors and witnesses of violence against women.

The chapter went on to consider the role of media in affecting widespread attitudinal change. It pointed out that media institutions may be allies or enemies of women's organisations' work. Although media institutions are often responsible for detrimental portrayals of women, they are potentially a powerful medium for educating a large numbers of people that violence is wrong. The chapter examined strategies that use mainstream mass media, and then considered alternative media such as drama and local-level campaigning

Some development organisations and women's organisations working on violence against women have concentrated their efforts on encouraging mainstream media providers to address violence, and to examine critically their portrayal of women. Other organisations, like PADV in Cambodia and the Information and Consultative Centre in Georgia, use television and radio as media for disseminating information to a large audience. The PADV project in Cambodia and NCPTE in Ethiopia illustrate the importance of government support for nationwide campaigns.

A final strategy considered to bring about attitudinal change was training in order to raise awareness of inequalities between women and men, the role of violence against women in perpetuating these inequalities, and strategies for ending violence. The chapter described strategies for training community-level workers who can act as catalysts for change. Gender training within organisations can underpin such initiatives, and enhance their sustainability. Learning and awareness changes about issues of violence against women can also be catalysed by processes such as the evaluation of programme activities, and sharing of knowledge and experience.

8 Challenging the State

In the context of norms recently established by the international community, a State that does not act against crimes of violence against women is as guilty as the perpetrators. States are under a positive duty to prevent, investigate and punish crimes associated with violence against women.

(Radhika Coomaraswamy, UN Special Rapporteur on violence against women, its causes and consequences, 1995, para. 72)

The State is an extremely important player in strategies to end violence. In terms of protection and support, state institutions are often a first port of call for survivors of violence. Governments and state institutions also have an important role in preventing violence against women from occurring.

The key role of the State in ending violence against women has been recognised in international agreements, described in Chapter 2. These oblige states to respond to the issue of violence against women. The Declaration on the Elimination of Violence against Women, adopted by the UN General Assembly in 1993, identifies three main categories of violence against women, namely physical, sexual, and psychological violence occurring within the family, within the community, and perpetrated or condoned by the State (Article 2). It also explicitly recognises that women in situations of conflict are especially vulnerable to violence (Preamble, para. 7). Article 4 outlines the measures that the State should take to address violence against women. For example, states should implement policies that include counselling, health and social services, and general preventative, punitive, and remedial measures.

In turn, the 1995 Beijing Platform for Action sets out the specific steps that governments must take to end violence against women, including violence against women in the home. Measures suggested by the Platform for Action include the condemnation of violence against women, regardless of customary, traditional, or religious considerations; refraining from engaging in violence against women; taking active steps to punish and redress such violence, including passing legislation; ratifying international human rights instruments; providing women who are subject to violence with access to mechanisms of justice; raising awareness about violence against women; and providing training to judicial, legal, medical, social, educational, police, and immigration personnel on how to respond to violence. The Platform for Action also demands that states report on the measures they take against violence against women, and that they co-operate with UN human rights monitoring bodies (Chapter IV, para. 4.9).

In many countries, the law deals with different forms of violence separately, and in different ways, as if they had no structurally related cause. Domestic violence, sexual assault, sexual harassment, and violence related to culture and tradition, have been treated by national law as unrelated crimes. The connections between different forms of violence against women tend to be ignored, and the common root cause of different forms of violence, the unequal relations between women and men, is not made explicit. Jane Connors, the current Secretary of the CEDAW Committee, has criticised this approach, stating that it has led to states developing fragmented and *ad hoc* strategies to address different forms of violence against women (Connors 1993). Considerable evidence of the failings in state responses to violence against women has been offered in earlier chapters of this book.

As the Special Rapporteur's quote at the start of this chapter suggests, the widening of state responsibility for violence against women in international human rights law, so that it includes abuses by private actors as well as agents of the State, has been a centrally important strategy for combating violence against women. Ensuring that national laws also widen their remit involves legal reform. With this in mind, the chapter emphasises the importance of the role of international and national NGOs in challenging state policy. To do this effectively, co-operation and strategic alliances between different kinds of NGOs are critical. Resulting coalitions have pooled their learning about the principles and use of the international agreements, declarations, and conventions that are relevant to violence against women. Development and humanitarian organisations can play a significant role in pressuring for change, through advocacy, lobbying, training, and the development of co-operative relations with state actors.

8.1 Strengthening legal responses to violence against women

Unless criminal law enshrines specific measures to protect women from violence, and to punish perpetrators, it is unlikely to provide an effective framework for the reduction of violence against women. Some national legal systems incorporate specific laws relating to violence against women. These laws potentially provide individual victims with remedies, and are a key indication of the level of government commitment to opposing violence (Council of Europe 1997). Women's organisations and other NGOs in various countries have lobbied their governments for legal reform, where the legal system does not provide adequate protection for women.

In Bolivia, for example, women's organisations worked with the government in drawing up a national law on violence against women. The law, which was passed in 1995, was the result of many years of work in defining violence against women, making recommendations on how to change existing laws, proposing new ones, creating new NGOs to work on violence against women, and making strategic alliances with national and international bodies. The result was a national plan for a law that would punish violent crime, ensure the compilation and dissemination of information about violence against women, create services for victims, and educate the public to alter patterns of behaviour that reinforce discrimination and violence. Diane Urioste of the Centro de Promoción de la Mujer Gregoria Apaza explained to the participants at the Oxfam international workshop on violence against women in Sarajevo in 1998 how the law came to fruition (see Box 8.1).

Box 8.1
Making violence against women a crime in Bolivia: the role of the women's movement

In Bolivia, the women's movement was instrumental in the development of state policy to combat violence. Up until 1995, the law did not recognise domestic violence against women as a crime. Section 276 of the Criminal Procedure Code stated that, 'As grounds for impunity, the law provides that no penalty will be applied when injuries are slight and where inflicted by the husband or wife, parents or children, siblings, relatives directly related or by marriage, and brothers-in-law, when living under the same roof.' Section 112 of the Criminal Procedure Code stated that, 'Children and parents may not bring legal action against one another; nor directly related cousins and uncles; husbands or wives.'

It has been difficult to work on violence against women in Bolivia. Critics have accused women's organisations of distracting public and government attention from the more important work of transition to a democratic system of government. However, an opportunity to promote human rights presented itself in 1993, when the new government came into power with a commitment to human development, and many women who had previously been working in NGOs went to work for the government. This meant it was possible to make allies in government who could apply pressure to institutionalise policies on violence against women.

The women's movement, which had emerged almost two decades beforehand, was experienced in lobbying for the passing of a new law. It used the Inter-American Convention on the Prevention, Punishment, and Eradication of Violence Against Women as a yardstick against which to measure and develop proposals for national legislation. The Convention was also used as a lobbying tool.

In 1994, the National Plan for the Prevention and Eradication of Violence Against Women was formulated and implemented. Formulated by the Under-Secretariat for Gender Affairs (SAG), it was put forward with the objective of 'overcoming the legal and socio-cultural obstacles, and providing adequate services for the population with the aim of tackling the many dimensions of the problem.' (National Plan for the Prevention and Eradication of Violence Against Women, Ministerial Resolution No. 139.94) The National Plan adopted the definition of violence against women used in the Inter-American Convention on the Prevention, Punishment, and Eradication of Violence Against Women. This defines violence against women as 'any gender based action or conduct that leads to death, injury or psychological or sexual suffering in private or public life' (Article 1). One of the central problems identified by the Plan was the absence of adequate legislation. One of the actions proposed included the formulation of adequate legal rules and proceedings for the prevention and punishment of violent crime.

The Inter-American Convention on the Prevention, Punishment, and Eradication of Violence Against Women was recognised by the government of Bolivia, and Sections 276 of the Penal Code and Section 112 of the Bolivian Criminal Procedure Code were abolished. A law was passed relating to domestic and family violence, which came into effect in December 1995. The Bolivian Penal Code was reformed in relation to sexual violence and violent crimes, and a law against Sexual Harassment was drawn up.

Source: Urioste 1998.

The successful example of the passing of laws and policies to combat violence against women in Bolivia demonstrates the importance of local and international women's movements working together to apply pressure on governments. It also points to the power of international conventions in promoting change at national level.

Very few countries have specific laws that deal with sexual harassment. When they do, their scope is often restricted to violence by those in positions of authority. Association Democratique des Femmes du Maroc (ADFM) is a member of Collectif 95 Maghreb Egalité. It promotes the protection of women in Morocco from violence in public spaces, including the workplace. In Morocco, victims of violence do not benefit from legal protection. Moroccan law does not sanction against sexual harassment as such; the legal provisions that may be used relate to public acts of indecency and incitement to debauchery (Collectif 95 Maghreb Egalité 1998).

In those countries that do not have specific laws on sexual harassment, labour law to deal with incidents that occur within the workplace, even though sexual harassment that occurs outside the workplace is not punishable in law. In India, the opposite is the case. 'Eve-teasing'[1] is prohibited in Indian legislation (Council of Europe 1997), but there is no protection against sexual harassment at work. Sakshi, a violence against women intervention centre based in New Delhi, India, has experience in lobbying for sexual harassment at work to be addressed in the Indian legal system (see Box 8.2).

The blame and doubt that women who have been raped often face means that many of them do not go to the police or courts for assistance. As previous chapters have shown, those who do often find that the police and judiciary fail them in some way. Women experience widespread failures on the part of police and legal officials to carry out the procedures necessary for supporting women and punishing their attackers. In presenting their case to the police and judiciary, women frequently find that they face extreme difficulty in providing evidence that is considered acceptable to prove their claims.

In India, prior to amendments to the Penal Code in 1983, the legal definition of rape was based on a notion of consent. Under this type of definition, women must provide evidence that they tried to resist the rape, in order for the attacker to be prosecuted. The coercion that women may feel as a result of the threat of violence is given no credence in this kind of legislation. In 1983, amendments to the Indian Penal Code shifted the burden of proving the lack of consent to the accused in cases of custodial rape – violations condoned or perpetuated by the State in situations in which the State serves as the physical keeper of an individual, such as in situations of compulsory psychiatric institutionalisation, medical and educational custody, police custody, and penal (criminal) custody. In 1997, the government approved a further amendment to the Penal Code so that neither the character, reputation, and conduct of the victim, nor a delay in the reporting time, should be adequate reason for imposing a sentence of less than seven years on the perpetrator. Despite this legislation, in practice, women's dress or their marital or social status are in some cases still used to provide evidence to show that the rape was in some sense justified (Nilofer 1998).

Box 8.2
Sakshi's work in lobbying for sexual harassment in the workplace to be addressed in Indian law

Sakshi was set up in October 1992 in response to the harassment and gang rape of a woman who was fighting to stop child marriages amongst upper caste families.[2]

Following her death, Sakshi, together with other women's organisations, filed a legal petition with the Supreme Court of India. The petition demanded the establishment of guidelines prohibiting sexual harassment. Following a long struggle, Supreme Court Guidelines on Sexual Harassment at the Workplace were passed in August 1997.

The guidelines define sexual harassment as any unwelcome physical contact and advances, requests for sexual favours, sexual innuendo, display of pornography, or any other unwelcome physical, verbal, or non-verbal conduct of a sexual nature. These guidelines are restricted to the workplace, but are broad enough to encompass violent behaviour from any colleague – not only those in positions of authority. They make the employer responsible for preventing sexual harassment, and sanctioning against it when it occurs. As a result, government and private institutions are legally obliged to treat sexual harassment as a crime that requires both redress and preventative measures to be undertaken by governments and employers.

Sakshi and other organisations have advocated that these guidelines should be implemented through the setting up of a complaints committee within each organisation, headed by a woman, and including a third party representative from an NGO who has expertise on the issue.

Sakshi is running training sessions on how to use the guidelines in different institutions. Whilst they are pioneering, these measures do not address violence outside the workplace and it is unclear how they will apply to the increasing numbers of women who work in the informal sector, often in exploitative conditions.

Source: Kapur 1998

Rape can be defined in a narrow way that leaves out many forms of violence. The Indian anti-rape campaign's focus on custodial rape meant that other forms of rape, such as marital rape and rape within the family were excluded or sidelined (Gangoli 1998). There has as yet been no amendment in law to include rape within marriage in India. The only exception is if the wife is below 16 years of age (Karlekar 1998).

Some countries have begun to recognise marital rape as a criminal offence, although others argue that rape does not exist between husband and wife. In Sri Lanka, recent amendments to the Penal Code recognise marital rape but only with regard to separated partners (Coomaraswamy 1996, para. 64). Other countries have legislated against marital rape between partners living together. For example, in Cyprus, the Law on the Prevention of Violence in the Family and Protection of Victims, passed in June 1993, clarifies that 'rape is rape, irrespective of whether it is committed within or outside marriage.' (ibid.) Similarly, Canada and various Australian states have altered their rape legislation. Previously, it was the task of the court prosecution to prove that a woman did not consent to sex. The law has been changed so that the burden of proof now falls on the accused, who must provide evidence that consent was sought and given (Council of Europe 1997).

The law can only be made to work for women if the judicial system allows it to do so. Women survivors of violence need support throughout the judicial process. In particular, cases of rape and sexual violence demand sensitivity to the fact that women who go to court almost certainly face stigmatisation and blame. Judicial procedures need to be critiqued in the light of this, and reformed where appropriate. A Council of Europe report on responses to violence against women details reforms introduced in New South Wales, Australia, in the 1980s, and in Canada (Council of Europe 1997).

In New South Wales, these reforms included:

- the restriction of evidence relying on the sexual history of the defendant;
- an overhaul of the prosecution process, including training of prosecutors about the realities of rape and rapists;
- the proper application of 'similar fact evidence' (in which, if the same man is accused of raping more than one woman, and the cases are similar, they can be tried together);
- the introduction of video recording of women's statements, and the use of screens in court to prevent women from having to face their attacker in open court;
- speedier processing of cases;
- the introduction of monitoring of trials and analysis of acquittal rates to monitor regional variation in outcomes.

Radhika Coomaraswamy, the Special Rapporteur on violence against women, its causes and consequences, describes some of the positive changes in Rape Law in some countries in her 1997 report on violence against women in the community:

> *The legal definition of rape in most countries is limited to non-consensual or forced vaginal penetration, so that the focus is on a male perspective of acceptable boundaries of heterosexual sex rather*

*than on the victim's experience of sexualized violence. Some
Commonwealth jurisdictions, however, have revised their definitions
of rape to focus more broadly on acts other than penile penetration,
such as the insertion of objects into the vagina and anus.
Consent has been defined as the legal dividing line between rape and
sexual intercourse. In court, the argumentation over consent,
however, often degenerates into a contest of wills and credibility.
Many courts are reluctant to find the defendant guilty of rape in the
absence of physical injuries. If consent forms an integral part of the
definition of rape as a crime, as in most legislation, prosecution must
assume the burden of proving the lack of consent beyond a reasonable
doubt. If, however, consent is provided as an affirmative defence
outside the definition of rape, the burden of proof of consent shifts to
the accused. In 1983, amendments to the Indian Penal Code shifted
the burden of proving the lack of consent to the accused in cases of
custodial rape. The latter still does not constitute mainstream legal
thinking on the subject, however.*

(Coomaraswamy 1997b, Section B para. 34)

International development and humanitarian agencies can also play a key
role in influencing the policy and laws of individual states. There have been
positive developments recently in relation to violence against women in the
realm of refugee law (see Box 8.3).

Box 8.3
Challenging states to 'engender' refugee law: the role of the UNHCR

The 1951 Convention relating to the Status of Refugees defines 'refugee'
as an individual who has 'a well-founded fear of being persecuted for
reasons of race, religion, nationality, membership of a particular group or
political opinion...' (Art. 1(2)). Although the Refugee Convention does not
recognise gender-based persecution as a grounds for granting refugee
status, the UNHCR document *Sexual Violence against Refugees: Guidelines
on Prevention and Response* (more commonly known as the Gender
Guidelines) encouraged states to recognise gender-based forms of
persecution as a part of the Refugee Convention definition. Rape and
sexual violence may be considered grounds of persecution within the
Convention definition if the State is unable or unwilling to provide
protection (Art. 1(A)2). Further, in 1993, the Executive Committee
(EXCOM) of the UNHCR condemned persecution through sexual
violence. It called on states to develop guidelines to address the needs of
women asylum-seekers, because women refugees are often persecuted in
different ways to men, and for different reasons.

EXCOM Conclusion 73 notes 'the widespread occurrence of sexual violence in violation of the fundamental right to personal security as recognized in international human rights and humanitarian law, which inflicts serious harm and injury to the victims, their families and communities, and which has been a cause of coerced displacement including refugee movements in some areas of the world.'

It also notes that 'refugees and asylum-seekers, including children, have in many instances been subjected to rape or other forms of sexual violence during their flight or following their arrival in countries where they sought asylum, including sexual extortion in connection with the granting of basic necessities, personal documentation or refugee status.'

Among other measures, the Conclusion urges states to develop training programmes for military and law enforcement officers that include training in offering protection from sexual violence; to implement legal systems for investigating complaints of sexual abuse; and to provide medical and psycho-social care, and counselling facilities to refugee victims of sexual violence and their families. The Conclusion also supports claims to refugee status based upon a well-founded fear of persecution through sexual violence, and stresses the importance of ensuring the presence of female field staff in refugee programmes.

The UNHCR's call has led to some progressive interpretations of refugee law by national governments. For example, Canada and the USA have incorporated FGM,[3] forced abortion, and sterilisation, as constituting gender-based persecution in the granting of refugee status (Coomaraswamy 1998, 60). The threat of such violence is now considered a legitimate ground to claim asylum in the USA or Canada under the 1951 Refugee Convention. The US *Guidelines on Gender Issues in Asylum Claims* recognise a variety of forms of gender-related persecution in addition to female genital mutilation, including sexual abuse, rape, infanticide, forced marriage, slavery, domestic violence, and forced abortion (ibid.). In March 2001, a US federal appeals court broadened the interpretation of grounds for political asylum when it ruled that a woman should not be deported to Mexico on the grounds that she would face abuse from her father if she returned (McDonnell 2001).

The ICTR and ICTY have also played an important part in influencing national governments, through setting standards for supporting women survivors of rape and sexual violence in conflict and their witnesses through the prosecution process (see Box 8.4). In conflict as in peacetime, lack of protection for victims and witnesses has been a central problem in prosecuting cases of rape and sexual violence.

Local women's organisations can play an important role in working with the legal system to bring forward cases of sexual violence. In the ICTR September 1998 Judgement in the case of Jean-Paul Akayesu, the Tribunal noted the important role played by women's organisations in bringing

---

Box 8.4
Best practice in protecting women survivors and witnesses of rape and sexual violence: the ICTY

As Rule 96 of the Rules of Procedures and Evidence for the ICTY on sexual assault demonstrates, evidentiary procedure affirms the women's testimony. Rule 96 defines rape and sexual assault in terms of the force applied by the defendant rather than the resistance offered by the victim; it requires no corroboration, and the victim's sexual history is inadmissible.[4] The text reads:

In cases of sexual assault:

(i)   *No corroboration of the victim's testimony shall be required.*

(ii) *Consent shall not be allowed as a defence if the victim:*

    (a) *has been subjected to or threatened with or has reason to fear violence, duress, detention or psychological oppression; or*

    (b) *reasonably believes that if the victim did not submit, another might be so subjected, threatened or put in fear.*

(iii) *Before evidence of the victim's consent is admitted the accused shall satisfy the Trial Chamber in camera that the evidence is relevant and credible.*

(iv) *Prior sexual conduct of the victim shall not be admitted in evidence.*

Rules 69 and 75 of the Rules of Procedure and Evidence are also important for the protection of witnesses and victims. Protective measures include the use of pseudonyms, the deletion of references to the victim's identity in court transcripts, the giving of testimony by camera and by one way closed circuit television, scrambling of victims' voices and images, and the prohibition of photographs, sketches, or videotapes of witnesses or victims. Provided certain conditions are met, the identity of the victims or witnesses can be withheld from the accused, even at the trial stage. A unit has been created to provide counselling and support to victims and witnesses.

---

sexual violence into focus as a crime under international law. In Rwanda, the participation of women's organisations and legal academics in the *amicus curiae* ('friend of the court', a third party invited to give impartial evidence on a particular case) process showed that there was evidence available to support the charges of sexual violence. In the experience of Rwandan NGO AVEGA-Agahozo's workers, the absence of adequate witness protection has been the most significant impediment to women testifying before the Tribunal. Many survivors of sexual violence have been inhibited from coming forward because of fear of death, harassment, and intimidation. In response to the problem, many women's organisations employ the services of female para-legal workers who have been able to advise and accompany women who wish to testify in war crime trials

(Rose Moukamusana, AVEGA-Agahozo, personal communication 1998). In the trial and prosecution of Jean-Paul Akayesu, South African Justice Navanethem Pillay, the Court's only female judge, played a critical role in the amendment of the indictment by encouraging women victims of rape to come forward as witnesses.[5]

8.2 Building the capacity of state workers to challenge violence

As we have seen in previous chapters, laws are not in themselves a solution to ending violence against women. Rather, they form a skeleton, or framework, that supports other strategies (Connors 1993). A key set of strategies used by women's organisations and other NGOs is to offer training and support to state officials, to build awareness and change attitudes about violence against women, and how to respond appropriately to the problem.

8.2.1 Strengthening police sanctions against violence

The police station is often the first point of contact with the State for women who are experiencing violence. They may go there because they want protection against violence. The response of the police is likely to have a marked influence on women's opinion of the assistance afforded by the State, and may affect their decision on whether or not to pursue a complaint.

Chapter 5 discussed the reasons why women often do not seek external help, including fear of blame and reprisal, and economic dependency on their attackers. Where a woman faces violence in the domestic or family context, she may want the violence, but not necessarily the relationship, to end. The police are unlikely to understand or be able to respond to the complexities of women's needs and fears. Deterrents against women lodging a complaint are even greater in countries where there is no clear government response to counter male violence or where the State and the judicial system are weak, as can be the case in contexts of armed conflict or rapid transition.

Special women's police stations, staffed with multi-disciplinary female teams, can be set up and equipped to ensure that the many needs of victims of violence are met, and to encourage women to report violence. A similar, more modest, strategy is to set up special women's desks in police stations.

In Brazil, the first *delegacia da mulher* (women's police station) was set up in 1985. This was a specialised unit that worked exclusively with victims of domestic violence, in São Paulo. Since then, similar units have been set up throughout most of the states in Brazil (Thomas 1994), and there are now around 200 women's police stations in the country (Chiarotti 1998).

It appears that women's police stations have led to an increase in the numbers of women reporting violence. The women's police stations attend to the woman or child victim of violence during the reporting of the incident, and also provide them with psychological support and legal advice. Additionally, the stations undertake follow-up monitoring of the abuser to ensure that punishment is carried out (Chiarotti 1998).

However, women's police stations normally operate on meagre resources, and their staff receive only a minimum training. Many women police officers prefer not to work in women's police stations. Widespread prejudice against work to combat violence against women creates the sense that work in a women's police station is a less-than-satisfactory appointment option (Aboim 1999).

Maria Luiza Aboim also found that the relationship between women's organisations and the police force in operating such stations is fragile. Originally, feminists and women's organisations were involved with the selection and training of staff for the stations, but gradually they have become marginalised, and local police forces have taken over these processes. There is now little collaboration between feminists and the women police stations, and women victims of violence rarely receive consistent treatment (Aboim 1999).

'Partnership projects' or 'one-stop centres' in police stations

As discussed in Chapter 5, women often face considerable difficulties in getting assistance from different support services to meet their needs after incidents of violence. These various needs may include health and medical care, lawyers, police, psychological counselling, and someone to listen, especially if they live in a rural area and the majority of services are located in a city. Women may look to the State for all, or some, of these needs, and may go to NGOs, friends, or relatives for others. Women's need for help from different institutions has led to the development of strategies that provide a co-ordinated response.

Partnership projects involving different institutional actors, or what are sometimes called one-stop centres, aim to address women's different needs within a single physical space. They have been set up in police stations, hospitals, and in other places within the community. Those in a hospital setting are discussed in the next section of this chapter.

The advantage of setting up such a project in a police station is that it gives the police, who may be mistrusted, credibility. It also gives the representatives of women's organisations the opportunity to make contact with women quickly. In the UK, the 'Domestic Violence Matters' (DMV) project involved a team of skilled 'crisis-interveners', located within the police service, whose job was to follow up police responses to domestic violence. The project aimed to establish 24-hour crisis intervention, to promote law enforcement, to encourage consistent and co-ordinated responses, and to identify gaps in provision (Kelly *et al.* 1999). The basic principle of the intervention was to make personal and immediate contact with women after a violent incident. One of the key conclusions of an evaluation of the intervention was that women supported the combination of police intervention and follow-up civilian support. The personal and immediate character of the contact was very important to the women.

However, although women's confidence in the police had increased, the evaluation found that attitudinal barriers and the routine trivialising of domestic violence by police continued. Co-operation between civilian staff and the police was problematic, although it did improve with time. There is an ongoing tension over whether such partnerships compromise women's organisations' independence and accountability. Ensuring accountability requires regular monitoring and evaluation of such projects according to women's identified needs (Kelly *et al.* 1999).

Partnership projects offering a full range of services, 24 hours a day, are only likely to be financially viable in towns and cities. As such, in many instances they are not an immediately accessible form of assistance. Financed largely by the State, and providing specialised services, they are not a substitute for the forms of support provided by peers and counsellors described in many of the women's organisations whose activities formed a chief focus in Chapter 5. Despite the ambition of partnership projects to provide an holistic response to women survivors of violence, it is possible that local women's organisations may be best able to respond effectively to women's needs and interests. Such organisations are likely to be informal, and to operate on a smaller scale, which places them in a better position to encourage women's self-help and group-related activities.

Ensuring police use legal sanctions

In cases of domestic violence, legal sanctions open to some police forces include mandatory arrest. Mandatory arrest policies have been developed in Canada, Australia, and the USA. These policies require police and prosecutors to treat domestic violence cases in the same way as any other criminal matter – i.e. to prosecute if they are made aware of the offence, regardless of the wishes of victims of violence. The intention of such policies is to relieve women from the responsibility, and thus the blame, for arresting a man. However, recent evaluations suggest that these 'pro-arrest' strategies can be counter-productive and even highly dangerous to women (Connors 1993). Arrest and prosecution does stop current violence in the short-term, and may deter men who have more to lose, for example, married men and employed men (Heise, Pitanguy, and Germaine 1994) but the effectiveness of arrest in preventing violence is still not known.

Another tool available to the police in countering domestic violence is the 'protection order'. This is a legally binding document that prevents a violent man from having any contact with a woman. It can exclude him from any residence he shares with her, and provides the police with a mechanism for arrest if further violence occurs. The South African Family Violence Act of 1994 accommodates both mandatory arrest and 'protection order' options. The Act requires the police to arrest and charge an attacker with assault or rape, and detain him in custody, pending bail. The police should also pursue a full investigation and prosecute him. The law also allows the police to decide to caution the man if the woman to whom he has been violent prefers this to arrest. In this situation, the police should help the women take out a 'protection order' against the man. If the man breaks the order he should be arrested and charged.

In Colombia, legislative advances in line with the Inter-American Convention on the Prevention, Punishment, and Eradication of Violence Against Women entitle women who have experienced emotional or physical violence from a family member to protection within ten hours. The protection measures include offering police protection to the victim at home and at work and removal of the offender from the home. Offenders are obliged to attend re-educative and therapeutic treatment, to pay damages, and face penalties according to Colombian law. In addition, legislation has been revised so that punishments for those who have committed sexual violence against a spouse are as severe as penalties for those who assault strangers. These and other changes have led to increased numbers of cases being reported and brought to court by women. Backlash includes calls to modify the law because it has been criticised as destroying family unity (Gonzalez-Sanchez 1998).

Women's organisations can play a key role in ensuring that police or judicial officers' interpretations of the law are in line with the spirit, and the letter, of legislation that is of potential use to women survivors of violence.

The Tshwaranang Legal Advice Centre to End Violence Against Women in South Africa plays a role in supporting and increasing the impact of the work of state and NGO service-provider organisations that are working to end violence. The organisation states that its main objective is to effect change in the legal system from the 'top down' so that NGOs and women's organisations do not simply send women into a legal system that is hostile to their needs. It aims to use the law to educate government and society at large that violence against women is unacceptable, and to make the legal system more user-friendly and accountable to women. In its work, the

Advice Centre does not deal with individual women, but acts as a liaison between NGO service-providers and the State (Tshwaranang Legal Advocacy Centre to End Violence Against Women 1996).

The organisation has identified many ways in which the work of service providers can be influenced positively, to ensure a good outcome for women survivors of violence. For example, women in South Africa can apply for protection orders on the basis of the 1993 Prevention of Family Violence Act. However, magistrates often do not receive copies of legislation that was enacted before the April 1994 election. Most magistrates who receive copies of the Prevention of Family Violence Act have not gone through any training workshops on how to implement it (Tshwaranang Legal Advocacy Centre to End Violence Against Women 1996). Magistrates seldom authorise the eviction of the perpetrator of violence from the shared home. Instead women, often with young children, are expected to leave the home and the protection order is used to keep the abuser from accosting her subsequently (Masimanyane CEDAW Working Group 1998).[6]

8.3 Achieving attitudinal change at the level of the State

Some women's organisations combine research into the extent and nature of violence against women with lobbying, advocacy, and media work, in order to achieve attitudinal change on the part of state officials. They see these activities as a complement to the service-provision to individual survivors of violence which is a more usual focus of women's organisations. Despite the critical importance of direct support, vital preventative and advocacy-related work must also continue, and NGOs and women's organisations may not always develop these activities as fully as they could.

8.4 Strengthening state provision of health and welfare

In a review of government measures to address violence in many countries throughout the world, Jane Connors, Secretary of the CEDAW Committee, argues that overall, the response of state health and welfare sectors to violence against women is disappointing. She suggests that this is because professionals in these sectors are not educated in the dynamics of violence against women, and have chosen to concentrate on victims rather than on offenders as the key to their response. As a result, health and welfare providers may view violence as an individual, rather than a structural, problem (Connors 1993). In addition, government responses in social sectors can fall short because they fail to understand the complex linkages between different strategies to deal with violence.

Box 8.5
Influencing government interventions through information-gathering and advocacy in South Africa

The Tshwaranang Legal Advocacy Centre to End Violence Against Women in South Africa has developed a programme of advocacy and research that aims to influence government interventions in combating violence against women. The Centre has created a database on violence, and monitors government policy and legislation. The first projects undertaken included the submission to relevant government departments of drafted policies on a range of subjects including anti-stalking laws and reform of the Violence Against Women Act. The organisation set up a system of distributing and collecting questionnaires from service-provider organisations to collect information on the prevalence of violence. It has produced a legal manual to help NGOs improve their legal advice. Finally, it has monitored the government's commitment to international obligations, sometimes submitting *amicus curiae* briefs to ensure that the voices of NGO service-providers are heard on issues that affect their work.

Source: Tshwaranang Legal Advocacy Centre to End Violence Against Women 1996

8.4.1 Partnership projects in hospitals

The principles underpinning the idea of partnership projects were outlined earlier in this chapter in relation to the police service. Such projects are sometimes also run from hospitals. An advantage to hospital-based partnership projects is that they are open 24-hours-a-day, so women can always get help.

Locating the service in a hospital can be especially useful in co-ordinating the procedures and investigations necessary for a rape trial (Coomaraswamy 1997b). In partnership projects, when a woman arrives at a hospital after having been raped, specially trained doctors will talk to her and collect evidence from her relating to the rape. The hospital then contacts the police to report the incident, lawyers are made available, and a staff member of a women's organisation can assist the victim. Women's different needs are addressed in one place.

A disadvantage of the hospital-based approach is that women who require information or emotional support, but do not have serious physical injuries, may not choose to go to a hospital. In addition, hospital-based services may use a medical model of the consequences of violence for the individual, which fails to account for the importance of social factors in women's recovery.

8.4.2 Ensuring medical tests are sensitive to women's needs

In rape cases in particular, women are often required to undergo medical examination in order to collect evidence of the violence against her. In hospitals, as in police stations, the behaviour of staff can determine whether a woman will go on to press charges. With the aim of accelerating and standardising this procedure, combined with the need to collect and preserve evidence in a sensitive manner, some countries – including Australia, Brazil, and Canada – provide special forensic examination kits. The kit provided in Canada provides women with information about legal procedures and trials, the medical examination, and victim services. It contains instructions for the police and doctors, and instruments for the collection of evidence (Coomaraswamy 1997b).

8.5 Lobbying for state provision of shelters

Most government social provision for survivors of violence is very limited. The majority of countries that have passed laws prohibiting violence against women have not implemented other kinds of action to prevent violence or to aid victims of violence. However, states do sometimes provide shelter for women. State-led shelter provision is likely to differ to the kind of shelter provision provided by development and women's organisations discussed in Chapter 5.

In Pakistan, state-run shelters, *Darul Amans* (literally, 'houses of peace'), cannot cope with demand. Their shortcomings have been highlighted by NGOs, who point out that since women can only gain access via a magistrate, the shelters are not easily accessible. Women have to get authorisation to leave *Darul Amans*, and there have been cases of women being held in these shelters against their will (Amnesty International 1999b). In addition, such shelters are unlikely to be able to address women's needs holistically. For example, rather than help women to develop skills to increase their autonomy once they leave, most shelters do not provide women with activities in which to engage (op. cit.).

In contrast, shelter provision by women's organisations typically starts from the stated needs of women themselves, and additionally seeks to encourage women to find solutions to end violence through counselling, income-generation, group or creative work, training, or legal advice. Many women's organisations therefore believe that the most effective shelter provision is initiated by women's organisations, and funded by government.

8.6 Transforming state-instigated research

The problem of the lack of information on the extent of violence against women has been highlighted throughout this book. Governments are the only bodies with the resources and capacity to produce national statistics on reported incidents of violence against women. Police, courts, hospitals and health care institutions, social security bodies, schools, universities, refuges, and hotlines should all be involved in the process of recording of national data.

Governments may aim to include data on violence against women as one aspect of general violent crime. However, the methods of enumeration and analysis used for violent crimes in general are unlikely to pick up incidents of violence against women, or to consider the nature of the violent event itself, and the motives and consequences that led up to the violence. This last failing results in partial or inaccurate portrayals of the nature of violence and the perpetrators (Dobash *et al.* 1992).

A recent large-scale government-organised study that has taken these criticisms seriously was a telephone survey undertaken by Statistics Canada, a national-level state body responsible for compiling statistics on, amongst other things, crime and violence, in 1993. This was a national-level investigation to examine the dimensions and nature of violence against women, and its correlation with other social and economic factors (Johnson 1998). See Box 8.6 for more details.

Quantitative data on violence against women is essential in order to demonstrate that it is widespread and systematic, but small-scale qualitative research carried out by community-level organisations is equally important. Situated at a remove from the State, such organisations may be in a better position to constructively criticise the response of state institutions. Non-state community-based institutions are likely to have close links with women in the community, to be trusted by women, and to involve participation by women themselves. There is a considerable need for detailed material that helps us to understand women's decisions to leave and return to violent partners, that tracks changes in violence in relationships over time, and that analyses men's motives for being violent and stopping violence when they do.

8.7 Training of state officials

Training programmes on gender and violence geared towards state officials have in the main focused on the police, because of the fact that they are usually the first point of contact for women who have been attacked. Evidence from many countries suggests that police officers are particularly

---

Box 8.6

State research on the prevalence and causes of violence in Canada

In 1993, a random sample of 12,300 women aged 18 years and over was interviewed by telephone. The survey sought information relating to women's experiences of violent acts, the physical and emotional consequences of such acts, and the decisions that women made to tell others, to use shelters and other social services, or to report the incidents to the police. The definitions of violence used conformed to the Canadian Criminal Code, and the opinions of academics, government policy-makers, the police, shelter workers, women's groups, and women victims of violence were sought in the design of the investigation. Ensuring the safety of the women interviewed was an important concern. Respondents could reschedule the interview and could phone free of charge to resume the interview at any stage. No call-backs were made to the respondents, who therefore controlled their own participation. Interviewers had a list of nearby shelters should the respondent become distressed. A psychologist was hired to provide debriefing for the interviewers.

The survey produced some of the most comprehensive national-level data on the extent and incidence of sexual assault. It demonstrated that sensitive and creative women-focused methods of research involving specialists in the community result in a higher response rate, and the improved reliability of results.

Source: Johnson 1998

---

at risk of applying misinformed stereotypical attitudes towards survivors of violence. For example, many are suspicious of complaints in cases where the victim knows the attacker, where there is no visible sign of injury, where the victim appears calm or unemotional, or where there is a delay in reporting the assault (Connors 1993). This hostility may cause a woman to drop her complaint. Where women persevere, if investigations are badly conducted by an ill-trained police force, attackers are less likely to be convicted.

In some countries, NGOs have played a significant role in effecting transformations in the attitudes and capabilities of state officials. Some women's organisations have developed co-operative relations with the police, and have offered courses to police personnel. The most effective training is both technical – for example, learning how to obtain the best evidence for conviction – as well as political – for example, leading to an awareness of the roots of violence in women's subordination. Box 8.7 discusses the example of the Musasa Project in Zimbabwe, which has been involved in providing training to police on issues of domestic violence.

Box 8.7
The Musasa Project, Zimbabwe: police training on domestic violence

Following a pilot study with the Zimbabwean Republican Police (ZRP), the Musasa Project was invited to conduct a five-day workshop with police Community Relations Liaison Officers (CRLOs). The workshop appeared successful, but Musasa Project staff realised that although the CRLOs had a role as the public relations specialists in the police force, the workshop was too small-scale to make a real difference to police policy on violence against women, or to the treatment of women who reported abuse.

As a result, Mususa began education work with other police branches, including with constables at local police stations. The work with the police was modelled on Freirean principles of public education.[7] It began with the police identifying the problems they encountered when dealing with cases of violence against women. With the help of Musasa's staff, police then began to suggest some solutions.

One problem identified by police was that women who made charges of domestic violence often subsequently withdrew their charges. Police performance is judged according to cases that are laid and then prosecuted, and police became unwilling to invest time and energy in domestic violence cases because of a fear that women would withdraw charges, leaving them with an unprosecuted case.

After identifying the problem, the police were organised into small groups, in which they listed the potential reasons why women withdraw charges. They then made recommendations on how to improve the situation, and put them into action. Consequently, proposals were submitted directly to the Zimbabwe Ministry of Justice on how to improve the situation for women victims of violence.

A further problem to emerge in the training was police frustration with the legal system. There was a back-log of cases, and cases were often felt to be badly prosecuted. A group of prosecutors was invited to participate in a workshop hosted and paid for by the police, and facilitated by the Musasa Project. From this workshop emerged strategies for better liaison between the police and prosecutors.

Source: Stewart 1995a

There are several important lessons from the Musasa Project's work in Zimbabwe. The first is the importance of understanding the internal structure of the police force, and working with crime units, as well as those police who liaise with the public. Secondly, it was felt by the Musasa facilitators of the training programme with the police that involving a legal professional in the process enhanced the training session's credibility (Stewart 1992). Thirdly, the Musasa Project found it useful to get officials from one part of the legal system – in this case, the police – to act as a conduit to those from another – the prosecutors. The final point is that the police needed constant reminders that their role was that of law-enforcement, not counselling. The programme facilitators noted that the police often mistakenly saw their role as being to sooth and comfort the women victims, when this is not a service that women expect from the police. In Zimbabwe, the sensitivity exhibited by the police involved in working with Musasa, and their willingness to learn, led to an increase in cases reported and prosecuted (Njovana 1994).

Another example of this kind of work is at regional level: in Latin America in 1997, women's organisations from Argentina, Bolivia, Brazil, Panama, and Peru came together with security forces to hold seminars on violence against women. This occurred in the context of a wider training campaign on women's and children's human rights (Chiarotti 1998).

The UNHCR was involved in supporting work of this nature in Kenya, from 1993. The Women Victims of Violence Project (WVV) was set up by the UNHCR in October 1993, in response to the high number of reported incidents of violence against Somali women and girls in the north-eastern refugee camps. In 1996, the name of the project was changed to 'Vulnerable Women and Children Programme', in recognition of the fact that using the term 'victims' carried negative connotations.

Early in the project, staff realised that they needed to address police-related problems, such as the lack of adequate numbers of police to patrol the area; police who lacked knowledge and supervision; and the fact that the police force consisted of men who had no awareness of gender-based inequalities, or the rights of refugees, and who were hostile towards refugees and insensitive in handling cases of violence against women. Police also lacked motivation in detecting and investigating suspected attackers, while some were actually compliant or directly involved in attacks.

Through consultation with the police and Kenyan authorities, the project implemented a number of measures. These included the construction of police posts inside strategic camps, the development of reliable communications networks, and an increase in the number of police officers in the camps (Gardner 1996). In addition, the WVV conducted training with local police forces. More details of this training are found in Box 8.8.

The WVV project shows the positive impact on violence against women that can be achieved through working with the police to raise their awareness of the effects of violence, as well as of their role in providing practical assistance to victims of violence. It also demonstrates the difference that can be made in camp security through several well-coordinated interventions.

Box 8.8
The Women Victims of Violence Project (WVV): police training in refugee camps in Kenya

WVV organised two rounds of police training workshops, held in camp locations through 1994 and 1995. The workshops involved over 160 police participants, ranging from the top District Chief Inspectors to the patrol sergeants. Participants also included magistrates, agency staff, and representatives from the refugee communities.

The workshops were devised and facilitated by an all-women team of trainers, including women from UNHCR's WVV project itself, protection officers, and representatives from the Kenyan branch of the International Federation of Women Lawyers (FIDA). The objectives of the workshops were to improve the working relations between police, refugee workers, and refugees, and to promote understanding of refugees' basic rights and the special needs of victims of violence.

The majority of participants welcomed the opportunity to learn how to work with women who had experienced violence, and the proper procedures to enable prosecution.

Some of the immediate outcomes of the project included:

- better co-operation between the police and other agencies, including UNHCR, on matters concerning refugees and camp security;
- agreements between police and other agencies to share strategy and policy plans;
- raised morale and motivation among individual police officers;
- police requests for copies of national and international laws;
- police recommendations for strategies for improving the protection of women refugees;
- police recommendations for women police officers to be posted in the area.

After one year of implementation, the number of reported rapes in the refugee camps had fallen by over two-thirds.

Source: Gardner 1996

However, the experience of the WVV project also shows that there is a need for more far-reaching reform within the legal system. Without an integrated approach that addresses the judicial system, strategies to eliminate violence will be limited.[8] One of the steps undertaken by UNHCR was to contract a Kenyan NGO, FIDA, to help refugee women seek legal redress. The effect of these measures was a fall in the average monthly number of rapes from more than 30 in 1993 to fewer than 10 in 1994

(Lawyers Committee for Human Rights 1995). However, the benefits of having a lawyer available to assist women can be curtailed by a cumbersome legal system, where there is a backlog of cases or where cases are badly prosecuted. For example, an evaluation conducted in Kenya in 1994 concluded that the provision of legal assistance through FIDA to individuals was a high-cost approach in a country where rape convictions are very difficult to obtain (Gardner 1996).

A case study from Brazil shows a different kind of training strategy to those used by WVV and the Musasa Project. This approach involved installing women in police stations, to deal specifically with cases of violence against women. The women were representatives from a network of women's organisations in the state of Pará in Amazonia.

Despite the rise in the number of cases reported, the benefits of the Brazil project, like those of the WVV refugee project in Kenya, were limited by the negative effects of the cumbersome judicial process. In Brazil, it can take many years to bring the perpetrators of violence against women to justice, during which time women can remain susceptible to further abuse.

Box 8.9
Training of women community para-legal workers in Brazil

Following lobbying of the local government by a network of women's organisations in Pará, Amazonia, 25 women received a four-stage training course for para-legal workers over a period of two years. The aim was to create women para-legal workers who could work within police stations, specialising in cases involving violence against women.

The first stage of the course dealt with basic concepts of law, the second concerned the Brazilian Penal Code, the third focused on civil law, and the fourth was about the structures of the legal system. After each student had received her training, she undertook an internship as a legal apprentice.

Following their training the women started work, on a voluntary basis, in the municipalities in the region. In most cases, the women knew much more about the law than the police themselves. As a result of appointing and training the women, there was a large increase in registered complaints, particularly involving cases of child and adolescent rape. However, the women's work is unpaid, jeopardising the sustainability of the project, as most of these women are poor women from small towns in the interior of the Amazon Basin.

Source: Sena 1998

The three examples in this section illustrate how some organisations in certain countries have recognised the importance of special police training initiatives that focus on violence against women. They also show that training the officials to whom women come for assistance does improve the rates of reporting of violence against women. Ideally, training should be extended beyond the police to other groups within the State, including judges, lawyers, and health, welfare, and social workers. It may, in addition, be appropriate for training to focus not only on violence against women, but to incorporate other related areas. For example, training of health professionals could address the links between women's subordination, sexuality, and violence against women.

As the section on training in the community in Chapter 7 emphasised, training is unlikely to make a difference if it is an isolated intervention. Staff within state institutions are working in environments where the culture, systems, and procedures are biased in men's favour. Training in these institutions is effective when it is a part of a wider strategy to render the institution 'right for women' (Goetz 1997).

8.8 State involvement in education campaigns

Some governments have recognised the role that stereotypical views of women and men can play in perpetuating violence against women, often as a result of lobbying on the part of women's organisations. As a result, these governments have engaged in popular education campaigns. While many elements of these are similar to those discussed in Chapter 7, state-led education campaigns can be held at national level, and as such have the potential to reach large numbers of people. Involvement of the government has the further advantage that it can add weight to the campaign's messages. However, in order to ensure that a government campaign is accurate and effective, it must be based on the views and analysis of organisations that have a history of working on these issues, and have developed knowledge and expertise. In addition, it is crucial to involve women who have faced violence themselves.

The Zero Tolerance campaign was the first crime prevention campaign to tackle violence against women at national level in the UK. Details are in Box 8.9.

Like the previous examples in this chapter, the Zero Tolerance campaign demonstrated the benefits of co-operation between state agencies and women's organisations. The impact of such a strategy could be increased still further by integrating it into the activities of schools, colleges, and universities.

Box 8.9
The 'Zero Tolerance' mass campaign to prevent violence against women in the United Kingdom

'Zero Tolerance' was first launched in 1992 by the Edinburgh District Council's Women's Committee, to highlight the nature and extent of abuse of women. The message of the Zero Tolerance campaign was that there is no acceptable level of violence against women and children. Originally an initiative developed by Edinburgh City Council, in Scotland, Zero Tolerance has since become an independent organisation.

The first phase in the campaign addressed the prevalence of violence against women, and stereotypes about women who suffer violence. The campaign aimed to challenge beliefs that most women are at risk from abuse by strangers in the street, and that most victims are from working class backgrounds. The second phase concentrated on gender stereotypes about men, and how these can lead to men's behaviour being excused and justified. The third phase targeted the criminal justice system. The fourth phase was directed at young people. The philosophy has been based on a threefold approach that has become commonly known as the 'three Ps': provision of support services, protection, and prevention.

Posters formed a main part of the campaign. They used uncompromising messages with powerful black and white visuals depicting settings inside the home, and images of predominantly middle-class, white women in seemingly comfortable and secure situations. The accompanying texts create a shocking contrast to the gentle imagery. For example,

She lives with a successful businessman, loving father and respected member of the community. Last week, he hospitalised her.

These messages are displayed on large bill-boards, on the sides of buses and at bus stops. Smaller versions are produced for workplaces and community venues, and other social marketing such as postcards, badges, bookmarks, buttons, and T-shirts, has also been developed.

Community involvement was instrumental in ensuring the success of the campaign. To sustain the local profile of the campaign, 12 implementation groups were established across Strathclyde, Scotland. The composition of these varied according to the areas, but most included representatives of the local government and health departments, women's groups, and rape crisis organisations.

Most Scottish cities, and an increasing number of English ones, have run at least one phase of the campaign. Local governments purchase the campaign materials and adapt them for their own use. They are responsible for running their own local campaign.

The Zero Tolerance campaign was criticised for failing to address the interests of ethnic minority and disabled women, and responded to this by producing a set of new posters and messages.

Source: Cosgrove 1996

8.9 NGO lobbying of governments to effect change

Regional and international networks of women's organisations and other NGOs have played an important role in lobbying governments to enshrine commitments to address violence against women in international instruments, and then in follow-up through monitoring and evaluating government strategies to eliminate violence against women.

There is a clear role for NGOs working on women's rights, civil and political rights, and development and humanitarian aid, to campaign at the international level for governments to push for change. In previous chapters, we have seen that inter-governmental initiatives can play an important role in creating conditions that can protect women from violence.

A network of women's organisations has noted the importance of continuing collaboration between governments and the NGO sector to ensure that governments continue to improve their policy and practices on violence against women in line with national and international legal agreements:

> *The assumption by governments is that once legislation is in place, things will change. There must be greater emphasis on implementation with clear guidelines on how to monitor this. Collaboration between government and NGOs must be strengthened. To achieve this would partly require governments to appropriately acknowledge NGOs' contribution in the fight against violence against women. Government reports must have clarity as to the amount of resources allocated for example to non-legislative initiatives, and the public must have access to this information .... Government must attend to the immediate need for services, such as shelters, social security benefits, setting up of victim assistance programmes at all courts and police stations, and the training of service providers.*

(Masimanyane CEDAW Working Group 1998).

8.9.1 National-level lobbying

The end of apartheid in South Africa and the start of a democratic regime has given women new opportunities to influence the processes of creating new legislation on violence against women. In a presentation made at the Oxfam international workshop on violence against women in Sarajevo in 1998, Futhi Zikalala from the Domestic Violence Assistance Programme in South Africa described the impressive legal machinery that South Africa has developed on gender equality. The new national constitution has provision to set up National Commissions, including one on gender equality. Parliament has women's caucuses at national and provincial levels. In national government, the office of the Deputy President has a sub-office on the status of women. Gender working groups are attached to local government structures (Oxfam GB 1998). This legal machinery is supported by a rich women's movement. There is for example, a national shelter movement, and a national network against violence against women. The National Network of Women against Violence operates at national and provincial levels and is comprised of both governmental and non-governmental representatives and organisations. The network is the first initiative in a strategy to involve the public, private, and non-governmental sectors in its fight to eliminate violence (Coomaraswamy 1997c).

However, progressive state policies in relation to violence against women may not be implemented and are vulnerable to changes in government and shifts in policy agendas. Diane Urioste, writing about Bolivia, cautions, 'Just because a proposal is technically good, it does not mean it carries political strength. The passing of proposals by the State does not necessarily imply their application or even the will to do it. Clear proof of this is that with the change in government in 1997, there was a pause, if not a step backward, in public gender policies.' (Urioste 1998, 7) For this reason, continued lobbying and advocacy by the women's movement is vital.

Using regional agreements as lobbying tools to change national policy is an effective strategy. The work of the women's movement in Bolivia, described earlier in this chapter, is an example of successful lobbying to incorporate international legislation – in this case the Inter-American Convention on the Prevention, Punishment, and Eradication of Violence Against Women – into national legislation. The Inter-American Convention was adopted by the OAS, and entered into force in 1995.[9] It states that discrimination against women is one of the fundamental causes of violence, and includes as a specific right, women's right to a life free of violence. Under the constitution, the State is held responsible for violent acts as well as for finding the means to avoid violence. Individuals and organisations can take cases to the Inter-American Commission on Human Rights. States that are parties to the instrument must provide information on the methods they have adopted to prevent and eradicate violence, and to assist women affected by violence, through submitting national reports.

Nicaragua is another country to have reformed legislation on domestic violence as a result of the Inter-American Convention on the Prevention, Punishment, and Eradication of Violence Against Women. In 1994, the Nicaraguan Network of Women against Violence presented 49,000 signatures to the National Assembly, demanding the ratification of the Convention. The success of the Network is in part due to the way it has negotiated broad strategic alliances with a range of social and political actors while also maintaining control of the process and wording of the law

Box 8.10
Women's regional networks monitor state commitments in the Maghreb region

The Collectif 95 Maghreb Egalité was founded in April 1992 by a group of feminist associations, researchers, lawyers, and activists. Since that time, the organisation has developed from being a loose confederation of NGOs and activists to being a well-established and structured network. It has developed strong links with governments and other NGOs in Algeria, Morocco, and Tunisia, and has achieved considerable success in placing gender equality at the centre of political and economic debates over the future of development through lobbying efforts directed mainly at governments.

The aim of the network was to pool the efforts of women in these three countries to prepare and submit monitoring reports on the implementation of international conventions, notably the Women's Convention of 1979. Prior to the Beijing conference, the Collectif produced a key lobbying document, demanding the adoption of 100 new measures and provisions towards reforming family laws on a more egalitarian basis. During the conference in Beijing, the Collectif organised a well-attended parliament of women from Muslim countries, and a series of seminars on violence against women.

The Collectif strives to be an effective lobbying group with three main objectives:

1. to advocate for the extension, consolidation, and respect of women's rights in the Maghreb region through the combination of research and information work as well as a strategy of proactive action and public events;
2. to strengthen women's movements in the Maghreb and in the wider Arab Muslim circle;
3. to help scale up this work and raise the public profile of women's organisations, and to act as an umbrella for those activities.

Since Beijing, the group has met on several occasions to evaluate its ongoing work. Encouraged by its achievements, the Collectif decided to extend and expand its mandate until the year 2000. The Collectif publishes annual monitoring reports on the implementation and violations of women's rights in the three countries. In addition, a committee has been set up to monitor and take forward the adoption of the 100 amendments of family laws.

Source: Traboulsi 1997

(Ellsberg, Liljestrand, and Winkvist 1997). Similarly, the women activists involved attribute the success of the lobbying in Bolivia, at least in part, to their co-operation with other groups of women at the Latin American regional level, as well as to good co-ordination within the Bolivian women's movement itself.

8.9.2 International-level lobbying

Strengthening the Beijing Platform for Action

The outcome of the UN Fourth World Conference on Women was rendered much stronger in relation to violence against women as the result of the activities of women's NGOs before, during, and after the conference. Women's organisations joined forces in order to lobby governments. Networks like the Collectif 95 Maghreb Egalité (see Box 8.10), which was founded in preparation for Beijing, played – and continue to play – a crucial role in monitoring state commitments to the promises made at Beijing.

The main aim of networks such as the Collectif Maghreb is to lobby governments to ensure that national legislation complies with international standards. Women's organisations are undertaking a tremendous amount of activity concerned with advocacy and lobbying on legal reform, organising tribunals and public events, writing parallel reports on the implementation of the Women's Convention, and monitoring abuses and violence. Mobilisation, training, and awareness-raising are at the heart of advocacy strategies to bring about desired changes.

International development and human rights organisations can play a key role in supporting and funding such work. Oxfam GB's programme in the Middle East responded to violence against women in its region by providing feminist regional networks, including the Collectif 95 Maghreb Egalité, with grants and training: 'In addition to its impact on learning, we see in networking a powerful means for breaking the isolation of local groups and NGOs particularly in the case of those working in contexts such as Algeria.'[10] (Lina Abou-Habib, Personal communication 1998)

Establishing acts of sexual violence as international crimes

The process through which sexual violence has come to be recognised as an international crime is a good example of the action of NGOs to effect international change.

Women's organisations and women's rights activists played a crucial role in the adoption of the Rome Statute establishing the ICC in 1998. (The adoption of the Statute, and the events that led up to it, were discussed in detail in Chapter 2.) Activists from the women's movement were instrumental in influencing the drafting process of the Statute of the ICC, lobbying delegates to ensure that the Court would be empowered to prosecute and punish the perpetrators of crimes of sexual violence. In the Preparatory Committees for the ICC, government delegates were for the first time openly and in detail discussing sexual crimes.

Together with the Women's Caucus and the worldwide NGO Coalition for the ICC, Oxfam lobbied the UK and other official country delegations to support expanded definitions of crimes against women in relation to crimes against humanity and war crimes. The eventual Statute (as outlined in Chapter 2) gives the ICC power to try cases of rape and other forms of sexual abuse as war crimes, and – when they are committed on a widespread or systematic basis – as crimes against humanity. A further achievement was made in relation to the provisions of the Statute governing the composition of the court and of the staff working in the office of the prosecutor. Women's groups and activists lobbied on the importance of having women judges, prosecutors, investigators, and staff, with expertise in gender-based violence. The Statute provides for victim and witness protection that is sensitive to women and sexual violence. The Statute further requires that judges have legal expertise on violence against women and children.

8.10 Summary and implications for development organisations

A key part of eliminating violence against women is state condemnation of violent acts. This sends out a clear message that violence against women is wrong (Connors 1993). From the perspective of the State, there are strong financial incentives to end violence against women, related to the economic costs of violence and the burden that it places on health care systems (discussed in Chapter 2), as well as human rights arguments. Having made commitments to protect women's human rights, for which they are held accountable, it is in the interests of national governments to be seen to be fulfilling their promises and taking steps to end violence against women.

This chapter has discussed a wide range of measures that states can take to condemn violence, and related these to strategies open to NGOs that wish to hold governments to account over this. Forms of state action against violence include legal reform, the provision of services, media campaigns, research, and training of officials. A frequent limitation of government responses is their fragmented nature. The most effective state responses address violence from a gender perspective, recognising the links between the various forms of violence against women, and the role of different institutions in perpetuating this violence.

Often, however, government responses are restricted to legal reform and pay little attention to implementation of the law. As Susan Chiarotti, Regional Co-ordinator of CLADEM in Argentina states: 'Governments should understand that discrimination and subordination are a cause of violence against women. Taking isolated measures to assist the effects of violence without confronting its causes, will always be only a band-aid strategy. This is like attacking an illness ignoring the elements that caused it.' (Chiarotti 1998, 14)

This chapter has emphasised the vital role played by women's organisations and development, humanitarian, and civil rights NGOs in challenging the State and holding it accountable for its actions – or lack thereof – to end violence against women. Networks and alliances of NGOs have made huge strides in ensuring that governments meet their commitments to end violence. These networks are typically made up of individual women and NGOs, as well as judges, police, health workers, and other specialists from a range of backgrounds, who together increase the legitimacy of the network in the eyes of the State and the general public. The networks are made up of individuals and groups that recognise the value of working at all levels – from grass-roots communities to parliament – to achieve change.

Ultimately, the effectiveness of state responses to violence against women will be determined by politics. Local women's and human rights organisations play an important role in actively pressuring governments to preserve existing areas of support. Continual lobbying and advocacy by women's organisations and networks is crucial in order to ensure that gender-sensitive reforms become an enduring feature of the way governments relate to women, and to keep violence against women on the political agenda. Continued dialogue with the State is also important for the identification of new areas of support.

9 Conclusion: planning for freedom from violence

I learned I can live up to my own identity, my husband cannot torture me; both of us have equal rights.

Perween on legal awareness training as part of Oxfam's Fair Trade income-generation project in Bangladesh (Barney, internal Oxfam document 1999).

Self-esteem, freedom from violence and the fear of violence, and the achievement of equal rights – Perween sums up concisely and simply what Oxfam aims for in its support for work on violence against women. The question is, how do we get there from where we are now? In relation to violence against women, we are still struggling with the private/public divide, and how to make policy reflect the insight that the personal sphere is a matter of public concern and political action. How do we overcome the obstacles that stand in the way of eradicating women's suffering and oppression in the personal and relational spheres through making the institutions, laws, and norms that govern people's lives responsive to these issues?

As we have seen in this book, violence against women is widespread and systematic, pervading all societies and cultures. How do we construct our response, as development agencies, in such a way that it is systematic and effective, and has an impact upon the systematic perpetration of crimes against women? How do we address not just the symptoms, but also the causes of this blight upon humanity? This concluding chapter will discuss some of the approaches and strategies which have been presented in this book, and some of the trends in relation to the reported increases in violence against women. In the light of these, it will go on to look at the policy implications for development agencies of attempting to have a significant impact on the incidence of violence against women worldwide.

This book has examined some of the commonly-articulated explanations of male violence against women, such as those referring to individual acts of a minority of psychotic men, or to the influence of alcohol and drugs, or to economic hardship and the context of war, and found these to be wanting. They do not explain the scope of the problem, its prevalence across class, race, age, and ethnic boundaries, and nor do they account for the violence of otherwise very ordinary men in unexceptional circumstances. These are only partial explanations, and similarly do not account for the fact that the criminal attacks attributed to these causes so often go unpunished. While these factors may exacerbate violence against women, this book has argued that the roots of violence against women are located in the fundamental structures of ideas, beliefs, and practice that constitute the edifice of gender inequality and support the institutions of patriarchy.

Gender inequality, expressed in relations of power that systematically undermine, restrict, and deny women's life choices and chances, is, as we have seen, maintained by social and cultural institutions and beliefs, and by fear. This may be fear of poverty and homelessness where women's only access to land, housing, and income is through property owned and controlled by men. It may be fear of social ostracism as the high price of challenging social and cultural norms. It may be fear of attracting male jealousy by taking initiatives that lead to women's higher status through education or political participation. It may be fear of losing children, along with everything else, where women have no independent right to custody. And underlying all of these is the fear of physical and sexual violence, which is associated with all the other forms of fear, and underpins them.

9.1 A rights-based approach to development

This book has presented a wide range of approaches to combating male violence against women. It has examined development and human rights approaches. Historically, development and human rights agencies have worked in very different ways, but in recent years the 'rights-based approach to development' has become common currency among international governmental and non-governmental agencies. Oxfam's development of this approach was described in the Preface. The different approaches and strategies employed in fighting violence against women described in this book demonstrate the value of working within a framework of internationally-agreed norms, both for the empowerment of individual women seeking to understand their situation, and for the development of policy to end the impunity that the perpetrators of violent attacks upon women have enjoyed, and still do enjoy, in all parts of the world.

However, while the language of international rights and law, both in peace and in wartime, helps to bridge the gaps between individual experience and the protection duties of the State, it is not the universal language that it should be. It is a language made by men. Feminist lawyers have argued that 'international law is both built on and operates to reinforce gendered and sexed assumptions' and that women have been marginal to the development of international law, which seems largely impervious to the realities of women's lives. Women are stereotypically viewed, mainly as victims, and especially as mothers, or potential mothers, in need of protection (Charlesworth and Chinkin 2000, 48). Thus, while the international legal system is a valuable strategic tool to be used by women, it is at the same time in need of reform to enable it to reflect better the specificities of women's experience, which become invisible when absorbed into what are male-defined norms. The rights-based approach to achieving women's empowerment and freedom from violence becomes even more important in this context – it is also part of a broader strategy to make existing international law more responsive to women, and to reform it.

This book has also pointed out the limitations of the implementation of legal measures, whether international or national. The Convention on the Elimination of All Forms of Discrimination against Women has more reservations than any other such international treaty. National law, even when it does enshrine principles that uphold women's rights to freedom from violence, is rarely implemented at its points of delivery – by the police, the courts, or the government departments responsible for implementing state policy for its citizens. The book relates some successful strategies to achieve legal reform – such as in the case of the women's movement's success in lobbying for national law on violence against women in Bolivia (see Chapter 8). Other examples show NGOs successfully training the police and judiciary to deal more appropriately with cases of violence against women, such as the Musasa Project in Zimbabwe (see Chapter 8). But these are ultimately dependent upon the political will of the State to monitor the implementation of the law and good practice by individuals. The accountability of these individuals on matters related to gender equity in general and violence against women in particular is simply not prioritised by government departments, in any country.

Despite the limitations of national and international legal systems, working with the law to protect women and to give women the chance for redress, as well as punishing the perpetrators of violent acts, is an essential part of combating violence against women. An important aspect of legal work is the empowering effect it can have upon women who have been accustomed to believe that their suffering is inevitable, or is ultimately their own fault. The shame and silence with which women themselves surround violent and sexual attacks upon them can begin to be broken by the realisation that these attacks are criminal and punishable by law. Of course there remain grave dangers, which have also been referred to in this book, of reprisal attacks upon women who attempt to seek legal or other support. The promotion of this kind of strategy to combat violence itself meets with violence, and vulnerable actors in the process need protection from harm.

9.2 Strategies for tackling violence against women

Giving direct support to women

This book describes a wide range of strategies used by women's organisations and NGOs to give direct support to women who are the victims of sexual or gender-based attacks. While these may not employ the international human rights framework as such, the reference point for responding to women's immediate needs for support, shelter, and protection is the set of fundamental human rights to life, security of person, and protection, which are violated by violent attacks on women.

A woman's first port of call may be members of her family or community, even when other members of these institutions are responsible for the attack. It is important for any external organisations to identify any existing forms of protection and redress when planning an intervention. Beyond this, organisations may provide crisis lines, counselling, safe houses, and shelters as an emergency response. The book considers these protective environments, along with refugee camps and resettlement centres for displaced people, and looks at ways in which short-term aid can also provide long-term support and rehabilitation for women who have been victims of violence. Longer-term strategies described in this context include the provision of housing, new economic options through training, and psycho-social support for the management of emotional damage.

Provision of this kind is essential support. As long as women continue to be subjected to violence, there will be a need for immediate welfare-based interventions. But in the longer run, gender relations have to change, along with perceptions of masculinity and femininity, and male and female roles. Both men and women have to accept fundamental changes in ideas and beliefs as well as behaviours, if violence against women is to be eradicated. The empowerment of women to resist violence and to seek redress is a key strategy, at the individual and community levels. Recalling Perween's statement at the beginning of this chapter, women's self-esteem is one of the first and deepest casualties of sexual and gender-based violence. Rebuilding this is a long process, but the book describes successful programmes in Brazil and India where support of other women and women's organisations enabled women to become more assertive within their relationships, to challenge violence, and to achieve more equitable and respectful relationships within the household.

Working with men

The issue of working directly with men is a complicated one. Do men perceive it to be in their interests to change their ideas and behaviours in relation to women? Should resources be diverted from women victims of violence to programmes that attempt to educate men or rehabilitate violent men? These are ongoing problems, but there is general agreement amongst those working on violence against women that men have to be challenged and must change, and that the perpetrators of violence must be punished and not ignored. The book describes some of the ways in which men can be challenged directly, including methods such as community sanctions against men who abuse women; training and awareness-raising with men; traditional and modern ways of healing or rehabilitating men; and men working with other men on issues of responsibility and behavioural change. Most of these strategies are small-scale and some have been shown to have an important, if local, impact. However, their impact is likely to remain limited unless they are situated within a context of broader societal or institutional commitments to tackling gender inequity. This means that governments and international organisations need to take the violence of men towards women seriously, and address it at the policy level, not only in relation to criminal justice, but also in relation to the economy, to political structures, to health, education, and welfare.

Challenging ideas and beliefs

The book considers a range of strategies to challenge ideas and beliefs through public education, campaigning, and work with the media to change the representation of women and violence. Popular theatre and drama, and large-scale advertising on billboards, buses, public places, government offices, and television, are some of the ways in which public awareness on violence against women can be raised. Training of community workers and women and men at community level is a more direct way to promote attitudinal change. Although there have been some successes, this kind of change is very difficult to measure and to sustain. It is probably, however, the most important aspect of the work on violence against women. It needs to be well integrated with direct support to women, work with men, and with strategies to strengthen governmental and legal responses to violence against women. Alliances are crucial to this work, and it needs to be broadly based to achieve impact. As Margaret Schuler states in the introduction to a key publication by UNIFEM in 1992 on strategies to tackle violence against women:

> *Education and consciousness-raising only achieve their purpose when gender violence becomes an issue of vital importance to people's lives. Mobilisation can only take place when people are willing to act, and*

people take action only when something is important to them. The educational process of making gender violence relevant to people essentially does three things: it challenges people at the individual level to re-examine and change their own views and behaviours; it builds a larger pool of people seeking solutions; and it creates a base of political support that functions to create pressure for change at the structural level. Thus, the key to success in any strategy, both short and long term, is making gender violence an issue of critical importance to everyone: women; men; the public; institutions; the state.

(Schuler ed. 1992)

Legal strategies

Some of the issues related to international law have been discussed above. The book presents a range of experience, mainly from women's organisations, of challenging governments and lobbying for legal reform. There are many success stories, from achieving national legislation on rape in Bolivia and India, to the lobbying of women lawyers and NGOs to give much stronger definition to crimes of sexual violence in the Statutes of the ICTR, ICTY, and ICC. The enactment of relevant law is however only half the battle; implementation is the real problem. Lobbying and advocacy, as well as public pressure, are essential to expedite and monitor the implementation of the law.

Research and documentation

Finally one area of work is essential for any type of intervention to tackle violence against women – research and documentation. One of the main obstacles to programming on violence against women in a more systematic way is the lack of information and hard data on the subject. Where statistics exist, for example where the police have collected data through cases reported to them, they are usually recognised as inaccurate because of the very low level of reporting of violence against women. Violence against women is a hidden crime. Women fear to report it because of the danger of reprisals. Men do not admit to it. The police do not always record it. National governments do not include it in national statistics. At the level of individual interviews, police around the world are notoriously crass in their approach to women who have been the victims of sexual violence, and there are innumerable accounts of the insensitivity or hostility of lawyers, magistrates, and judges dealing with such cases in court. Distorted messages about cases of violence are thus conveyed to the press and then to the public, feeding misconceptions and prejudice, and discouraging women from taking legal action.

There is an important role for NGOs to counteract these distorted messages, and one strategy is to research and document the incidence and severity of violence against women accurately and rigorously. Much more comprehensive statistical evidence is needed. When particular cases are documented, information must be collected in such a way that it would stand up in court. Good research and documentation is the basis not only of sound legal challenges however, but of effective lobbying for policy change, for public awareness raising, and for the policy formation of governments, international agencies, and national and local organisations. Planning in the field of violence against women requires accurate base-line information against which to measure the effectiveness of interventions, and the analysis of trends.

9.3 Identifying trends

Is violence against women increasing? The evidence is anecdotal and fragmented. In some parts of the world, reporting of violence has increased, in others it has not. All estimates of rates of violence against women assume a very high level of under-reporting. The Gender Empowerment Index now adopted by some countries to show progress in the development of women, and women's participation in political structures, could well include an index on violence against women against which achievements would be adjusted. There has been recent work on 'counting the cost' to national budgets of violence against women. This calculates the damage to national institutions and to business, but not to women themselves, their children, and ultimately to the quality of life of all human society.

While it may be difficult to identify an increase in violence, this book has nevertheless cited instances where such an increase has been observed, for example, during armed conflict and after it, as a society recovers; and more broadly as a result of macro-economic, social, and political crisis. The difficulty of measuring these increases is due to the fact that little comparative data exists that would indicate with any accuracy the incidence of violent attacks against women before the conflict or crisis. Highly visible large-scale attacks such as those documented in Rwanda and Bosnia during the wars there, and in Indonesia during the economic crisis, tend to obscure the picture of the situation of women beforehand, and thus give no indication of the 'normal' rate of violence against women.

Nonetheless, we can identify certain global and regional trends that appear to increase the incidence of violent crimes perpetrated against women. Recent conflicts have highlighted the extent to which sexual violence against women is used as a war strategy, and the planned use of violence against civilian women in this way seems to be a feature of modern conflicts. The UNDP has in several reports made links between economic crisis and human insecurity, at all levels. Structural inequalities brought about by globalisation generate violence at the household, community, and national levels (UNDP 1999). In East Asia, while national economies show signs of recovery from the collapse of the financial markets during the Asian Financial Crisis of 1997-8, the human costs of the crisis include continued social stress and fragmentation. Increasing domestic violence, street crime, and suicides have been reported in Malaysia, Thailand, and Korea. In Korea, a hotline for women received an escalating number of calls from women suffering from domestic violence – seven times as many as during the previous year (UNDP 1999, 40).

International trade and the advent of the Internet have led to an expansion of the global sex industry, including trafficking in women, prostitution, and sex tourism. The opening up of borders within the former Soviet bloc together with the shrinking of opportunities for women in the formal economy in the region, have caused many women to migrate to other parts of Europe looking for work. However, restrictive immigration policies in Western Europe increase women's vulnerability to sexual exploitation by the organised criminal groups on which they often depend for movement.

In Pakistan, crises in national and religious identities have turned urban populations to fundamentalist models of law. This has been linked to the increased incidence of 'honour-killings' where the perception of what defiles honour is continually widening so that male control does not simply extend to a woman's sexual behaviour, but to all of her behaviour, including her movements, her language, and her actions. In any of these areas, any form of defiance by women is perceived as undermining male honour, and women may be killed by men for such trivial matters as answering them back, bringing their food late, and going on forbidden visits (Amnesty International, 1999b).

During periods of social upheaval, violence against women may be tolerated to an even greater extent as social norms that control men's behaviour break down. The sanctions against violence that may be applied by family and community, or the protection that they may offer, can be disrupted by migration, displacement, and economic strain on individuals. Women may also be afforded less protection by the State as crime and justice systems divert their attention to general criminal matters, deprioritising still further what continues to be seen predominantly as the 'private' crime of domestic violence. When the State is under pressure to cut social spending, provision for victims of gender and sexual violence may be withdrawn. The options available for women to challenge attacks upon them may therefore become far fewer, so that violence can be perpetrated with impunity.

For development agencies this entails developing responses that address violence in different and changing contexts, on the basis of sound analysis. The integration of examination of the incidences of violence against women, and of the factors and indicators that may point to its increase, into the analysis of the external context, is essential. An internal analysis of the institutional context and of the composition and culture of the development agency is equally important. Even though there is a trend within international organisations and development agencies to identify violence against women as a corporate priority for action, much work remains to be done within these organisations before staff will see violence against women as a development concern as legitimate as the more 'traditional' areas such as production, education, or public health. Violence against women is probably still regarded as an important, but fairly marginal, concern by most staff in most international development and relief agencies.

9.4 Policy implications for international NGOs

It has been stressed throughout this book that violence against women is a systematic strategy to maintain women in a state of subordination and fear, and that systematic and strategic measures are need to combat it. This final section does not go into the detail of specific recommendations for criteria for strategies; indeed these are always best worked out in context. Instead, it presents three broad policy areas that international organisations should consider in their programming on violence against women:

1. 'mainstreaming' awareness of violence against women into all development, relief, and advocacy interventions;
2. developing an integrated organisational strategy for interventions;
3. using broad and strategic alliances.

9.4.1 Mainstreaming awareness of violence against women

The point has been made in the Preface to this book, and throughout the text, that changes in policies and practices on violence against women depend for their sustainability upon more profound changes in the ideas and beliefs that determine attitudes and behaviours in any culture. Culture is of course highly changeable, and ideas and beliefs can and do change, but change will always be strongly resisted by those who have the greatest stake in the status quo, and change is not always positive. When international agencies support the challenge to violence against women, and thus to inequitable gender relations, they may sometimes expose partner organisations to risk, and the women involved in the programme to greater risk still. Less obvious in development planning is the risk of backlash and reprisals from women who stand to benefit in similar ways to men from the status quo. Development policy and practice needs to take all of this into account.

All development agencies need to be aware of the risks of increasing violence against women and factor them into all of their planning and interventions. We know that women are at most danger from men they know. Development projects need to account for this when they provide women with access to economic resources, family planning, new networks, and altered status outside the household. All of these interventions may increase women's status, which can result in violent reactions from men.

One way to address this is by involving women in the planning of interventions so that potential violence can be identified and strategies put into place to prevent it. For example, interventions that allow women to develop self-esteem, a critical awareness of power relations, and a network of support help equip women with the resources they need to challenge violence. Development organisations can ask what mechanisms are already in place to challenge violent men and support women. Is there a way to bring men on board so that they see a woman's empowerment project not as a threat but as a positive development?

International NGOs and government agencies need clear policy, not only with regard to reducing the incidence of violence against women and protecting women from violence through specifically targeted programmes, but also to ensure that all development, humanitarian, and advocacy interventions are alert to the possibilities of exacerbating violence against women.

Standards might be set to guide this, for example:

- All interventions are based upon a sound gendered analysis, not only of poverty and suffering, but also of the ideas, beliefs, and attitudes of men and women, and the impact of these on violence against women.
- Women are involved in the planning of such interventions.
- All interventions and policy positions are informed about their possible impact upon violence against women.
- All interventions include measures to protect women from violence if it is likely to be a by-product of women's development.

9.4.2 Developing an integrated organisational strategy

In an institutional policy environment in which international NGOs have been facing declining incomes and increased donor demands for accountability and impact, there is a powerful pressure to focus interventions on areas where the results will be visible within at least the medium term. Within the array of possible strategies to address violence against women, some results may be more visible than others – for example, the passing of a law against rape is more measurable and visible than gradual changes in attitudes within a given society. NGOs may be tempted to go for the demonstrable impact, both for their own sense of achievement and to be able to reassure donors that their money is well spent.

It is however clear from this book that violence against women needs to be tackled on many fronts, and that it is a deeply-rooted problem. Gender relations and all the beliefs and attitudes and behaviours associated with them do indeed change, and can be changed – but not overnight, and often not in immediately visible ways. To deal only with the symptoms of violence against women by providing shelter and protection to the women who are attacked, or legal redress to punish the perpetrators, will do little to reduce or prevent further instances of violence. As we have also seen, the violence to which women are subjected is not random, or abnormal, or defined by specific circumstances alone. It is used as a weapon to punish women for stepping beyond the gendered boundaries set for them, and to instil fear of even considering doing so. It is a systematic strategy to maintain women's subordination to men.

As we said in the Preface, this needs a strategic and systematic response. International organisations need clear policy objectives that tackle this systematic violation of women's rights in all spheres, and at many levels, involving the key actors and institutions. Thorough research and documentation must form the basis of policy-making and the planning of specific interventions, and strategies in the three main areas identified in this book must complement each other: direct support to survivors of violence, challenging and changing legal institutions, and working at the level of changes in attitudes and beliefs of women and men. This does not mean that only organisations working on all these fronts should be supported, or that all of these strategies will be appropriate in all circumstances. Rather, it means that appropriate strategies are defined, on the basis of sound research and understanding, for specific contexts; and that overall, in any context, there are complementary strategies that help to build a 'critical mass' of action against violence against women. Working only in one of the sectors – direct provision, or legal reform, or public education – is unlikely to have much impact in isolation. International agencies thus should plan their support in such a way that the work delivered by different organisations adds up to an integrated programme in any given country or region. This should include development, humanitarian, and advocacy interventions.

Standards set to ensure this might be:

- International agency support of systematic research and analysis of violence against women is the first step in programme planning.
- International agency frameworks for programming always include direct responses to the effects of violence, institutional and legal reform, and changing social and cultural values propping up violence against women.
- International agency strategic programme options are defined by their context but always include complementary strategies within a programme area.
- Development, humanitarian, and advocacy interventions on violence against women work to common goals and standards.

9.4.3 Using broad and strategic alliances

It is clear from the complex and wide-ranging nature of the problem, that no single organisation will be able to achieve significant results in reducing or eradicating violence against women on its own. Broad alliances are needed, in order to tackle the problem from all sides. A wide range of expertise is essential – that of service-providers, counsellors, health professionals, lawyers, economists, campaigners, educationalists, and so on. Networks are important for mobilising on specific issues. In the Preface we referred to the alliance built by ten different 'Oxfams' around the world, forming a single 'family' that is now beginning to plan its work on violence against women. This alliance potentially brings together the wide range of partners the different Oxfams support. A recent initiative by one of the organisations in the Oxfam family is the creation of an email network of partners working on violence against women, and Oxfam GB will add its own partners to this. This will enable discussion and learning to take place amongst a relatively small group on topics decided by the steering group, and will be moderated by an international women's organisation.

Alliances with international agencies in the UN system, such as UNDP, UNIFEM, UNHCR, UNRISD, the ILO, and with staff working on violence against women in the World Bank, are important in increasing the scale and scope of work on violence against women. Human rights organisations such as Amnesty International and Human Rights Watch have been active on violence against women in recent years. Important allies for international NGOs are the feminist activist lawyers who have been particularly influential in the drawing up of the Statute of the ICC, and the functioning of the two International Criminal Tribunals. Numerous national and regional organisations, alliances, and networks exist on specific forms of violence, such as trafficking and female genital mutilation, as well as on violence against women more generally. Women's Courts and Tribunals have been organised by feminist organisations in many parts of the world to draw the attention of the public to the violence inflicted on women. A recent Tribunal was held in Tokyo, the Women's International War Crimes Tribunal on Japan's Military Sexual Slavery organised by the Asian Centre for Women's Human Rights. This Tribunal put the Japanese government into the dock for the institution of 'comfort women' during World War II, and while the Centre knows there will never be a conviction, the Tribunal enabled women who had been silent for half a century to speak out, and was widely covered by the media.

International development and relief organisations are sometimes slow to work with these coalitions and networks, but if they are to take on the issue of violence against women, and have a significant impact upon it, joint work with key alliances is essential.

Standards relating to this area might be:

- All programme planning on violence against women demonstrates awareness of key actors in the field.
- All programme planning on violence against women identifies key partnerships and alliances for wider impact.
- All programmes on violence against women work with key strategic allies at national, regional, and/or international level.

9.5 Ending violence against women?

Ultimately, our vision is to end violence against women. In the meantime, we need to set realistic and achievable goals, with sustainable results, which represent the steps to the realisation of this vision. Many of these steps have been set out by the United Nations. The Beijing Platform for Action adopted by the Fourth World Conference on Women in 1995 includes violence against women as one of its Critical Areas of Concern, and states that, 'Violence against women both violates and impairs or nullifies the enjoyment by women of their human rights and fundamental freedoms. The long-standing failure to protect and promote those rights and freedoms in the case of violence against women is a matter of concern to all States and should be addressed.' (United Nations 1995b, 73) The document then lists a comprehensive set of actions to be taken by governments, non-governmental actors, the public and private sector, and the mass media.

All of this work needs resources. Recommendation (p) exhorts governments to:

> *'allocate adequate resources within the government budget and mobilise community resources for activities related to elimination of violence against women, including resources for the implementation plans of action at all appropriate levels'.*

In the end, the allocation of resources will determine the success or failure of the world community to end violence against women. Within NGOs, where resources are limited and competition for them is fierce, priority given to violence against women often comes and goes – flavour of the month now, forgotten tomorrow. As this book goes to print, there is a momentum and a widespread concern with the problem amongst many international organisations, governmental and non-governmental. The challenge to them, and to ourselves, is to recognise that eradication of violence against women is complicated, difficult, and entails tackling some of the most deeply-entrenched beliefs in human society; that it is a long-term project and will need sustained allocation of resources over a long period of time; that it requires commitment and dedication to continue, when results seem elusive and hard to demonstrate; and that we must keep faith with those millions of women who are subjected to torture of all kinds, just because they were born female.

Appendix 1

The three phases of Rape Trauma Syndrome

1. Impact phase

Duration: Immediately following assault until approximately 24-48 hours post-assault.

Survivors may exhibit a wide range of emotional reactions. Memory gaps are common; responses are likely to reflect automatic coping styles. The survivor may have concerns about pregnancy, venereal diseases, and AIDS. In general, responses can be divided into two broad categories:

i. Expressed, in which feelings of fear, anger, and anxiety are shown through such behaviour as crying, laughing, restlessness, and tenseness.

ii. Controlled, in which feelings are contained and a calm, composed, or subdued effect is demonstrated.

Interventions: When working with a survivor during the impact phase, it is extremely important to emphasise three things:

a. she has been through an extremely frightening experience;

b. she is not to blame for what has happened;

c. she is now in a safe place (if it is true).

2. Acute phase

Duration: Variable – from a few days to six weeks or more. Period of disorganisation; predominate feeling is fear; physical symptoms are especially troubling.

Physical reactions: Skeletal muscle tensions, fatigue, sleep disturbances, stomach pains, nausea, vaginal discharge, itching, burning, and generalised pain.

Emotional reactions: Flashbacks, sleep disturbances, nightmares, poor concentration, memory loss, guilt/self-blame, shame, anger, vulnerability, appetite change, fear, anxiety, moodiness, denial, obsessions with details of rape, lack of trust.

Interventions: Some survivors are ready to talk about what has happened. It is important to reassure the survivor that she is experiencing normal, expected reactions to a traumatic event. It is also important to reassure the survivor that with time she will get better. Support a non-judgemental attitude that places blame on the rapist.

Some rape survivors are not ready to talk immediately. The survivor should not be forced to discuss the incident, and it will be reassuring for her to know that whatever she chooses to do – talk or not talk – is okay.

3. Reorganisation phase

Duration: Long-term process lasting from one to two years. The effectiveness of the reorganisation phase is dependent on many variables, such as ego strength, social supports, and prior history of victimisation.

Emotional Reactions: With support and/or counselling, the survivor gradually regains control and is able to trust herself and place blame on the perpetrators. Without support, the acute trauma symptoms tend to lessen over time but the survivor is likely to suffer from one of the following symptoms:

i. isolation/withdrawal;

ii. lowered self-esteem: feels shameful, dirty, powerless, naïve, stupid;

iii. restricted mobility: phobias, fear of being alone, fear of darkness;

iv. depression/restricted effect: wary, clamping down of emotions, holding things inside;

v. sexual dysfunction: fear of sex, numbing, sometimes promiscuity.

Intervention: Help her to identify the ways in which her existing symptoms are connected to the rape.

Source: New York City/Balkan Rape Crisis Response Team 1993, pp. 1-3

Appendix 2

The KwaZulu Natal Programme for the Survivors of Violence framework for understanding the effects of political violence and responding to it

Table 1
Effects of violence: fragmentation and disempowerment

	Fragmentation	Disempowerment
Effects on individuals	Loss of memory of traumatic events	Sense of loss of control of life
	Efforts to avoid stimuli (including thoughts) associated with traumatic events	Decreased ability to fulfil social roles (parent, teacher, priest, breadwinner, child)
	Dissociation of affect	Loss of education, training, personal development opportunities
	Inability to contain feelings of hopelessness, frustration, and anger	High stress, inability to concentrate, sleep disturbances, poor eating habits, substance abuse, impaired ability to function
		Loss of interest in significant activities
		Sense of foreshortened future resulting in decreased long-term planning or vision
Effects on small groups	Generalised distrust and suspicion of others	Small groups become unable to fulfil their role in community (e.g., prayer groups, youth clubs)
	Lack of intimacy and emotional support	
	Reduced caring behaviour	
	Envy towards friends and family	

	Fragmentation	Disempowerment
	Undermining attempts to heal by family and friends Breakdown in community communication structures leading to individual isolation	Loss of meaningful supportive, healing, and development resources within community (e.g., sports and recreation facilities, skills training opportunities)
Effects on communities	Destruction of valuable and scarce infrastructure and resources Division within community prevents resources from being optimised. Generalised distrust of 'outsiders' Reduced ability to access resources outside of community or to repair/replace damaged infrastructure Non-functional community structures prevent community being represented in local government structures (breakdown in democracy) These can result in frustration and anger and further conflict	Local structures lose their ability to represent and govern (teachers cannot enforce discipline in schools, break-away political structures form, conflict between civic and political structures emerges)
Effects on society	Isolation of communities hinders peacemaking and facilitates conflict Proliferation of weapons Proliferation of paramilitary training	Intolerable strain on virtually all services results in the reduced ability of essential services to function (e.g., policing, emergency services, health services, welfare services) Development programmes are undermined, leading to a generalised disillusionment with processes of social change

	Linking	Empowerment
Individual interventions	Individual and group counselling aimed at: • processing traumatic events • learning adaptive coping techniques • learning to contain and express emotion in a controlled and adaptive manner	Individual and group counselling aimed at: • understanding individuals' personal narratives • developing decision-making skills • planning for the future • relearning social skills necessary to continue life in a peaceful society • opportunities for personal development • opportunities to develop self-esteem
Small group interventions	Group work aimed at building relationships: • recognising and naming 'distrust' • exploring barriers to trust • learning how to negotiate trusting relationships Opportunities to develop intimacy and social support Developing caring behaviour: • exploring barriers to caring • learning caring behaviour Rebuilding fragmented social structures	Rebuilding small groups and assisting them in carrying out their original purpose
Community-level interventions	Rebuild infrastructure and other resources Employ peace-making and negotiation to ensure that resources are available to the entire community	Build the capacity of local leaders, and service providers to provide an effective and accountable service to the community

Table 2
Goals of interventions: linking and empowerment

311

	Linking	**Empowerment**
	Facilitate links with resources outside of communities. Empower community structures to work responsibly with outside agencies	
	Facilitate the development of proper democratic local government and other community structures	
Society-wide interventions	Foster links between communities, and between different levels of government	Support the functioning of different social services (extra training and resources for police, and other services)
	Lobby against proliferation of weapons	Support broader development and public works programmes that offer economic relief to survivors of violence
	Lobby against paramilitary training	

Source: KwaZulu Natal Programme for the Survivors of Violence (1997) 'Models of Interaction'. Available on-line at http://www.geocities.com/hotsprings/spa/3028

Notes

Introduction

1   The term 'gender' is used in this book to refer to all the socially ascribed attributes, roles, and responsibilities that are connected with being a man or a woman in any society. Our gender identity shapes the ways in which other individuals and institutions perceive us, as well as the ways in which we perceive ourselves. The distinction between 'sex' and 'gender' continues to be the subject of heated debate (see for example, Baden and Goetz 1998, for a summary of debates on 'gender' arising from the UN World Conference on Women in Beijing).

2   Commission on Human Rights Resolution 1994/45 of 4 March 1994.

3   The 1998 Rome Statute of the International Criminal Court gives it jurisdiction to try people responsible for genocide, crimes against humanity, war crimes, and the crime of aggression. As in the case of the two *ad hoc* Tribunals, the definition of genocide contained in the Rome Statute is the same as the definition provided for in the Genocide Convention. The definition of crimes against humanity (which do not need to be perpetrated in the context of an armed conflict to fall within the ICC jurisdiction) includes – when committed as part of a widespread or systematic attack against any civilian population with knowledge of the attack – 'rape, sexual slavery, enforced prostitution, enforced sterilisation, or any other form of sexual violence of comparable gravity' (United Nations 1998, Article 7(1(g))). For the first time under international law, the ICC Statute explicitly codifies rape, sexual slavery, enforced prostitution, forced pregnancy, enforced sterilisation, and other forms of sexual violence as war crimes, whether committed in the context of a conflict of an international or internal character.

4   Globalisation has been defined as 'a process whereby producers and investors increasingly behave as if the world economy consisted of a single market area with regional or national sub-sectors, rather than a set of national economies linked by trade and investment flows.' (UNCTAD 1996, 6, cited in Panos 1999)

5   The workshop was part-funded by the British government's Department for International Development (DfID).

6   CLADEM and Oxfam GB (July 2000) *Cuestión de vida: balance regional y desafíos sobre el derecho de las mujeres a una vida libre de violencia* (A question of life: a regional account of achievements and challenges relating to women's

right to a life free from violence), Lima: CLADEM, Apartado Postal 11-0470, Lima, Peru.
Tel: 00-51-1-463-9237; fax: 00-51-1-463-5898; e-mail: cladem@chavin.rcp.net.pe

Chapter 1

1   Other definitions of violence against women employ the terms 'sexual violence' or 'domestic violence':

> *[Sexual violence covers] any physical, visual, verbal, or sexual act that is experienced by the woman or girl, at the time or later, as a threat, invasion or assault, that has the effect of hurting her or degrading her and/or takes away her ability to control intimate contact.*
> (Kelly 1988)

> *[Sexual violence covers] all forms of sexual threat, assault, interference and exploitation, including molestation without physical harm or penetration.*
> (UNHCR 1995)

> *Domestic violence… refers to the use of physical or emotional force or threat of force including sexual violence, in close adult relationships. In the majority of incidences of violence or sexual assault against women, the attacker is known to the woman and is likely to have had an intimate relationship with her.*
> (Dublin Task Force on Violence against Women 1997)

2   See pp. 89-90 for a more detailed discussion of FGM.

3   For examples of this approach see West, Roy, and Nichols (1978) and Gelles (1972).

4   Later, Caroline Moser adapted these concepts for use as planning tools for development policy-makers and practitioners, translating the language of 'interests' into that of 'needs'. For a full discussion of practical and strategic gender needs, see March, Mukhopadhyay, and Smyth (1999).

5   'Collective empowerment' is a similar concept, sometimes used to refer to the power that women can harness through mobilising in groups or organisations.

6   The term 'economic empowerment' is currently used by many development interventions seeking to increase women's income-generation. Most of these interventions are informed not by a commitment to supporting women's empowerment, but by a welfare or anti-poverty perspective.

7   The providers are the Grameen Bank, the Bangladesh Rural Advancement Committee (BRAC), Thangemara Mahila Sebuj Sengstha, and the Bangladesh Rural Development Board.

8   A fatwa is a formal legal opinion delivered by an Islamic religious authority.

Chapter 2

1   Cited in the 'Report on the Situation of Human Rights in Haiti', prepared by Adama Dieng, independent expert to the 53rd Session of the Commission on Human Rights, A53/355, 10 September 1998, para. 25.

2 However, this notion of the family as entitled to protection from external interference is made permeable by the recognition that the State has a responsibility to take action against human rights abuses by private persons that is implicitly recognised in core human rights instruments. For example, the ICCPR requires States Parties (states legally bound to the treaty by virtue of having become a party to it through ramification or accession) to undertake 'to respect and ensure' the rights in the Covenant to all without discrimination. In this connection, the UN Human Rights Committee has extended this obligation to include protection and redress against acts inflicted by individuals acting in a private capacity.

3 The 'certain circumstances' alluded to are 'when the State is complicit in acts of violence, has acquiesced in them or has failed to take the necessary measures to prevent them, and when the violence is intentionally inflicted and causes severe pain and suffering' (Amnesty International 2001a, 3). Thereby, the torture prohibition is extended, in certain cases, to acts by private individuals.

4 This refers to the American Convention on Human Rights (Pact of San José), signed 22 November 1969, entered into force 18 July 1978.

5 Velásquez Rodríguez Case, Judgement of 29 July 1988, Inter-American Court of Human Rights, Series C, no. 4, paras. 174-5. Available online at http://www1.umn.edu/humanrts/iachr/b_11_12d.htm

6 CEDAW is used to refer to both the Convention and the Committee. For the purposes of clarity, this book will refer to the Convention as 'the Women's Convention', and to the Committee as 'the CEDAW Committee'. The CEDAW Committee is a body of 23 independent experts established pursuant to Article 17 of the Women's Convention and charged with examining States Parties' compliance with and implementation of the provisions of the convention.

7 Article 1 of the Women's Convention defines discrimination against women as:

Any distinction, exclusion or restriction made on the basis of sex that has the effect or purpose of impairing or nullifying the recognition, enjoyment or exercise by women, irrespective of their marital status, on the basis of equality of men and women, of human rights and fundamental freedoms in the political, economic, social, cultural, civil or any other field.

8 The phrase 'due diligence' first appeared in the case of Velásquez Rodríguez v. Honduras, International-American Court of Human Rights (1998) Series C no. 4, Judgement of 29 July 1988, paras. 174,175.

9 The OTP is shared by the ICTY and ICTR, with the Office of the Prosecutor in The Hague and the Deputy Prosecutor in Kigali.

10 The following excerpt is the definition of rape used by the Chamber. These paragraphs are taken from the Judgement of the International Criminal Tribunal for Rwanda in the case of Jean-Paul Akayesu:

The Chamber must define rape, as there is no commonly accepted definition of this term in international law. While rape has been defined in certain national jurisdictions as non-consensual intercourse, variations on the act of rape may include acts which involve the insertion of objects and/or the use of bodily orifices not considered to be intrinsically sexual .... The Chamber considers that rape is a form of aggression and that the central elements of the crime of rape cannot be captured in a mechanical description of objects and body parts. The Convention against Torture and Other Cruel, Inhuman and Degrading Treatment or Punishment does not catalogue specific acts in its definition of torture, focusing rather on the conceptual frame work of state sanctioned violence. This approach is more useful in international law. Like torture, rape is used for such purposes as intimidation, degradation, humiliation, discrimination, punishment, control or destruction of a person. Like torture, rape is a violation of personal dignity, and rape in fact constitutes torture when inflicted by or at the instigation of or with the consent or acquiescence of a public official or other person acting in an official capacity....

The Chamber defines rape as a physical invasion of a sexual nature, committed on a person under circumstances which are coercive. Sexual violence which includes rape, is considered to be any act of a sexual nature which is committed on a person under circumstances which are coercive.

(ICTR decision of 2 September 1998, the Prosecutor v. Jean-Paul Akayesu, case no. ICTR-96-4-T paras. 596-8. Available on-line at http://www.un.org/ictr)

Poignantly, in relation to the finding of rape and sexual violence as constitutive elements of the crime of genocide in the Akayesu Judgment, Hilary Charlesworth has critically pointed out that that decision 'simply illustrates the inability of the law to properly name what is at stake: rape is wrong, not because it is a crime of violence against women and a manifestation of male dominance, but because it is an assault on a community defined only by its racial, religious, national or ethnic composition. In this account, the violation of a woman's body is secondary to the humiliation of the group. In this sense, international criminal law incorporates a problematic public/private distinction: it operates in the public realm of the collectivity, leaving the private sphere of the individual untouched. Because the notion of the community implicated here is one defined by men within it, the distinction has gendered consequences.'(Charlesworth 1999, 387)

11 The establishment of an international criminal court was first proposed in the 1950s, but was obstructed by four decades of Cold War. The issue was raised again in 1989, and by 1994 a draft statute was produced, with jurisdiction over genocide, war crimes, crimes against humanity, and aggression (Williams 1999a).

12 United Nations 1998, Article 7g

13 United Nations 1998, Article 8, 2bxxii

14 United Nations 1998

15 These Principles were prepared under the direction of the Representative of the UN Secretary-General on Internally Displaced Persons, and presented to the 54th session of the Commission on Human Rights. The Principles are concerned with protection from displacement, protection during displacement, humanitarian assistance, and return, resettlement, and reintegration.

16 For an elaboration of the distinction between rights and the law and the need to put the law into context, see Smart (1989). Other useful books on women and human rights include Kerr (1993) and Tomasevski (1993).

17 Chapter 3 discusses the consequences of violence for women's health.

18 Social Investment Funds were developed in order to mitigate the social impact of Structural Adjustment Programs.

19 See pp. 16-17 for a discussion of this study and the methodologies it employed.

20 Moser focuses on 'assets' because it conveys what the poor have rather than what they don't have. It suggests that just like the non-poor, the poor are managers of a complex portfolio of resources and skills. 'Assets' include tangibles such as labour, land, housing, and human capital, and intangibles such as household relations and social capital. The more assets individuals, households, and communities possess, the less vulnerable they become. Where assets are eroded, insecurity, violence, and poverty will tend to increase.

21 Chapter 4 looks in detail at why violence may increase in the contexts of structural adjustment policies, and poverty more generally.

22 FIDA and WVV are part of the Women's Advocacy Support Group. This group represents specific issues of importance to women in Kenya at NGO and UN fora, as a basis for future programme work on violence towards refugee women and the empowerment of pastoralist women's groups.

Chapter 3

1 The UNDP Human Development Report includes a Gender-Related Development Index (GDI), which 'attempts to capture achievement in the same dimensions as the HDI... but adjusts the results for gender inequality', and a Gender Empowerment Measure (GEM), which 'captures gender inequality in key areas of economic and political participation and decision-making'. (UNDP 1999, 132)

2 For a recent report providing a compilation of studies on the prevalence of child sex abuse, see Heise, Ellsberg, and Gottemoeller 1999, 12.

3 For a critique of the 1993 Asia Watch and Women's Rights Project report on trafficking of women to Thailand, see Murray (1998).

4 The practice started among the upper castes in the Bihar region in the early 1980s, and later spread to a wider section of the population. Adithi attributes the emergence of female infanticide to increases in dowry, poverty, and destitution (Strinivasan *et al.* 1995).

5 For example, the Jordanian Penal Code includes several articles providing for reduced penalties for men who kill their wives or female relatives because of adulterous relationships. It further appears that in these cases Jordanian courts often pass reduced sentences ranging from two years to six months of imprisonment (Jahangir 1999). Amnesty International reported that in December 2000 the Jordanian Upper House voted to repeal Article 340 of the Penal Code (which exempts from penalty males who murder wives or female relatives on grounds of adultery or reduces the penalty if the victim is found in an 'adulterous' situation). However, the repeal was later rejected by the lower house (Amnesty International 2001b).

6 Traditionally, dowry referred to wealth given to a woman by her family on her marriage. Most prevalent in North India, it was a Hindu practice that enabled parents to pass on family assets to their daughters, who were not allowed by law or custom to inherit property (Desjarlais *et al.* 1995). Dowry has now been transformed into a premarital transaction referring to the money or goods that the bride's parents agree to present to the groom and his family as a condition of the marriage settlement. Lori Heise argues that it is increasingly seen as a 'get rich quick' scheme by prospective husbands (1993). For two differing analyses and instances of dowry, see Ursula Sharma's (1984) account of customary Hindu and Sikh practices in the states of Himachal Pradesh and Punjab, India, and Ernestine Friedl's (1975) analysis of dowry in a Greek village.

7 See Appendix 1 for more information on the three phases of Rape Trauma Syndrome.

Chapter 4

1 Some development practitioners consider that the community does not fit the description of an institution in the same way as does, for example, the household (see March, Smyth, and Mukhopadhyay 1999).

2 In contrast, Naila Kabeer's (1994) discussion of the Social Relations Framework examines a different list of institutions, namely, the household, the community, the State, and the market.

3 A recent report from the UN Special Rapporteur on violence against women, its causes and consequences, examines state policies that prevent women from making reproductive choices. The report discusses the failure to address violence against women perpetrated by health care workers; the failure to provide contraceptive information; the denial of contraception; forced sterilisation, forced abortion, forced use of contraception; and the provision of unsafe or inappropriate contraception (Coomaraswamy 1999b).

4 Note that although a link between violence and alcohol consumption is often made, we should exercise caution in employing alcohol or drug use as a direct or independent explanation of men's violence towards women (Dobash and Dobash 1992).

5 For these and other examples, see Copelon 1995; Swiss and Giller 1993, 613; Americas Watch and Women's Rights Project 1992; Asia Watch and Women's Rights Project 1992; and Swiss 1991.

6 See www1.jca.apc.org/vaww-net-japan for the Tribunal judgement.

7 A series of international standards and decisions support this argument. See, for example, the Preliminary Report of the Special Rapporteur on the situation of systematic rape, sexual slavery and slavery-like practices during periods of armed conflicts, 'Contemporary Forms of Slavery', UN Document E/CN.4/Sub.2/1996/26, 16 July 1996, 6; and the Final Report of the United Nations Commission of Experts established pursuant to Security Council Resolution 780 (1992), 'Annex II: Rape and Sexual Assault: A Legal Study', UN Document S/1994/674/Add.2, vol. I, 28 December 1994, 5.

8 Thanks to Oliver Sprague for directing me to this research.

9 *Afghantsi* is the Russian word used to describe Russian army veterans who fought in Afghanistan.

Chapter 5

1 United Nations (1998), Article 7(g)

2 United Nations (1998), Article 8, 2bxxii

3 Significantly, the war crime provisions contained in the Rome Statute of the ICC pertaining to rape, sexual slavery, enforced prostitution, and forced pregnancy, prohibit these acts both in the context of armed conflict of an international and non-international character (United Nations 1998).

4 The Sphere Project *Humanitarian Charter and Minimum Standards in Disaster Response*, published in 2000 by the Sphere Project and Oxfam GB, has gone some way to integrating gender-awareness into its wide-ranging minimum standards guidelines for humanitarian actions.

5 'Musasa' is the Shona word for a large tree, connoting temporary shelter.

6 See Chapter 1 for more information on the ways in which these para-legal workers are challenged and threatened as a result of the work they do, and Chapter 8 for a description of the training involved.

7 As noted in Chapter 3, 'Rape Trauma Syndrome' (RTS) has been used as a diagnostic category by women's crisis centres such as People Opposing Women Abuse in South Africa and Medica Zenica in Bosnia.

8 Also significant in this regard are occasions when the State names events in the past as violent, for example, the case of state-sanctioned prostitution as experienced by Japanese 'comfort women' during World War II.

9 Increasing numbers of Guatemala's indigenous people call themselves Maya – referring to their part in a broader community of eight or nine million people who speak different Mayan languages across four countries – Mexico, Belize, Honduras, and Guatemala. Since the first half of the nineteenth century the Mayan struggle for civil and political rights against the *ladinos* (the politically dominant group in Guatemala) has aimed to redefine Guatemala as a multicultural nation in which the much older Maya nations can take an equal place (Wearne 1994).

10 The town of Tuzla was located in Bosnian government-held territory in the north-east of Bosnia, where local authorities upheld an explicit commitment to multi-ethnicity. A large proportion of the Serb population had fled from Tuzla at the beginning of the fighting, leaving a Muslim majority.

11 Some defaulted due to factors beyond their control such as bad harvests, the stealing of products, a lack of knowledge about simple accounts, or being overwhelmed by cash needs such as the need for medical treatment.

12 See Chapter 2, note 5.

13 Press release issued by the Office of the UN High Commissioner for Human Rights, 22 December 2000. Available on-line at http://www.unhcr.ch

14 The World Bank defines social capital as 'reciprocity within communities and between households based on trust derived from social ties. The extent to which a community can itself be considered an asset depends on its 'stocks' of social capital, identified as the networks, norms and trust that facilitate co-ordination and co-operation for mutual benefit. These are the reciprocal exchanges that exist first and foremost, between individuals and households, but that then extend into the social institutions at the community level.' (Holland and Moser 1997, 4)

Chapter 6

1 This material was prepared by the Planned Parenthood Association of South Africa and the Medical Research Council. Thanks to Linnea Renton, the Co-ordinator of the Stepping Stones Training and Adaptation Project. For more information on Stepping Stones, the project, or the gender violence training module, contact her at: ActionAid, Hamlyn House, Macdonald Road, London N19 5PG, UK.

2 'Civil violence' is in inverted commas because the term is often used to refer to violence in the public sphere between men, and not violence against women.

Chapter 7

1 This study is based on interviews with 207 women and men, in four different areas of Lusaka, on the subject of violence against women.

2 Gramsci uses the word 'hegemony' to denote the relationship between the ruling class and other social forces. A hegemonic class is 'one which gains the consent of other classes and social forces through creating and maintaining a system of alliances by means of political and ideological struggle' (Simon 1991, 23).

3 A 'soap opera' is a serialised radio or television drama in which, typically, ordinary domestic situations are given melodramatic or sentimental treatment.

4 For example, see Miller and Razavi (1998); Goetz (1997); Jahan (1995).

Chapter 8

1 'Eve-teasing' is a term used in India to denote sexual harassment, especially on public transport and in the street.

2 See Chapter 1 for a description of the case.

3 See: re Fauziya Kasinga, Applicant, US Department of Justice Executive Office for Immigration Review Board of Immigration Appeals, File A73 476 695 – Elizabeth Interim Decision: 3278, Department of Justice Board of Immigration Appeals, 1996 BIA LEXIS 15, 13 June 1996, Decided. Fausiya Kasinga was 17 years old, and escaped FGM and an arranged marriage in Togo.

4 *Rules of Procedure and Evidence*, (IT/32/REV.19), Rule 96: Evidence in Cases of Sexual Assault. Available at: http://www.un.org/icty/basic/rpe/IT32_rev20.htm#Rule%2096 The ICTR has a similar rule.

5 'Landmark first women's definition of rape in International Law – Urgent Action Alert', Sisterhood is Global Institute, September 30, 1998, available at http://www.sigi.org/Alert/rape0998.htm

6 The Act is a piece of legislation riddled with problems that makes it unworkable in practice for women (Fedler 1995). It was not drafted by experts on domestic violence. These criticisms have been acknowledged and a Committee has been established to develop a Domestic Violence Bill. See the Shadow Report to the CEDAW Committee for recommendations for the Bill (Masimanyane CEDAW Working Group 1998).

7 See the section on training in Chapter 7 for a description of the principles of Paulo Freire's work.

8 See UNHCR's recent report on developing a community-based response to sexual violence against women for further lessons on training with police and other officials in refugee camps (UNHCR 1997).

9 See pp. 50-1 for more information about the Inter-American Convention and on inter-governmental organisations that operate at the regional level and are active in human rights and democratic development work.

10 A second important network in the Middle East region is the Permanent Arab Court to Resist Violence Against Women.

Bibliography

Abdalla, R. (1983) *Sisters of Affliction: Circumcision and Infibulation of Women in Africa*, London: Zed Books.

Abdullah, R. (1997) 'Gender Based Violence as a Health Issue: The Situation and Challenges to the Women's Health Movement in Asia and the Pacific', paper presented at the 8th International Women and Health Meeting, Rio de Janeiro, Brazil.

Aboim, M. (1999) *Brazil: Domestic Violence and the Women's Movement*, San Francisco CA: Family Violence Prevention Fund.

Abou-Habib, L. (1998) 'The use and abuse of female domestic workers from Sri Lanka in Lebanon', *Gender and Development* 6(1).

Abreu, A. (1998) 'Mozambican women experiencing violence', in M. Turshen and C. Twagiramariya (eds), *What Women Do in Wartime: Gender and Conflict in Africa*, London: Zed Books.

Abu-Dayyeh, S. (1998) 'Case Study', Jerusalem: Women's Centre for Legal Aid and Counselling.

Acsadi, G. and G. Johnson-Acsadi (1993) 'Socio-economic, Cultural, and Legal Factors Affecting Girls' and Women's Health and their Access to and Utilisation of Health and Nutrition Services in Developing Countries', background paper for the World Bank Best Practices Paper on 'Women's Health and Nutrition', Population, Health, and Nutrition Department, Washington DC, draft of 17 March.

Adams, A. (1993) 'Dyke to dyke: ritual reproduction at a US men's military college', *Anthropology Today* 9(5), pp. 3-6.

Ahuya, M. (1996) *Widows – Role Adjustment and Violence*, New Delhi: Wishwa Prakashan.

Aleksanyan, M. (1998) 'The Work of TRUST: Research into Attitudes to Violence against Women, TRUST (Armenia Social Work and Sociological Research Centre)', paper presented at Oxfam international workshop on violence against women, Sarajevo, November.

Alvarez, S. (1990) *Engendering Democracy in Brazil: Women's Movements in Transition Politics*, Princetown: Princetown University Press.

Americas Watch (1984) *Guatemala: A Nation of Prisoners*, New York: Human Rights Watch.

Americas Watch and Women's Rights Project (1992) *Untold Terror: Violence against Women in Peru's Armed Conflict*, New York: Human Rights Watch.

Amnesty International (1991) 'Women in the Frontline', New York: Amnesty International.

Amnesty International (1995a) 'Women in China', *AI Index*, ASA 17/29/95.

Amnesty International (1995b) 'Women in Kenya', *AI Index*, AFR 32/06/95.

Amnesty International (1995c) 'Women in Pakistan: disadvantaged and denied their rights', *AI Index*, ASA 33/23/95.

Amnesty International (1996a) 'United Arab Emirates: Sarah Balabagan (f) Filipina national', Urgent Action, 9 February, *AI Index*, MDE 25/03/96.

Amnesty International (1996b) 'Chad: Cases for appeal', AFR 20/05/96, 18 September.

Amnesty International (1997) 'Breaking God's commands', *AI Index*, AFR 59/01/97.

Amnesty International (1998) 'Guatemala: all the truth, justice for all', AMR 34/02/98.

Amnesty International (1999a) *Amnesty International Report*, London: Amnesty International.

Amnesty International (1999b) 'Pakistan: violence against women in the name of honour', *AI Index*, ASA 33/17/99.

Amnesty International (1999c) 'Trinidad and Tobago: Indravani Pamala Ramjattan – battered woman faces death penalty', *AI Index*, AMR 49/12/99.

Amnesty International (2001a) 'Broken bodies, shattered minds: torture and ill-treatment of women', *AI Index*, ACT 40/001/2001, 8 March.

Amnesty International (2001b), *Annual Report 2001, AI Index* POL 10/001/2001, London: Amnesty International Publications.

Anderson, M. and P. Woodrow (1989) *Rising from the Ashes: Development Strategies in Times of Disaster*, Boulder CO: Westview Press.

Anti-Slavery International (1994) *Early Marriage*, London: Anti-Slavery International.

Arnig, E. (1993) 'Child prostitution in Cambodia: did the UN look away?', *International Children's Rights Monitor* 10(3).

Aron, A. (1992) '*Testimonio*, a bridge between psychotherapy and sociotherapy', *Women and Therapy* 13, pp. 173-89.

Aron, A., *et al.* (1991) 'The gender-specific terror of El Salvador and Guatemala – post-traumatic stress disorder in Central American refugee women', *Women's Studies International Forum* 14(1/2), pp. 32-47.

Asia and Pacific Women's Resource Collection Network (1990) *Asia and Pacific Women's Resource and Action Series: Health*, Kuala Lumpur: Asia and Pacific Development Centre.

Asia Pacific Forum on Women, Law, and Development (1990) *My Rights, Who Controls?*, Kuala Lumpur: Asia Pacific Forum on Women, Law, and Development.

Asia Pacific Forum on Women, Law, and Development (2000) 'The Women's International War Crimes Tribunal on Japan's Military Sexual Slavery', *Forum News* 13(3), December. Available on-line at http://www.apwld.org/vol133-07.html

Asia Watch and Women's Rights Project (1992) *Burma: Rape, Forced Labour, and Religious Persecution in Northern Arkan*, Washington DC: Human Rights Watch.

Asia Watch and Women's Rights Project (1993) *A Modern Form of Slavery: Trafficking of Burmese Women and Girls into Brothels in Thailand*, Washington DC: Human Rights Watch.

Asia Watch and Women's Rights Project (1995) *Rape for Profit: Trafficking of Nepali Girls and Women to India's Brothels*, Washington DC: Human Rights Watch.

Asling-Monemi, K., *et al.* (1999) 'Violence against women increases the risk of infant and child mortality. A case reference study in Nicaragua', cited in UNICEF (2000).

Association of Female Lawyers of Liberia (1998) 'Hundreds of victims silently grieving', in M. Turshen and C. Twagiramariya (eds), *What Women Do in Wartime: Gender and Conflict in Africa*, London: Zed Books.

Baden, S. and A. Goetz (1998) 'Who needs [sex] when you can have [gender]? Conflicting discourse on gender at Beijing', in C. Jackson and R. Pearson, *Feminist Visions of Development: Gender Analysis and Policy*, London: Routledge.

Banks, L. and S. Hobson (1993) *Informal settlements in the Eastern Cape, Border and Transkei Regions. A Pilot Study.* Grahamstown: Rhodes University Institute of Social and Economic Research.

Banwell, S. (1994) *Law, Status of Women and Family Planning in Sub-Saharan Africa: A Suggestion for Action*, Nairobi: The Pathfinder Fund.

Barron, J., Dobash, R., McWilliams, M., and S. Watt (1994) 'Violence to women from known men', in J. Hanmer and J. Hearn (eds), *Final Report on Research Strategy on Violence, Abuse and Gender Relations*, report to the ESRC, Research Paper 11, Bradford: Violence Abuse and Gender Relations Research Unit, University of Bradford, March.

Bateman, C. (1998) 'Ubuntu justice', *Cape Town Insight*.

Beales, S. (2000) 'Why we should invest in older women and men: the experience of HelpAge International', *Gender and Development* 8(2).

Benería, L. and M. Roldán (1987) *The Crossroads of Class and Gender: Industrial Homework, Subcontracting and Household Dynamics in Mexico City*, Chicago: University of Chicago Press.

Bennett, O., Bexley, J., and K. Warnock (1995) *Arms to Fight, Arms to Protect: Women Speak Out about Conflict*, London: Panos.

Bhasin, K. (1997) 'Gender workshops with men: experiences and reflections', *Gender and Development* 5(2).

Bolles, L. (1983) 'Kitchens hit by priorities: employed working class Jamaican women confront the IMF', in J. Nash and M. Fernandez-Kelly (eds), *Women, Men and the International Division of Labour*, Albany NY: State University of New York Press.

Borger, J. (1997) 'In cold blood', *The Guardian*, 4 November.

Bradley, C. (1994) 'Why male violence against women is a development issue: reflections from Papua New Guinea', in M. Davies (ed.), *Women and Violence: Realities and Responses Worldwide*, London: Zed Books.

Brett, R. and M. McCallin (1996) *Children: The Invisible Soldiers*, Stockholm: Rädda Bärnen.

Broadbent, L. (1999) *Macho*, video, available from lucinda@cqm.co.uk

Brown, J (1992) 'Introduction: definitions, assumptions, themes, and issues', in D. Counts, J. Brown, and J. Campbell (eds), *Sanctions and Sanctuary: Cultural Perspectives on Beating of Wives*, Boulder CO: Westview Press.

Brownmiller, S. (1975) *Against Our Will: Men, Women and Rape*, Harmondsworth: Penguin.

Bruce, J. (1989) 'Homes divided', *World Development* 17(7).

Brush, L. (1990) 'Violent acts and injurious outcomes in married couples: methodological issues in the National Survey of Families and Households', *Gender and Society* 4, pp. 56-67.

Bullock, L. and J. McFarlane (1989) 'The battering low-birthweight connection', *Am. J. Nurs.* 89, pp. 1153-5.

Bunch, C. and R. Carrillo (1991) *Gender Violence: A Development and Human Rights Issue*, New Brunswick NJ: Centre For Women's Global Leadership, Douglas College.

Bunch, C., Carrillo, R., and R. Shore (1998) 'Violence against women', in N.P. Stromquist (ed.), *Women in the Third World: An Encyclopedia of Contemporary Issues*, New York and London: Garland.

Bunch, C. and N. Reilly (1994) *Demanding Accountability: The Global Campaign and Vienna Tribunal for Women's Human Rights*, New York: Center for Women's Global Leadership, Rutgers University and UNIFEM.

Burns, J. (1992) 'A Serbian fighter's trail of brutality', *New York Times*, 27 November.

Callaghan, N., Hamber, B., and S. Takura (1997) 'A triad of oppression: violence, women and poverty,' *NGO Matters: Poverty Special*, South African NGO Coalition, August.

Cameron, D. and E. Frazer (1987) *The Lust to Kill*, London: Polity Press.

Cameron, J. and K. R. Anderson (1998) '"Circumcision", culture, and health-care provision in Tower Hamlets, London', *Gender and Development* 6(3).

Campbell, J. (1992) 'Wife-battering: cultural contexts versus western social sciences', in D. Counts, J. Brown, and J. Campbell (eds), *Sanctions and Sanctuary: Cultural Perspectives on the Beating of Wives*, Boulder CO: Westview Press.

Carrillo, R. (1992) *Battered Dreams: Violence Against Women as an Obstacle to Development*, New York: United Nations Fund for Women (UNIFEM).

Carucci, L. (1992) 'Nudging her harshly and killing him softly: displays of disenfranchisement on Ujelang Atoll', in D. Counts, J. Brown, and J. Campbell (eds), *Sanctions and Sanctuary: Cultural Perspectives on the Beating of Wives*, Boulder CO: Westview Press.

Castelli, D. (1998) 'Sexual Exploitation of Adolescent Girls in Chile', paper on the work of Colectivo Raices Santiago presented at the Oxfam international workshop on violence against women, Sarajevo, November.

Castelo-Branco, V. (1997) 'Child soldiers: the experience of the Mozambican Association for Public Health (AMOSAPU)', *Development in Practice* 7(4)

Castle, S. (1998) Editorial, *The Independent on Sunday*, 10 May.

CEDAW (1979) *Convention on the Elimination of All Forms of Discrimination Against Women*, United Nations Organisation, General Assembly Resolution 34/180, December.

CEDAW (1992) *Violence against Women*, General Recommendation no. 19, Eleventh session, UN Document CEDAW/C/1992/L.1/Add.15, New York: United Nations.

Center for Reproductive Law and Policy (1996) 'Rape and Forced Pregnancy in War and Conflict Situations', New York: Center for Reproductive Law and Policy, 30 April.

Center for Reproductive Law and Policy and Latin American and Caribbean Committee for the Defence of Women's Rights (1999) *Silence and Complicity: Violence against Women in Peruvian Public Health Facilities*, New York: Center for Reproductive Law and Policy; Argentina: CLADEM.

Chant, S. (1991) *Women and Survival in Mexican Cities: Perspectives on Gender, Labour Market and Low-Income Households*, Manchester: Manchester University Press.

Chant, S. (1994a) 'Women and poverty in urban Latin America: Mexican and Costa Rican experiences', in F. Meer (ed.), *Poverty in the 1990s: The Responses of Urban Women*, Oxford/Paris: Berg/ISSC in co-operation with UNESCO.

Chant, S. (1994b) 'Women, work and household survival strategies in Mexico, 1982-1992: past trends, current tendencies and future research', *Bulletin of Latin American Research* 13(2), pp. 203-33.

Chant, S. and M. Gutmann (2001) *Mainstreaming Men into Gender and Development: Debates, Reflections, and Experiences*, Oxford: Oxfam Publications.

Charlesworth, H. (1999) 'Feminist methods in international law', *American Journal of International Law* 93:2, pp. 379-94.

Charlesworth, H. and C. Chinkin (2000) *The Boundaries of International Law: a Feminist Analysis*, Manchester: Juris Publishing/Manchester University Press.

Charlesworth, H., Chinkin C., and S. Wright (1991) 'Feminist approaches to international law', *American Journal of International Law* 85(4), pp. 613-45.

Chiarotti, S. (1998) 'Violence against Women in the Private Sphere in the Latin American and Caribbean Region', paper presented at Oxfam international workshop on violence against women, Sarajevo, November.

Chowdhry, G. (1995) 'Engendering development? Women in development (WID) in international development regimes', in J. Parpart and M. Marchand (eds), *Feminism/Postmodernism/Development*, London: Routledge.

Clayton, L. (1998) interview with Jane Origolo, Director of Sinaga, internal Oxfam document.

Coalition to Stop the Use of Child Soldiers (1998) *Stop Using Child Soldiers* Stockholm: Rädda Bärnen on behalf of the International Save the Children Alliance.

Cock, J. (1989) 'Keeping the home fires burning: militarisation and the politics of gender in South Africa', *Review of African Political Economy* 45-6.

Cockburn, C. (1998) *The Space Between Us: Negotiating Gender and National Identities in Conflict*, London: Zed Books.

Collectif 95 Maghreb Egalité (1998) 'Violence against women and violation of their rights in the Maghreb', in *Annual Report 1996–7*, Morocco: Collectif 95 Maghreb Egalité.

Collins, A. (1998) *Shielded from Justice: Police Brutality and Accountability in the United States*, New York: Human Rights Watch.

Commission for Historical Clarification (1999) 'Guatemala: Memory of Silence. Report: Conclusions and Recommendations', available online at http://hrdata.aaas.org/ceh/report/english/

Connell, R. (1995) *Masculinities*, Oxford: Polity Press.

Connors, J. (1989) *Violence against Women in the Family*, New York: United Nations.

Connors, J. (1993) 'Combating Violence Against Women', a report by the International League for Human Rights, March.

Cooke, R. and D. Maine (1987) 'Spousal veto over family planning services', *American Journal of Public Health* 77(3), pp. 330-44.

Coomaraswamy, R. (1995) 'Preliminary Report submitted by the Special Rapporteur on Violence Against Women, Its Causes and Consequences to the Human Rights Commission', Human Rights Commission, E/CN.4/1995/42, November.

Coomaraswamy, R. (1996a) 'Report of the Special Rapporteur on Violence against Women, its Causes and Consequences', Commission on Human Rights, fifty-second session, item 9, E/CN.4/1996/53, 6 February.

Coomaraswamy, R. (1996b) 'Report of the Special Rapporteur on Violence against Women its Causes and Consequences, Addendum, Report on the Mission to Poland on the Issue of Trafficking and Forced Prostitution of Women (24 May to 1 June 1996)', Commission on Human Rights, E/CN.4/1997/47/Add.1, 10 December.

Coomaraswamy, R. (1997a) 'Report of the Special Rapporteur on Violence against Women, its Causes and Consequences on Violence Against Women in the Community', Commission on Human Rights, fifty-third session, item 9(a) of the provisional agenda, E/CN.4/1997/47, 12 February.

Coomaraswamy, R. (1997b) 'Report of the Special Rapporteur on Violence against Women, its Causes and Consequences, Addendum Report on the mission of the Special Rapporteur to South Africa on the Issue of Rape in the Community (11-18 October 1996)', Commission on Human Rights, fifty-third session, item 9(a) of the provisional agenda, E/CN.4/1997/47/Add.3, 24 February.

Coomaraswamy, R. (1998) 'Report of the Special Rapporteur on Violence Against Women, its Causes and Consequences', Commission on Human Rights, fifty-fourth session, E/CN.4/1998/54, 26 January.

Coomaraswamy, R. (1999a) 'Report of the Special Rapporteur on Violence against Women, its Causes and Consequences, Addendum: Communications to and from Governments', Commission on Human Rights, fifty-fifth session, item 12(a) of the provisional agenda, E/CN.4/1999/68/Add.1, 11 January.

Coomaraswamy, R. (1999b) 'Report of the Special Rapporteur on Violence against Women, its Causes and Consequences, Policies and Practices that Impact Women's Reproductive Rights and Contribute to, Cause or Constitute Violence against Women', Commission on Human Rights, fifty-fifth session, item 12(a) of the provisional agenda, E/CN.4/1999/68/Add.4, 21 January.

Coomaraswamy, R. (1999c) 'Report of the Special Rapporteur on Violence against Women, its Causes and Consequences, Addendum Report of the Mission to the United States of America on the Issue of Violence in State and Federal Prisons', Commission on Human Rights, fifty-fifth session, item 12(a) of the provisional agenda, E/CN.4/1999/68/Add.2, 4 January.

Coomaraswamy, R. (1999d) 'Report of the Special Rapporteur on Violence against Women, its Causes and Consequences', Commision on Human Rights, fifty-fifth session, item 12(a) of the provisional agenda, E/CN.4/1999/68, 10 March.

Coomaraswamy, R. (2000) 'Report of the Special Rapporteur on Violence against Women, its Causes and Consequences on Trafficking in Women, Women's Migration and Violence against Women', Commission on Human Rights, fifty-sixth session, item 12 of the provisional agenda, E/CN.4/2000/68, 29 February.

Copelon, R. (1995) 'Gendered war crimes: reconceptualising rape in time of war, in perspective', in J. Peters and A. Wolper (eds), *Women's Rights Human Rights: International Feminist Perspectives*, New York: Routledge.

Corcoran-Nantes, Y. (1997) 'Chattels and concubines: women and slavery in Brazil', in R. Lentin (ed.) *Gender and Catastrophe*, London: Zed Books.

Cosgrove, K. (1996) 'No man has the right', in C. Corrin (ed.), *Women in a Violent World: Feminist Analysis and Resistance Across 'Europe'*, Edinburgh: Edinburgh University Press.

Counts, D. (1987) 'Female suicide and wife abuse: a cross cultural perspective', *Suicide: Life Threatening Behaviour* 17, p. 194.

Counts, D., Brown, J., and J. Campbell (eds) (1992) *Sanctions and Sanctuary: Cultural Perspectives on Beating of Wives*, Boulder CO: Westview Press.

Council of Europe (1997) 'Final Report of the Group of Specialists for Combating Violence against Women, including a Plan of Action for Combating Violence against Women', EG-S-VL, Strasbourg, 25 June.

Crewe, E. and E. Harrison (1998) *Whose Development? An Ethnography of Aid*, London: Zed Books.

Cullen, C. (1994) 'Experiences of female Republican prisoners', in C. Fischer (ed.), *Policing a Divided Society*, Belfast: Research and Documentation Centre.

Dairiam, S. (1992) 'Violence against Women: A Development Issue', paper presented at gender training workshop held at the National Planning Academy, December, mimeo..

Dasgupta, M. (1987), 'Selective discrimination against female children in rural Punjab, India', *Population and Development Review* 13(1).

Davies, M. (ed.) (1994) *Women and Violence: Realities and Responses Worldwide*, London: Zed Books.

DAWN (1987) *Development Crises and Alternative Visions*, London: Earthscan.

Day, S. (1994) 'What counts as rape? Physical assault and broken contracts: contrasting views of rape among London sex workers', in P. Harvey and P. Gow (eds), *Sex and Violence: Issues in Representation and Experience*, London: Routledge.

de Oliveira, T. (1998) 'What is the Colectivo Mujer Vida?', paper presented at Oxfam international workshop on violence against women, Sarajevo, November.

Dean, J. (1996) *Solidarity of Strangers, Feminism after Identity Politics*, Berkeley: University of California Press.

Deng, F. (1997) 'Internally Displaced Persons – Report of the Secretary General', United Nations document, E/CN.4/1997/43, 4 February.

Desai, M. (1996) 'Human rights in an unglobal civil society', *Moving Pictures Bulletin*, issue 25.

Desjarlais, R., Eisenberg, L., Good, B., and A. Kleinman (1995) *World Mental Health: Problems and Priorities in Low-Income Countries*, New York: Oxford University Press.

Dobash, E. and R. Dobash (1992) *Women, Violence and Social Change*, London: Routledge.

Dobash, E., Dobash, R., Wilson, M., and M. Daly (1992) 'The myth of sexual symmetry in marital violence', *Social Problems* 39(1), pp. 71-91.

Dorkenoo, E. (1994) *Cutting the Rose: Female Genital Mutilation the Practice and its Prevention*, London: Minority Rights Publications.

Dublin Task Force on Violence against Women (1997) *Report of the Task Force on Violence against Women*, Dublin: Office of the Tainiste, Brunwick Press.

Dunkle, K. and A. Potter (1997) 'Rape: the basic facts', in K. Dunkle and A. Potter, *POWA Information Package – Gender and Violence Against Women*, Johannesburg: POWA.

Dwyer, D. and J. Bruce (1988) *A Home Divided: Women and Income in the Third World*, Stanford CA: Stanford University Press.

Eade, D. and S. Williams (1995) *The Oxfam Handbook of Development and Relief*, Oxford: Oxfam Publications.

Eade, D. and S. Williams (1997) 'Building bridges in South Africa: conflict, reconstruction and reconciliation in times of change', *Development in Practice* 7(4).

ECN (1998) 'More rapes since ANC came into power', *ANC News Briefing*, 25 July.

El-Bushra, J. and C. Mukarubuga (1995) 'Women, war and transition', *Gender and Development* 3:3.

El-Bushra, J. and E. Piza-Lopez (1994) 'Gender, war and food', in J. Macrae and A. Zwi (eds), *War and Hunger: Rethinking International Responses to Complex Emergencies*, London: Zed Books in association with Save the Children (UK).

Ellsberg, M., *et al.* (1996) *Confites en el infierno: prevalencia y características de la violencia conyugal hacia las mujeres en Nicaragua*, Managua: Asociación de Mujeres Profesionales por la Democracia en el Desarrollo.

Ellsberg, M., Liljestrand, J., and A. Winkvist (1997) 'The Nicaraguan Network of Women against Violence: using research and action for change', *Reproductive Health Matters* 10, November, pp. 82-92.

El Saadawi, N. (1993) 'Women's resistance in the Arab world and in Egypt', in H. Afshar (ed.), *Women in the Middle-East: Perceptions, Realities and Struggles for Liberation*, Basingstoke: Macmillan.

Elson, D. and R. Pearson (1981) 'The subordination of women and the internationalization of factory production', in K. Young, *et al.* (eds), *Of Marriage and the Market: Women's Subordination in International Perspective*, London: CSE Books.

Enloe, C. (1988) *Does Khaki Become You? The Militarisation of Women's Lives*, London: Pandora/HarperCollins.

Enloe, C. (1993) *The Morning After: Sexual Politics at the End of the Cold War*, Berkeley: University of California Press.

Fedler, J. (1995) 'Lawyering domestic violence through the Prevention of Family Violence Act 1993 – an evaluation after a year in operation', *South African Law Journal* 231.

Fischbach, R. and E. Donnelly (1996) 'Domestic violence against women: a contemporary issue in international health', in J. Subedi and E. Gallagher (eds), *Society, Health and Disease: Transcultural Perspectives*, Upper Saddle River NJ: Prentice Hall.

Fisher, J. (1994) *Out of the Shadows: Women, Resistance, and Politics in South America*, London: Latin America Bureau.

Forced Migration Monitor (1997) 'Trafficking in Women from the Former Soviet Union', no. 19, September.

Ford-Smith, H. (1993) 'No! To sexual violence in Jamaica', in M. Davies (ed.), *Women and Violence: Realities and Responses Worldwide*, London: Zed Books.

Francis, R. (1995) 'An overview of community based intervention programmes for men who are violent or abusive in the home', in R. Dobash, E. Dobash, and L. Noaks (eds), *Gender and Crime*, Cardiff: University of Wales Press.

Freeden, M. (1991) *Rights – Concepts in the Social Sciences*, Milton Keynes: Open University Press.

Freiberg, P. (1991) 'Condom use: burden shouldn't be women's', *Christian Science Monitor*.

Freire, P. (1973) *Pedagogy of the Oppressed*, Harmondsworth: Penguin Education.

Friedl, E. (1975) *Women and Men: An Anthropologist's View*, New York: Holt, Rinehart & Winston.

Gallin, R. (1992) 'Wife abuse in the context of development and change: a Chinese (Taiwanese) case', in D. Counts, J. Brown, and J. Campbell (eds), *Sanctions and Sanctuary: Cultural Perspectives on the Beating of Wives*, Boulder CO: Westview Press.

Gangoli, G. (1998) 'The right to protection from sexual assault: the Indian anti-rape campaign', in D. Eade (ed.), *Development and Rights*, Oxford: Oxfam Publications.

García-Moreno, C. (1999) 'Violence Against Women, Gender and Health Equity', paper prepared under the Global Health Equity Initiative project on Gender and Health Equity, Harvard Center for Population and Development Studies, Family Violence Prevention Fund, September.

Gardam, J. (1993) 'The law of armed conflict: a feminist perspective', in K. Mahoney and P. Mahoney (eds), *Human Rights in the Twentieth Century*, Dordrecht: Kluwer Academic Publishers, pp. 419-36.

Gardner, J. (1996) 'Case Study: UNHCR's Women Victims of Violence Project, Kenya', paper prepared for CODEP (Conflict, Development and Peace Network) Gender and Conflict subgroup workshop, Oxford, September 1996.

Gelles, J. (1972) *The Violent Home*, Newbury Park: Sage Publications.

George, S. (1997) 'Female infanticide in Tamil Nadu, India: from recognition back to denial', *Reproductive Health Matters* 10, November.

Gerwertz, K. (1995) 'Bride burning conference set: seeks to address true dimensions of a growing problem', *Harvard University Gazette*, 28 September, p.5.

Getiashvili, K. (1998) 'The Work of the Women's Information and Consultative Centre, Tblisi, Georgia', paper presented at Oxfam international workshop on violence against women, Sarajevo, November.

Giller, J. and S. Kabaganda (1990) 'Women and rape in a war-torn country', *Action for Development Newsletter* 2(3), September.

Gilmore, G. (1990) *Manhood in the Making: Cultural concepts of Masculinity*, New Haven: Yale University Press.

Goetz, A. (1992) 'Gender and administration', *IDS Bulletin* 23(4).

Goetz, A. (1994) 'From feminist knowledge to data for development: the bureaucratic management of information on women and development', *IDS Bulletin* 25(2), pp. 27-36.

Goetz, A. (1995) 'Institutionalizing women's interests and gender-sensitive accountability in development', *IDS Bulletin* 26(3).

Goetz, A. (1997) *Getting Institutions Right for Women in Development*, Brighton, Sussex: IDS Publications.

Goetz, A. and R. Sen Gupta (1996) 'Who takes the credit? Gender power and control over loan use in rural credit programs in Bangladesh', *World Development* 24(1), pp. 45-63.

Goldblatt, B. and S. Meintjes (1998) 'South African women demand the truth', in M. Turshen and C. Twagiramariya (eds), *What Women Do in Wartime: Gender and Conflict in Africa*, London: Zed Books.

González de la Rocha, M. (1991) 'Family well-being, food consumption, and survival strategies during Mexico's economic crisis', in M. González de la Rocha and A. Escobar Latapí (eds), *Social Responses to Mexico's Economic Crisis of the 1980s*, San Diego: Centre for US-Mexican Studies, University of California.

González de la Rocha, M. (1994) *The Resources of Poverty: Women and Survival in a Mexican City*, Oxford: Blackwell.

Gonzalez Sanchez, P. (1998) 'Violence and Gender in Colombia: Community Based Options for its Eradication', paper presented at Oxfam international workshop on violence against women, Sarajevo, November.

Guyer, J. and P. Peters (1987) 'Conceptualising the household: issues of theory and policy in Africa', *Development and Change* 18(2).

Hanmer, J. and M. Maynard (eds) (1987) *Women, Violence, and Social Control*, Basingstoke: Macmillan.

Harrel, A. (1991) *Evaluation of Court Ordered Treatment for Domestic Violence Offenders*, Washington DC: The Urban Institute.

Hartmann, B. (1987) *Reproductive Rights and Wrongs. The Global Politics of Population Control and Contraceptive Choice*, New York: Harper & Row.

Hartstock, N. (1985) *Money, Sex and Power: Towards a Feminist Historical Materialism*, Boston: Northeastern University Press.

Hasan, Z. (1994) 'Introduction', in Z. Hasan (ed.), *Forging Identities: Gender, Communities and the State*, Delhi: Kali for Women.

Hashemi, S., Schuler, S., and A. Riley (1996) 'Rural credit programs and women's empowerment in Bangladesh', *World Development* 24(4), pp. 635-53.

Hashim, I. (1999) 'Reconciling Islam and feminism', *Gender and Development* 7(1), pp. 7-14.

Hastie, R. (1996) 'Bosfam Review', internal Oxfam document, August.

Hearn, J. (1996) 'A critique of the concept of masculinity/masculinities', in M. Mac An Ghaill (ed.), *Understanding Masculinities: Social Relations and Cultural Arenas*, Milton Keynes: Open University Press.

Hearn, J. (1998) *The Violences of Men: How Men Talk About and How Agencies Respond to Men's Violence to Women*, London: Sage Publications.

Hecht, D. (1999) 'Ban on female circumcision backfires', Dakar: *InterPress Third World News Agency*, 8 February.

Heise, L. (1993) 'Violence against women: the missing agenda', in M. Koblinsky, J. Gay, and J. Timyan (eds), *Women's Health: A Global Perspective*, Boulder CO: Westview Press.

Heise, L. (1995a) 'Freedom close to home: the impact of violence against women on reproductive rights in perspective', in J. Peters and A. Wolper (eds), *Women's Rights Human Rights: International Feminist Perspectives*, New York: Routledge.

Heise, L. (1995b) 'Overcoming Violence: a background paper on violence against women as an obstacle to development', in G. Reardon (ed.), Power and Process: A Report from the Women Linking for Change Conference, Thailand, Oxford: Oxfam Publications.

Heise, L., *et al.* (1989) 'International dimensions of violence against women', *Response* 12(1), 3-11.

Heise, L., Ellsberg, M., and M. Gottemoeller (1999) 'Ending violence against women', *Population Reports*, Series L, no. 11, Baltimore: Johns Hopkins University School of Public Health, Population Information Program, December.

Heise, L., Pitanguy, J., and A. Germaine (1994) 'Violence Against Women: The Hidden Health Burden', World Bank Discussion Paper 225, Washington DC: World Bank.

Herman, J. (1992) *Trauma and Recovery: The Aftermath of Violence – From Domestic Abuse to Physical Terror*, New York: Basic Books.

Hetherington, B. (1998) 'Memorandum on the UK government's policy on the recruitment of young persons to the armed forces and on the engagement of young persons in conflict', London: Peace Pledge Union, April.

Heyzer, N. (1998) 'Working towards a world free from violence against women: UNIFEM's contribution', *Gender and Development* 6(3).

Hicks, G. (1995) *The Comfort Women: Japan's Brutal Regime of Enforced Prostitution in the Second World War*, New York: W.W. Norton.

Hirschmann, D. (1998) 'Civil society in South Africa: learning from gender themes' *World Development* 26(2), pp. 227-38.

Holland, J. and C. Moser (1997) *Urban Poverty and Violence in Jamaica*, Washington DC: World Bank.

Huber, G., Donaldson, M., Robertson, M., and M. Hlongweni (1997) 'Demand for Instant Gratification an Important Factor in many Rape Cases', Johannesburg, South Africa: Centre for the Study of Violence and Reconciliation (CSVR).

Hughes, D. (1997) 'Protecting the Dignity of Women', paper presented at a conference on Policing the Internet: Combating Pornography and Violence on the Internet – A European Approach, 13-14 February.

Human Rights Watch (1996) *Shattered Lives: Sexual Violence during the Rwandan Genocide and its Aftermath*, New York: Human Rights Watch.

Human Rights Watch (1999) *Crime or Custom: Violence against Women in Pakistan*, New York: Human Rights Watch.

Hussain, A. (1999) 'Report of the Special Rapporteur on the Protection and Promotion of the Right to Freedom of Opinion and Expression', Commission of Human Rights, fifty-fifth session, item 11(c) of the provisional agenda, E/CN.4/1999/64, 29 January.

Hyman, B. (1993) 'Economic Consequences of Child Sexual Abuse in Women', unpublished Ph.D. dissertation, Heller School of Policy, Brandeis University, Massachusetts.

International Planned Parenthood Federation (IPPF) (1996) 'A New Look at Male Involvement', Briefing Paper, London: IPPF, 4 November.

Interpress (1999) 'UN sees link between AIDS and gender violence', 3 March, IPS-Interpress News Service, www.ips.org

Jackson, C. (1996) 'Rescuing gender from the poverty trap', *World Development* 24(3), pp. 489-504.

Jacobson, J. (1991) *Women's Reproductive Health: The Silent Emergency*, Washington DC: Worldwatch Institute.

Jahan, R. (1988) 'Hidden wounds, visible scars: violence against women in Bangladesh', in B. Agarwal (ed.), *Structures of Patriarchy*, London: Zed Books.

Jahan, R. (1995) *The Elusive Agenda: Mainstreaming Women in Development*, London: Zed Books.

Jahangir, A. (1999) 'Report of the Special Rapporteur on Extrajudicial, Summary or Arbitrary Executions', Commission on Human Rights, fifty-fifth session, E/CN.4/1999/39, 6 January.

Jani, P. (1995) 'The necessity of a reconciliation process in north Albania', *Anthropology of Eastern Europe Review* 13(1).

Jenkins, J. (1991) 'The state construction of affect – political ethos and mental health among Salvadoran refugees', *Culture, Medicine and Psychiatry* 15(2), 139-67.

Jehl, D. (1999) 'Arab honor's price: a woman's blood', *New York Times*, 20 June.

Jeong, Y. (1997) *Cases of Crimes Committed by US Military Men: Yoon Keum E Murder Case*, Seoul, Korea: National Campaign for Eradication of Crime by US troops in Korea.

Jha, M. (1999) *India: Chappal, Sticks and Bags*, Family Violence Prevention Fund, available from http://www.igc.org/igc/womensnet

Jilani, H. (1998) *Human Rights and Democratic Development in Pakistan*, Lahore: Human Rights Commission of Pakistan.

Joekes, S. (1987) *Women in the World Economy*, Oxford: Oxford University Press.

Johnson, H. (1998) 'Rethinking survey research on violence against women', in E. Dobash and R. Dobash (eds), *Rethinking Violence Against Women*, London: Sage Publications.

Kabeer, N. (1994) *Reversed Realities: Gender Hierarchies in Development Thought*, London: Verso Books.

Kabeer, N. (1998) '"Money Can't Buy Me Love"? Re-evaluating Gender, Credit and Empowerment in Rural Bangladesh', IDS Discussion Paper 363, Brighton: Institute of Development Studies, University of Sussex.

Kalichan, S., Williams, E., Cherry, C., Belcher, L., and D. Nachimson (1998) 'Sexual coercion, domestic violence, and negotiating condom use among low-income African American women', *Journal of Women's Health* 7(3), pp. 371-8.

Kandiyoti, D. (1988) 'Bargaining with patriarchy', *Gender and Society* 2(3).

Kanji, N. (1995) 'Gender, poverty and economic adjustment in Harare, Zimbabwe', *Environment and Urbanization* 7(1), pp. 37-55.

Kapur, A. (1998) '"I am witness to…". A profile of Sakshi Violence Intervention Centre in New Delhi, India', *Gender and Development* 6(3).

Kar, U. (1999) 'Much ado about knitting: the experience of Bosfam (Bosnia)', in F. Porter, I. Smyth, and C. Sweetman (eds), *Gender Works,* Oxford: Oxfam Publications.

Kardam, N. (1991) *Bringing Women In: Women's Issues in International Development Program,* Boulder CO: Lynne Rienner Publishers.

Karkal, M. (1985) 'How the other half dies in Bombay', *Economic and Political Weekly,* 24 August.

Karlekar, M (1998) Domestic Violence, *Economic and Political Weekly,* July 4.

Katz, S. (1995) 'The rise of religious fundamentalism in Britain: the experience of Women Against Fundamentalism', *Gender and Development* 3(1).

Kelkar, G. (1992) 'Stopping the violence against women – fifteen years of activism (India)', in M. Schuler (ed.), *Freedom From Violence: Women's Strategies from Around the World,* New York: Women, Law and Development/UNIFEM.

Keller, B. (1994) 'In Mozambique and other lands, children fight the wars', *New York Times,* 9 November, p. A14.

Kelly, L. (1988) *Surviving Sexual Violence,* Cambridge: Polity Press.

Kelly, L. (1996) 'Wars Against Women: Gender, Heterosexuality, Militarism and the State', paper presented at the Political Studies Association conference, Engendering Conflict, London School of Economics, February.

Kelly, L. (1997) 'Women's Perspectives', paper presented at a conference on Policing the Internet: Combating Pornography and Violence on the Internet – A European Approach, 13-14 February.

Kelly, L., Bindel, J., Burton, S., Butterworth, D., Cook, K., and L. Regan (Child Abuse and Women's Studies Unit) (1999) 'Domestic Violence Matters: An Evaluation of a Development Project', Home Office Research Study 193, Research Development and Statistics Directorate Report, London: Home Office.

Kelly, L. and J. Radford (1996) '"Nothing really happened": the invalidation of women's experiences of sexual violence', in L. Kelly, M. Hester, and J. Radford (eds.), *Women, Violence and Male Power,* Milton Keynes: Open University Press.

Kelly, L. and J. Radford (1998) 'Sexual violence against women and girls: an approach to an international overview', in E. Dobash and R. Dobash (eds), *Rethinking Violence Against Women,* London: Sage Publications.

Kelly, L., Wingfield, R., Burton, S., and L. Regan (Child Abuse and Women's Studies Unit) (1995) Splintered Lives: Sexual Exploitation of Children in the Context of Children's Rights and Child Protection, London: Barnardos.

Kempadoo, K. (1998) 'Introduction: globalising sex workers' rights', in K. Kempadoo and J. Doezema (eds), *Global Sex Workers: Rights, Resistance, and Redefinition,* London: Routledge.

Kerns, V. (1992) 'Preventing violence against women: a Central American case', in D. Counts, J. Brown, and J. Campbell (eds), (1992), *Sanctions and Sanctuary: Cultural Perspectives on Beating of Wives,* Boulder CO: Westview Press.

Kerr, D. (1997) 'Co-operation from the Police and the Legal System: Internet Watch Foundation', paper presented at a conference on Policing the Internet: Combating Pornography and Violence on the Internet - A European Approach, 13-14 February.

Kerr, J. (ed.) (1993) *Ours By Right: Women's Rights as Human Rights,* London: Zed Books/ North-South Institute.

Khodyreva, N. (1996) 'Sexism and sexual abuse in Russia', in C. Corrin (ed.), *Women in a Violent World: Feminist Analysis and Resistance Across 'Europe',* Edinburgh: Edinburgh University Press.

Kibitskaya, M. (2000) '"Once we were kings": male experiences of loss of status at work in post-communist Russia', in S. Ashwin (ed.), *Gender, State and Society in Soviet and Post-Soviet Russia,* London: Routledge.

Korac, M. (1998) 'Linking Arms: Women and War in post-Yugoslav States', Uppsala: Life and Peace Institute, June.

Kristof, N. (1993) 'Peasants of China discover new ways to weed out girls', *New York Times,* 21 July, p. 1.

Kumkum, A. and S. Vaid (1996) 'Institutions, beliefs, ideologies: widow immolation in contemporary Rajasthan', in K. Jayawardena and M. de Alwis (eds), *Embodied Violence: Communalising Women's Sexuality in South Asia,* London: Zed Books.

Kusnir, D. (1993) 'The use of family therapy with victims of torture', in V. Iacopino and E. Holst, *Preventing Torture and Treating Survivors: A Challenge to Health Professionals,* workbook from the 121st meeting of the American Public Health Association, San Francisco.

Kutzin, J. (no date given) 'Obstacles to Women's Access: Issues and Options for More Effective Intervention to Improve Women's Health', background paper for the World Bank Best Practices Paper on Women's Health and Nutrition, Population, Health, and Nutrition Department, Washington DC: World Bank.

KwaZulu Natal Program for the Survivors of Violence (1997a) 'Bridging the Theory Gap', unpublished paper, KwaZulu Natal, South Africa.

KwaZulu Natal Program for the Survivors of Violence (1997b), unpublished background paper, part of a funding submission to Oxfam, KwaZulu Natal, South Africa.

Lackey, B. and K. Williams (1995) 'Social bonding and the cessation of partner violence across generations', *Journal of Marriage and the Family* 57, 295-305.

Large, J. (1997) 'Disintegration conflicts and the restructuring of masculinity', *Gender and Development* 5(2).

Lateef, S. (1992) 'Wife abuse among Indo Fijians', in D. Counts, J. Brown, and J. Campbell (eds), *Sanctions and Sanctuary: Cultural Perspectives on Beating of Wives*, Boulder CO: Westview Press.

Lawyers Committee for Human Rights (1995) *African Exodus: Refugee Crisis, Human Rights and the 1969 OAU Convention*, New York: The Lawyers Committee for Human Rights.

Lee, R. (1993) *Doing Research on Sensitive Topics*, London: Sage Publications.

Levinson, D. (1989) *Family Violence in Cross-Cultural Perspective*, Newbury Park: Sage Publications.

Lewis, D. (1990) 'Tungaru conjugal jealousy and sexual mutilation', *Pacific Studies* 13(3), pp. 115-26.

Lira, E. (1997) 'Guatemala: uncovering the past, recovering the future', *Development in Practice* 7(4).

Longwe, S. (1995) 'Institutional opposition to gender-sensitive development: learning to answer back', *Gender and Development* 3(1).

Lukes, S. (1974) *Power: A Radical View*, London: Macmillan.

Macey, M. (1999) 'Religion, male violence, and the control of women: Pakistani Muslim men in Bradford, UK', *Gender and Development* 7(1).

Machel, G. (1996) 'Report by the Expert of the United Nations Secretary-General on the Impact of Armed Conflict on Children', United Nations Document, A/51/306, 26 August.

MacKinnon, C. (1993) 'On torture: a feminist perspective on human rights', in K. Mahoney and P. Mahoney (eds), *Human Rights in the Twenty-First Century*, Amsterdam: Kluwer Academic Publishers.

Made, M. (2000) 'Globalisation and gender training for the media: challenges and lessons learned', *Gender and Development* 8(1).

Maguire, S. (1998) 'A Family Affair: A Report of Research into Domestic Violence against Women in Albania, Bosnia and Herzegovina, Croatia, Federal Republic of Yugoslavia', internal Oxfam document, July.

Mahajan, V. (1994) 'In Search of "Asmita"', paper presented at international Oxfam gender and development conference, Women Linking for Change, Thailand, January.

Malange, N., McKay, A., and Z. Nhlengetwa (eds) (1996) *On Common Ground Isiselelo Esifanayo*, KwaZulu Natal, South Africa: KwaZulu Natal Program for the Survivors of Violence.

March, K., Smyth, I., and M. Mukhopadhyay (1999) *A Guide to Gender Frameworks and Analysis*, Oxford: Oxfam Publications.

March, K. and R. Taqqu (1986) *Women's Informal Associations in Developing Countries – Catalysts for Change?* Boulder CO: Westview Press.

Masimanyane CEDAW Working Group (1998) 'South Africa Violence Against Women', NGO shadow report to CEDAW, co-ordinated by Masimanyane Women's Support Centre, East London, South Africa, June. Available on-line at http://womensnet.org.za/pvaw/campaigns/cedawsh.htm

Match International (1990) *Linking Women's Global Struggles to End Violence*, Ottawa: Match International Centre.

Matin, N. (1998) 'Against Domestic Violence: Women's Response and Resistance in Bangladesh', paper presented at the Oxfam international workshop on violence against women, Sarajevo, November.

Mazumdar, V. (1989) 'Peasant Women Organise for Empowerment: The Bankura Experiment', Occasional Paper no. 13, New Delhi: Centre for Women's Development Studies.

McClintock, M. (1985) *The American Connection, Volume II: State Terror and Popular Resistance in Guatemala,* London: Zed Books.

McCollom, H., Kelly, L., and J. Radford (1994) 'Wars against women', *Trouble and Strife* 28, Spring, pp. 12-18.

McDonnell, P. (2001) 'Ruling allows asylum for foreign victims of abuse court: panel blocks deportation of woman who said she would be beaten if she returned home to Mexico', *Los Angeles Times,* 22 March.

McWilliams, M. (1998) 'Violence against women in societies under stress', in E. Dobash and R. Dobash (eds), *Rethinking Violence Against Women,* London: Sage Publications.

McWilliams, M. and J. McKiernan (1993) *Bringing it Out in the Open: Domestic Violence in Northern Ireland,* Belfast: HMSO.

Medica Zenica Women's Therapy Centre (1995) 'Research: Dominant Gynaecological and Psychological Consequences of Rape', unpublished report, Zenica, Bosnia and Hercegovina: Medica Zenica.

Medica Zenica Women's Therapy Centre (1996) 'Surviving the violence: war and violence against women are inseparable', *Bulletin 1.*

Medica Zenica Women's Therapy Centre (1997) *Rape – A Specific Trauma, a Specific Type of Violence, Zenica,* Bosnia and Hercegovina: Special Edition, Infoteka Project, Medica Zenica.

Medica Zenica Women's Therapy Centre (1999) 'Women's Human Rights to Life Without Violence', unpublished report, Zenica, Bosnia and Hercegovina: Medica Zenica.

Mehra, M. (1998) 'Exploring the boundaries of law, gender and social reform', *Feminist Legal Studies* vi(1).

Meintjies, S. (1997) Truth and Reconciliation Commission Human Rights Violations Women's Hearing, 29 July, CALS submission, Day 2, available on-line at http://www.truth.org.za

Meursing, K., Vos, T., and O. Coutinho (1994) 'Child sexual abuse in Matabeleland, Zimbabwe', *Social Science and Medicine* 41, pp. 1693-704.

Miller, C. and S. Razavi (1998) *Missionaries and Mandarins: Feminist Engagement with Development Institutions,* London: ITDG Publications.

Mitchell, W. (1992) 'Why men don't beat their wives: constraints towards domestic tranquility in a New Guinea society', in D. Counts, J. Brown, and J. Campbell (eds), *Sanctions and Sanctuary: Cultural Perspectives on Beating of Wives,* Boulder CO: Westview Press.

Mladjenovic, L. (1992) 'Dear women, pacifists from Belgrade', in S. Zajovic (ed.), *Women for Peace Anthology,* Belgrade: Women in Black.

Mladjenovic, L. (1996) 'Ethics of Difference: Politics of Feminists from Divided Former Yugoslavia', paper presented at a conference on 'Violence, Abuse and Women's Citizenship', Brighton, UK, 10-15 November.

Mladjenovic, L. and D. Matijaševic (1996) 'SOS Belgrade July 1993-1995: dirty streets', in C. Corrin (ed.), *Women in a Violent World: Feminist Analysis and Resistance Across 'Europe'*, Edinburgh: Edinburgh University Press.

Mohanty, C. (1991a) 'Under western eyes: feminist scholarship and colonial discourses', in C. Mohanty, A. Russo, and L. Torres (eds), *Third World Women and the Politics of Feminsim*, Bloomington IN: Indiana University Press.

Mohanty, C. (1991b) 'Cartographies of struggle: Third World women and the politics of feminism', in C. Mohanty, A. Russo, and L. Torres (eds), *Third World Women and the Politics of Feminism*, Bloomington IN: Indiana University Press.

Molyneux, M. (1985) 'Mobilisation without emancipation? Women's interests, state and revolution in Nicaragua', *Feminist Studies* 11, Summer, pp. 227-54.

Moore, H. (1986) *Space, Text and Gender: An Anthropological Study of the Marakwet of Kenya*, Cambridge: Cambridge University Press.

Moore, H. (1988) *Feminism and Anthropology*, Cambridge: Polity Press

Moore, H. (1994) *A Passion for Difference: Essays in Anthropology and Gender*, Cambridge: Polity Press.

Morrow, J. (1995) 'Rural Indian women protest rape verdict', *India News Network Digest* 2(721), 15 December.

Moser, C. (1989a) 'The impact of recession and structural adjustment policies at the micro-level: low income women and their households in Guayaquil, Ecuador', in UNICEF (ed.), *Invisible Adjustment* Vol. 2, pp. 137-62, New York: UNICEF.

Moser, C. (1989b) 'Gender planning in the Third World: meeting practical and strategic needs', *World Development* 17(11), pp. 1799-825.

Moser, C. (1993) *Gender Planning and Development: Theory, Practice and Training*, London: Routledge.

Moser, C. (1996) *Confronting Crisis: A Comparative Study of Household Responses to Poverty and Vulnerability in Four Poor Urban Communities*, Environmentally Sustainable Development Studies and Monographs Series, no. 8, Washington DC: World Bank.

Mrševic, Z. and D. Hughes (1997) 'Violence against women in Belgrade, Serbia: SOS Hotline 1990-1993', *Violence Against Women* 3(2), April, pp. 101-28.

Muchenga Chicuecue, N. (1997) 'Reconciliation: the role of truth commissions and alternative ways of healing', *Development in Practice* 7(4).

Murray, A. (1998) 'Debt-bondage and trafficking: don't believe the hype', in K. Kempadoo and J. Doezema (eds), *Global Sex Workers: Rights, Resistance and Redefinition*, London: Routledge.

Murray, C. (1981) *Families Divided: The Impact of Migrant Labour in Lesotho*, Cambridge: Cambridge University Press.

Murthy, R. (1996) 'Fighting female infanticide by working with midwives: an Indian case study', *Gender and Development* 4(2).

Murthy, R. (1998) 'Power, institutions and gender relations: can gender training alter the equations?', *Development in Practice* 8(2).

Musasa Project (1997) *Musasa News* 7(1), May.

Mzungu, M. (1998) 'Violence against Girl Domestic Workers', paper presented at Oxfam international workshop on violence against women, Sarajevo, November.

Narasimhan, S. (1992) *Sati Widow Burning in India*, New York: Doubleday.

Nashwan, K. (1998) *A Wife's Right to a House*, Palestinian Model Parliament, April.

National Committee on Violence Against Women (1994) *Position Paper*, Canberra: Australian Government Publishing Services.

Nduna, S. and L. Goodyear (1997), *Pain Too Deep for Tears: Assessing the Prevalence of Sexual and Gender Violence Among Burundian Refugees in Tanzania*, New York: International Rescue Committee.

Nelson, E., and C. Zimmerman (1996) *Household Survey on Domestic Violence in Cambodia*, Phnom Penh, Cambodia: Project Against Domestic Violence with the Ministry of Women's Affairs.

New York City/Balkan Rape Crisis Response Team (1993) *Training Manual*, New York: St. Lukes Roosevelt Hospital Centre.

NGO Coalition Against Exploitation of Women (1995) 'Petition Against Sexual Exploitation', paper presented at UN Fourth World Conference on Women in Beijing, February.

Nilofer, S. (1998) 'Reforming Rape Law in India', paper presented at Oxfam international workshop on violence against women, Sarajevo, November.

Njovana, E. (1994) 'Gender-based violence and sexual assault in African Women', *Oxfam Reports*, May, pp. 17-20.

Njovana, E. and C. Watts (1996) 'Gender violence in Zimbabwe: a need for collaborative action', *Reproductive Health Matters* 7, May.

Nordstrom, C. (1992) 'The backyard front', in C. Nordstrom and J. Martin (eds), *The Paths to Domination, Resistance and Terror*, Berkeley: University of California Press.

North, D. (1990) *Institutions, Institutional Change and Economic Performance*, Cambridge: Cambridge University Press,

Oller, L. (1994) 'Domestic violence: breaking the cycle in Argentina', in M. Davies (ed.), *Women and Violence: Realities and Responses Worldwide*, London: Zed Books.

Ong, A. (1987) *Spirits of Resistance and Capitalist Discipline*, Albany NY: State University of New York Press.

Organisation of American States (1994) *The Inter-American Convention on the Prevention, Punishment, and Eradication of Violence against Women* (Convention of Belém do Para), AG/RES 1257 (XXIV-O/94). Available on-line at http://www.oas.org

Ouattara, M., Sen, P., and M. Thomson (1998) 'Forced marriage, forced sex: the perils of childhood for girls', *Gender and Development* 6(3).

Oxfam GB (1998a) 'Conflict and Democratic Transition in Central America and Mexico', workshop report, Guatemala, February 24–6.

Oxfam GB (1998b) 'Nothing Can Stop Me Now', report of the Oxfam international workshop on violence against women, Sarajevo, November.

Padarath, A. (1998) 'Women and violence in KwaZulu Natal', in M. Turshen and C. Twagiramariya (eds), *What Women Do in Wartime: Gender and Conflict in Africa*, London: Zed Books.

Pandian, H. (1999) E-mail contribution to UNIFEM End Violence Working Group. Available on-line at http://www.undp.org/unifem

Panos (1998) 'The intimate enemy: gender violence and reproductive health', *Panos Briefing* 27, London, March.

Panos (1999) 'Globalisation and employment: new opportunities, real threats', *Panos Briefing* 33, May.

Payne, L. (1998) *Rebuilding Communities in a Refugee Settlement: A Casebook from Uganda*, Oxford: Oxfam Publications.

Pearson, R. and S. Theobald (1998) 'From exporting processing zones to erogenous zones: international discourses on women's work in Thailand', *Millennium: Journal of International Studies* 27(4), pp. 983-93.

Peled, I., Jaffe, P., and J. Edleson (eds.) (1995) *Ending the Cycle of Violence: Community Responses to Children of Battered Women*, Thousand Oaks CA: Sage Publications.

Pellecer, C. (1998) 'The Work of Tierra Viva', paper presented at Oxfam international workshop on violence against women, Sarajevo, November.

People Opposing Women Abuse (POWA) (1998) *Rape Trauma Syndrome*, June, Johannesburg: POWA.

Petchesky, R. (1998) 'Introduction', in R. Petchesky and K. Judd (eds.), *Negotiating Reproductive Rights: Women's Perspectives across Cultures and Countries*, London and New York: International Reproductive Rights Research Action Group and Zed Books.

Petchesky, R. (1990) *Abortion and Women's Choice: The State, Sexuality and Reproductive Freedom*, Boston MA: Northeastern University Press.

Peterson, V. and L. Parisi (1998) 'Are women human? It's not an academic question', in T. Evans (ed.), *Human Rights Fifty Years On: A Reappraisal*, Manchester: Manchester University Press.

Pisklakova, M. (2000) 'No excuse for violence', interview with Marina Pisklakova, *The Moscow Times*, 5 February, p. 10.

Plata, M. (1996) 'Interview: Maria Isabel Plata, Executive Director of Profamilia, talks to Caroline Sweetman about the work of the organisation in Colombia', *Gender and Development* 4(2).

Population Council (1994) *Gender-based Violence and Women's Reproductive Health*, New York: Population Council.

Porter, F. with I. Smyth (1998) 'An Overview and Gender Analysis of Male and Female Social Exclusion', internal Oxfam document.

Potts, D. (1996) *Why do Men Commit Most Crime? Focusing on Masculinity in a Prison Group*, Wakefield: West Yorkshire Probation Service.

Poudel, P. (1994) 'Trafficking in women in Nepal', *International Movement Against Discrimination and Racism Review for Research and Action*, May.

Poudel, P. and J. Carryer (2000) 'Girl-trafficking, HIV/AIDS, and the position of women in Nepal', *Gender and Development* 8(2).

Price, J. (no date given) 'Notes on workshops conducted with women in North India: exploring health, sexuality and control over our bodies', *GADU Newspack* 14.

Project Against Domestic Violence (1996) *Annual Report*, Phnom Penh, Cambodia: Project Against Domestic Violence.

Project Against Domestic Violence (1998) *Monologue,* Phnom Penh, Cambodia: Project Against Domestic Violence.

Pyne, H. (1995) 'AIDS and gender violence: the enslavement of Burmese women in the Thai sex industry', in J. Peters and A. Wolper (eds), *Women's Rights Human Rights: International Feminist Perspectives,* New York: Routledge.

Radwan, E. and M. Emad (1997) *The Early Marriage in the Palestinian Community: Causes and Effects,* Gaza: Women's Affairs Centre, Gaza Research Program, see http://www.wacgaza.org

Rahayu, R. and J. McAvoy (1998) 'Investigating Mass Rape in the Indonesia Riots of May', paper presented at Oxfam international workshop on violence against women, Sarajevo, November.

Rao, V. and F. Bloch (1993) *Wife-beating, its Causes and Implications for Nutritional Allocations to Children: An Economic and Anthropological Case Study of a Rural South Indian Community,* Washington DC: World Bank, Poverty and Human Resources Division.

Razack, S. (1994) 'What is to be gained by looking white people in the eye? Culture, race and gender in cases of sexual violence', *Signs: Journal of Women in Culture and Society* 19(4), pp. 5–27.

Razavi, S. and C. Miller (1995) 'From WID to GAD: Conceptual Shifts in the Women and Development Discourse', Occasional paper no. 1, UN Fourth World Conference on Women, February, Geneva: UNRISD.

Regmi, S, and B. Fawcett (1999) 'Integrating gender needs into drinking-water projects in Nepal', *Gender and Development* 7(3).

Richards, P. (1995) 'Rebellion in Liberia and Sierra Leone: a crisis of youth?' in O.W. Furley (ed.), *Conflict in Africa,* New York: IB Tauris.

Richters, A. (1994) *Women, Culture and Violence: a Development, Health and Human Rights Issue,* Women and Autonomy Series, Leiden, Netherlands: Netherlands Women and Autonomy Centre (VENA), Leiden University.

Ringelheim, J. (1996) 'Gender and genocide: a split memory', in R. Lentin (ed.), *Gender and Catastrophe,* London: Zed Books.

Rodley, N. (1998) 'The evolution of the international prohibition of torture', in Amnesty International (ed.), *The Universal Declaration of Human Rights 1948-1988, The United Nations and Amnesty International,* London: Amnesty International.

Rose, P., Yoseph, G., Berihun, A., and T. Nuresu, (1997) 'Gender and Primary Schooling in Ethiopia', report of a joint team from the Institute of Development Studies, Sussex, and the Ministry of Education, Addis Ababa, Research Report 31, Sussex: IDS.

Roth, K. (1998) 'The court the US doesn't want', *New York Review of Books,* 19 November, p.45.

Rowlands, J. (1997) *Questioning Women's Empowerment: Working with Women in Honduras,* Oxford: Oxfam Publications.

Rowlands, J. (1998) 'A word of the times, but what does it mean? Empowerment in the discourse and practice of development', in H. Afshar (ed.), *Women and Empowerment: Illustrations from the Third World,* London: Macmillan.

Roy, P. (1998) 'Sanctioned violence: development and persecution of women as witches in South Bihar', *Development in Practice* 8(2).

Royal Netherlands Embassy (1995) 'External Evaluation of People Opposing Women Abuse (POWA)', unpublished report, 6 October.

Russell, D. (1982) 'The prevalence and incidence of forcible rape and attempted rape of females', *Victimology: An International Journal* 7, pp. 81-93.

Russell, D. (1990) *Rape in Marriage*, Bloomington IN: Indiana University Press.

Said, E. (1979) *Orientalism*, New York: Vintage Books.

Sancho, N. (1997) 'The 'comfort women' system during World War II: Asian women as targets of mass rape and sexual slavery by Japan', in R. Lentin (ed.), *Gender and Catastrophe*, London: Zed Books.

Schmink, M. (1985) 'Women and urban industrial development in Brazil', in J. Nash and H. Safa (eds), *Women and Change in Latin America*, South Hadley: Bergint Garvey Publishers.

Schopper, D., van Praag, E., and S. Kalibala (1996) 'Psychosocial care for AIDS patients in developing countries', in S. Carr and J. Schumaker (eds), *Psychology and the Developing World*, Westport CT: Praeger.

Schuler, M. (ed.) (1992) *Freedom from Violence: Women's Strategies from Around the World*, New York: Women, Law, and Development/UNIFEM.

Schuler, S., Hashemi, S., Riley, A., and S. Akhter (1996) 'Credit programs, patriarchy and men's violence against women in rural Bangladesh', *Social Science and Medicine* 43(12), pp. 1729-42.

Schuler, S., Hashemi, S., and S. Badal (1998) 'Men's violence against women in rural Bangladesh: undermined or exacerbated by microcredit programmes?', *Development in Practice* 8(2).

Segel, T. and D. Labe (1990) 'Family violence: wife abuse', in B. McKendrick and W. Hoffman (eds), *People and Violence in South Africa*, Oxford: Oxford University Press.

Sen, A. (1990) 'Gender and co-operative conflicts', in I. Tinker (ed.), *Persistent Inequalities: Women and World Development*, Oxford: Oxford University Press.

Sen, A. (1999) *Development as Freedom*, Oxford: Oxford University Press

Sen, G. and C. Grown (1987) *Development, Crises and Alternative Visions: Third World Women's Perspectives*, New York: Monthly Review Press.

Sen, P. (1997a) 'A Basket of Resources: Women's Resistance to Domestic Violence in Calcutta', doctoral thesis, University of Bristol, UK.

Sen, P. (1997b) 'Domestic Violence Against Women as Torture', paper presented at Amnesty International Expert Meeting on Women and Torture, February.

Sen, P. (1998a) 'Development practice and violence against women', *Gender and Development* 6(3).

Sen, P. (1998b) 'Violence in intimate relationships: a research project in India', in H. Afshar (ed.), *Women and Empowerment: Illustrations from the Third World*, London: Macmillan.

Sena, E. (1998), 'Experiences of How Organised Women's Movements have Confronted Violence Against Women in the State of Pará, Northern Brazil', paper presented at Oxfam international workshop on violence against women, Sarajevo, November.

Shackman, J. and J. Reynolds (1996) 'Training of indigenous workers in mental-health care', in S. Commins (ed.), *Development in States of War*, Oxford: Oxfam Publications.

Shallat, R. (1993) 'Violations on trial', *Women's Health Journal* 3(93), pp. 45-51.

Sharma, U. (1984) 'Dowry in India: its consequences for women', in R. Hirschon (ed.), *Women and Property, Women as Property*, London: Croom Helm.

Shikola, T. (1998) 'We left our shoes behind', in M. Turshen and C. Twagiramariya (eds), *What Women Do in Wartime: Gender and Conflict in Africa*, London: Zed Books.

Showstack-Sassoon, A. (ed.) (1987) *Women and the State*, London: Hutchinson.

Siddiqui, H. (1996) 'Domestic violence in Asian communities', in C. Corrin (ed.), *Women in a Violent World: Feminist Analysis and Resistance Across 'Europe'*, Edinburgh: Edinburgh University Press.

Simon, R. (1991) *Gramsci's Political Thought: An Introduction*, London: Lawrence & Wishart.

Simpson, G. (1992) 'Jack-Asses and Jackrollers: Rediscovering Gender in Understanding Violence', Occasional Paper written for the Centre for the Study of Violence and Reconciliation, Johannesburg, South Africa.

SINAGA Women and Child Labour Resource Centre (1997) 'Domestic Child Workers: Selected Case Studies on the Situation of the Girl-Child Domestic Workers', Oxfam GB working paper series 1, July.

Sisterhood is Global Institute (1998) 'Landmark first women's definition of rape in international law', *Urgent Action Alert*, 30 September. Available on-line at http://www.sigi.org/alert/rape0998.htm

Sistren (1998) *Profile of Sistren Theatre Collective: Where Theatre is Education and Education is Theatre*, Kingston, Jamaica: Sistren.

Sistren (no date given) *Sistren's Way Forward*, Kingston, Jamaica: Sistren.

Smart, C. (1989) *Feminism and the Power of the Law*, London: Routledge.

Smith, S. (1998) 'Wise up, guys', *Links: A Newsletter on Gender*, Oxfam GB, July.

Smyth, I. (1999) 'A rose by any other name: feminism in development NGOs', in F. Porter, I. Smyth, and C. Sweetman (eds), *Gender Works: Oxfam Experience in Policy and Practice*, Oxford: Oxfam Publications.

Smyth, I. and F. Porter (1999), 'Gender training for policy implementers: only a partial solution', in F. Porter, I. Smyth, and C. Sweetman (eds), *Gender Works: Oxfam Experience in Policy and Practice*, Oxford: Oxfam Publications.

Soh, C.S. (2000), *The Comfort Women Project*, available on-line at http://online.sfsu.edu/~soh/comfortwomen.html

Spadacini, A. and P. Nichols (1998) 'Campaigning against female genital mutilation in Ethiopia using popular education', *Gender and Development* 6(2).

Standing, H. (1990) *Dependence and Autonomy: Women's Employment and the Family in Calcutta*, London: Routledge.

Stanko, B. (1998) *Counting the Costs: Estimating the Impact of Domestic Violence in the London Borough of Hackney*, London: Crime Concern.

State Commission for Gathering Facts on War Crimes in the Republic of Bosnia and Herzegovina (1992) 'Sexual Crimes of the Aggressor in Bosnia and Herzegovina', *Bulletin* 1, Sarajevo, October.

Sternberg, P. (2000) 'Challenging *machismo:* promoting sexual and reproductive health with Nicaraguan men', *Gender and Development* 8(1).

Stewart, S. (1992) 'Working the system: sensitising the police to the plight of women in Zimbabwe', in M. Schuler (ed.), *Freedom From Violence: Women's Strategies from Around the World,* New York: Women, Law, and Development/UNIFEM.

Stewart, S. (1995a) 'Working with a radical agenda: the Musasa Project', *Gender and Development* 3(1).

Stewart, S. (1995b) 'Bringing the law home: action on gender and rights in Asia', internal document, Oxfam UK/I, Sri Lanka.

Stiglmayer, A. (1994) *Mass Rape: The War Against Women in Bosnia-Herzegovina,* Lincoln and London: University of Nebraska Press.

Straus, M. and R. Gelles (eds) (1990) *Physical Violence in American Families,* New Brunswick NJ: Transaction Publishers.

Straus, M., Gelles, R., and S. Steinmetz (1980) *Behind Closed Doors,* Newbury Park CA: Sage Publications.

Strinivasan, V., *et al.* (1995) *Female Infanticide in Bihar,* Bihar: Adithi.

Summerfield, D. (1992) 'Charting Human Response to Extreme Violence and the Limitations of Western Psychiatric Models: an Overview', paper presented at World Conference: Trauma and Tragedy, Amsterdam, June.

Summerfield, D. (1995) 'Assisting Survivors of war and atrocity: notes of psycho-social issues for NGO workers', *Development in Practice* 5(4).

Sweetman, C. (1995a) *The Miners Return: Changing Gender Relations in Lesotho's Ex-Migrants' Families,* Gender Analysis in Development Series no. 9, Norwich: University of East Anglia.

Sweetman, C. (1995b) 'Editorial', *Gender and Development* 3(2).

Sweetman, C. (1996) 'Editorial', *Gender and Development* 4(2).

Sweetman, C. (1997) 'Editorial', *Gender and Development* 5(2).

Sweetman, C. (1998) 'Editorial', *Gender and Development* 6(3).

Sweetman, C. (2001) '"Sitting on a rock": men, socio-economic change, and development policy in Lesotho', in C. Sweetman (ed.), *Men's Involvement in Gender and Development Policy and Practice: Beyond Rhetoric,* Oxford: Oxfam Publications.

Swift, A. (1998) 'Lifting the black woman's burden', *The Independent,* South Africa, 26 January.

Swiss, S. (1991) *Liberia: Women and Children Gravely Mistreated,* Boston MA: Physicians for Human Rights.

Swiss, S. and J. Giller (1993) 'Rape as a crime of war', *Journal of the American Medical Association* 270, 4 August.

Swiss, S., *et al.* (1998) 'Letter from Monrovia: violence against women during the Liberian Civil Conflict', *Journal of the American Medical Association* 279(8).

Tanzania Media Women's Association (1994) 'How common is sexual harassment in Tanzania?', in M. Davies (ed.), *Women and Violence: Realities and Responses Worldwide*, London: Zed Books.

Thomas, D. (1994) 'In search of solutions: women's police stations in Brazil', in M. Davies (ed.), *Women and Violence: Realities and Responses Worldwide*, London: Zed Books.

Thomas, D. and R. Regan (1994) 'Rape in war: challenging the tradition of impunity', *SAIS Review* 81(89), Winter-Spring.

Thomas, H. (1997) 'Enslaved black women: the politics of reproduction and infanticide', in R. Lentin (ed.), *Gender and Catastrophe*, London: Zed Books.

Tomasevski, K. (1993) *Women and Human Rights*, Women and World Development Series, London: Zed Books.

Toubia, N. (1993) *Female Genital Mutilation: A Call for Action*, New York: United Nations.

Traboulsi, O. (1997) 'Maghreb Tour Report (Morocco, Algeria, and Tunisia)', internal Oxfam document, March.

Tresnjevka Women's Group (1992) Report, Zagreb: Tresnjevka Women's Group, 28 September.

Tripp, A. (1994) 'Gender, political participation and the transformation of associational life in Uganda and Tanzania', *African Studies Review* 37(1), pp. 107-32.

Tshwaranang Legal Advocacy Centre to End Violence against Women (1996) Financial proposal submitted to Oxfam, February.

Twagiramariya, C. and M. Turshen (1998) '"Favours" to give and "consenting" victims: the sexual politics of survival in Rwanda', in M. Turshen and C. Twagiramariya (eds), *What Women Do in Wartime: Gender and Conflict in Africa*, London: Zed Books.

Ugwu-Oju, D. (1995) *What Will My Mother Say? A Tribal African Girl Comes of Age in America*, Chicago IL: Bonus Books, Inc..

UNDP (1990) *Human Development Report*, New York: Oxford University Press.

UNDP (1994) *Human Development Report*, New York: Oxford University Press.

UNDP (1995) *Human Development Report*, New York: Oxford University Press.

UNDP (1999) *Human Development Report*, New York: Oxford University Press.

UNDP (2000) *Human Development Report*, New York: Oxford University Press.

UNFPA (1997) *The State of World Population*, New York: United Nations Publications.

UNHCHR (no date given) 'Discrimination against women: the convention and the committee', *Fact Sheet* no. 22, Geneva: Office of the High Commissioner for Human Rights. Available on-line at http://www.unhchr.ch/

UNHCR (1986) *Statistical Review of the Situation of Children in the World*, Geneva: UNHCR.

UNHCR (1990) *Policy on Refugee Women*, Geneva: UNHCR.

UNHCR (1991) *Guidelines on the Protection of Refugee Women*, Geneva: UNHCR.

UNHCR (1992) *Handbook on Procedures and Criteria for Determining Refugee Status*, Geneva: UNHCR.

UNHCR (1995) *Sexual Violence against Refugees: Guidelines on Prevention and Response*, UNHCR: Geneva, March.

UNHCR (1997) 'A community-based response on sexual violence against women', *How To Guide: Reproductive Health in Refugee Situations*, Geneva: UNHCR Tanzania Desk.

UNHCR (1998) 'Building a team Approach to the Prevention and Responses to Sexual Violence', *How To Guide: Reproductive Health in Refugee Situations*, report on the technical assistance mission, Kigoma, Tanzania, September, Geneva: UNHCR Tanzania Desk.

UNICEF (2000) 'Domestic violence against women and girls', *Innocenti Digest* 6, May, Florence.

UNICEF (2001) 'Early marriage: child spouses', *Innocenti Digest* 7, March, Florence.

United Nations (1948) *Universal Declaration of Human Rights*, General Assembly, Resolution 217A (III), adopted on 10 December, 3rd session.

United Nations (1951) *Convention Relating to the Status of Refugees*, signed 28 July 1951, entered into force 22 April 1954, 189 UNTS 150.

United Nations (1966) *International Covenant on Economic, Social and Cultural Rights*, General Assembly Resolution 2200A (XXI), 21 UN GAOR, Supp. no. 16 at 49, UN Document A/6316 (1966), 993 UNTS 3, reprinted in 6 ILM 360 (1967).

United Nations (1976) *International Covenant on Civil and Political Rights*, General Assembly Resolution 2200A (XXI), 21 UN GAOR, Supp. no. 16 at 52, UN Document A/6316 (1966), 999 UNTS 171.

United Nations (1979) *Convention on the Elimination of All Forms of Discrimination against Women*, General Assembly Resolution 34/180, 34 UN GAOR, Supp. no. 46 at 193, UN Document A/34/46, reprinted in 19 ILM 33 (1980).

United Nations (1984) *Convention against Torture and Other Cruel, Inhuman or Degrading Treatment or Punishment*, General Assembly Resolution 39/46, Annex, 39 UN GAOR, Supp. no. 51 at 197, UN Document A/39/51, reprinted in 23 ILM 1027 (1984), minor changes reprinted in 5 HRLJ 350 (1984), 24 ILM 535 (1985).

United Nations (1989) *The Convention on the Rights of the Child*, General Assembly Resolution 44/25, Annex, 44 UN GAOR, Supp. no. 49 at 167, UN Document A/44/49, reprinted in 28 ILM 1448 (1989).

United Nations (1993a) *Strategies for Confronting Domestic Violence: A Resource Manual*, Vienna: United Nations and Centre for Social Development and Humanitarian Affairs.

United Nations (1993b) *Declaration on the Elimination of Violence Against Women*, adopted 20 December 1993, General Assembly Resolution 48/104, UN Document A/48/29, reprinted in 33 ILM 1049 (1994).

United Nations (1995a) *The World's Women 1995: Trends and Statistics*, New York: United Nations.

United Nations (1995b) *Beijing Declaration and Platform for Action, Report of the Fourth World Conference on Women*, Beijing 4-15 September, UN Document A/CONF 177/20, New York: United Nations.

United Nations (1998) *Rome Statute of the International Criminal Court*, UN Doc. A/CONF.183/9*, 17 July, reprinted in 37 ILM 999. Available on-line at http://www.un.org/law/icc/statute/romefra.htm

United Nations Centre for Human Rights (1994) 'Discrimination against Women: the Convention and the Committee', Human Rights Fact Sheet no. 22, Geneva: United Nations.

United Nations Centre for Human Rights (1995) 'Integration of a Gender Perspective into United Nations Human Rights Activities and Programmes', report of an expert group meeting on the development of guidelines, Geneva, 3-7 July.

United Nations Commission of Experts for the International Tribunal for the Former Yugoslavia (1994) 'Annex II Rape and Sexual Assault: A Legal Study', UN Document S/1994/674/Add.2 (vol. I), 28 December.

United Nations World Conference on Human Rights (1993) *Vienna Declaration and Programme for Action*, adopted 25 June 1993, UN Document A/CONF.157/24, reprinted in 32 ILM 1661 (1993), 14 HRLJ 352 (1993).

United Nations Centre for Human Rights (1994) *Human Rights –The New Consensus*, London: Regency Press (Humanity) Ltd.

Urioste, D. (1998) 'The Bolivian State and the Movement of Women in the Fight for the Elimination of Violence', paper presented at Oxfam international workshop on violence against women, Sarajevo, November.

Van der Wijk, D. (1997) 'The Human Side of Conflict: Coping Strategies of Women Heads of Households in Four Villages in Sri Lanka and Cambodia', unpublished report, Oxfam GB, August.

Vandenberg, M. (1997) 'The invisible woman', *The Moscow Times*, 8 October.

Vandenburg, M. (1997) 'Trafficking of women to Israel and forced prostitution', report by the Israel Women's Network, November.

Vasquez, R. and G. Tamayo (1989) *Violencia y Legalidad*, Lima: Concytec.

Veno, A. and D. Thomas (1996) 'Psychology and the process of social change', in D. Thomas and A. Veno (eds), *Community Psychology and Social Change: Australian and New Zealand Perspectives* 2e, Palmerston North, New Zealand: The Dunmore Press Ltd..

Vetten, L. (1998) 'War and the making of men and women', *Sunday Independent*, South Africa, 16 August.

Volunteers for Humanity (1998) 'Mass Rape in the Recent Riots: The Climax of an Uncivilised Act in a Nation's Life', paper presented at the Oxfam international workshop on violence against women, Sarajevo, November.

Vulliamy, E. (1993) 'Pope warns raped women on abortion', *The Guardian*, 1 March.

Wahra, G. and M. Goldring (1994) 'Women Refugees and Refugee Women', paper presented at international Oxfam gender and development conference, Women Linking for Change, Thailand, January.

Walby, S. (1990) *Theorising Patriarchy*, Oxford: Blackwell.

Walker B. (1991) 'Working Guidelines for Gender and Emergencies', internal document, Oxfam GB.

Walker, J. and L. McNicol (1994) *Policing Domestic Violence: Protection and Prevention or Prudence*, Newcastle: Relate Centre for Family Studies.

Walley, J. (1997) 'Searching for "voices": feminism, anthropology and the global debate over female genital operations', *Cultural Anthropology* 12(3), pp. 405-38.

Wandita, G. (1998) 'The tears have not stopped, the violence has not ended: political upheaval, ethnicity, and violence against women in Indonesia', *Gender and Development* 6(3).

Wartemberg, L. (1992) 'Entre el maltrato y el repudio: dilema de las mujeres del altiplano cundiboyacense en Colombia', in A. Defossez, D. Fassin, and M. Viveros (eds), *Mujeres de los Andes. Condiciones de Vida y Salud*, Colombia: Instituto Francés de Estudios Andinos (IFEA)/Universidad Externado de Colombia.

Wearne, P. (1994) *The Maya of Guatemala*, United Kingdom: Minority Rights Group.

Weekly Mail and Guardian (1999) 'Get a life…', *Weekly Mail and Guardian*, South Africa, 8 October.

Welsh, J. (1992) 'Documenting Torture: A Human Rights Approach', paper presented at a meeting on Science of Refugee Mental Health: New Concepts and Methods, 29 September-1 October, Harvard University, Harvard MA.

West, A., Roy, C., and F. Nichols (1978) *Understanding Sexual Attacks*, London: Heinemann Educational.

White, S. (1997) 'Men, masculinities and the politics of development', *Gender and Development* 5(2).

Wijers, M. and L. Lap-Chew (1997) *Trafficking in Women, Forced Labour and Slavery-like Practices in Marriage, Domestic Labour and Prostitution*, Utrecht: The Dutch Foundation Against Trafficking in Women (STV).

Williams, R. (1977) *Marxism, Literature and Politics*, Oxford: Oxford University Press.

Williams, S. (1995) 'Oxfam and Basic Rights', internal Oxfam document.

Williams, S. (1999a) 'Ending impunity for sexual violence', *Links Newsletter*, special issue on violence against women, Oxfam GB, March.

Williams, S. (1999b) 'Gender and Human Rights in the Macedonian Refugee Camps, Report of Visit to the Refugee Camps in Macedonia, 26-29th April', internal Oxfam document.

Williams, S. (1999c) 'Protection of Refugee Women in the Macedonian Camps: Key Concerns', internal Oxfam document, May.

Williams, S., Mwau, A., and J. Seed (1994) *The Oxfam Gender Training Manual*, Oxford: Oxfam Publications.

Women 2000 (1998) 'Sexual Violence and Armed Conflict: United Nations Response', report of the United Nations Division for the Advancement of Women, Department for Economic and Social Affairs, April.

Women's Commission of the Human Rights League of Chad, Turshen, M., and C. Twagiramariya (1998) 'Women denounce their treatment in Chad', in M. Turshen and C. Twagiramariya (eds), *What Women Do in Wartime: Gender and Conflict in Africa*, London: Zed Books.

Women's Global Network for Reproductive Rights (1993) *Newsletter*, January-March, Amsterdam, Netherlands.

Wood, K. and R. Jewkes (1997) 'Violence, rape and sexual coercion: everyday love in a South African township', *Gender and Development* 5(2).

Wood, K., Maforah, F., and R. Jewkes (1998) '"He forced me to love him": putting violence on adolescent sexual health agendas', *Social Science and Medicine* 47, 233-42.

World Bank (1993) *World Development Report 1993: Investing in Health,* New York: Oxford University Press.

World Health Organisation (1997) *Information Pack,* Geneva: WHO.

Wulf, D. (1994) 'Refugee women and reproductive health care: reassessing priorities', in S. Zajovic (ed.), *Women for Peace Anthology,* Belgrade: Women In Black.

Young, K. (1997) 'Gender and development', in N. Visvanathan, L. Guggan, L. Nisonoff, and N Wiegersma (eds), *The Women, Gender and Development Reader,* Cape Town and London: David Phillip and Zed Books.

Yuval-Davis, N. (1987) 'The Jewish collectivity', in Khamsim Collective (ed.), *Women in the Middle East,* London: Zed Books.

Yuval-Davis, N. (ed.) (1992) *Unholy Orders: Women Against Fundamentalism,* London: Virago.

Yuval-Davis, N. (1997) *Gender and Nation,* London, Thousand Oaks CA, New Delhi: Sage Publications.

Yuval-Davis, N. and F. Anthias (eds) (1989) *Women-Nation-State,* London: Macmillan.

YWCA (1994) 'Violence Against Women: Zambian Perspectives, An Evaluation Report of the Initiatives of the YWCA of Zambia', May, Lusaka, Zambia: YWCA Council of Zambia.

YWCA (1995) *Femicide Register,* July, Lusaka, Zambia: YWCA Council of Zambia.

YWCA (1997) 'Tips on family violence', *Voices of Women* 1(11), p. 10.

Zabelina, T. (1996) 'Sexual violence towards women', in H. Pilkington (ed.), *Gender, Generation and Identity in Contemporary Russia,* London: Routledge.

Zajovic, S. (ed.) (1993) *Women for Peace Anthology,* Belgrade: Women in Black.

Zimmerman, C. (1994) *Plates in the Basket Will Rattle: Domestic Violence in Cambodia,* Phnom Penh, Cambodia: Project Against Domestic Violence.

Zimmerman, C. (1997) *Domestic Violence in Cambodia: Survey Summaries of Plates in a Basket will Rattle and Household Survey on Domestic Violence,* Phnom Penh, Cambodia: Project Against Domestic Violence.

Zur, J. (1996) 'Reconstructing the self through memories of violence among Mayan Indian war widows', in R. Lentin (ed.), *Gender and Catastrophe,* London: Zed Books.

Index

abortion
  may be denied to rape victims 97
  sex-selective 79, 89
abuse 11
  'naming', power to destroy abusers 185
abusive relationships, why women decide to
    stay 173, 203, 204
advertising 297
advocacy and research programme,
    Tshwaranang Legal Advocacy Centre
    (South Africa) 277B
Africa
  Central, Reproductive Health
    Programme 25
  West, collective shaming of violent men
    207
  'wives of the lineage' 66
  see also South Africa and other named
    countries
African Charter on Human and People's
  Rights, women's rights protocol 51
Akayesu, Jean-Paul, conviction of 3, 58,
    271-2
Albania, gun removal projects 144
Amazon Women's Forum, provision of
    para-legals in police stations 42-3
AMEPU (Uruguay) 66
American Convention on Human Rights,
    State responsibilities 50
Amnesty International 49-50, 304
anti-discrimination provisions 51, 61
Arab women's liberation movement 65-6
armed conflict
  and crisis, investigating violence against
    women in context of 240-1
  girls in 94-5
  protection of women and girls during
    55-9
  and violence 131-48
armies
  motivation to join 132-3
  and violence against women 134-8
Asia Pacific Forum on Women, Law and
    Development, definition of violence 14
Asian Centre for Women's Human Rights
    303

Asian Financial Crisis, 298
attitudes, challenged 241-51
attitudinal change 251-61
  achievement of at State level 276, 277B
  through training 297
Australia
  community costs of violence against
    women 68
  'Men's Houses' programme, Victoria
    164, 222
  New South Wales, judicial reforms 268
AVEGA-Agahozo see Rwanda, AVEGA-
    Agahozo
awareness-raising, on violence against
    women 232
Azerbaijan, Association for the Defence of
    Women's Rights, on drug smuggling
    sentences 130

Balkans, institutional responses to domestic
    violence 236-7
Bangladesh 164
  acid attacks, dowry related 92
  Burmese refugee camps 171, 172B
  domestic violence and fair trade projects
    211, 213
  impact of credit
    on gender relations 72, 189
    on violence 128
  leaving *purdah*, transgresses norms of
    female decency 24
  measures to counteract violent backlash
    40-1
  paramilitary forces, violence against
    women 140-1
  shaming perpetrators of violence 36
  violence and loans 39, 128
  war of secession, rape of Bengali women
    83
  wife-beating 81
bargaining power, in households 117
Belgrade
  network of organisations addressing
    needs of refugee women 177
  see also SOS Hotline, Belgrade

masculinity 18, 20, 138, 206, 208, 224, 226
military, needs constant reproduction 132
maternal altruism 108
media 241, 295
  public education through 245-51
Medica Zenica 137
  crafts classes for residential project 191
  each woman seen as an individual 180-1
  education provision 194
  helper-client relationship vital 181
  new project on post-war domestic
    violence 144
  report on pschological impact of rape
    98-9
  reporting 'the assassination of self' 37
  sewing workshop, gives a minimum
    income 191-2
  value of therapeutic work for the
    traumatic effects of violence 180
medical care 118
medical violence 122-3
men 35, 37, 205
  development of critical consciousness
    225, 226
  effects of loss of sole-breadwinner status
    126-9
  financial situation, and violence against
    women 129-31
  resistance to women's efforts to meet
    together 171, 172B
  returned from war, signs of frustration
    148
  use violence to restore/reinforce power
    149
  working with 204-5, 224-7, 297
  young
    entry into the army attractive 132-3
    socialisation into the military 132-3
    violence against their mothers 147
Men Against Violence (Nicaragua), combats
  machismo and male violence 42
men's consciousness raising groups 226-7
men's work with men 224-7
mental health, and 'naming' violence 184-8
Mexico 118
  increase in domestic violence 71-2, 127
  scarcity and less household conflict 129
migrant communities, honour-killings in 91
military strategy, violence against women
  an integral part 135, 186B, 299-300
Morocco
  Association Democratique des Femmes
    du Maroc, protection of women from
    violence in public spheres 265-6
  women use strikes to protest 210B

Moser, Caroline, different approaches to
  development (WID/GAD matrix) 23,
  31-2
Mozambique
  beliefs, purification rituals heal negative
    effects of bad spirits/war traumas
    214-15
  children kidnapped for military service
    94-5
  psycho-social approach to demobilised
    child soldiers 218-19
mutilation
  in Zambian killings 234B
  see also female genital mutilation (FGM)
'naming' violence 184-8
  Northern Ireland 209
natal families, may protect women from
  violence 115-16
national liberation movements, strict rules
  against sex 138
nationhood 132
Nepal, *deukis* system 88
Netherlands, sexual violence against girls 86
NGOs 233, 236-7, 247, 259
  co-operation and alliance between
    critical 263, 302-3
  developing an integrated organisational
    strategy 303-4
  lobbying governments to effect change
    287-91
  mainstreaming awareness of violence
    against women 301-2
  may reinforce unequal gender relations
    258
  role in transforming attitudes and
    capabilities of state officials 280, 295
  use of Women's Convention 195
Nicaragua 288
  CISAS
    championing human rights 225
    and development of men's critical
      consciousness 225, 226, 226B
Nigeria, sexually transmitted diseases in
  children 86
Northern Ireland 143, 209
  women prisoners abused by female
    officers 22-3

occupational therapy 188, 189B, 192-3
opposition groups, armed, violence against
  women 139-41
organisational strategy, integrated,
  development of 303-4
ostracism, of rape victims 104, 207-8, 215
Oxfam GB 5-6, 294